Gender and Development

A History of Women's Education in Kenya

Emily Awino Onyango

Langham
ACADEMIC

Published 2018 by Langham Academic (Previously Langham Monographs)
An imprint of Langham Publishing
www.langhampublishing.org

Langham Publishing and its imprints are a ministry of Langham Partnership

Langham Partnership
PO Box 296, Carlisle, Cumbria CA3 9WZ, UK
www.langham.org

ISBNs:
978-1-78368-489-2 Print
978-1-78368-490-8 ePub
978-1-78368-492-2 PDF

British Library Cataloguing-in-Publication Data
A catalogue record for this book is available from the British Library

ISBN: 978-1-78368-489-2

Cover & Book Design: projectluz.com

Contents

List of Abbreviations

AAWORD	African Association of Women in Research
ABC	analysis tool of gender
ADC	African District Councils
AGHS	Alliance Girls High School
AIDS	acquired immune deficiency syndrome
AIM	African Inland Mission
CMS	Church Missionary Society
CSM	Church of Scotland Mission
DAWN	Development Alternatives with Women in a New Era
DC	district commissioner
EFA	Education for All
FAIM	Friends African Industrial Mission
FAO	Food and Agricultural Organization
FAWE	Forum for African Women Educationists
FEMNET	African Women Development and Communication Network
FGM	female genital mutilation
GMS	Gospel Missionary Society
HIV	human immunodeficiency virus
ICHDR	International Centre for Health Development and Research
KAU	Kenya African Union
KCA	Kikuyu Central Association
KCAN	Kenya Coalition for Action in Nutrition
KISE	Kenya Institute of Special Education
KNDI	Kenya Nutritionists and Dieticians Institutes

KPU	Kenya Peoples Union
KTWA	Kavirondo Tax Payers Welfare Association
KYA	Kiambu Youth Association
LNC	Local Native Council
LPK	Labour Party of Kenya
LPT	Lower Primary Teachers Course
MA	master's of arts
MP	Member of Parliament
MU	Mothers Union
MYW	Maendeleo Ya Wanawake
MYWO	Maendeleo Ya Wanawake Organization
NARC	National Alliance Rainbow Coalition
NCCK	National Council of Churches in Kenya
NCWK	National Council of Women in Kenya
NFLS	Nairobi Forward-Looking Strategies for the Advancement of Women
NGO	Non-Governmental Organization
ODM	Orange Democratic Movement
PC	provincial commissioner
PHD	doctor of philosophy
PKP	Progressive Kikuyu Party
SWAG	Senior Women's Advisory Group on Sustainable Development
UN	United Nations
UNEP	United Nations Environmental Program
UNESCO	United Nations Educational Scientific and Cultural Organization
UNICEF	United Nations Children's Fund
USA	United States of America
USIU	United States International University
WB	World Bank
WTO	World Trade Organization
YWCA	Young Women Christian Association

Introduction

The focus of this book is a reconstruction of African, women's, and religious history of Kenya. The book privileges the African voice, women's voice, and religion in the reconstruction of the history. This is based on Professor Ogot's assertion that Africans participated in the construction of their identity and history in the precolonial period.[1] This was done through the formal schools, where history was constructed through the different specialists. Africans continue to participate in the construction of their history and identity through recitation and performance. Oral traditions have developed through such history, and they have changed in response to new challenges and situations.

The first written sources were mainly accounts from administrators and missionaries. Johnston, Hobley, Northcote, Leakey, and Tate wrote on different aspects of the material cultures and religious beliefs of the African communities.[2] Their main focus was on the strangeness of the beliefs. They wrote that most of the beliefs were based on ignorance and were unchristian. However, they did not relate the beliefs to the environment. Most of these

---

1. Bethwell Ogot, "The Construction of Luo Identity and History," *African Words and Voices*, eds. L. White, S. Miescher, and D. Cohen (Indianapolis: Indiana University Press, 2001), 31–52.

2. Sir H. Johnston, *The Uganda Protectorate* (London: Hutchinson, 1902); C. W. Hobley, "Kavirondo," *The Geographical Journal* 12, no. 4 (1898): 361–372; C. W. Hobley, "Eastern Uganda Occasional Papers No. 1," *The Journal of the Anthropological Institute of Great Britain and Ireland*, 1902; Hobley, "British East Africa: Anthropological Studies on the Kavirondo and Nandi," *The Journal of the Anthropological Institute of Great Britain and Ireland* 33 (1903): 325–359; Hobley, *Kenya from Chartered Company to Crown Colony* (London: Witherby, 1929); G. A. S. Northcote, "The Nilotic Kavirondo," *Journal of Royal Anthropological Institute of Great Britain and Ireland* 37 (1907): 58–66; Louis Leakey, *The Stone Age Races of Kenya* (London: Oxford University Press, 1935); Leakey, "Southern Kikuyu before 1903," (1939) Mss.Afr.s.1117 (Rhodes house); H. R. Tate, "Notes on the Kikuyu and Kamba Tribes of British East Africa," *Journal of the Anthropological Institute of Great Britain and Ireland* 34 (1904): 130–148; H. R. Tate, "The Native Law of Southern Gikuyu of British East Africa," *Journal of the Royal African Society* 9, no. 35 (April 1910): 233–254.

works were authentic sources of history because they were mainly based on African informants. Africans continued to control their history because the first written sources were either written by Africans or written by missionaries in vernacular and therefore authentic African voices: Okola and Were;[3] Mboya;[4] Mayor, who wrote *Thuondi Luo* or *Luo Heroes*[5] which became a classic textbook in primary and intermediate schools; and Kenyatta, who wrote *Facing Mount Kenya*[6] which was a classic text on the culture and history of the Kikuyu.

The first anthropologists who did sketchy work on African cultures, were still authentic sources as their works were mainly based on information given by African experts. Evans-Pritchard's work in 1949 and 1950, was mainly based on information by Archdeacon Owen and Ezekiel Apindi.[7] Southall's work was mainly based on information by Paul Mboya.[8] Malo, who was the president of the African Tribunal court was a major contributor to Wilson's work.[9] There was consensus that these were genuine traditions and cultures of the African people as proved through further research. The traditions therefore constitute authentic evidence for ideas, values, and mentality of the different communities.

There has been ongoing work on the reconstruction of African history from the 1940s, by professional historians whose work is based on primary data. Ayany's work was on the history of Luo clans.[10] Malo focused on historical traditions of Central Nyanza, based on field research between

---

3. Zablon Okola and Michael Were, *Weche Moko Mag Luo* [Luo Traditions, Customs, and Folklore], (Nairobi: CMS, 1936).

4. Paul Mboya, *Luo Kitgi Gi Timbegi* [Luo Customs and Tradition] (Nairobi: East African Standard, 1938).

5. A. W. Mayor, *Thuondi Luo* [Luo Heroes] (Maseno: CMS, 1938).

6. Jomo Kenyatta, *Facing Mount Kenya: The Tribal Life of the Gikuyu* (London: Heinemann, 1938).

7. E. E. Evans-Pritchard, "Luo Tribes and Clans," *Rhodes-Livingstone Journal* 7 (1949): 24–40; E. E. Evans-Pritchard, "Marriage Customs of the Luo in Kenya," *Africa* 20, no. 2 (1950): 132–142.

8. A. W. Southall, "Lineage Formation among the Luo," *International African Institute Memorandum* 26 (London: Oxford University Press, 1952).

9. G. M. Wilson, *Marriage Laws and Customs: Report to Kenya Government* (Nairobi: Government Printers, 1955).

10. Samuel Ayany, *Kar Chakruok Mar Luo*, 2nd ed. (Kisumu: Equatorial Publishers, 1951).

1940 and 1951.[11] Snell studied the traditions and customs of the Nandi as a means of reconstructing African history.[12] This was on research from Nandi Chiefs and elders. Ogot, Muruiki, Were, Osogo, Ochieng, and Ayot have reflected on oral traditions and their significance as historical texts and used them for the reconstruction of precolonial history.[13] Reconstruction of history based on field research was also done by the University of Nairobi historical department.

However, despite the extensive research, most of the African historiography does not focus on gender. But as Doyle recommends, women constitute local sources and are important for historical analysis.[14] Doyle also advocates for an engendered history based on linguistic analysis. This book uses both gender and linguistics as a tool of analysis. Most of the scholars researching on African women in the 1980s were outsiders. These included Gross and Bingham, Bay, and Hay and Wright.[15] In 1984, the first work on African women's history was published,[16] followed by Berger and White.[17] These were largely by western female scholars and they were mainly concerned with recovering African women's histories on a wide range of socio-economic and political subjects. Geiger, Musisi, and Allman[18] focused on the study of

---

11. S. Malo, *Dhoudi Mag Central Nyanza* [Clans of Central Nyanza] (Kampala: Eagle, 1953).

12. G. S. Snell, *Nandi Customary Law* (London: Macmillan, 1954).

13. Bethwell A. Ogot, "Social and Economic History of the Luo of Kenya 1870–1910," Arts Research Prize Essay (Kampala: Makerere University Library, 1950); Bethwell A. Ogot, *A History of the Southern Luo*, vol. 1 (Nairobi: EAPH, 1967); Godfrey Muruiki, *A History of the Gikuyu, 1500–1900* (Nairobi: Oxford University Press, 1974); Gideon Were, *A History of Abaluyia of Western Kenya* (Nairobi: EAPH, 1967); John Osogo, *A History of Baluhyia* (Nairobi: Oxford University Press, 1966); William R. Ochieng, *An Outline History of Nyanza Up to 1914* (Nairobi: EALB, 1974); Henry Ayot, *History Texts of the Lake Region in East Africa* (Nairobi: KLB, 1977); Henry Ayot, *A History of Luo Abasuba of Western Kenya from 176–1940* (Nairobi: KLB, 1979).

14. Shane Doyle, *Crisis and Decline in Bunyoro: Population and Environment in Western Uganda 1865–1955* (Oxford: James Currey, 2006).

15. Susan Gross and Majorie Bingham, *Women in Africa of the Sub Sahara* (Hudson, WI: GEM Publications, 1982); Edna Bay, *Women and Work in Africa* (Boulder, CO: Westview Press, 1982); Margaret Hay and Marcia Wright eds., *African Women and the Law: Historical Perspectives* (Boston: Boston University, African Studies Centre, 1982).

16. Margaret Hay and Sharon Stichter, *African Women South of the Sahara* (New York: Longman, 1984).

17. Iris Berger and Frances White, *Women in Sub-Saharan Africa: Restoring Women to History* (Bloomington: Indiana University Press, 1999).

18. Susan Geiger, Nakanyike Musisi, and Jean Marie Allman, eds., *Women in African Colonial Histories* (Bloomington: Indiana University Press, 2002).

African women's histories, mainly limiting their papers to selected parts of a single country or one ethnic group; they were able to do in depth, culturally-sensitive studies of African women during the colonial period.

In Kenya, several scholars have produced women's history including Tabitha Kanogo and Carolyn Shaw, who revisit the extensively researched area of Kenyan history and excavate women's history.[19] They give Kenyan women agency[20] and contextualize ethnically the experiences of these women. Scholars like Atieno-Odhiambo and Cohen, apply gender as a tool of analysis to their research and pose questions relating to gender to their respondents in the field.[21] Musandu engages Kenyan historical and ethno-historical data to demonstrate female socio-economic and political agency, with a major focus on the political.[22] This book recovers women's history, affirms women's socio-economic and political agency from the precolonial period, and underlines the role of religion in women's agency.

This book also contributes to mission history and African religious history. The early mission historiography had focused on European strategies and efforts in planting churches. Richards, in her book on fifty years of Church Mission Society work in Nyanza, concentrates on the heroic work of male European missionaries in the establishment of mission stations and schools.[23] She rarely mentions African converts by name. However, there is now a consensus that African initiative played a considerable role in the expansion of Christianity. This book demonstrates that both African men, women, and women missionaries played a key role in the establishment and expansion of the church. Women also played a key role in leadership and socio-economic development of their societies. This is in agreement with

---

19. Tabitha Kanogo, *Squatters and the Root of Mau-Mau 1905–1963* (London: Ohio University Press, 1987); Tabitha Kanogo, *African Womanhood in Colonial Kenya 1900–1950* (Oxford: James Currey, 2005); Carolyn M. Shaw, *Colonial Inscriptions: Race, Sex and Class in Kenya* (Minneapolis: University of Minnesota Press, 1995).

20. By "agency" I mean an individual's ability to make effective choices and to transform those choices into desired outcomes.

21. E. S. Atieno-Odhiambo and David W. Cohen, *Siaya: The Historical Anthropology of an African Landscape* (London: James Currey; Athens, OH: Ohio University Press, 1989), 85–110.

22. Phoebe Musandu, "Daughter of Odoro: Grace Onyango and African Women's History" (Master's thesis, Miami University, 2006).

23. Elizabeth Richards, *Fifty Years in Nyanza, 1906–1956: The History of the CMS and the Anglican Church in Nyanza* (Maseno: CMS Jubilee Committee, 1956).

Hastings' and Ranger's argument that African agents played a critical role in the expansion of Christianity.[24] Many of them had little contact with the institutional church and appropriated religious information through informal channels. This kind of Christianity was appropriated within the culture and worldview of the people. The teacher-evangelists responded to and also stimulated mass demand for spiritual change. Missions therefore came across congregations gathered around schools and churches that had been founded by labour migrants and only later brought to the fold of the church. Urban-Mead argues that African initiatives altered the course of the original mission establishment.[25]

One major focus of mission literature is the interaction between Christianity and African culture. This book argues that Africans interacted with the missionaries and the colonial government within the context of their own worldview and culture. Mudimbe views colonialism as a socio-cultural phenomenon and missionaries as important in creating and representing the colonial world in Africa.[26] Peel argues that missionaries did not recognize African cultures.[27] They felt that heathenism was a kind of absence, not something with a durability of its own, embedded in an all-encompassing system, thought, style, and ethos. However, it is evident that Africans reflected the teachings within their own context. By translating the Scriptures into vernacular, every engagement was done in the context of African culture. Translation work greatly enhanced the interaction between the Christian worldview and African cultures. Bediako and Sanneh emphasize the importance of translation of Scripture into African languages, as it facilitated

24. Adrian Hastings, *The Church in Africa 1450–1950* (Oxford: Clarendon, 1994); Terrence Ranger, "Taking on the Missionary Task: African Spirituality and Mission Churches in Manicaland in 1930," in *Christianity and the African Imagination*, ed. David Maxwell (Boston: Brill, 2002).

25. W. E. Urban-Mead, "Religion, Women and Gender in Brethren in Christ Church, Matabeleland, Zimbabwe 1898–1978" (PhD diss., Columbia University, 2004).

26. Valentine Y. Mudimbe, *The Invention of Africa: Gnosis, Philosophy and the Order of Knowledge* (Bloomington: Indiana University Press, 1988).

27. J. D. Y. Peel, "Gender in Yoruba Religious Change," *Journal of Religion in Africa* 3, no. 2 (May 2002): 138.

engagement with people's worldview and thought patterns.[28] This resulted in rooting Christianity and making it authentic.

This book adapts a historical approach to the study of African traditional religions. I concur with Ranger and Kimambo and Spear, who argue that African religion played an important role in African's appropriation of Christianity.[29] This appropriation was within the context of their existing experience and beliefs; these appropriations should also be understood within the wider socio-economic and political context. Due to both the translation of Scripture in vernacular and the use of vernacular in the curriculum, there was interaction between Christianity, western culture and African worldviews and ideas. This is in line with Lonsdale's argument that there has been long conversation between Christianity and African cosmologies.[30] He argues that the Kikuyu read the Bible as an allegory of their own history.

This book illustrates that women missionaries and local women were central to mission work and also to leadership and development in both church and society. This is in contrast to Kirkwood's findings on the marginalization of women in the mission field.[31] The focus of Ng'iya Mission Station was work among women and girls. By coincidence, the mission station was established in the vicinity of the shrines of one of the feminine ancestral spirits. This book therefore affirms the ideas of Labode and Urban-Mead that gender issues were central to mission work.[32] The Ng'iya Mission Station focused on all kinds of issues relating to gender. This book therefore reclaims women's presence in history.

---

28. Kwame Bediako, *Theology and Identity: The Impact of Culture on Christian Thought in Second Century and Modern Africa* (Carlisle: Regnum Books, 1999); Kwame Bediako, *Jesus in Africa: The Christian Gospel in African History and Experiences* (Akropong: Regnum Africa, 2000); Lamin Sanneh, *Translating the Message: The Missionary Impact on Culture* (New York: Orbis, 1989).

29. Terrence Ranger and I. N. Kimambo, eds., *The Historical Study of African Religion* (London: Heinemann, 1972); T. Spear and I. N. Kimambo, eds., *East African Expressions of Christianity* (Oxford: James Currey, 1999).

30. John Lonsdale, "Kikuyu Christianities: A History of Intimate Diversity," in *Christianity and the African Imagination*, ed. David Maxwell (Boston: Brill, 2002).

31. Deborah Kirkwood, "Protestant Missionary Women: Wives and Spinsters," in *Women and Missions: Past and Present*, eds. F. Bowie, S. Ardener, and D. Kirkwood (Oxford: Berg, 1993).

32. M. Labode, "From Heathen Kraal to Christian Home: Anglican Mission Education for Girls 1850-1900" in *Women and Missions*, eds. F. Bowie, D. Kirkwood and S. Ardener (Oxford: Berg, 1993); Wendy Urban-Mead, "Religion, Women and Gender in Brethren in Christ Church, Matabeleland, Zimbabwe 1898–1978" (PhD diss., Colombia University, 2004).

CHAPTER 1

The Argument

This book is a reconstruction of an engendered history of missionary education in colonial Kenya. The central argument is that Kenyan women used resources from the Christian faith, their culture, and mission education to bring change and transformation in both the church and society. They managed to negotiate positions of leadership in both the church and society and contributed to the general development of these societies. Equipped with their new identity as African-Christian women, they challenged hegemonic forces within African culture and in the wider society to work towards justice, peace, and reconciliation. Although African societies were patriarchal, some women had the opportunity to reach positions of leadership.

The second chapter illustrates that African women played a central role in leadership, in the economy, and the society in general during the pre-colonial period. This was first due to their understanding of God. God created both men and women with dignity. Second, according to African understanding, the attributes of God were both masculine and feminine. This meant that both male and female roles were valued in the society. Women also played a central role in the society because of their philosophy of life. Africans viewed seniority as central to knowledge, economic empowerment, and leadership. Rank, authority, and prestige were all based on seniority of age and descent.

African marriage relationships were key to understanding their philosophy and thought forms. The marriage system was a springboard to understanding the political, social, and economic systems of the people. The marriage process gave individual women the opportunity to make decisions, accumulate property for their houses, and seek redress in cases of injustice. The polygamous marriage system was key to understanding African society.

The polygamous marriage system was an expression of the respect of both community and kinship ties, but also respect for individuality.

The institution of the senior wife or *Mikayi* was the locus of women's empowerment. *Mikayi* was a position of power, prestige, and status in the home. All the other wives viewed her with respect, and she referred to them as "daughter of my house." *Mikayi* was involved in decision-making and leadership of the home. *Mikayi* was a position of advantage economically. She was allocated more property by virtue of her position. However, through the concept of *Ot* or the household, the polygamous marriages gave all the other women opportunity for economic empowerment. First, this was because distribution of property was done through the household. In the polygamous system, the woman was the head of the household. Second, the polygamous marriage created the opportunity for individual initiative and competition between the houses.

However, despite the opportunities for empowerment, African societies disempowered women. This was mainly due to patriarchy and also some of the religious practices and rituals. However, all women underwent cultural education. Through cultural education, women were empowered with knowledge and skills. Through education, they had resources which they would use not only to critique society, but also to empower themselves.

The third chapter looks at colonial rule as a watershed for African women. The onset of colonial rule was disastrous for African women. Women were marginalized from leadership positions, economic development, and the judicial processes. This marginalization was a major departure from the pre-colonial societies. The marginalisation of women was due to both complex changes facilitated by colonial rule and through colonial policies. First, the main aim of colonial administration was to establish power in Kenya. They therefore re-organized and re-structured the leadership system. The British established direct and autocratic rule, in which they were completely in control. However, they used indigenous institutions to achieve their aims. They also used ethnicity by appointing traditional chiefs, but re-organized those positions. Through this process of centralization, women were excluded from leadership structures.

Women were also excluded from other instruments of power like access to education and other symbols of authority like the administrators and the missionaries. Women could therefore not participate in leadership roles in the nationalist movements, which were important in the empowerment of the emerging elite. African women could also not be appointed to administrative positions like the local native councils. They were also locked out of government employment. Women were also excluded from participation in the new judicial systems. They therefore had no opportunity to make decisions on issues affecting them.

The establishment of European rule also greatly affected the environment and the ecological systems. This resulted in new plagues and cattle diseases like rinderpest. This had a direct impact on women's participation in agriculture, which was their main economic activity. In the process of establishing colonial rule, British punitive actions mainly targeted African property and wealth. This resulted in a great set-back both to women's property rights and economic independence. Through their policies and re-organisation, the British also brought in a new idea of property rights, which relegated women as part of men's property. Women were also side-lined from the practice of agriculture through the rise of the petty-bourgeois, who could use their money to employ labour in agriculture for economic purposes. A new land tenure, the Swynnerton plan, introduced title deeds to men, who could now access loans and engage in cash-crop farming.

The methods used in tax collection by administrators led to corruption. Taxation policies and methods of collection also led to a lot of violence – especially against women. Both taxation and labour policies contributed to the changing role of men and women in society. Compulsory labour for women in the Chief's camps and the roads, labour migration of men, the demand for women to entertain tax collectors, and women's attempt to produce their own food and to survive resulted in women being the beasts of burden.

The labour policies also had a great effect on both the social and economic status of women. African women had to take over agricultural and livestock work previously done by men. Since men were the ritual agricultural leaders, and no agricultural season could begin without their presence, this had a great effect on farm production. Labour migration led to the separation of families and had a negative effect on the moral values. Most of the men felt de-humanized at their places of work, and this had a far-reaching effect on their families. The introduction of cash and the wage-earning economy resulted in women's disempowerment as they were not considered as wage earners. Women had no opportunity for getting income and also no opportunity for investment. Women were also excluded from trade. Colonial economic policies, like cash crops through peasant production also targeted men. Women had no access to technology.

Chapter 4 illustrates that women recaptured their dignity, gained the opportunity for leadership, and reconnected with some aspects of their past traditions through the establishment of the Christian faith and mission work. Although the mission work during the pre-colonial period was predominantly done by male missionaries, they laid the foundation for future empowerment of women. African women participated in the leadership and establishment of the church. This was mainly due to Mission policies, which emphasized lay leadership and also the development of local leadership. African women also used their Christian faith to challenge some of the ideas and rituals from African religion and culture, which had contributed to their dis-empowerment.

Second, African women participated in church leadership in places where the focus was on the Christian home or village and not on church structure and organization. Christianity was seen in terms of the establishment of a new society, and the teacher-evangelists were viewed as the leaders of the new clans. They were leaders in both church and society. Women were leaders in these villages and homes. Christian women using their faith went against custom to set up homes in the absence of men who were away due to labour migration or World War I. However, women could also rise to clan or sub-clan leaders in pre-colonial society. Women also participated in leadership and decision-making because of their perception of the nature of authority in the church. Most of the African Christians maintained that authority for Christian leadership came through possession of the spirit of God and not from sphere of influence as held by missions. Second, it came through credibility, which resulted from being a member of the community of faith. Third, they felt that Christian identity was important for membership and leadership of the church.

The establishment of Christianity and missions led both to the socioeconomic empowerment of women and also avenues for fighting for justice.

First, some of the missionaries were involved in fighting for justice for women. They raised issues like women's involvement in forced labour and administration of justice. They also challenged some of the cultural practices that seemed to violate individual freedom. Women were also empowered by their faith to stand for their own rights and to work towards peace and reconciliation. Christian mission work gave women an opportunity to access basic literacy skills and also Christian education. The Christian leaders emphasized having reading skills as basic to being accepted for baptism. Christian converts were expected to attend catechism classes, which were later turned into normal schools. African women through Christian education became agents of new ideas.

While most of the missionaries had great fear of materialism and urbanization, most of the women used their faith as agents of new ideas and economic development. The church was the sole provider of education for girls, which was the main tool of socio-economic and political development. This gave women the opportunity to recapture their participation in agriculture.

African women felt affirmed and Christianity became part of their new identity because of the engagement between Christian faith and African thought-forms, worldview, and culture. Most of the missionaries were evangelicals and never recognized other cultures as a result of individualism and Christian universalism. During the colonial period, missionaries were important in creating and representing the colonial world in Africa.[1] According to Peel, most missionaries did not recognize African culture.[2] They felt that "heathenism was a kind of absence, not something with a durability of its own, embedded in an all compassing system, thought, style and ethos."[3] However, by emphasizing on the use of African languages, they gave African cultures and ideas a lot of credibility. By translating Scriptures into the vernacular and oral teachings of the Bible, there was engagement between Christianity and African cosmologies. The Africans read the Bible as an allegory of their own history, and generated discussions which brought dialogue, confrontation, and compromise. Translation work greatly enhanced the interaction between the Christian worldview and African cultures. Bediako and

---

1. Mudimbe, *Invention of Africa*, 1–23.
2. Peel, "Gender in Yoruba Religious Change," 1.
3. Peel, 140.

Sanneh emphasize the importance of translation of Scriptures into African languages as it facilitated engagement with people's worldview and thought patterns.[4] This resulted in rooting Christianity and making it authentic. Scriptures were made available as a basic reading text and was also central to the oral instructions being given to the Christians. There was similarity between the Biblical narratives and some of the African narratives. African women therefore felt affirmed by Scriptures.

The Scriptures also became an authoritative basis for challenging some of the ideas and rituals from African religion and culture. Women used the Christian faith to recapture their dignity. They sought help from European officials who championed their cause. However, the most effective transformation came as a result of courageous women challenging some of the practices. As Hodgson and McCurdy show, women escaping to the mission station generated discussions and debates in the society, which led to change of ideas and attitudes.[5]

Women could also participate in leadership and establishment of the church because of the policy of lay leadership and also development of local leadership. Pirouette and Hastings point out that African agents, especially catechists and evangelists played an important role in the expansion.[6] Most of them had little contact with the institutional church and appropriated religious information through informal channels. They therefore came up with a Christian faith, which either adopted aspects of the traditional beliefs or challenged the behaviour that follows traditional belief. The teacher-evangelists responded to and stimulated mass demand for change. Missions, therefore came across congregations gathered around schools and churches, which had been founded by African agents and only later brought to the fold of the church. As a result of this agency, there was a popular expression of Christianity. African initiatives therefore altered the course of the original mission establishment.

4. Bediako, *Jesus in Africa*, 65; Sanneh, *Translating the Message*, 51.

5. D. L. Hodgson and S. A. McCurdy, *'Wicked' Women and the Reconfiguration of Gender in Africa* (Oxford: James Currey, 2001).

6. M. L. Pirouet, *Black Evangelists: The Spread of Christianity in Uganda 1891–1914* (London: Rex Collings, 1978); Hastings, *Church in Africa*.

The teacher-evangelists used ideas from the Bible, western ideas through literacy and ideas from African culture to found new societies and were seen as both secular and religious leaders in the community, which was in continuity with African leadership. However, authority for leadership in these new communities was first and foremost through possession of Spirit of God. This was both a biblical appropriation and continuity from African culture. Second, leadership was as a result of having a clear multiple identity, both as member of the African and Christian community. This is what gave people credibility for leadership. Missionaries who established the first mission stations were also perceived as having multiple identities. Their mission stations were seen as clans, and they as leaders of those clans.

Third, women participated in leadership because of the example set by the first African converts and women missionaries. Although the official structures of the church were patriarchal and exclusive, women were leaders in the Christian village even before the establishment of some of the mission stations by the European missionaries. There is a consensus that the missionaries' wives and African initiatives played a key role in the expansion of Christianity. The original leaders of the church were mainly the African catechists. The Bombay Africans or those who had received the message either at Frere-Town, Nairobi or Uganda. The spouses of the Bombay Africans played a key role in this expansion. When the mission stations were set up, both African women and the women missionaries played a central role in the leadership of the mission station. There were even instances when the women missionaries were actually the people in charge of the mission station. Gender issues were also central to mission work. An example is Ng'iya Mission Station, whose focus was to work among Luo women and girls. By coincidence the mission station was established in the vicinity of the shrines of the feminine ancestral spirits. Ng'iya Mission Station focused on all kinds of issues relating to gender. Alego, in which Ng'iya was situated, housed the shrine of one of the Luo feminine ancestral spirits. This meant that there was also engagement with feminine issues at the spiritual level.

Chapter 5 focuses on mission interaction with African culture, specifically focusing on African marriages and marriage processes. In an attempt to re-organize African marriages, the missionaries and administrators were not only re-organizing the women's lives but were also re-working key structures of the society. This is because African marriage structures and processes reflected their philosophy of life, power structures, and socio-economic systems.

African women therefore had to find new ways of dealing with complex issues arising from the new situations and also maintain their multiple identities as African and as Christian women. African marriage systems and processes were at the core of African women's identity. Female circumcision gave women self-determination and was also a mark of ethnic identity. The payment of bride-wealth gave the marriages credibility. It also gave the women status, dignity, and voice in society, and gave legal status to the children. The process of payment brought the families together, and since payment of bride-wealth was a lifelong process, it facilitated continuous dialogue between the two communities. African marriages reflected their respect for both individuality and community cohesion. The process of bride capture, and the role of the *go-between* in marriage reflected respect for both individual rights and freedom of choice as well as respect for community. The processes ensured that people followed normative beliefs and values of society. However, the process also offered safe space and provided a way out for people who could not cope but ensured that their dignity and integrity was maintained.

However, through social change and mission work, African women acquired multiple identities. They had to work out how to maintain their identities as African Christian women. Bride-wealth was viewed by Europeans as enslavement of women and was also believed to be the reason behind many forced marriages. Marriage was also increasingly being viewed by some of the Africans as an individual affair and not a community issue. However African Christians had still to dialogue with non-Christian members of the family over payment of bride-wealth. Bride-wealth became a major point of conflict. The introduction of a cash economy further complicated the issue as most of the bride-wealth was being paid in cash. This was mainly paid to the girl's father as an individual. Therefore in cases of marriage break up, it was difficult to pay back the money. Most of the parents therefore forced their children to stick to oppressive marriages.

African marriage processes were also central to the economic empowerment of women. Bride-wealth facilitated accumulation of wealth for the household by the woman. Through the process of bride capture, a woman could also acquire livestock. In the African polygmous marriage set-up, women headed the household and through household they had individual property rights. African women could also accumulate property through personal initiative, which was encouraged through competition between the houses. African widows had their property rights secured through widow inheritance. African marriages also reflected their power structures. *Mikayi* had decision-making powers in the home, and it was also a stepping stone to leadership in the society. All women had decision-making power in their houses. African marriage systems had within them systems of justice, arbitration, and reconciliation.

The mission's emphasis on monogamous marriage was therefore a real point of conflict with African philosophy of life. In the new marriage set-up, a man was supposed to head the house, while the woman's position was relegated to the kitchen. This was different from the African philosophy where power was shared. The man headed the home and made decisions at the wider level, including decisions on the running of the household. African Christian women were advocating monogamous marriages but wanted to retain the position of *Mikayi*. Most of the girls running to the mission station wanted to recapture this position. African women were also fighting a new invention of tradition, that of rural-urban polygamy, which entrenched patriarchy. The teaching against polygyny also had an adverse economic implication on African women. Through the new monogamous system, most of the women lost their property rights. There was a re-organization of gender roles. The emphasis on monogamy also meant that some of the women had to stay single. However, both the African culture and also the missions had no respect for the single status. Most of the single women had no means of economic empowerment. The teaching on monogamy therefore in some instances contributed to the low social status and oppression of women.

The fight against polygamy resulted in divorce cases, which had been rare in precolonial society. Although the missionaries criticized polygamy, they failed to address pertinent issues like childlessness in marriage. In most cases, missions resorted to colonial legal systems of justice to deal with marriage-related issues. Paradoxically, African women often went to mission stations so that they could access new systems of justice. They were also looking for protection from adverse situations since the missions had attacked the cultural systems which offered these.

However, the colonial legal system could not deal adequately with marriage-related issues as they also touched on faith and identity. African Christian women had a major challenge to deal with the issues and at the same time maintain their multiple identities as African Christian women. African Christian women had also to deal with rituals, which were not only an assault to the dignity of women, but also disempowered them socially and economically. African women were assisted by the women missionaries to organized *Buch Mikayi*, or the women's council. The women's council facilitated the empowerment of Christian women. *Buch Mikayi* was initially started as a part of Ng'iya Girls' School. It offered an opportunity for women to come together and discuss issues affecting them and seek solutions. *Buch Mikayi* also facilitated individual agency work of various women. It gave women an opportunity for leadership and decision-making in church and society. It also created a foundation for women's social and economic empowerment through education. *Buch Mikayi* therefore helped women to fight against oppression resulting from mission work and social change as well as oppression resulting from cultural practices. *Buch Mikayi* fought patriarchy in both church and society.

Women went to the mission station to recapture their dignity and recapture position of *Mikayi* by being able to make decisions over their lives. They gained empowerment by accessing education, which was the new source of power. They gained new skills in agriculture and sewing, which they could use for their economic empowerment in the new system. The women also went to the mission station as a way of accessing the new system of justice. Women who were caught up in the system also sought help from European officials who championed their cause. The most effective transformation came through women escaping to the mission stations and generating discussions and debates, which led to a change of ideas and attitudes. Christian women also defied some of the cultural practices like widow inheritance, which dehumanized them. Women were courageous to do this because of the resources from both their Christian faith and culture.

Chapter 6 focuses on educational practices and empowerment of girls through Ng'iya Girls' School. The educational practice had been greatly influenced by the educational philosophies and policies of the different actors. All the actors agreed on the focus on education, namely emphasis on marriage, centrality of religion in the curriculum, and the use of the vernacular. However, each group had a different philosophy behind their emphasis. The major concern of the Africans was training girls for marriage. However, African marriages entailed their social and economic systems. This implied that education addressed all those aspects of life. Most of them argued that there was great need for proper literary grounding on the domestic subjects. The use of vernacular meant interacting with African philosophy, thought-forms, and ideas.

African women negotiated mission education to deal with complex issues during and after the colonial period. They used resources from their faith, mission education, and culture in ways unintended and unexpected by the authorities. The women used their faith, education, and African culture to recapture the position of *Mikayi*, which was a position of leadership and economic empowerment. African women used mission education to recapture the two most influential positions in the pre-colonial society. Those were the positions of *Pim*, or teacher, and the position of *Ajuoga*, or medical specialist. These positions were also very influential and essential during the colonial period.

African women used their faith and education to challenge some of the cultural practices, which gave them low social status. They also challenged some of the agricultural rituals, which gave men power to declare the onset of agricultural seasons. They also challenged widowhood practices, accompanied by sexual rituals, which dehumanized women. The widowhood rites also denied many women their property rights. African Christian women also challenged the rural-urban polygamy that developed in the early 1930s. This kind of polygamy was described by Christian women as *chode*, or prostitution, which was a newly coined term.

African women also used sewing and domestic science skills in unintended ways. Instead of just enhancing domestic skills, the sewing classes became a way of transcending language and cultural barriers. They used sewing skills to recapture their dignity. They also used sewing skills as a means of income generation. This gave them economic independence and enabled them to challenge taboos. They used sewing and domestic science skills to entrench themselves as agents of new ideas and of change. The new dress code ushered in changes, which were a challenge to the traditional idea of authority. The new dress code therefore caused contradiction in society, which created opportunity for debate on power and authority.

African women used resources from mission education and culture as a stepping stone to economic empowerment. They were enabled to generate income to invest and achieve economic independence. Ng'iya Girls' School graduates used their income as teachers to pay taxes for their parents. Some built corrugated iron sheet houses for their parents, elevating them to a higher class in society. The women took roles traditionally preserved for men, and they were referred to as *chuo*, or male.[7] Luo women also used the gardening skills they received at Ng'iya to improve their crop yields. Some of the women established themselves as large-scale cash-crop farmers. Through the work ethic instilled in them, the women took the initiative and participated in community development. The women participated in trade and in some of the instances, assisted the community to set up village banks.

African women used resources from their faith and mission education to access positions of leadership in the church, both as ordained and as lay women. The women used their leadership positions to build relationships and to work towards peace and reconciliation between different ethnic groups. Ng'iya graduates were among the first women in Nyanza to be elected to the Diocesan synod. All the women lay canons in the Dioceses in Nyanza are graduates of Ng'iya. The first woman to be appointed director of Christian community services and the first woman to be elected a Diocesan chancellor in the church in Kenya were both graduates of Ng'iya. The first woman to be an ordained priest in the Anglican Church in Kenya was also a graduate of Ng'iya Girls' School.

Luo women also used resources from mission education and their culture to access leadership positions and to make decisions over their lives. They recaptured the Luo idea of *thuon* and the biblical imagery of soldiers of Christ to take risks and bring transformation in society. Luo women used their reading skills to gain status and power in the society. They took the example of their teachers and other Christian women as role models

---

7. "Male" among the Luo was not biological but referred to power.

for leadership. Some of the Luo women recaptured the position of *Mikayi* by becoming political figures in the society. Grace Onyango, Grace Ogot, and Lucia Okuthe used their education to access political leadership and church leadership.

Chapter 7 focuses on girls' education at Alliance Girls' High School and the establishment of the women's movement. Alliance offered an elite education to a few girls drawn from all over Kenya. The education at Alliance was based on the Christian ideals of the alliance of missions. Alliance of missions brought together Christian missionaries working together on common areas of interest like education and social work. The government worked together with the Christian missions to provide higher education for girls. The focus of Alliance Girls' High School was both scholarship and Christian values. The girls sat for both the Kenya African Secondary School Certificate and the Cambridge High School Certificate Examination. The girls were eventually enrolled for high-school certificate from Cambridge. Alliance produced women academics, administrators, politicians, and other professionals.

The education of girls at a higher level led to the establishment of the women's movement in Kenya. The movement was built on the foundation of African traditional society and the women's movement. The women's movement became the springboard for women's empowerment in Kenya, which enabled the fight against injustices, and for gender equality. The movement became the avenue for economic development. One of the main bodies for women's empowerment was the Maendeleo Ya Wanawake Organisation (MYWO). During the colonial period, the agenda of MYWO was to divert women from participating in the Mau Mau liberation movement. Their focus was on community development, especially of women in the rural areas, through women's clubs. The clubs gave women the opportunity to come together, exchange experiences, acquire new information and skills, and cooperate to promote common good. Phoebe Asiyo became the first African president of MYWO.

The women used the women's movement as a fighting tool for the liberation of women and gender equality. They fought against gender-based violence. In the United Nations Conferences, they emphasized the need to focus on African women's voices and priorities. At the UN Conference in Mexico in 1975, Julia Ojiambo who headed the government delegation, underlined the need to focus on the issues of want before clamouring for emancipation. The main focus for the Kenyan women was on development. One of the major issues was on women's health especially on reproductive health and family planning. The women's movement took a leading role in promoting the advancement of women during the UN's Decade for Women 1976–1985. One of the biggest debates at the UN Women's Conference at Copenhagen in 1980 was on female circumcision. The women from the Northern Hemisphere claimed that the African women were complacent. The African women pointed out that female circumcision could not end through militarization, but through dialogue. Militarization could only drive it underground. They argued that in the long term, female circumcision could only end through education and economic empowerment of women. The African women insisted that there was need to deal with more pertinent issues like poverty, malnourished children, and death at childbirth.

The women's movement in Kenya played a key role in leading the preparations for the UN conference in Nairobi in 1985. They pointed out the need for African women to have their own framework for women's empowerment instead of focusing on women in development. They were concerned that African women should be participants in the development process. They insisted that there was need to listen to the less-privileged women's voices. The African women underlined that economic development was key to African women's liberation. They felt that issues of drought and famine should take precedence over controversy, which characterized some of the meetings. There was a need for more constructive dialogue. They maintained the need for women to participate in public affairs. The conference in Nairobi emphasized on the need for equality between men and women. Gender language was born in this conference. The women also came up with alternative report focusing on Development Alternatives with Women in a New Era (DAWN). The main thrust of this report was that development was not serving the needs of women and did not correspond with women's values and aspirations. They questioned the framework of women in development.

In Beijing at the sidelines of the conference, African women came up with an analysis of the constraints that have hindered the achievement of development goals. These included gender inequality, poverty, structural adjustment programs, militarization, deforestation, dumping of toxic waste and pesticides that destroy the environment, high population growth, poor governance, indifference of donors to gender issues, biased use of resources, language barriers, and exclusion of young people from leadership.

Eddah Gachukia worked for women's empowerment through the African Women Development and Communication Network (FEMNET) and the Forum of African Women Educationalists (FAWE). The aim of FEMNET was to remove all of the obstacles to women's active participation in all spheres of public and private life. This was through equal share in economic, social, cultural, and political decision making. Their focus was on women's empowerment through the principals of gender equality and respect for human rights. They also focused on the girl child's education. FEMNET came up with an African Woman's Journal. Their framework for women's empowerment was gender and development. Gender was about women and men, and therefore men were incorporated in their programs. FAWE's main focus is the education of girls. They underline the importance of education for participation in development. Girls have to access education if gender equity is to be achieved.

CHAPTER 2

Women during the Precolonial Period

Education of Girls

Education was very central to maturity, responsibility, and leadership in most African societies. The belief in God was the foundation of African life, and therefore religion was tied to the whole system of education. Acquisition of knowledge had several dimensions to it. Education was therefore both formal and informal, both theoretical and practical.[1] The aim was to inculcate knowledge but also to empower people with different skills. Another aim of education was building character.[2] Education started at the time of birth and only ended with death. The parents were the first teachers, who educated their children until they were ready for a wider education. Education was defined for every age group. Education of the young children was entirely in the hands of the mother and the nurse. The medium of teaching was through lullabies, and as they grew older songs were used. They played games imitating adult roles and were also taught stories and legends of their communities.[3] The specific objective of education at this stage was to provide a child with a wide range of knowledge for overall development, morally, mentally, physically, and socially.

The second stage of education was when the youngsters grew older and the boys were taught by the men; while the girls learned from the womenfolk essential skills befitting their role in the society. The focus of this education

---

1. Muruiki, *History of Gikuyu*, 19.
2. Kenyatta, *Facing Mount Kenya*, 121.
3. Kenyatta, 104–105.

was on child-care, house-work, and agricultural activities. The instilling of gender roles and identity was the main factor in this education. The major method of passing knowledge at this stage was through participation and observation. The girls were absorbed in the domestic routine at home, and by the age of twelve, they were expected to be proficient and able to manage most of the domestic affairs on their own. When their mothers went to the garden, they were expected to prepare a meal for the family. Girls were expected to have sufficient knowledge of agriculture and were basically given the necessary instruction by their mothers. By the age of twelve, they were supposed to go to the garden from around six in the morning till around ten. The girls were also given some livestock training and would follow the brothers as they went to herd animals. They would also learn milking skills

The most important channel for education was the initiation ceremony. Young people underwent formal education in the hands of experts. Among the Kikuyu this was done in a temporary hut built in the home of the sponsor. Instruction was very key at this stage, as it marked transition from childhood to adulthood. Some of the subjects covered included tribal traditions, religion, norms and values of the society, sex education, health and hygiene, roles, and responsibilities in the society. Young people were also taught special skills by different experts. They learned the history and geography of their society. After the initiation ceremony, girls continued to learn informally by assuming their responsibilities in the homestead and being taught more about their roles as girls and mothers under more experienced women.[4]

Education was also tied to specific economic activities in the society. The young girls were empowered with skills to assist in production of material wealth. Education in general technology was open to all children. However, there were special professions that were inherited from parents. Medicine would be inherited by a son if the medicine man was a man, and inherited by the daughter if she was a woman. It was inherited by the child who had the best memory. The parent would show the child all different kinds of medicine and instruct them over their use. Whenever, a patient or client came, the child sat beside the parent as she did the work. The child would be asked to help grind or mix the medicine, which was to be used. When

---

4. Muruiki, *History of the Gikuyu*, 9.

the parent was going to work in a different location, the parent would carry a bag containing the implements. Education and inheritance therefore went together. There was a similar pattern of education with the rainmakers and a potter. Most of the professions were only affected when children became adults. There was a rite performed and the skills dedicated to the ancestors of the clan.

Case-Study of *Siwindhe* as a Locus for Girls' Education

Siwindhe, or girls' dormitory, was the major forum for formal education of girls among the Luo. *Siwindhe* was a circular building with a thatched, cone-shaped roof and its walls were always decorated with paintings of animals. In the *siwindhe* a warm, cozy, and perpetual fire burnt on the hearth. The girls started getting specialized and more detailed instructions in the *siwindhe* at the onset of puberty, immediately after undergoing the initiation. Sleeping in the *siwindhe* was compulsory at this stage, and absence was upbraided and rebuked. Culprits were punished by being made to attend to the fire. The importance of the *siwindhe* was captured in the Luo saying that "You are 'unschooled' as a person who never slept in the *Siwindhe*." Each *siwindhe* had a cohort of twelve to fifteen girls from the same home, clan, or neighboring clans. They would only leave the *siwindhe* for marriage.[5]

The main aim of education was inculcation of *rieko*[6] or knowledge, which was central to maturity, responsibility, and leadership. The belief in God was the foundation of life, hence religion was tied to the whole system of education. The aim of education was both to inculcate knowledge and impart different skills. Education was to empower the young girls to meet the challenges of the future, socially, economically, and politically. The girls would learn the history and philosophy of their people. The Luo emphasized head knowledge or *Obwongo,* or the work of the brain. This had to do with critical thinking and memory.

Education was also to help foster identity. Young girls were taught about their kinship structures and things that pertain to life in general. The aim was to maintain community cohesion. It was to help children be good and

---

5. Asenath Odaga, *Poko Nyar Migumba* (Kisumu: Lake Publishers, 1978), 6.

6. *Rieko*: an expansive term which refers to knowledge, intelligence, being skilled, wisdom, experience, and exposure. The older a person became, the more *rieko* they acquired.

responsible members of the society that is both brave and respectful. Respect, honour, and integrity were central virtues in the society. Education promoted respect for elders, and elders also respected young people. Through education the norms of the society were passed down to successive generations. The aim of education was also to inculcate moral values and assist in developing virtues within the society. This would assist the young people in making the right decisions in life.

Education was also central to character formation. Individuals were trained, mentored, and exposed so that they could develop *chuny motegno*, or a strong heart. *Chuny* or heart was the site of deep intellect, ethical emotions, and wisdom of a person. Virtue was the main feature for right conduct. Virtues were tied with feelings, thoughts, beliefs, intentions, and attitudes. *Pakruok*, always translated as "virtue boasting," or publicly naming virtues was central in helping to cultivate virtues. The Luo referred to people not by their given names, but by virtue names. Names had magical power, and the character of a person was believed to be in their names. Women were called by their clan names, which was believed to have a bearing on their personality. People could also be referred to using particular colours, which were symbolic of particular virtues. *Rateng*, or black, symbolized courage, while *silual*, or brown, symbolized decency – a highly respected virtue among the Luo.[7]

The individual was seen as part of the wider community. People were contextualized, hence not just referred to by their virtue names but virtue names of relatives and friends, community deeds, or place of origin. This was very important for mentoring. Social models were always brought to the attention of young people. This greatly influenced the ideals and other personality traits. Dances and other community occasions gave opportunity for *pakruok*. The harpist would stop his song and ask the girl, "Who are you?" to which she might respond: "I am the courageous or brave one," or "I am the sister of the strong one, who has reserved his strength and will dig his own grave"; or "I am the lover of the strong, brave, and generous man, who dared the wild buffalo. All blind men can peacefully wash their hands and wait for meat." Virtue could also be praised through song and other

---

7. Mboya, *Luo Kitgi Gi Timbegi*, 176.

poetic performances. A common praise song was, "There are many men who are wealthy; however, wealthy Otieno cannot be compared with others who shrink like roasted meat." This implied that most rich people were thrifty and stingy; however, Otieno was generous and hospitable. Another common song was in praise of Adoyo, a lady who had a pure, strong, and calm heart.[8]

The learning process also took place through general interaction within the community. Knowledge was passed through traditional methods of communication. These skills and techniques were sharpened in the *siwindhe*. Communication skills were used as means and techniques of passing on philosophy and planting ideals in the members of the society. They were also an important tool of inculcating norms and values. Communication was important because through it people became aware of their identity. Primary techniques of education included language, songs, proverbs, stories, and riddles. Poetic performances were also central in teaching. Language was central in communication as in it philosophy, norms, and values of the society were revealed. Verbal stereotyping was a very important tool for the education of children. Children were called names like *Thuon* or courageous, *Jaber* or beautiful one, *Nyaduse* or humble or graceful. These names imposed certain ideas on the child's mind.[9]

Ngeche or proverbs were used extensively for education, and all children were expected to learn them. *Ngeche* were statements or expressions that made indirect reference to issues. They were integrated into speech to enhance their aesthetic appeal. *Ngeche* captured the morals of the community poetically. They were the embodiment of the community ethos. They were also the code of the community's worldview and philosophy of life. The proverbs were derived from the immediate environment. The main function was to comment on situations or behaviours as a way of cultivating understanding on the system of thought of the community. *Ngeche* was a way of re-stating the community's norm by ridiculing deviant behaviour, counselling or advising. Most of the *Ngeche* emphasized the value of kinship and gave the impression of an egalitarian society. However, egalitarianism was defined within certain bounds and left a lot of space for individualism.

---

8. S. O. Miruka, *Oral Literature of the Luo* (Nairobi: EAEP, 2001).

9. A. B. C. Ochola-Ayayo, *Traditional Ideology and Ethics Among the Luo* (Upsalla: Upsalla University Press, 1976), 58, 67.

Among the Luo, individualism and communalism were allowed to co-exist and complement each other. They emphasized on individual rights and justice.[10]

Poetic performances were also central in the education system. Poetry was an important medium of expressing powerful feelings, thoughts, and ideas. The culture was replete with poetic performances both in public and private. These were expressed through poems, songs, dance, drama, and choral performances. Poetry was important for both socialisation and passing down information. Poetry was also a source of cultural historical records. Poetic performances provide an avenue for social commentary. People would use poetry to critique individuals and institutions and to debate over issues. Poetry provided an avenue for critiquing adults and even sacred institutions. It also offered people an opportunity to use taboo words especially for education. Drama or non-verbal articulation could be used by persons to express deep thoughts or emotions. People could also use satirical poems.[11]

The use of humour, satire, and symbols was very important in the education. Satire was the result of using devices like irony and sarcasm. Satire was an integral part of poetic performances and narratives. The *huwege* concept of education was common among the Luo. *Huwege* was a discussion carried across ridges in song form. This was a kind of debate, a person in one ridge singing and getting a response from the other side in song. *Huwege* song was used as a commentary, for ridicule, or as a critique of a person or individuals. The songs were composed and sung in the fields, hill-tops, forests, rivers, and other people would join in song. This was an effective way of passing down information. It was also a very important forum for discussion. It tackled very sensitive issues like anti-social behaviour, or difficult situations in the society. However, the singing made the discussions interesting, and there were no direct confrontations. Narratives were important in teaching Luo philosophy and thought-forms. They were also a means of passing down community history. Narratives were used to discuss the norms and values of the society. The use of beast convention or animals to substitute human characters was very common in narratives. This arose out of the

---

10. Mboya, *Luo Kitgi Gi Timbegi*, 238–240.
11. Miruka, *Oral Literature of the Luo*, 89.

need for open teaching and discussions but at the same time community cohesion. The use of narratives was an important peace-building technique. Moral castigation was therefore handed over discreetly instead of through the open court.[12]

Pim, an elderly woman past child-bearing age, and in most cases a widow, was the main teacher in the *siwindhe*. *Pim* was a position of leadership, and she had maximum respect in the society. The grandmother among the Luo had moved from the role of production and reproduction to increasing authority and freedom. *Pim* had a lot of knowledge, wisdom and skills to pass on to the youth. This was due to her seniority and position in the hierarchy and being widely exposed. Luo women never married within their patrilineal group, hence *pim* provided young people with knowledge beyond their patrilineal group. The main role of *pim* was to live with, teach, and nurture young people in the clan and neighbourhood. She in turn found companionship, support, food, and protection. *Pim* was also central to the teaching of the youth because of amity between grandmother and children.[13]

Pim could freely discuss all subjects. The girls learned the cultural history, plus the history of clans and settlements. They learned about the environment and the geography of their area. In the *siwindhe*, the girls also learned the philosophy and thought-forms of their people. They were taught more advanced customs and traditions of the society. The *siwindhe* was also a place for learning the beliefs, norms, and values of the society. *Pim* also discussed with the girls issues of marriage and family life, cookery and gave them basic medical tips. *Pim* was also the main instructor on sex-education. She prepared the girls under her care for marriage. Girls were encouraged to interact with people of the opposite sex. However, they were not supposed to lose their virginity before marriage. *Pim* gave girls practical tips on how to handle themselves. She occasionally gave the senior girls permission to go and visit their lovers after the rest had retired. This was top secret between *pim* and the young people. *Pim* was the chief confidant of the girls entrusted

---

12. B. Onyango-Ogutu and A. Roscoe, *Keep My Words: Luo Oral Literature* (Nairobi: EAPH, 1982), 32.

13. Paul Wenzel Geissler and Ruth Jane Prince, "Shared Lives: Exploring Practices of Amity between Grandmothers and Grandchildren in Western Kenya," *Africa* 14, no. 1 (2004): 96.

to her care. She would also discuss dressing and ornaments. In addition, *Pim* was involved in their marriage arrangements and had to receive gifts from the men came for the bride capture.[14]

Girls went to the *siwindhe* at around seven o'clock after supper. They first had an opportunity to learn from each other through informal discussions. The girls also practiced new songs and dancing skills. Dancing was very important in Luo social life and was also a very important tool in communication. They composed songs praising the clan, and especially those who had died in war defending the clan. They also practiced *oigo* or love songs. The girls who were married but were visiting the homestead would share their experiences with the unmarried girls. The program in the *siwindhe* would begin by fastening the door. The girls would then spread their mats and bedding, then each would take their place. *Pim* would take her place at her bed referred to as *uriri*, which was located apart from youth. *Pim* would declare that it was time for total silence in the house

The formal part would be started by a performance of riddles. Riddles were statements, questions or sounds that have meaning. Riddles use metaphors in which reality is referred to in a veiled manner. Riddles were rational and were de-coded. They were the method through which the young people were taught to define concepts. It started with the description of a concept, and people were asked to say the concept which had the characteristics described. This was both to enhance critical thinking and memory. Riddles enhanced the power of observation of the environment. They entertained, socialized, and stimulated the mind. Riddles also enhanced understanding of phenomena and trained memory. They facilitated language use and gave commentary on life. Old riddles were removed as new ones were coined. Riddling gave an opportunity for mock marriage games. If people could not answer a riddle, the riddler would ask the others to offer her a man for marriage. She would accept or reject the boy given, for example on the grounds that he was lazy, feeble, ugly, or stingy. The mock marriage provided normative outlets for issues that would be disruptive in marriages. Mockery of people was otherwise disapproved in society.

---

14. Mboya, *Luo Kitgi Gi Timbegi*, 122.

Riddles were also important for socialization. It was a group activity, and young people would learn to see each other as doers, receivers, and challengers. They initiated action to test others' wits, but they acted also as recipients as their wits were being tried. The whole activity was both inclusive and reciprocal. It required compliance with certain rules, and everyone who had a riddle had to start with a specific formula. Offering a prize to a person whose riddle was solved was of high social value. It offered recognition and therefore motivated people to come up with their own new riddles. Refusal to accept the prize indicated the value of choice in the community. Themes of riddles would also be commentaries on life and behaviour. Story-telling or narrative session followed riddling. Riddles pointed out the essential complexity and disorder in life which narratives tried to simplify and explain. *Pim* would be the first one to tell stories and after the narratives, a debate would erupt in the *siwindhe*.

Women in Religious Leadership

Women played a key role in leadership in precolonial Kenya. This is first evident in the study of African religions, which is important in understanding the worldview and culture of the people. Hierarchy and seniority were very central elements of leadership in society. Knowledge, wisdom, experience and skills, which were central to leadership in society, came with age. God was the most senior and on top of the hierarchy. God was creator and originator of all life. God was an inalienable part of human beings and gave them dignity.

Women played a central role in religion as a result of understanding of the attributes of God, which were both masculine and feminine. God exercised paternal authority over everything. This supernatural paternalism was related to situation where ownership, leadership, and inheritance had been predominantly linked to male roles and patrilineal descent. God also had a feminine role, especially as creator, molder or maker in the idiom of pottery or basketry, which were predominantly female activities.[15] God was also the supreme spiritual power, and life-force of all living creatures.

---

15. Grace Ogot, *Miaha* (Kisumu: Anyange, 1983).

Below God, there were other spirits in the spiritual world. These included divinities, natural spirits, ancestors, heroes, and other mythological figures. They were both masculine and feminine and controlled human destiny. Seniority was central to participation in all kinds of leadership, including worship and sacrifice. The ancestral spirits – both male and female – were viewed as the most senior members of the society. They played a key role as mediators between God and humanity. Ancestral spirits could be petitioned to save people from evil forces and sickness, and they were asked to paralyze magic. The ancestral spirits needed honor and respect, and people would take gifts and offerings to them. Ancestors were also regarded as guardians of tribal ethics and spiritual welfare.

There were specific ancestral spirits belonging to specific lineages and were clan members, both male and female, who had died in the past. Various aspects of human life were controlled by these spirits.[16] Ancestral spirits would dwell in large rocks or would come in the form of a large snake. The most famous of these among the Luo was *Nyagidi*, the feminine ancestral spirit. *Nyagidi* moved gaily decked in the necklace of *gagi*, which is a type of Lake Shell. She lived in the river *Kanyaboli* in Alego, which flowed into Lake Victoria. *Nyagidi* would visit the mainland once every five years. The visit would be followed by a good harvest and long periods of prosperity. If *Nyagidi* was not welcomed, she would wreck vengeance by bringing famine and drought to the land. When rain was needed, *Nyagidi* would stand on the surface of the lake, like a great rainbow and puncture the skin of heaven.

Another ancestral spirit was embedded in the tale of *Nyamgondho*. This was a commentary on one of the physical features, a rock by the lake in Southern Nyanza. *Nyamgondho* caught a shriveled woman spirit from the lake. He built for the woman a hut, and she brought with her from the lake a large number of cattle, goats, and chicken. *Nyamgondho*, who was *msumba*, an unmarried land tenant, became rich overnight and married several wives. *Nyamgondho* could now sit and drink among the elders. One day, after a drinking spree, *Nyamgondho* returned home and all the wives refused to open the gate. He was annoyed and insulted the elderly woman, claiming

---

16. Nancy Schwartz, "Active Dead or Alive: Some Kenyan Views about the Agency of Luo and Luhyia Pre- and Post-Moterm," *Journal of Religion in Africa* 30, no. 4 (November 2000): 466.

that even the shriveled one whom he had retrieved from the lake was not responding. Next morning as *Nyamgondho* woke from his drunken stupor, the woman left and all her property followed. *Nyamgondho* followed and gazed at the lake speechless, but it was too late. *Nyamgondho* was transformed into a rock, his chin resting on his walking stick. He had encountered the vengeance of a feminine lake spirit.[17]

In most African societies, possession by the supernatural spirit was a prerequisite to access authority and positions of leadership and responsibility. Through spirit possession, people received the power needed to perform certain tasks. One such religious position was that of a medicine man/woman, a position occupied by both men and women. These people received both knowledge and mystic powers. They were empowered to prophesy, administer healing, and even becoming war leaders. They were the most prominent religious leaders in the society. They had a protective medico-charm used for the good of individuals, families, or community as a whole. Medicine-men/women had both mystic powers and religious medicine. They were religious experts who took a latent role in the preparation for wars, raids, and during the planting season. Medicine-men/women divined fortune for war, cursed the enemy, and made magic to secure victory and safety for warriors. They dealt with all the evil things that affected the nation and prophesied about the future, and nobody could disobey their word. Medicine-men/women would bring peace between two warring sides. They also dealt with many aspects of family life and relationships; they were also ritual and political advisers to the elders and chiefs. They combined both ritual and political leadership and sometimes the tribal state was led by a medicine man/women who assumed power during the war. The African narratives were full of women medicine men/women. The medicine men/women were viewed as friendly people in the community, but they had a very complicated role. They fulfilled their roles in collaboration with other specialists in the community. Women were also rainmakers, who were consulted in time of drought and rain. They used both mystic powers and skills, who could either be supernatural or inherited. The rainmakers were paid for their services, and most

---

17. Onyango-Ogutu and Roscoe, *Keep My Words*, 142.

of them were respected people in the society. Among the Luhyias, most rainmakers were women and came from the family of Nganyi.

However, despite women's empowerment, women were also disempowered by the culture. First, this is because most of the societies were patriarchal societies, and power was invested on men. Second, most of the societies had myths that showed women were the source of sin and other negative issues. Third, some of the rituals were very dehumanizing and degrading to women.

Leadership in Society

Leadership in most African communities was determined by seniority. This is best illustrated in the polygamous marriage set-up, where the senior wife was consulted on all important decisions in the home. Women, specifically the senior wife could head clans, be religious leaders, and even warriors if they possessed the necessary gifts and skills. Second, although the societies in Kenya were patriarchal, there were opportunities for women to exercise leadership and power. This was due to both flexibility and dynamism within the culture and the opportunity for negotiating positions.

In most of the traditional cultures, power, decision-making, and ownership were male attributes, but women could be male.[18] Second, in most of the societies, a woman's life consisted of two different life ages. As a wife and mother, she was at the center of production and reproduction, but initially had little authority in the home. In the later stage after menopause, as a mother-in-law and grandmother, she enjoyed much authority in the home and in the community. After menopause, for example, among the Luo women ceased to be female, they became male. They could therefore participate in activities that females were banned from. Third, according to traditional myths women held positions of leadership, and they determined what was to be done. This confirms that Africans had ideas of women in leadership.[19]

---

18. Ifi Amadiume, in her book *Male Daughters and Female Husbands* (London: Zed Books, 1987), discusses gender among the Igbo, which is quite similar to many African cultures. She distinguishes gender from biology and sex. The women are not men, which is biological, but male which stands for power.

19. E. R. Holmes and L. D. Holmes, *Other Cultures, Elder Years* (London: Sage, 1995); Geisler and Prince, "Shared Lives," 97.

In most African communities, leadership and social relations were based on age and other status positions. The most senior member of the society was the most respected because wisdom and good judgement come with age. In some of the societies, women were among the council of elders. Among the Luo, they could rise to the level of *Okebe*, a person who rose to position of leadership because of hard work, wealth, and responsibility, and who was consulted on several issues.[20] The hierarchy included chiefs, warriors, medicine women, and war heroes. Women could be part of the hierarchy, and one of the kikuyu women, Wangu wa Makeri even rose to the position of chief during the colonial period, which affirms that women could hold such positions.

In most African societies, women also participated in leadership because there was no centralized leadership in most of the societies. Most of the communities were egalitarian with no single group completely charged with the responsibility of maintaining the social and political institutions as they existed. Everyone safe-guarded the part of the society in which he was involved at any given time. Therefore, authority and power were widely diffused through the varied components.[21] Also to hold position of leadership, there were certain qualities and abilities of individuals that were recognized and developed. There were women judges and orators as part of the leadership structure.

Socio-Economic Empowerment

Precolonial Kenya was basically an agricultural country and the most important possession for most communities was land and livestock. Land was in most cases owned by the community, and no individual or group could sell community land. The basic land right stemmed from membership of the clan.

The Kikuyu believed they were given land by God, and therefore ownership of land was basically by fact of being a Kikuyu. First, land was used to establish a homestead and then for cultivation. The community land was

---

20. A. Oginga Odinga and Henry Odera Oruka, *Oginga Odinga: His Philosophy and Beliefs* (Nairobi: Initiative, 1992), 37.

21. Muruiki, *History of the Gikuyu*, 110.

acquired through clearing and cultivation of virgin land. The portion given to the wife to cultivate became her property. If a man married another wife, he could clear another portion of land. The Kikuyu could also acquire land through purchasing as a community or individuals from Ndorobo. This became the property of both the husband and the wife. Among the Kikuyu, land could be allocated to daughters for use. If the girl married a poor man, they would continue using the land allocated to the girl (wife) while she was still young. Among the Luo and Luhya, unmarried women had usufructory right.[22]

Among the Luo and the Luhya, land was owned on clan basis. Each family had exclusive occupational and usufruct rights over its own holding. There was no concept of individual ownership, as all ownership was derived from clan membership.[23] However, on another level, there was the concept of ownership of land. The person with allocative rights was referred to as the owner of the land and held the land in trust for the community. Second, the family who guaranteed the use of land was also referred to as the owner of land. In most African communities, women were the owners of the cultivated fields. They made decisions regarding these fields and decided which crops to plant. They could exchange or give out the plots for a period of time. The woman controlled the products accruing from her efforts.

Allocation of land was central to the economic status of women, as agriculture was traditionally a woman's activity. Among the Luo, this was reinforced by myths, and according to one of the myths, there was original bliss, and people did not have to work. People just had to take their hoes to the farm, which would automatically get dug. However, *miaha*, the newly married wife, was disobedient and instead of just placing the hoe in the farm, she decided to dig. From that day of a woman's disobedience, God cursed people to dig and work for their livelihood. According to another version of the myth, originally people were not obliged to work as God gave them food, and they in turn sacrificed. However, there was a time when God did not receive the sacrifice on time. First, the chameleon and then the

---

22. Achola O. Pala, "Women Access to Land and Their Role in Agriculture and Decision Making: Farm Experiences of Joluo of Kenya," *Journal of Eastern African Research and Development* 13 (1983): 77; Muruiki, *History of the Gikuyu*, 74.

23. Ogot, *History of the Southern Luo*, 147.

tortoise were sent, but they failed to deliver the sacrifice as they were very slow animals. At that time, women ruled and made decisions. However, after the failure of the sacrificial expedition, the woman and man spent time arguing as to who was responsible. During the war of words, the sacrifice was further delayed, and God was further annoyed. God therefore decreed that human beings should work, especially dig for their livelihood. Women among the Luo were therefore central to agricultural activities. According to the Luhyia, rainmaking is key to agriculture, and according to myths, rainmaking myths are traced to women.[24]

Another major possession among Africans was livestock. Cattle, sheep, and goats played a significant role in the economy. They were used as a means of exchange, and among the Kikuyu, sheep and goats were the major currency and the greatest investment. Livestock also served in social transaction and ceremonies. They were mainly used for paying bride-price. They served as a source of meat, milk, and blood in the diet. Livestock produced hides used for bedding, making sandals, and straps for carrying loads. Livestock also played a key role in religious sacrifice. Having livestock gave an individual prestige in the society.

The household headed by a woman was central in understanding economic arrangements in the African societies. The house was the matrifocal unit, which included mother, son, and her unmarried daughters. This formed the basic economic unit. All the sons would inherit property associated with their mother's hut, which included cultivated land, livestock and other movable property. The woman was the guardian of this property until the sons got married. The household or hut was therefore the springboard for the economic empowerment of women in African societies. African societies were patriarchal but within the polygamous set up, there was balancing of power. The man was the head of the home while the woman headed the hut.[25] The hut was the central unit for organizing the process of production, distribution, and consumption. Women had decision-making power over

---

24. Atieno-Odhiambo, "Hegemonic Enterprises and Instrumentalities of Survival: Ethnicity and Democracy in Kenya," *African Studies* 61, no. 2 (2002): 223–249.

25. A typical Luo home, or *dala*, was an enclosure that consisted of several huts. The man had his own house, or *duol*, centrally situated in the home. Each woman had her own hut, which consisted of her household, the woman, and all her unmarried children. The man was the head of the home, however, the woman headed the household.

the activities of the hut. The hut was also central for economic development because it was the major unit that encouraged competition. Most of the African societies put a lot of emphasis on communal relationship and ownership. However, *nyiego*,[26] or competition, defined the relationship between households. At an economic level, the hut therefore stood for individuality, competition, and accumulation of wealth. Each household received their basic inheritance, and it was up to them to develop their resources. The woman's hard work and organizational skills eventually determined her social and economic status in the society.

The hut also played a central role in the accumulation and distribution of livestock, the most important form of investment. In the polygamous set-up, livestock was distributed according to the household. Women also had the opportunity to accumulate livestock for their household through their own efforts. One such opportunity was through the marriage process. Among the Luo and Luhyia, bride-wealth was one of the major methods women used to accumulate livestock. Most of the livestock acquired from the bride-wealth belonged to the house of the bride's mother. They would use the milk and other resources from the livestock. These livestock would later be used by the bride's brother for their own marriage. This was very important as the brother's wife would participate in the economic development of their house through agriculture.

Women also accumulated bride-wealth through the cow given specifically to the mother as bride-wealth. Second, virginity was highly valued, and a girl who was a virgin at marriage would receive a cow. Among the Luo, a woman would receive a calf, an ox, two goats, and a hoe from her father for investment in her house during the final marriage ceremony. The woman would also receive a goat and hoe from the husband. This was done after the birth of her first child. Later, when the woman started to cook in her house, she would get household goods from the mother-in-law. During the initiation ceremonies (e.g. female circumcision), the guardian and the female operators would be given livestock. Women, who had excess grain

---

26. *Nyiego*, from the root word jealousy, characterized the relationship between the wives in a polygamous marriage. The woman referred to the co-wife as *Nyieka*, or my competitor. This has largely been interpreted as competition for the husband's attention. However, on a deeper level, it was competition for resources.

by the end of the agricultural season, exchanged them for livestock. Women therefore had several avenues for accumulation of livestock and for economic development of the household.

Bride-capture was an important method of accumulating cattle and also enhancing the social status of women among many African communities. In the marriage ceremony, after all the bride-wealth was paid, the men would organize to capture the girl, which would lead to a spirited fight by the girl and by her brothers. A girl who staged a spirited fight during the capture could demand payment of livestock. She would therefore start accumulating livestock for her household. Bride-capture would also enhance the social status of women as a girl who staged a spirited fight was viewed as a hero. Bride-capture also gave the girl the final opportunity to communicate her final decision over marriage. If a girl had changed her mind, she would communicate this during the process of capture. Among the Luo, she would do this by holding a Euphorbia tree; she could also eat Sodom apple or climb an ant-hill. Bride-capture also gave the girls an opportunity to deal with problematic situations without losing their social status. If a couple had something to hide, they would organize an earlier capture to avoid public humiliation and embarrassment. This would be for example in a situation where the girl was pregnant out of wedlock, or if the boy was too poor to pay dowry.

Women were also involved in industries and trade. Pottery and making baskets and beads were exclusively women's industries. Women were also involved in both internal and external trade. Inter-tribal trade was mainly done by women, who would pass with immunity through other territories. The Kikuyu had large markets and traded in iron and iron objects, tobacco, gourds, honey, ochre, pottery, baskets, and livestock. Excess grain was stored and sold when there was scarcity. In western Kenya, there was a lot of trade at two levels, between two neighbouring clans and inter-tribal trade. Inter-tribal markets were established at the foot of a big tree in the boundary. Various commodities like grain, livestock, craft work, pottery, and pot implements were sold. Women also participated in local hawking of fish. Trade was mostly through the barter system. Marriage and kinship ties played a key role in trade in Africa. Marriage brought together women from different clans. This formed an important market base, as people would visit their relatives and participate in trade in the process. Homes would therefore serve as temporary markets.

However, African women's socio-economic empowerment was balanced off by cultural ideas, which contributed to the low social status of women. Most communities had myths, where women were initially in control and their authoritarian rule overthrown by men. Thus, their emphasis was establishing patriarchal societies. In most African societies, although women had control over cultivated land, men controlled the farming season.[27] The clearing of fields in readiness for planting was done exclusively by men. Men were also the agricultural ritual leaders. Among the Luo, all agricultural seasons were accompanied by sexual rituals, which required the presence of both husband and wife. The sexual rituals therefore controlled women's economic autonomy. A widow could not meaningfully participate in agricultural activities until she had undergone widow inheritance.

Widows were also disadvantaged and experienced low social status through death and widowhood rituals. When the man died, the wives were supposed to mourn silently, until evening, when official mourning would be declared. The wives would tear off their clothes and remain naked because the person who was clothing them had died. The women would also powder themselves with ash and remove all the man's wealth from the house. They would pour out all the millet and other grain for the cattle to eat and destroy granaries. The family would resort to poverty, and would henceforth be fed by neighbours.[28] After three days, the women would be shaved, and the period of mourning would be declared. They were declared to be ritually unclean. During this period, the women were not supposed to move freely in the society; hence all social and economic activities were suspended.

27. John Middleton and Kershaw Greet, *The Kikuyu and Kamba of Kenya* (London: International African Institute, 1965), 21.

28. Mboya, *Luo Kitgi Gi Timbegi*, 131–132.

CHAPTER 3

Colonial Period as a Watershed for African Women

Leadership during the Colonial Period

African women were marginalized from leadership during the colonial period due to the policies adopted by the colonial government. First, this was due to the British policy of centralization. In 1895, Arthur Hardinge was appointed the first British Commissioner in the Protectorate. He relied on John Ainsworth, Francis Wall, and Charles Hobley, the provincial commissioners for the consolidation of British power. They became Provincial Administration Officers across the country.[1] The main aim of the British was to pacify the region, establish law and order, and entrench British power. There was need for a more centralized administrative structure in order to achieve this policy.

The British adopted Lord Lugard's policy of indirect rule. Therefore, chiefs were adopted as agents of local administration. In most African communities, the position of the chief had evolved into a territorial leader during the period of migration and settlement. These chiefs, however, had to work with other elders in leadership. In 1902, the British introduced the chief's ordinance and re-organized the position to serve their needs.[2] Although, some communities like the *Kamba* did not have chiefs but were ruled by the council of elders. Chiefs were introduced everywhere as convenient

---

1. William R. Ochieng, *A History of Kenya* (London: Macmillan, 1985), 102.

2. Bethwell A. Ogot, "British Administration in the Central Nyanza District of Kenya 1900–1960," *Journal of African History* 4, no. 2 (1963): 250.

for colonial rule. The chiefs were put in charge of several areas. They were to maintain law and order, keep the roads clear, and hear petty cases.[3] All of these chiefs were men, except Wangu Wa Makeri, who used culture to negotiate her position as a chief.

Wangu wa Makeri (1856–1930) was the first wife of Makeri wa Mbogo, a wealthy man from Muranga. In 1901, she was appointed by Francis Hall as Assistant Chief in Weithaga. This was at the recommendation of the Paramount Chief Karuri. Chief Karuri had first earmarked the position for Wangu's husband, Makeri, who was his friend and of the same age. Makeri however declined to take the position as he wanted to concentrate on the care of his livestock. Wangu took over the position, as the first wife could access positions of leadership in African societies, especially after menopause.

Wangu wa Makeri was a very strict administrator, and her implementation of the British colonial laws made her very unpopular. She was very brutal in her dealing with tax evaders and those who were found drinking *muratina*, a potent, locally-brewed gin. The tax evaders were dragged, whipped, and incarcerated in solitary confinement by Wangu's footmen. In some instances, people's sheep were impounded if they failed to pay taxes. The people who were confined acted as porters, and their work included carrying the chief and other British administration officials. Wangu also devised treatment to sober up drunk people. A case in point is when she dealt with a drunk man who wanted to disrupt the elders' meeting. The man was made to kneel before the whole village, and made a subject of ridicule. When Wangu visited the villages, people had to dot the pathways with calabashes of yams, sweet potatoes, and arrow roots for her consumption.

In 1909, people plotted for Wangu's downfall. She was accused of going against Kikuyu culture. Wangu had decided to join the male warriors in *kabati dance*. This was a dance organized by male warriors when they wanted to discuss battle plans. The dance could also be organized as a crowd-puller when a major announcement was to be made. Wangu had joined the *kabati dance*, when she saw Chief Karuri join in. This was a taboo, as women were not supposed to join the male warrior's dance. As she was dancing to the rhythm of the song, her skirt rose up and exposed her thighs, which was

---

3. Robert Maxon, *John Ainsworth and the Making of Kenya* (New York: University of America Press, 1980), 181.

also taboo. The people exaggerated and spread rumours that she had danced naked. In 1909, Wangu was summoned by Karuri to answer to the charges that she had danced naked, and she offered to resign.[4]

Further marginalization of women from leadership came under the policies of Sir Charles Eliot, who was appointed governor in 1902. Eliot instituted a policy of white settlement. According to this policy, power was with the white administrators: "One fundamental as regards this rule is that the white-man is paramount. This means that in reality the white minority will form an oligarchy and consequently, ninety percent of the population comprising black will remain without a say in their own affairs."[5] This resulted in the formation of an all-white legislative council in 1907. In 1909, the provincial administration was also reorganized. The provincial commissioner was given wider responsibility and power over the territory. They reorganized the position of the chief, appointed new ones, and excluded those who had been elected by their own people. When the provincial commissioners were appointed, many chiefs had sent their emissaries to negotiate with the Europeans. However, the young men who were sent were employed as chiefs surpassing the elders.[6] This situation was confirmed in Ainsworth's assertion: "It is not clear, who are recognized by the British as chiefs and headmen. There were those people who set themselves up as rival chiefs and headmen. They refused to recognize the authority of existing chiefs. Individuals used the opportunity to rival those who had political power and influence before the onset of colonial rule, reinforcing their claims by bringing problems directly to the European office."[7]

By the end of 1909, the provincial administration drew a comprehensive list of recognized chiefs. These people were given new symbols of power like cloth and copper rings. The chief's power was redefined, and they were given regular salaries. However, in the process the provincial administration by passed the traditional system of electing new chiefs and elders. There were elaborate consultations before the elections. This ensured that the chief

---

4. "Wangi wa Makeri" in Standard Digital, Sunday 12 February 2012.

5. John Ainsworth, "Black and White Man in East Africa," 1916, RH Mss.Afr.s., 382 (1).

6. Paul Mboya, interview with Crispin Onyango, 21 December 1967. SPA.

7. Ainsworth, "Nyanza Province Special Report," 1909, KNA PC/NZA/1/3/38.

ruled by consensus and involved other elders. The process was captured in Owen's letter:

> Ruoth among the Luo embodied all that the people held as dear to them. When a Chief was chosen, his installation was a ceremonious affair, including his investment with insignia of office. The stuff of justice called luth was also an object of ceremonials of an elaborate kind. In effect under the tribal system both tribal elders and elder women yielded allegiance to their head, which cemented them together and gave them the best possible guarantee of a peaceful society.[8]

By 1912, the position of the chief had been completely reorganized. The responsibility of the chief was to maintain the spirit of loyalty to the British crown and inculcate that spirit in his people. He was to discover people's opinion on the issues. The chief was to maintain order, prevent offenders, and bring offenders to justice; the chief also seized and kept property. The chief assisted the government in the execution of their duties like collecting taxes.[9] This was a departure from the traditional idea of a chief as a leader of people, who worked with other leaders.

The evolution of a separate judicial system by passing the traditional elders marginalized women from leadership. In 1907, the Native Court Ordinance, created courts in every location. The court was to try both criminal and civil cases under the chairmanship of the chief. In 1930, the Native Tribunal Ordinance created divisional tribunals. These had jurisdiction over four locations. In 1935, Division Courts were set up to hear both criminal and civil cases, and the members were chosen from the panel of elders. By 1951, there was a complete reorganization of the African court system. The panel system was abolished and in its place was a bench of four or five permanent members. In 1951, the African Courts Ordinance granted additional powers to these courts. In excluding traditional specialists, women were left out of the judicial system.[10]

---

8. Owen to Sir Joseph Byrne, Governor, 30 May 1932, CMS: G3/A5/01932 f 99.

9. Ochieng, *History of Kenya*, 105.

10. Ogot, "British Administration," 254.

African women were marginalized from leadership by being alienated from new instruments of power. Education provided by the missionaries was viewed as the new source of power. It was even challenging to the power of *jobilo*: "People were amazed that it was possible to discover what somebody had written by reading a person's thinking. Those who could read were also said to be talking to papers. This was branded as a new kind of magic."[11] Mission education initially targeted sons of chiefs whom they viewed as future leaders. The chiefs were encouraged to send their sons to school, where they were taught to read and write and also learned Swahili. Such youths would be used as administrators to assist in the administration of natives. Ainsworth had advocated a kind of education that would empower the boys with skills like carpentry, masonry, and new farming techniques. In 1909, after the Fraser Report, the government began a project in conjunction with the missions to offer both general and technical education at Maseno.[12] The progressive boys were employed as interpreters and clerks for the colonial officials. The educated boys therefore became the new elite in society. In 1926, the Alliance Boys' School was started as an elite school for African boys. The younger men also enlarged their power base due to their proximity to the new sources of powers, namely, the administrators and missionaries. Women were, however, excluded from these instruments of power. During the colonial period, the only education offered for the girls was mission education. However, the main aim of the missions was to train wives for the emerging elite. Despite this marginalization, some women used resources from their culture to participate in the nationalist movement. Mekatili Wa Menza, of Giriama from the Coast, rallied her people to revolt against the British before 1920, she even recruited two members from what was left of the male-led council of elders.[13]

Mekatilili, the first independent fighter, was born in 1860 in Giriama land in Kilifi. She was the only daughter in a family of five children. Mekatilili was named Myanzi wa Menza but became Mekatilili when she had her first boy, Katilili. She was a member of the traditional women's fellowship and

---

11. Reuben Omullo, interview with Crispin Onyango, 15 June 1967. SPA.

12. Memoirs of J. J. Willis Reflections of Uganda 1872–1954 Mss.Afr.s.1296 Box 5/14.

13. Cynthia Brantley, *The Giriama and the Colonial Resistance in Kenya 1800–1920* (Berkley: University of California Press, 1981).

later became the leader of the group. Mekatalili was greatly influenced by the stories told by her grandmother on the intervention by foreigners. The coming of the British had been foreseen by a prophetess. A Giriama foreseer had also foretold the coming of strangers, who would bring with them things that flew over people's heads, and a Giriama woman, who would lead resistance against them.[14]

Initially the major concern of Mekatilili was the breakdown of Giriama culture and the British influence. She called upon her people to save their sons and daughters from getting lost in British ways. Mekatilili led her people in the context of British colonial rule and likened herself to the mother of chicks in defence of her people. She created a resistance to the authority of the British and their appointed headmen. Mekatilili accused the headmen of betraying the Giriama for cheap rewards. Mekatilili's bravery and oratory power earned her a huge following.

Mekatilili fought the labour, taxation, and land policies of the British colonial government. She mobilized the Giriama to take oaths and offer sacrifices in order to restore their sovereignty, and she urged people not to fear Europeans. Mekatilili was against labour recruitment and opposed forced labour in British-owned rubber and sisal plantations. The British were putting increasing economic pressure on the Giriama through taxation, attempts to control trade in palm wine and ivory, and by recruitment of young men to work on plantations and public works projects. Mekatilili also opposed the recruitment of Giriama youth to serve as carrier corps during World War I.

In 1912, the British wanted to forcibly take about 100,000 acres of fertile land, north of Sabaki River. Mekatilili and Wanje wa Madori, led a meeting in Kaya Fungo, the ritual centre for the Giriama in July and August 1913. The Giriama refused to move from their land by oath, and the British decided to use force. About 250 Giriama were killed, and 70 percent of their houses were burnt or razed, and about six thousand goats were seized. The rebellion lasted for over a year, and although the British won the war, in the long-term, they removed land restrictions and lightened the labour demands. Charles Hobley, the provincial commissioner at the coast, was

---

14. Celia Nyamweri, "Reinventing African National Heroes: The Case of Mekatilil, a Kenyan Popular Heroine," *African Affairs* 115, no. 461 (October 2016): 619.

in charge of the eviction project. He attributed the responsibility of the Giriama resistance against the British to a blind rascal (due to his opposition of British) named Ngongo, who instigated a half-mad woman, Mekatilili, to tour the country, preaching resistance to the government. Mekatilili was also described by the British as a "witch" and a prophetess, who spread the gospel of violence. Mekatilili and Wanje wa Madori were arrested in October 1913 and sentenced to five-years imprisonment in Kisii. In April 1914, they escaped from prison and walked back to Giriama land where they received a hero's welcome.[15]

Despite the opposition by Mekatilili and others, Kenya was established as a British Colony and a white man's country. The colonial government gave priority to the white settlers. The colonial government therefore developed land, taxation and labour policies, which oppressed Africans. The leadership of the country was in the hands of the Europeans. The education policy focused on giving Africans such an education that would prepare them as labourers. This led to the formation of a nationalist's movement led by the political elite.

The political elite arose out of protest or a nationalist movement. These were mainly graduates of the mission schools, all of them male. Underlying most of the political protests was the quest for control of the means of modernization. In 1920, four chiefs – Mbiyu Koinange, Josiah Njonjo, Philip Karanja, and Waruhui Wakungu – formed the Kikuyu Association. The aim was to defend Kikuyu land from settler encroachment and gain title deeds. In 1921, Harry Thuku and other educated elite products of mission schools founded an alternative movement. They felt that they were in a better position to talk for the Africans than the chiefs who had been appointed by the colonial office. They founded the Young Kikuyu Association. They demanded the marginalization of women from political leadership came as a result of the emergence of an African abolition of Kipande, lower taxes, abolition of forced labour, increased education for Africans, and title deeds for land owners. Later, Young Kikuyu Association (YKA) was renamed the East African Association, so as to command a wider appeal from different ethnic groups. In 1924, a new movement the Kikuyu Central Association

---

15. Wanyiri Kihoro, *The Price of Freedom: The Story of Political Resistance in Kenya* (Nairobi: Mvule Africa, 2005), 17.

was formed. In 1927, Kenyatta joined the KCA and became the secretary and editor of the newsletter. The KCA mainly attracted the young Kikuyu educated elite.

The Kamba elite also formed a protest movement led by James Mutua and James Mwanthi. The movement was comprised of mission-educated elite, who were the main critiques of chiefs. They communicated effectively the feelings and discontent of the people, better than the chiefs. An example was the expulsion of Kamba cattle from Yatta Plateau grazing fields.[16] The marginalization of women from leadership came as a result of the rise of Young Kavirondo Association, also referred to as *piny owacho*, a mass resistance movement which was demanding more consensus and participation. This is seen even in the coining of the term *piny owacho*: "*Piny owacho*, translated 'the public asserts' or 'the people's will' was a term coined by one of the clan elders Ogutu Ahalo from Rangala, Gem. He advocated the use of the title as an explanation to the authorities of the precise name and object of the meeting held at Lundha, Gem."[17] Lundha, which was chosen as the venue, was the traditional centre for social and war time deliberations. The area was referred to as *Kar Buch Tong*, literally translated as "the place where people met with spears." The meeting was summoned by using traditional methods of communication by sending the message round verbally through the chiefs. Around nine thousand people from all over Nyanza attended the meeting.[18] The meeting of several chiefs gave the meeting credibility with the Luo people, the administration, and the missions. Most of the people who attended the meeting felt that this was an opportunity to give back the leadership to the Luo traditional leaders.[19]

The emerging elite however did not view *piny owacho* as a mass resistance movement. According to Jonathan Okwirry,[20] the first chairman, the idea

---

16. Maxon, *John Ainsworth*, 103.

17. Simeon Nyende, interview with Okaro-Ojwang, 1967. SPA.

18. Keith Kyle, *The Politics of Independence in Kenya* (London: MacMillan, 1999), 20.

19. Rosbella Otako, interview with Okaro-Ojwang, 1967. SPA. Rosbella was the wife of the assistant chief, in whose home *piny owacho* meeting took place.

20. Jonathan Okwirry was the first chairman of *piny owacho*, later registered as Kavirondo Tax-Payers Welfare Association. During the *piny owacho* meeting, Okwirry was a teacher at Maseno school. He was later appointed senior chief in Uyoma from 1945–1957. He was the African District Council chairman between 1945–1948. Benjamin Owuor was elected as secretary of *piny owacho*. He had earlier worked in the provincial commissioner's

of *piny owacho* was conceived and implemented by teachers at Maseno School: "It is the teachers at Maseno School, who held secret meetings and organized the resistance. I took the initiative to establish the meeting and drove the matter to the fore. I had more contact with the newspaper reports and therefore was more acquainted with the developments taking place."[21] Okwirry argued that the main reason for summoning people was to inform them of the new developments in the country. Kenya was being turned into a British colony, and there was an imposed system of administration. One of the major issues raised at the meeting had to do with leadership. The Luo were raising issues about centralized administration and the lack of authority by the African leaders. People also felt that their leaders lacked dignity and status. The leadership structure also excluded elders.[22] However, there was a difference of opinion between the general population and the emerging elite, as to the solution of the problem. The general Luo population wanted to revert back to the traditional leadership structure, but with a paramount chief to chair the meetings. Their major concern was the scornful attitude towards African leaders:

> Traditional African leaders, namely the clan elders, the Chiefs and the customary advisors were no longer consulted. They were deprived of authority and influence. This was transferred to colonial lackeys whose basic merit was unquestioning loyalty, obedience and submission. The newly appointed leaders had no confidence with the people. They were figureheads and instruments of colonial rule. Chiefs were simply used as messengers and overseers to supervise forced labor. They were mere puppets, hence the need for representative leadership.[23]

The traditional leadership style that the Luo were asking for would have been inclusive of women. However, the emerging elite proposed a system that would divert power both from the colonial administrators and

---

office. During the meeting, he was a teacher at Maseno. Simeon Nyende was elected as the treasurer of the movement. He had been a teacher at Maseno from around 1916, and a pastor from 1927. He was also an advisor to the Luo union East Africa.

21. Jonathan Okwirry, interview with Okaro-Ojwang. 1967. SPA.
22. Rosebella Otako, interview with Okaro-Ojwang. 1967. SPA.
23. Mariko Okungu, interview with Okaro-Ojwang. 1967. SPA.

traditional leaders. At a meeting with Tate, the provincial commissioner, and later with Governor Northey, at Nyahera in 1922, they proposed a president for Nyanza. This would be a leader of an autonomous government in Luo land: "Direct administration was the chief cause of the evils which beset the Luo community. There was need for a President of the entire Luo community as opposed to the paramount Chief. We needed a President of a semi-independent Nyanza, as opposed to a fragmentary system of rule based on Chieftainship."[24] The emerging elite cited the example of an outstanding Luo leader, by the name of Odera Ulalo, who had controlled the whole of Nyanza, plus a good part of what is currently the Rift Valley. They also wanted a block title deed for the whole of Nyanza. This was to be granted to the president, who would in turn distribute the land.[25] This would take away decision-making over land distribution from both the elders and the colonial government. The elite felt that the chiefs, due to their polygynous status would demand more land and more wealth. The chiefs, in their submission to the Carter Land Commission, however, demanded individual land tenure on a lease-hold basis.[26]

Jonathan Okwirry reiterated they were looking for a president in anticipation of a possible republic built along the same lines as Ankole, Toro, or Baganda Kingdoms. The emerging elite only put forward the idea of a paramount chief, when the colonial administration insisted that they could grant only this and not a president. In a memorandum to the Chief Secretary, the Kavirondo Tax-payers Welfare Association (KTWA), put forward the following request: "We are young educated people. Our method of thinking is based on books and white man's ideas and influenced by several years of government service. We would like your Excellency to arrange for three educated impartial natives to be appointed as paramount Chiefs in three Kavirondo Districts of Nyanza Province, whose work would be checking on native development."[27]

It was only in 1945 when Sir Philip Mitchell, the governor, outlined the government policy that the demands for a paramount chief and president

---

24. Jonathan Okwirry, interview with Okaro-Ojwang. 1967. SPA.
25. Simeon Nyende, interview with Okaro-Ojwang. 1967. SPA.
26. Benjamin Owuor, interview with Okaro-Ojwang. 1967. SPA
27. "Memorandum of KTWA to Chief Secreatary," 17 May 1939 KNA DC/CN8/2/71.

were put to rest. The governor held a big provincial *baraza* or meeting, in Kisumu and stated that:

> For years Africans have been clamoring for paramount Chiefs and administrative Chiefs. Such appointments had no place in the planned future. The intention is to strengthen the local government until it became largely responsible for administration in reserves. The government is going to introduce the position of administrative assistants. They would function as junior administrative officers. The Local Native Councils would also appoint African secretaries in the near future.[28]

The emerging elite's view of leadership, therefore, did not have room for women in leadership. Their main aim was to sideline the participation of elders, which would have ensured the position of women as leaders. The general Luo population had also noted that the emerging elite did not carry the aspiration of the masses. The elite were derogatively referred to as *jomemorandum,* or people of memorandum. They were very fond of issuing memorandums, and in their opening statements, they paid allegiance to England.

In 1924, in response to the demands of the emerging elite, the colonial government introduced Local Native Councils (LNC). This process further sidelined women from political leadership. The aim of the LNC was to capture the voice of the Africans and co-opt the emerging elite in running the country. Most of the people who could occupy administrative positions had to have education. The mission-educated group therefore produced the first political leaders and administrators. Among the first people co-opted to the LNC were Rev Simeon Nyende, Rev Ezekiel Apindi, Rev Reuben Omullo, Rev George S Okoth, Jonathan Okwirry, Mathayo Otieno, Benjamin Owuor, and Joel Omino. In Ukambani, James Mutua and James Mwanthi were elected to the LNC. Kangethe and John Mbuthia were elected to the Muranga LNC.[29] All chiefs were also nominated members of the LNC. A few women like Zeruya Adhiambo, educated at Ng'iya Girls' School became

---

28. "Administration: Report on Native Affairs," 1945 RH: Mss.Brit.Emp.S.390 Buxton, Box 7.

29. Maxon, *John Ainsworth*, 100.

members of LNC.[30] LNCs were later turned to African District Councils (ADC), which had more power to run African affairs. The major condition for membership of ADC was education and training. Women were therefore locked out of leadership because they lacked the required education and training. Most of the members of the emerging elite, however, asserted that leadership was open to women, it was only that they did not have the interest and the education.[31]

Women were also locked out of both the grass-roots and nationalist movements, which were the springboards of political leadership. After World War II, there was a new political atmosphere in the country. At the National level, there was the Kenya African Union (KAU). The main leaders of KAU were W. W. Awori, James Otiende, Achieng Oneko and Walter Odede, Harry Thuku, James Gichuru, Jomo Kenyatta, Kaggia and Kubai. Most of them had attained higher education. The other organization was the Luo Union, which brought together Luo from Central and Southern Nyanza. In 1954, the Luo Union East Africa was formed with Oginga Odinga as first *Ker* or President. The Luo Union became an important power base for political leadership. Oginga was also manager of the Luo Thrift and Trading Corporation. In 1944, Eliud Mathu was elected as the first African member of the legislative council. In 1948, the number of African nominated representatives to the legislative council rose to four. In 1954, The Lyttelton Constitution ushered in a multi-racial government. B. A. Ohanga was elected as a minister in the multi-racial government. However, African women were excluded from participation in party politics and political leadership due to lack of a higher education and an economic base.[32]

Priscilla Abwao was the only woman nominated member of the legislative council. She was a graduate of the Friends Girls' Boarding School in Kaimosi. Abwao taught in the school for two years before she entered social work. In 1951, she stopped teaching and began work in community development in North Nyanza. In 1954, she won a scholarship to study community

30. Barasa Samson Omachar, "The Development of Education: A Case-Study of Ng'iya Girls' School 1923–1927," (Master's thesis, Moi University, 2014), 90.

31. Simeon Nyende, interview with Ojwang Okaro, 1967, SPA; and Reuben Omullo, interview with Ojwang Okaro, 1967, SPA.

32. Ogot, "British Administration," 271.

development in Britain. She graduated with a diploma in Domestic Science after one year of study. On her return to Kenya, she was nominated to the legislative council in 1961. Abwao was the only nominated member to attend the Lancaster Conference during the negotiation for independence.[33]

Abwao actively participated in business motions of the legislative council. In line with MYWO, they emphasized the importance of educating the rural women so that the development goals of the country could be achieved. Abwao spoke against increased prices for household goods without a corresponding increase in family income. She argued that the Swahili term of respect for a European woman, *memsahib*, should be extended in its use for African women too. Abwao underlined that African women could not be respected by people of other races, unless African men changed their attitude. African women had not only rejected traditional rules of inequality but had also reversed the status hierarchy. Men must show equality to women.[34] Abwao started a women's federation, which invited women from Tanzania and Uganda, and worked towards the development in both rural and urban areas.

In 1962, Abwao attended the second Lancaster Council. She argued that women were not asking for a special position for themselves. What women wanted in the soon-to-be-independent Kenya was to be treated as partners in the new society, which they were part of creating. Abwao was representing women who had been marginalized from politics.[35] Abwao also noted that the African women represented two-thirds of the registered voters in Kenya; however, women had not been able to translate their demographic advantages into female electoral victories. The main concern of Kenyan women was the proper care and development of Kenya's human resources. As mothers, women perform the traditional role of guiding the young, keeping

33. Esther Mombo, "A Historical and Cultural Analysis of the Position of Abaluhyia Women in Kenyan Quaker Christianity 1902–1979" (PhD diss., University of Edinburgh, 1998), 173.

34. Audrey Wipper, "Equal Rights for Women," *Journal of Modern African Studies* 9, no. 3 (October 1971): 435.

35. Musandu, "Daughter of Odoro," 66.

the home, and contributing to the general social welfare of the community. Powers inherent in keeping the home are broad and far reaching.[36]

Socio-Economic Changes during the Colonial Period

Changes in the Practice of Agriculture

Agriculture was predominantly a woman's activity in traditional African societies, while men were herders. However, due to changes brought by migration and settlement, men began to participate in agriculture. The climatic conditions in the new places were suitable for agriculture, so people started mixed farming. Second, during the onset of the colonial period, cattle rinderpest, small pox, and sleeping sickness killed many cattle. This was followed by punitive action by the British.[37] The British decided to establish their rule by invading people, taking their animals and other property. This led to men completely moving to agriculture or participating more in agriculture in order to rebuild their herds.[38] Colonialism generally led to the marginalization of pastoralism and expansion of agriculture. The Christian missionaries also used agriculture as a tool for evangelism. They taught new farming methods to men who went to mission schools.

Further marginalization of women from agriculture as an economic activity was a result of colonial policies. Sir Charles Eliot and the governors who followed him favoured the settler mode of production. This resulted in the Crown Lands Policy, which stated that all land was owned by the Europeans. Settlers, who were initially tenants eventually became landlords, while the Africans became tenants. The precolonial land tenure could no longer work. Many people were displaced from their lands and either had to be resident laborers in their own land or move away permanently from the reserves and

---

36. Priscilla Abwao, "Memorandum on Behalf of African Women to Kenyan Constitution," Conference in London, 1962.

37. R. M. Maxon, *A Political History: The Colonial Period* (Oxford: Oxford University Press, 2002), 94.

38. Margaret Jean Hay, "Luo Women and Economic Change during the Colonial Period 1890–1945" in *Women in Africa: Studies in Social and Economic Change*, eds. N. Hafkin and G. B. Edna (Stanford, CA: Stanford University Press, 1976), 90–93.

go to the settler farm as squatters. In this case, the men obtained land for residence and cultivation in exchange for labour.[39]

In 1907, the colonial administration encouraged the growing of sesame and groundnuts in Western Kenya, on a large scale for export. These were traditionally crops grown by women. Women would always obtain seeds of new varieties through their relatives married in different parts of the territory. However, the chiefs now supplied the new variety of maize seed. In 1909, a West Indian was assigned to give men instruction on how to grow new varieties of crop and distribute cotton seeds and carry out inspections in the reserves. Indians and Swahilis were given small plots in parts of the territory to grow crops, and their farms would act as an example. By 1910–1914, there was great improvement in African peasant farming for export.[40] However, through this process agriculture as an economic activity was dominated by men.

Women were also sidelined from agriculture through the introduction of new technology. People were being encouraged to adopt better methods of preparing the land for planting. To enhance agricultural productivity, new implements were introduced, and elders and chiefs were already buying such implements.[41] There was introduction of heavier hoes, purchased mostly by men because it was only accessed through distant markets and was purchased using livestock.[42] Eventually, there was introduction of ploughs drawn by oxen. The chiefs were encouraged to open centres where demonstration in the use of ploughs was given to men. In 1912, a centre was opened in Kabete where farmers were sent to receive instruction on new methods of farming and the use of the plough. Women were therefore excluded from agriculture through lack of training opportunities in the use of new technology.

In the 1930s, the rise of the petty-bourgeois further marginalized women from the practice of agriculture. The educated elite employed as teachers,

---

39. R. M. Maxon, "The Years of Revolutionary Advance, 1920–1929," in *A Modern History of Kenya, 1895–1980*, eds. W. R. Ochieng and B. A. Ogot (Nairobi: Evan Brothers, 1989), 96.

40. Zeleza Tiyambe, "The Establishment of Colonial Rule," in *A Modern History of Kenya, 1895–1980*, eds. W. R. Ochieng and B. A. Ogot (Nairobi: Evans Brothers, 1989), 47–49.

41. Ainsworth, "Kisumu Province Annual Report," 1907–1908, KNA: PC/NZA/1/4.

42. Ochieng, *Outline History*, 68.

preachers, and clerks used money obtained from their wages to buy land and employ wage labour, thus practicing agriculture for economic purposes. In Central Province, they produced a food surplus, which they could sell in Nairobi. There was also an expanded market for maize and maize flour among the plantation workers. Around 1938, the depletion of land in the reserves led to the policy of destocking. Destocking the reserves especially in Ukambani led to compulsory sale of livestock.[43] This led to men practicing more agriculture.

After World War II, the policies of colonial administration further marginalized women from agriculture. Africans returning from the war were very militant against imperialism. The colonial office therefore came with the idea of creating a middle class to ease the tension. Macmillan, the under-secretary in the colonial office, proposed that the government should purchase smaller farms from the Europeans, with a view of selling them to the Africans. These farms were sold to the petty-bourgeois. Finally, the Swynerton plan in 1954 put agriculture for economic development exclusively in the hands of men.[44] First, this was through survey and enclosure of family land. The traditional land tenure systems were therefore reversed. The men were issued with title deeds as security for investment. African men could now grow cash-crop, be given technical assistance, and gain access to all marketing facilities.

Taxation policies

The introduction of tax was a major blow to the property rights and economic independence of African women. Taxation targeted *ot*, or hut, which was a springboard for women's economic empowerment. In 1901, a hut tax was introduced, to be paid by the male head of the hut. Each hut had to pay a goat for tax. Later, with the introduction of a money economy, the payment was two rupees per adult male per hut. In 1903, it was increased to three rupees per hut. In 1909, the poll tax was introduced on top of the hut tax, to be paid by every male adult in the hut. By 1913, the poll tax was being used as a way of registering men to go to work. A receipt was issued

---

43. Tabitha Kanogo, "Kenya and Depression," in *A Modern History of Kenya, 1895–1980*, eds. W. R. Ochieng and B. A. Ogot (Nairobi: Evans Brothers, 1989), 129.

44. Wunyabari Maloba, "Nationalism and Decolonization, 1947–1963," in *A Modern History of Kenya, 1895–1980*, eds. W. R. Ochieng and B. A. Ogot (Nairobi: Evans Brothers, 1989), 190.

for payment, and people who had paid the hut tax were not liable to pay the poll tax.[45]

Taxation became a major burden to women because some men generally resisted, or just avoided payment of the hut tax because they were not made liable.[46] Failure to pay tax always resulted in the sale of women's property. At first tax was paid in the form of ground flour, taken from the women's stock. Later, failure to pay tax would result in the sale of two whole granaries of maize harvest, which in most cases were women's property. Sale was done with a neighbour who could in turn pay money for taxation. The sale was mainly done to the younger men who worked in European farms and colonial employees like clerks and chiefs. These younger people had money, which was the new economic base. Through the introduction of a money economy and taxation, the economic arrangement of the African was reorganized. Greater property ownership was transferred from women to younger men. This had a great impact on the economic independence and social status of the women.[47] Some of the men working outside the reserves took hut tax receipts – paid by people back home – to show evidence of payment. They were therefore not made liable to pay poll tax.[48]

The introduction of the hut tax was not only an attack on women's economic base and property rights, but the process also reinforced the conception of women as property. Hut tax was a property tax levied according to huts owned by the tax payer. The colonial administrators assumed that huts were owned by men. The members of the local native council tried to point out that all the proceeds accrued through the hut belonged to women. They emphasized that to target the hut with taxation, was to target the woman who was the owner of the hut. Dobbs, a provincial commissioner, was sceptical and was convinced that the woman was herself property.

45. Anthony Clayton and C. D. Savage, *Government and Labour Policies in Kenya 1895-1963* (London: Frank Cass, 1974), 41.

46. Rosebella Otako, interview with Ojwang Okaro. 1967. SPA.

47. Rosebella Otako, interview with Ojwang Okaro. 1967. SPA.

48. Financial Commissioner, "Native Taxation Report," May, 1932. Mss.Brit. Emp.s.392.

Dobbs concluded that:

> A woman cannot own a hut in the sense that she could sell it.
> A woman is herself property and can only sue for property.
> She can only sue for property before the elders. A woman is
> given a hut by her husband, and if the woman died, the hut
> was destroyed and not used by another woman. It is difficult
> for native members to differentiate ownership from the right
> to occupy.[49]

Discussion on the status of women was further heightened by the debate over the taxation of widows. According to the taxation ordinance, the hut tax was payable by the owner of the hut. Women were technically not liable because native women were believed to only hold properties as trustees of their families. However, the financial commissioner maintained that widows had to be taxed because they were evidence of property ownership of the person who died. He maintained that:

> Women are a popular form of capital investment. Their value
> had appreciated owing to the relative increase of cattle which
> still remained the form of local currency. Women also yielded
> valuable income by working with their children in the fields
> and therefore could be taken as a simple measure of taxable
> capacity of the hut owner. A man with many huts will have a
> proportional number of people to work for him and contribute
> towards his taxable resources.[50]

The administration concluded that there was no more reason to exempt from taxation wealth produced by the agricultural work of a young and able-bodied widow than there was to exempt the same woman's produce before the death of the husband. The administrators also maintained that exemption of huts occupied by widows from tax would result in a great loss of revenue difficult to measure. They argued that hut tax discriminated between rich and poor, and maintained that the man who inherited the woman would pay the tax.

---

49. Minutes of LNC Meeting, 5–7 August 1930, KNA: PC/NZA 3/33/8/28.

50. Native Financial Commissioner, "Taxation Report," May 1932, RH: Mss.Brit. Emp.s.392.

The methods used in tax collection by the agents and colonial administrators were unjust and brutal and had a negative impact on the economic
and social status of women. The soldiers and agents were ordered to raid the
villages and set the houses on fire if tax could not be paid.[51] The women felt
the greatest impact over burning of the hut, since the hut was the woman's
abode. The process also led to large-scale confiscation of property in the
form of food-stuff – especially grains, beans, bananas, and cassava. Apart
from targeting women's economic bases, unfair methods of tax collection
led to the overworking of women. Failure to cooperate in the confiscation of
property would lead to forced labour either in the chief's home or administration camp. Colonial agents, tribal police, and chiefs also took advantage
of African generosity and tribal values. Whenever the officials went to collect
taxes they were treated like princes at the expense of women: "Chiefs and
sub-chiefs ordered women to prepare pots of beer and slaughter animals
and chicken. Women were also compelled to offer bags of flour, bananas,
dozens of eggs and firewood. The woman acted as the hosts of the colonial
administrators as they made rounds to collect taxes."[52]

Women therefore spent a lot of their time doing work which had no
direct economic value. They also had to use their own resources to entertain
the administrators. This was extra work on top of their daily chores in their
houses and farms. Although the methods of tax collection were brutal and
unjust, women could not register complaints as noted by Owen: "Laws are
published in English, natives are therefore ignorant of the actual terms of
the ordinance, which nowhere lays it down that a tax collector is empowered
to collect tax using unjust means. The district offices should explain the
ordinance so that there is no room for injustice."[53]

---

51. Reuben Omullo, interview with Crispin Onyango, 15 December 1967. SPA. The
administrators were nicknamed people with wings of fire because they used to carry match-
boxes in their shirt pockets, from where they removed them to burn houses.

52. Rosebella Otako, interview with Okaro-Ojwang, 1967. SPA.

53. Letter from Archdeacon Owen, *East African Standard*, 6 March 1928. A note by
P. C. Dobbs in his letter to the Chief Native Officer, Kisumu, 22 March 1928. RH: Mss.
Afr.s.665 (1).

Labour policies

The social and economic status of women was also greatly affected by the labour policies in economic development. In the new colonial dispensation, wage earning was the greatest stepping stone to economic development. The imperial policy encouraged economic development of the country through European settler farming. In 1908, the settlers maintained that it was unfair to invite the European farmer and at the same time do away with the foundation on which the whole of his enterprise and hope was based, namely, cheap labour.[54] The administration therefore had to devise some means of encouraging labour migration. One method of compelling men to move out of their reserves to find work was taxation. In 1908, settlers proposed the introduction of a poll tax, which was paid in cash. Receipts on payment were introduced as a means of registering people to work. This encouraged able-bodied men to work out of the reserves in order to earn money for taxation. Men therefore became the chief wage earners in the new dispensation.

Labour migration, especially of able-bodied men, was a great injustice to the African communities. Too heavy a burden was being laid on the women and children who had to do most of the work in the reserves. The cultivation and production even of food crops was suffering. First, this was due to the absence of men, who had traditionally done most of the clearing of the farms. Second, most of the men who were ritual leaders[55] were absent or delayed in coming for the onset of the agricultural seasons. There was therefore a decline in food production in the reserves. There was also an increase in social and economic evils. The proportion of men absent was detrimental to community life. It had an effect on both social organization and morality.[56] This also led to men keeping concubines and a new kind of polygamy, which was detrimental to the socio-economic organization. African men were also dehumanized by the kind of treatment they received from the administrators. African men were recruited as porters and had to

---

54. Maxon, *John Ainsworth*, 196.

55. In some of the African communities, sexual rituals preceded the planting of crops, hence the need for a man to be present.

56. "Labour Matters," 1925, RH: Mss.Afr.1117. Box 2 Orde Brown OB 24.

carry loads, including missionaries and administrators on their backs.[57] Men also felt dehumanized in their working place:

> They have a wretched hut and a minimum amount of mealie and mtama meal diet unaccompanied by any kind of condiment . . . salt or fat. A person from Kavirondo is turned out and works heavily the whole day, then he has to sleep in a leaky or wind exposed hut with possibly one blanket to cover him, with no one to cook his food, bring him wood or water . . . The day's toil is done and nobody is interested in him beyond getting as much work out of him as possible, and beating him if the employer is not satisfied with the amount of work performed . . . such a miserable life.[58]

The government policy on compulsory labour also had a great effect on the socio-economic status of women. People had to spend a lot of time on compulsory work, which diverted them from participation in their economic activities. In 1902, the Village and Headmen Ordinance was established. Under this ordinance, the headman was required to direct people to keep public roads in good condition and repair. In 1906 when Ainsworth arrived in Kisumu, he introduced compulsory work as part of the health measures. Ainsworth undertook systematic cleaning of bush and grass outside Kisumu and along the lake front. There was continued draining and filling of holes in the township. Measures were also introduced to deal with soil erosion.[59] Also, due to outbreaks of the bubonic plague on a yearly basis, the administration introduced what they termed as rat tax, as a means of keeping the region under quarantine. Each person was expected to hand over several rat tails to the headman as evidence that they had hunted for and killed rats.

In 1910, a Native Reserves Ordinance was established. This ordinance provided for compulsory labour on roads or any other work. Men in a given area could be directed to turn out and work for not more than six days per quarter on communal projects. They could work on water courses, minor irrigation, and dams. Compulsion by chiefs was allowed in order to

---

57. Sarah Ongeche, interview with Tolo, December 1966. SPA.

58. Maxon, *John Ainsworth*, 226.

59. Ainsworth, "Kisumu Province Annual Report," KNA: PC/NZA 1/4.

provide government officials with safari porters. But there was an abuse of the system, for it went beyond six days per quarter, and the work included women and children. Although forced labour was abolished in 1922 by the Native Labor Commission, people were still compelled to do community work. According to the 1922 ordinance, people were supposed to give a total of forty-eight days for unpaid and unfed community work. The other days were supposed to be paid labour. However, the colonial administration maintained that non-waged people among the Africans had to be forced to do compulsory work, unless they were producing economic crops for export. All male workers working on food production had to be considered for forced labour.[60] Due to the labour laws, men were more occupied with building roads in the reserves instead of working in their fields for food production or on cash crops.[61] In 1933, Simeon Nyende pointed out in the meeting that the LNC had voted money for road works, therefore all road works should be paid for. The chairman however pointed out that lack of funds could not permit payment of road works.[62]

Due to the abuse of power by the colonial administration, labour even went beyond what could be called public service. Compulsory unpaid labour laws were being applied oppressively. Women were being used in compulsory labour despite the law stating that it was for able-bodied men. There was forced labour for women on roads, and in chiefs and administrative camps:

> Women and children are being compelled by askaris to go out every morning to work on roads, paving them and sweeping them. They were also compelled to go to the Chiefs camp which was the local administrative center, where they did manual work . . . Women collected huge bundles of grass and carried them for long distances to be used in thatching in government Centre's, work camps . . . hewing firewood to be used by the Chiefs wives and fetching water for government workers.[63]

---

60. Amey, "Forced Labour," 1925, RH: Mss.Afr.S.1427.
61. LNC Minutes, 29–30 March 1932, KNA: PC/NZA/4/1/11.
62. LNC Minutes, 11 July 1933, KNA: PC/NZA/4/1/11.
63. Kungu Mariko, interview by Okaro-Ojwang, 1967.

The provincial commissioner, Dobbs,[64] however, argued that women volunteered for labour. Dobbs maintained that: "In the reserves natives had to do a certain amount of forced labor to keep their own roads clean, of course the obligation is on the adult male, however women and children come out of their own will to help their husbands, fathers and brothers to weed the road."[65]

Arch-deacon Owen had demanded that the girls who had been forced to carry thatching granary to the administration camp must be paid.[66] The LNC meeting in 1930 also pleaded that forced labour should be discouraged, especially the practice of bringing wood and water to the camps by women. They proposed that porters be employed in the camp for this purpose.[67] The practice of forced labour on women and girls demoralized them by making them beasts of burden. Also women would not have enough time to participate in economically viable activities.

Formation of class system

A major factor which led to the marginalization of women was the formation of class system. There was a gradual development of a middle class. First, this was done through redistribution of wealth. In 1895, the first agenda of the British was to bring different parts of the protectorate to submission through punitive action. To achieve this, the Europeans had to work through allies. Most of these collaborators were chiefs and headmen, who ceded their sovereignty through signing of paper treaties. Second, they were empowered economically by being made the sale of suppliers of food to the British officials. The British also used them in punitive actions, especially in lifting livestock and granaries of grain. The auxiliaries and agents were given some livestock to increase their standing and secure their co-operation.[68]

---

64. Dobbs worked in Nyanza between 1906–1931; 1906–1910, as assistant tax collector and later African District collector; 1925–1926 Senior commissioner Kisumu; 1928–1929 Acting Native Commissioner; and 1929–1931 Provincial Commissioner.

65. Papers of C. M. Dobbs, "Dobbs Dairy," 11 November 1929, RH; Mss. Afr.S.665/1.

66. Papers of C. M. Dobbs, Archdeacon Owen to *East African Standard*, 6 March 1928; "Forced Labour of Girls," quoted by P. C. Dobbs in his Letter to the Chief Native Officer, Kisumu, 22 March 1928, RH: Mss.Afr.s.665/1.

67. Minutes of LNC Meeting, 1930, KNA: PC/NZA/3/33/8/28 LNC.

68. Hobley, Dairy, 1899, RH: Mss.Afr.s.147b; Jonathan Okwirry, interview with Crispin Onyango, 18 December 1967. SPA.

Punitive action was therefore a major setback to women's economic independence. Through this process, grains that were owned by women were redistributed by chiefs to themselves or other members of the society who had more income.

Women were also sidelined from the economy through the development of a new class of traders. Indians had developed trade with Africans and gradually introduced the use of rupees. The introduction of a money economy had a great effect on the social and economic landscape of the protectorate. Barter trade, which was the mainstay of women was being replaced by retail shops. There was scarcity of food in 1906, in the protectorate, and Indian traders who had been granted licenses were doing a booming trade. Indian traders were involved in the sale of livestock, eggs, fowls, ghee (butter), millet, and maize.[69] The colonial authorities encouraged Indian traders because they stimulated both trade and consumption of important commodities among Africans leading to both increased production in the rural areas and Africans seeking employment in settler farms.[70] Ainsworth had maintained that Africans had to be made familiar with various objects. Bicycles were introduced in large numbers, and window shops were introduced in order to attract people to goods. There was an increase in the demand for imported goods. The encouragement of consumerism therefore established labour migration and a wage-earning economy among the men.

In 1910, African men entered retail trade. Initially, most of them were itinerant traders, selling simple consumer goods in exchange of produce as employees of the Indians. The Indians had established a *duka*, or shop-based enterprise, throughout the protectorate. By the 1920s, an indigenous trading class was formed. Wealthy Africans like chiefs, headmen, and clerks established maize mills in the reserves. After 1923, the LNCs provided capital for African men for the inauguration of water mills. They also encouraged people to get involved in trades, shops, and grind-mills under collective ownership.[71]

In 1923, the Devonshire Declaration proposed the development of an African middle-class. This was a result of the challenge posed by Asians in the empire, leading to the declaration of African paramountcy. The colonial

---

69. Ainsworth Papers, "Trade," 1909. RH Mss.Afr.s.382(1).
70. Zeleza, "Establishment of Colonial Rule," 57.
71. Maxon, "Years of Revolutionary," 95.

administration therefore came up with a dual policy of development. This was adopted by governor Corydon in Kenya. The aim was to encourage both African production in the reserves and settler production in a complementary fashion. African men were encouraged to work in their farms as a springboard for economic development. In the precolonial set up, women had used their agricultural lands to support the household and use excess products as investment. The men on the other hand used their farms wholly for investment. With this new policy therefore, men were in a position to invest in cash-crop production or growing of staple food for exports.

Finally, there was a gradual development of the middle class, through the establishment of a group of wage earners. There were different kinds of migrant labour, most of them men. First, there were unskilled laborers who lacked education and mostly did manual labour. Second, there were those who were conscripted to go and fight during the war as members of the Kenya Africa Rifles and others as carrier corps. Third, there was a group of mission educated men who did white collar jobs as clerks, teachers, and preachers. The wage earners created the foundation for the development of the petty-bourgeoisie. These were mainly people whose income was mainly from more than one source. They improved their economic position in the reserves through the purchase of seeds, ploughs, and additional land. Chiefs and other members of the LNC were in this group. They had regular employment, better access to land and made decisions on whom to grant permission to trade. In 1946, some of the ex-soldiers invested in business, joining the petty-bourgeois class of successful traders.[72] However, some of the women used opportunities given by culture for economic empowerment. For example, there were women traders and women house owners in urban areas like Pumwani.

---

72. Tiyambe, "Establishment of Colonial Rule," 163.

CHAPTER 4

The Establishment of Christianity in Kenya

Precolonial Period at the Coast as the Foundation for Mission Work

The establishment of mission work at the coast of Kenya during the pre-colonial period laid the foundation for mission work in the interior during the colonial period. Although the mission work was predominantly done by male European missionaries, they laid the foundation for later empowerment of African women. First, this was achieved through interaction between Christianity and African culture. The missionaries had no regard for African culture, but their translation of Scriptures and use of vernacular led to the interaction between Christianity and an African worldview. Second, the application of Venn's Policy led to local lay people participating in leadership. This also led to indigenization of the message. Although the missionaries were against materialism, Christianity was used for socio-economic empowerment. This was mainly facilitated by missions emphasizing on education as a tool of evangelism. Christianity was also understood in the context of fighting for social justice. Women played a key role in mission work from th e beginning.

Christianity was established at the coast of Kenya by Johann Ludwig Krapf who was born in 1810 to a German farmer. After conversion to Christianity, he attended a Missionary Training College at Basle. In 1837, Krapf was appointed by the Church Missionary Society to work in Ethiopia. The aim of Krapf was to convert the Galla, a feared group of people. He believed that the conversion of the Galla would lead to the conversion of Africa as they would influence others.[1]

The resolve of Krapf to continue with mission work in Africa was greatly influenced by Rosine. In 1842, Krapf travelled to marry a missionary, Rosine, who was working in Egypt, but on their return they were denied entry into Ethiopia. She refused to retreat or join other German missions. Rosine was expecting and gave birth to a baby girl in the Shoho desert. The father baptized the girl, Eneba, but she died the same evening. Rosine rested for only three days, and they started the journey again. They were refused entry at Tigre, so they took another vessel and eventually sailed to Zanzibar. The Sultan granted them permission to work in Mombasa. Rosine was brave and steadfast in her call.

In 1844, Krapf and Rosine arrived in Mombasa and shortly after their arrival, gave birth to their second daughter. Unfortunately, Rosine and their little baby died. The death of Rosine, however, only strengthened and confirmed Krapf in his purpose to devote all his life to the mission cause. Krapf gives a moving account of Rosine's death – stating that devoted companion of his travels and perils for a short while lost heart and wondered whether her life had been regulated by mere personal desires or by the spirit of sacrifice for the glory of God. She however ended in great peace and perfect submission to the divine will. Rosine desired to be buried in the mainland so that the sight of her tomb could constantly remind the passersby, of the object which had brought the servants of Christ to their country. According to Krapf, she wished to be preaching to them by the lonely sport which encloses her remains. Krapf wrote to the CMS:

> Tell the committee that there is on the East African coast, a lonely grave of the mission cause, connected with your society. This is a sign that you have commenced the struggle with this part of the world, never mind the victims who may fall, only carry it forward till the East and West Africa be united in the bonds of Christ.[2]

---

1. Robert Strayer, *The Making of Mission Communities in East Africa* (London: Heinemann, 1978), 10.

2. E. C. Dawson, *Missionary Heroines in Many Lands: True Stories of the Intrepid Bravery and Patient Endurance of Missionaries in their Encounter with Uncivilized Man, Wild*

Although Krapf had no regard for African culture, his missionary methods led to an interaction between Christianity and the African worldview, laying a strong foundation for missionary methods adopted during the colonial period. Krapf settled in Rabai Mpya, a few miles from Mombasa, and in 1846 was joined by another German missionary, Johann Rebmann. Both of them were influenced by German pietism, whose focus was winning individuals into personal devotion to Jesus Christ. To achieve this, their first project was to establish a mission station by erecting a school and a church. The main aim of education was to empower people to read, so that they could read the Bible in their language and come to personal salvation. They were not keen on establishing an institutional church or a social welfare. The main agenda of Krapf was to establish a chain of mission stations across Africa.

In Rabai, the missionaries lived in the midst of the Miji-kenda, and their first approach was to invite people to come and attend a worship service at the mission station. Fifteen people joined them in the first worship, but after the service made it clear that if they provided the right things such as rice and a bull, they would be happy to attend every week. The Mijikenda praised God through feasts, and the greatest blessing was plentiful harvest. However, the main interest of Krapf was in a Savior who would save them from their sins. Krapf and Rebmann also disagreed with Rabai elders over the defeat of evil. When a dangerous spirit was about, Rabai elders circulated with a roaring *muansa*. A *muansa* was like a large drum with a type of rope pulled through a hole in it – it producing a terrifying sound. All people had to go to their homes and shut their doors. Krapf and Rebmann deliberately opened their doors, and when elders came to ask them why they did not observe the rite, the missionaries told them of the deception of such things. Krapf, instead advised them to burn *muansa* and build and attend schools. The shocked elders responded that Krapf was a true medicine man.[3]

However, both the translation of Scripture and teaching literacy in the vernacular led to the interaction between Christianity and the African worldview. Krapf reduced Swahili and other coastal dialects to writing. He

---

beasts and Forces of Nature in all Parts of the World (London: CMS, 1924), 179.

3. William B. Anderson, *The Church in East Africa 1840–1974* (Dodoma: CTP, 1977), 3.

compiled the grammar and produced a Swahili dictionary. Krapf learned and published the vocabularies of six other local languages including Kiduruma and Kigiriama. Krapf also set on translation work and in two years, had translated the New Testament into Kiswahili. Rebmann continued with linguistic work after his colleague's departure. They laid a foundation, which was followed by subsequent missionaries.

However, the establishment of the Christian faith was mainly done through the agency of the Africans, namely Bombay Africans and other local leaders. African agency, especially laid the foundation for participation of lay African women in the church in the interior. This was also enforced by the fact that the Bombay Africans were accompanied by their wives who taught other women and mentored them. Although the missionaries were against materialism, the Bombay Africans worked hard and were economically empowered, which set an example for economic progress to the local Christians. The Bombay Africans acted as role models for Christians. The Bombay Africans used both their Christian faith, their training, and their empathy with the Africans to be able to preach.

The Church Missionary Society posted two African freed slaves, who had been trained in Bombay, to assist Rebmann in Rabai. William Jones and Ishmael Semler and their wives were sent to the coast of East Africa as a way of implementing Henry Venn's policy. Henry Venn's policy (he was the CMS secretary) focused on setting up local or indigenous institutions. The aim of Henry Venn was to set up local churches run by African pastors and African church workers. They were to be autonomous, making their own decisions, and handling their own finances. According to Henry Venn, the object of the Church Missionary Society mission was the development of native churches, with the view of their ultimate settlement upon a self-supporting, self-governing, and self-extending system. When this system is achieved the missions will leave and go to new grounds.[4]

William Jones was born in 1840 among the Yao people of Malawi. When he was ten years old, his stepfather sold him to an uncle, the stepfather's brother, in payment for his debt. The uncle tried to sell him in a slave market at Kilwa but failed, and so was taken to an expedition inland and was

---

4. Collin Reed, *Pastors, Partners and Paternalists* (New York: Brill, 1997), 6.

put up for sale in the slave market of Zanzibar. He was sold to an Omani Arab, who shipped him overseas. However, the slave dhow was intercepted by the British Royal Navy. Ishmael Semler was also a boy from Yao and was taken as a slave at the same time with Jones. He was taken to Mozambique, where he was bought and employed to work on an Arab sailing vessel. He was rescued by the British navy and landed in Bombay in 1850.

William Jones and Ishmael Semler were both placed at the Indo-British Institution. This was a government agriculture and trade school but run by the missionaries. Rev Candy, the secretary of the CMS corresponding committee in Bombay, was in charge of the institution. The boys were brought to the attention of Rev Candy by Mr and Mrs Isenberg, stationed at Bombay to take care of the freed slaves. The boys were taught religious studies, English, and Swahili among other subjects at the institution. After completion of the school, Rev Gottfried Deimler and his wife took the boys into their home and organized further education for them. Rev Deimler had planned to serve in Africa and had gone to Mombasa in 1856, but was taken ill and had to return to Europe. Later he was sent to India but was still interested in Africa and his colleagues Krapf and Rebmann, who had started the work there.[5]

According to Deimler, Jones and Semler loved reading the Bible and private prayer, and therefore it was important to give them further instructions to fit them as Catechists. He felt that first, they would serve their country men in India and eventually in the providence of God to East Africa. Deimler felt that Rebmann would rejoice to have native help. Jones and Semler therefore, attended money schools from 1859–1861. Money schools were modelled on the British public-school system catering to the elite in the Indian society. It had a Christian basis and aimed at academic excellence. The aim of the school was to train the upper class in English with daily Bible reading as an essential part of the curriculum. The wider aim was to create schools in which the whole education was imbued with Christian philosophy, so that patterns of thought would ultimately be changed.[6] The

5. Reed, *Pastors*, 8.
6. Reed, 20.

aim was not just to provide secular education, but also to prepare people for Christian ministry in their own country.

The subjects studied included English, classical history, Indian history, algebra, geometry, arithmetic, chemistry, practical mechanics, and religious education. At the school, they mixed with wealthy Indians and so were educated to be elites in the Indian society. They were being educated for leadership, lived in European homes, and were accustomed to European culture and thought-forms. For ten years, they went through western education, converted to Christianity and lived in a multicultural society. The aim of this was to equip them to go and assist the CMS missionaries in Mombasa.

After the studies in the money school, Jones and Semler were moved to the CMS mission Centre at Sharanpur, near Nasik. They were joined by George David who had only trained at the Indo-British school. The Centre at Nasik, under William Price played the most important role in the education of ex-slaves from Africa. Saharanpur was an orphanage and industrial training centre. The main trades taught were carpentry and blacksmithing. The three men were moved to the centre to assist in the training of other Africans as well as further their own education. Jones trained as a blacksmith, while Semler trained as a carpenter.[7] The aim of their training was to send them back to Africa in order to help the development of the African church. The three also met their spouses at Saharanpur, where the ladies were also being trained. Jones got married to Jemima, Semler to Grace, while David's future wife Priscilla and her sister Polly were also at Saharanpur. The ladies also underwent vocational training in Saharanpur where they were given education to prepare them for their roles as wives of future leaders. Apart from being taught literacy and the Bible, they were given skills in housecraft. They were taught sewing, cookery and agriculture. This empowered them to go and work among women.[8]

In 1864, the CMS sent William Jones and Jemima, Ishmael Semler and Grace, and George David and Priscilla (plus Polly who was going to marry Isaac Nyondo) to start a new venture in East Africa. They were sent to work under Rebmann in Rabai. Their main focus was teaching literacy and

---

7. Reed, 22.
8. Reed, 32.

preaching salvation. The wives taught the women and the girls. In 1866, Semler's wife died, and therefore he had to return to Saharanpur. In 1867, Mr and Mrs Jones were sent to work with the University Missions of Central Africa (UMFCA), founded by David Livingstone. The focus of UMFCA was setting up centers for Christianity and civilization for the promotion of true religion, agriculture, and lawful commerce. Livingstone believed that if people had another source of income, slavery would become less profitable. UMFCA focused on transformation of the society and not just individuals. In 1870, Mr and Mrs Jones moved back to Rabai, where Mrs Jones died of fever, and in 1871 Jones went back to India.[9]

By 1871, George David was the only one of the three men from Bombay left in East Africa. David was very influential with the African Christians but had a lot of tension with the missionaries. David, both from his African background and mission training, advocated for a more holistic approach to missions. David acquired a farm out of the desire for more involvement in the local community and culture and expressed a sense of belonging. He also saw the need for farming for socio-economic development. David was also appointed by the CMS to assume responsibility over the church in Rabai. He was later given responsibility over the locally founded freed slaves' settlements. David was therefore a mentor both on African leadership and socio-economic development.

The establishment of Christianity at the Coast of East Africa laid foundation for the empowerment of women, through the Christian faith being established in the context of a Christian village. The Christian village gave opportunity for traditional methods of leadership and gave Christian opportunity for leadership in the interior. Abe Sidi had formed an indigenous Christian village among the Giriama in Godoma. Sidi had set up a Christian group in response to the prevalent problem of domestic slavery. Swahili people had kept slaves to work in their homes and plantations. The coastal people also owned slaves, either those who were spoils from the war, or people who were unable to pay their debts. Domestic slavery was very harsh and runaway slaves ran into the bush and often formed their own villages. Many formed lawless or even militant groups because they did not want

---

9. Reed, 35.

to be recaptured. Some allied themselves to M'Baruk, a local Swahili, who led resistance to Arab domination of Mombasa area. However, one of the groups, led by Sidi chose to adopt a Christian life-style.[10]

Sidi was a leader in his own community and was converted to Christianity, which led him to the periphery of the community. He became a leader of a community of the runaway slaves. In 1870, thirty-five people in Sidi's village had openly proclaimed the Christian faith. Many more were openly adherents to Christianity, so they formed a Christian village with a new identity. They adopted Christian practices like monogamy and maintained faith despite persecution by Arabs. Rev Harry Kerr Binns, the missionary in charge of Mombasa, visited and did baptisms but he did not do so or send anyone to teach. Eventually, David had oversight of the community. Sidi led regular services using the Anglican prayer book. The services were not only attended by the villagers in Godoma, but also by the neighboring Wanika who had not heard the gospel. Godoma was therefore a completely indigenous community, and CMS proposed that Sidi be recognized as the lay pastor.

In 1880, Sidi moved the village a distance away to Fulladayo, also called Jilore. Not all adherents moved with him, which resulted in two Christian villages. Sidi moved out because he was looking first for more fertile land, and second a place which was more secure from the slave owners. Robert Keating, a Bombay African was eventually sent to Godoma. Binn sent some of the fugitive slaves to Fulladayo, thus CMS maintained a strong link with the church in Giriama but did not staff them. Fulladayo was a well-ordered community; they had morning and evening prayer, and the praise and worship was well organized. It was a very industrious community, with well-built houses and flourishing gardens. David was sent to a centre not far from Jilore, and in a short while he had gathered several adherents. In 1885, David suddenly died leaving a leadership gap. In the same year Sidi was attacked and died in the hands of the Swahili.

The establishment of Christianity at the coast also laid the foundation to women's empowerment due to its focus on social justice and liberation. In 1871, a parliamentary committee was set up by the British government

---

10. Strayer, *Making of Missions*, 37–39.

to investigate the issue of slave trade at the coast of East Africa. Sir Bartle Frere, Governor in Bombay, was chosen as special emissary to the Sultan to discuss the end of slave trade. Frere, also a member of CMS committee, had discussed with them the possibility of setting up a freed slave settlement. He signed a treaty with the Sultan to end slave trade.

Frere visited major coastal towns and mission stations to assess the effect of the slave trade. In 1873, Frere visited Rabai and was not very impressed by their approach to mission work. He found only eight Christians in Rabai, five of whom had been sent from Bombay. During his time at Rabai, Frere held discussions with David whom he described as an intelligent catechist. David was convinced that industrial mission similar to that in Nasik would have great success in East Africa. Frere in his report recommended the establishment of a freed slave settlement at the coast of Kenya. He proposed that William Price, who had headed the Centre at Nasik, and was now a vicar in England, be asked to establish the freed slave settlement.

In 1874, William Price and a team of freed slaves from Bombay set out for Frere-town. Jones and Semler, who were both remarried, were part of the team. William Price on his arrival made the following observation on the plight of the slaves:

> In one day from my window I have seen a poor woman with heavy chains on her legs so that she could only jerk herself a few inches at a time, bearing a load upon her head; a little girl of about 8 or 9 years with iron chain on her neck, several feet in length and at the same time carrying a burden on her hand; a little boy of the same age in the same condition; and a poor man emaciated and covered with sores, who in consequence of his heavy chain and extreme weakness could only move in a sitting position.[11]

These stories led to advocacy so that such people could be liberated and placed in a settlement. As a result, two centres were set up for freed slaves – in Rabai and Frere-town. The emphasis at Frere-town was on education as the major tool of evangelism. The initial focus was literacy or the 3-Rs: Reading, Writing, and Arithmetic. Reading was key in the curriculum so that

---

11. Reed, *Pastors*, 49.

people could learn how to read the Bible. The foundation of the curriculum was religious education and catechism. Most of the teaching was initially done in English and included writing and dictation. The boys were taught up to the upper primary level. Most of the teachers were Bombay Africans, who had received their training in Bombay. They also acted as mentors to the young people. Frere-town even introduced night classes for those who were employed, since literacy was an important prerequisite to catechism. Later on, the institution focused on industrial education, and agriculture and trade were introduced in the curriculum.

Frere-town became the training ground for teachers and evangelists and later the clergy. Some of the teacher-evangelists in the interior like Ezekiel Apindi and Daniel Mkuba were trained at Frere-town. They set up churches and schools for both boys and girls even before the founding of mission stations in their communities. In 1885, Bishop Hannington arrived in Mombasa as the first Bishop of Eastern Equatorial Africa. He underlined the importance of high-level training for African church leaders. The bishop made James Deimler, who had been trained at Frere-town, a lay reader. Deimler worked both as a teacher at the school and as an evangelist. He led the African leaders in advocacy work, by setting up an African workers council. The aim of the council was to draw attention of the missions to the practical grievances of the African agents. Second, it was to provide the African leaders with a forum for discussion of different issues in the life of the church. They also hoped to communicate to the rest of the society on different aspects of Christianity. Deimler was concerned about setting up structures which would enable African leaders to share in power in the church. In 1886, Bishop Parker, the new bishop instituted the Native Church Councils.[12]

Frere-town also focused on education of girls. The aim of education for girls was to make them good Christian wives. The girls were divided into different classes and were taught literacy in the morning and sewing and handicraft in the afternoon. In 1886, the first single woman missionary, Miss Mary Harvey joined Frere-town. Harvey joined a group of seven Bombay African women already working at Frere-town. Harvey taught the

---

12. Reed, 148.

girls sewing, domestic skills, and Scripture. Mrs Downes Shaw joined and was officially in charge of the girls, while Polly, Isaac Nyondo's widow, was the matron of the girls' dormitory. Nyondo was one of the first Christian converts at Rabai and later assisted Rebmann. He was appointed the first African teacher and evangelist at Rabai.

Frere-town laid the foundation for socio-economic empowerment. This was both through the use of industrial training and the example set by the Bombay African leaders. Although the missionaries were against economic development, which they termed as materialism, both Jones and Semler worked on their personal economic empowerment. Jones was placed at Rabai, where he used the agricultural expertise he had acquired in a farm in Bombay. Jones also purchased a considerable amount of land and built himself a stone house. He rented some of the land to the Indian shopkeepers. And he sent his children to India for education. Jones had a lot of influence in Rabai as he also fought for the rights of the freed slaves.

The Establishment of Christianity in Central Kenya

The African Inland Mission

The focus of the African Inland Mission (AIM) was on evangelism and not civilization, which was the nineteenth-century idea of social liberation and progress. However, due to the reality on the ground, the mission had to engage in social work and education as a tool of evangelism. They had to teach literacy so that their converts could read the Bible. And they used medical work, the establishment of orphanages, and runaway centres for girls as tools of evangelism. AIM therefore acted as a source of socio-economic empowerment for women. The AIM had a very large number of women missionaries. Although, the mission deployed them in seemingly secondary roles, they acted as mentors and modeled leadership to the African women. The women missionaries were teachers, administrators and medical practitioners, which were key leadership roles occupied by women in precolonial society. The women missionaries also had a great impact because they had direct impact with the community.

In 1895, AIM under the leadership of Peter Cameron Scott, established its work in Ukambani and later moved to Kikuyu land. The group was supported by the Philadelphia Missionary Council, whose major focus was evangelism rather than education or social work. The vision of AIM in Kenya is captured well in the work of John Stauffacher, "Side-tracked for two thousand years."[13] Stauffacher, the extension director of AIM, maintained that the sole purpose of mission is to preach the gospel in obedience to God's command. The primary task of AIM was therefore militancy in evangelism. This was in contrast to civilizing the world, symbolized in education. AIM was therefore opposed to education for its own sake, but education was to be used as a tool of evangelism. They opposed the teaching of English and sponsoring schools because they believed this would not only detract from evangelism but would also lead to materialism and worldliness.[14]

Most of the women who joined the AIM mission in Kenya subscribed to the official AIM policy. They were not influenced by the ideas of the women's wing whose missiological ideas were captured in the Woman's Work for Woman movement. The Woman's Work for Woman was established to evangelize the women and bring them to salvation. This evangelization was intertwined with civilization and being elevated to equality with western women, and into positions of respect in their own society. Woman's Work for Woman assumed that the non-Christian religions led to degradation of women. On the other hand, Christianity not only provided salvation but also civilization. The main interest of most of the women who joined the AIM mission station in Kijabe was evangelistic work. In 1902, Anne Campton, who had completed a course in the Bible school and had done evangelistic work for two years, joined the mission. Julia McClary joined Kijabe in 1903 in order to do evangelistic work among women. McClary was a graduate of the Moody Bible Institute and was in charge of the mission station among the miners near Johannesburg. Dr Florence Newberry, a trained pediatrician, joined AIM in 1908, and her main passion was to preach the Bible to the African tribes.[15]

However, the reality of the field was that the Africans were in most urgent need of education and were more responsive to the gospel if taught to read

---

13. Dana Lee Robert, *American Women in Mission: A Social History of Their Thought and Practice* (Macon, GA: Mercer University Press, 1996), 121.

14. Robert, *American Women*, 121.

15. Robert, 131.

the Bible. The missions had also to respond to some urgent needs of the society as a means of preaching the gospel. African women running away from unhappy forced marriages were open to the Christian message but needed somewhere to live in the mission premises. Agricultural projects were a necessary means to attain the goals of the mission. Hence, if the preaching of the word had to be effective, then the mission had to teach reading and provide homes for the runaway girls. The missions had no option but to undertake education and social work.

Several women missionaries were assigned tasks viewed to be secondary to evangelism by AIM. According to AIM, care giving and educational ministries were viewed as optional and outside the realm of true evangelism. In 1896, Margaret Scott, one of the founder missionaries and sister to Scott, founded the first school. However, she realized that if women's work was to be achieved, there was need to reduce the local language into writing. In 1897, Scott changed her focus and undertook dispensary and medical work among the women, and in 1900, she was joined by Emily Messenger. In an article on "Motherhood and Heathenism," Scott compared the life of the "heathen" woman with that of slavery in contrast to the happy domestic situation of the Christian mother. In 1902, Anna Campton was approached as an administrator in Mr Hulburt's office and spent time teaching children. In 1903, Julia McClary established work among the orphans. In 1907, Mrs Emil Sywulka started a day nursery school in Kijabe with the hope of reaching the mothers through the children. The mission also started a home for native girls in Kijabe in order to shelter young girls who had run away from arranged marriages. In 1908, Dr Florence Newberry was appointed to do medical work among Africans, missionaries, and Africans in Kijabe.

Women missionaries were also assigned translation and educational work at AIM. In 1905, Josephine Hope joined the mission and was assigned to teach in a school in Kijabe. Hope was the only AIM missionary who had received normal school training despite having limited equipment. Hope enjoyed teaching and found it a good way of entering into the lives and feelings, and understanding the ways, of the people. She was charged with the responsibility of teaching Africans, and the children of the missionaries and the settlers. In 1909, she requested to leave this teaching post and took charge of Rift Valley Academy, the AIM school for missionaries' children.

Most of the women missionaries involved in teaching opposed education in theory but found themselves involved in it. Rose Horton, a Methodist educated at the Moody Bible Institute joined the mission in 1915. Although a trained teacher, she continually opposed the missiology of education believing that to support school with money collected from church was sin. Horton noted that she had been given teaching as part of her work, but had to pray to continue on, as she waited for the situation to change so that she might be involved in the ministry of the word. Clara Guilding was a Canadian, but a member of the Moody Methodist Church in Chicago. She and her husband believed that education was the work of the government. However, due to a shortage of government schools, they reluctantly took on educational work in Machakos. This was to enable the children to read the Bible in their language. The woman's Bible class at Moody Memorial Church, who were supporting her, were opposed to school and girls' work which according to them was not part of the business of the church.[16]

However, Dr Helen Blakeslee, an osteopath, articulated that education as a means of evangelism. Blakeslee joined AIM in 1911, and her mission work included medical, evangelistic, and educational components. In her work, church and school were synonymous. The main motive of the bush schools was to teach people to read the word of God. They were evangelizing centres, rather than schools in the true sense of the word. In 1912, the AIM mission in Matara established a girls' home and education especially tailored for them. This was opposed by the local community and a delegation of parents complained to the district commissioner that girls were being alienated from their families. This led to tension between missions and the families over runaway girls.[17] Helen also used her medical work as a tool of evangelism. She told people that the medicine she was giving them was blessed by God. As a doctor, challenging Kikuyu's attitude towards the sick and the dying was part of her evangelistic work. In the 1920s, she was outraged by the way women were treated in Kikuyu society, through her interactions with them in medical work. Helen believed that one way to liberate women from customs like female circumcision was for them to marry

---

16. Robert, 27.

17. Cora Ann Presley, *Kikuyu Women: The Mau Mau Rebellion and Social Change in Kenya* (Stanford: Westview, 1992), 87.

Christians, establish Christian homes, and transform Kikuyu society from within. In 1927, she established a girls' training school, whose focus was to train Christian wives, mothers, teachers, nurses, and mid-wives. Kijabe was a boarding institution where girls were taught how to run Christian homes. In 1933, Blakeslee reported that they saw girls setting new standards of motherhood and influencing their communities through testimony and service.

The Gospel Missionary Society

The Gospel Missionary Society (GMS) was one of the first missions to establish its work in the interior of Kenya. Peter Scott sold the missionary idea to Fredrick Krieger, who accompanied the first group of AIM missionaries to Ukambani. Peter Scott died in 1896, and in 1897 Krieger resigned from AIM on account of the doctrinal basis adopted by AIM. Krieger was supported by the Peoples Church and Christian Union Association and continued with work in Ukambani but later moved to Kikuyu land. The GMS later merged with the Church of Scotland Mission to form the Presbyterian Church of East Africa. In 1898, Krieger established a mission station in Thembigua, and in 1899 he was joined by Rev William Porter Knapp, Myrtle Isabelle Knapp from New England, and Gertrude Wheeler. In 1902, another mission station was established in Kambui by the Knapps and Henderson.

Education was the main tool for evangelism for GMS. The main aim of education was to teach literacy so that the students could read the Bible. The missionaries hoped that after they became literate, they could read the Bible like the Bereans, who searched the Scriptures. Education was also for the formation of Christian character, so that the converts could grow in the fear of the Lord. Another aim of education was to train teacher-evangelists to spread the gospel. Education was therefore indispensable for aggressive evangelism. In 1903, GMS launched educational work in Thembigua and Kambui with morning school for children and evening school for adults. The teachers at Thembigua were Bertha Krieger and Eva Atwood, while Myrtle Knapp was stationed at Kambui. The missions clothed, fed and taught children for free in order to motivate them to go to school. Most of the young people who received education were destitute and orphans. They also got refuge in the mission.[18]

---

18. Evanson Wamagatta, "The Presbyterian Church of East Africa: An Account of Its Gospel Missionary Society Origins," (PhD diss., West Virginia University, 2001), 97.

One major focus of education for GMS was the education of girls. Apart from literacy and character formation another aim of education for girls was for them to get married and establish Christian homes. Christian homes were considered to be a powerful influence unto themselves, inspiring non-believers to desire the things of God. Christian weddings were the greatest indicators of the success of mission work. The girls, however, struggled to go to school because of opposition from their parents and the society. Many Kikuyus believed that misfortune would befall them if girls went to school. This is because the girls would leave the customs of their society. Second, such girls would refuse to marry polygamous men. The Kikuyu therefore used propaganda to scare girls from school. For instance, girls were warned that they would become barren if they went to school. Myrtle Knapp on the other hand attributed low attendance of girls to lack of initiative and being wedded to their customs. However, this was not true, as when boarding schools were set up in Kambui (1914) and Ngenda (1917), girls escaped to the mission station to attend school. The girls who escaped to the mission station were those who were converted against their parents will. The mission stations were also a safe haven for girls who were escaping marriages or customs, which they viewed as oppressive. Education was also key to the girls as it was the new source of power and socio-economic empowerment. Converted polygamous men would also send their wives to the mission station where they would stay until they found someone else to marry them.

However, the girls' escape to the mission stations created a lot of tension and debate in the society. Both the colonial state and the Kikuyu were not happy with the mission harbouring their daughters. On one occasion irate relatives of a fugitive girl at Ngenda abducted the four-year-old son of the missionary Kehreins Gordon and demanded their daughter back in exchange of the son. The colonial state issued an order that such disputes should be submitted to the District Commissioner (DC) for settlement.

The girls' work was conducted in a simple way with minimal expense on food and clothing. The girls grew most of their food on the mission land and shared the same house with Mary Gamerts Fielder. The main focus of the curriculum was religious instruction and literacy skills. After the morning school, the pupils went to fetch firewood, draw water, and prepare lunch. Knapp was in charge of women's work, and taught the sewing class on

Monday afternoons, followed by the women's meeting. On Tuesdays, she conducted the weekly Bible study and on Wednesdays visited the villages.

GMS also used both relief and medical work as means of evangelism. The establishment of GMS in 1898 coincided with a great famine, locust invasion, out-break of rinderpest, and small pox epidemics. Krieger secured financial support for famine relief. The missions cared for the hungry, sick, dying, and destitute who sought refuge in the mission station. Knapp estimated that about a third of the people died of small pox and other diseases. The missionaries equated personal care to the sick with love in action, and they used this to convince the Africans that the missionaries truly cared for them. Through medical work, the missionaries gained the confidence of the people. GMS had several female missionary nurses, namely Mary Gamertsfelder (1906–1937), Margaret Gough (1923–1939), Bessie Lovell (1925–1935), and Elnora Boda (1935–1945).

Medical work grew very rapidly and brought several people in touch with the gospel. Missions especially won converts when they healed those whom the witchdoctors had failed to heal. A case in point is that of Kiarie who had killed a snake in their homestead contrary to Kikuyu custom. Snakes were not supposed to be killed when they visited homes as it was believed that the spirit of the ancestors inhabited snakes. Kiarie was supposed to sacrifice to appease the offended spirit, but he did not sacrifice. The witchdoctor predicted that his younger sister would die as a consequence of the action. Kiarie's little sister fell ill, and everything the witch did failed to save her life. Kiarie's father finally allowed him to take her to Kambui, where she eventually recovered. The miraculous recovery undermined the power of the witch doctor and paved the way for the gospel. Successful treatment of incurable diseases also attracted people to the missions. A case is that of a barren woman at Kijabe who conceived and bore children after an operation. Her success attracted other barren women to the missions with the hope that they would receive similar treatment.

GMS also empowered women through offering employment or by being a place of refuge for those who were oppressed. Mukami, the wife of Kimani Wa Mugekenyi, was a woman worker with the mission. Although Mukami had a husband and two children, she attended school for two hours each morning. She had, as a result, learned to read Kikuyu, Swahili, and English, and offered herself to work among women in surrounding villages. Mukami was a hardworking woman and when she died in 1913, the missionaries eulogized her, how she had worked the whole Saturday before being taken ill in the evening of the same day. Her death was a big blow as the missions had regarded her marriage as a good example of an ideal Christian home. Knapp doubted whether there was any woman who had not heard about Christ from her.

Another Christian woman, Wairimu, stood for her faith and refused to be inherited by the husband's brother. In 1920, Warui, who was Wairimu's husband, had died of pneumonia. While in hospital, Warui, who was a Christian, warned his non-Christian brothers not to molest his wife after his death. He had given the wife permission to get remarried to a Christian of her choice. But as soon as the husband died, his younger brother began demanding that Wairimu should become his third wife. Wairimu ran away and sought refuge at the mission station but died before the issue could be resolved.[19]

Church of Scotland Mission

In 1889, Sir William Mackinnon, chairman of the Imperial British East African Company, and Alexander Low Bruce conceived the idea of a private Christian mission in the heart of the territory called the East African Scottish Mission. The aim was to focus on four-fold missions namely evangelism, medical, education, and industrial or commercial ends. In 1891, the first group of missionaries settled in Kibwezi. However, one of them, George Wilson, felt a special call to set up a mission station in Dagorreti to serve both Masailand and Kikuyu land. In 1899, the East African Scottish Mission set up a mission in Thogoto, with Thomas Watson as the evangelist and Dr Homer who was a medical doctor. On arrival there was a heavy locust invasion, devastating drought, cattle rinderpest, and a small pox epidemic. The focus of the mission was to set up a famine relief camp for children and old people. They also cared for small pox victims, and the mission attracted up to three hundred people. The mission set up a day school for children and an evening school for those who worked in the mission during the day.

---

19. Wamagatta, "Presbyterian Church," 165.

In 1901, the mission was transferred to Kikuyu and was taken over by the Church of Scotland Mission (CSM). The East African Scottish Mission workers transferred their services to CSM. Rev Dr Clement Scott was the superintendent, and Minnie Cummington Watson was engaged as a teacher. The focus of Scott was on agriculture, and he applied for three thousand acres of land from the government and planted experimental crops like potatoes, beans, and other cash crops. In 1903, Arthur Ruffelle Barlow arrived at Kikuyu as Scott's personal secretary. In 1905, Watson officially joined the mission as a teacher and a linguist. In 1908, Barlow was posted to establish CSM at Tumu-Tumu. He mainly concentrated on translation work and worked alongside Harry Leakey and Leonard Beecher of CMS missions; they translated Scripture into Kikuyu. Barlow also wrote the Kikuyu grammar. In 1910, Barlow was joined by Dr Philip to establish medical work at Tumu-Tumu. Clement Scott was succeeded by Dr Henry Scott in 1908. Henry Scott was a trained medical doctor and theologian but maintained that his medical work was subordinate to evangelism. Henry Scott's main legacy was the formation of the Alliance of Missions. In 1907, Dr John William Arthur opened the first mission hospital in Kikuyu. Arthur was a medical missionary and Church of Scotland priest. In 1912, he took over from Henry Scott as the head of the mission. He also played a very key role both on the issues of government and establishment of the Alliance of Missions.

Minnie (Cumming) Watson was the first woman missionary in the East African Scottish Mission. She was born in Dundee, Scotland, in 1867 and had long expressed a desire to be a missionary in Africa. Minnie came to Kenya to marry Rev Thomas Watson, one of the original six missionaries to Kenya in 1897. Minnie was married to Watson in December 1899, at Frere-town in Mombasa and travelled back to Dagorretti. They moved to Thogoto where they started a relief camp. Thomas Watson died on 4 December 1900, and Minnie assumed responsibility of running the mission, focusing on both evangelism and teaching. In 1901, Watson transferred her services to CSM. Watson was engaged as a teacher and started a system of tuition-free boarding school. She taught the most promising students in the morning to be teachers and worked with the teacher trainees to teach the day and boarding school students in the afternoon and mission workers at night. She directed the school expansion and supervised the native teachers. Village schools and out-schools were planted by the native teachers who also acted as evangelists. Watson frequently visited the out-schools. People like Jomo Kenyatta began their classes at the Kikuyu mission at one of Watson's classes. Watson insisted that girls be included in boys' boarding schools as day students. The education of Kikuyu girls immediately aroused fierce opposition as the Kikuyu believed that education would make a girl unmarriageable. A girl who is not married would not bring income to the family. Watson held meetings in the villages to encourage families to send their daughters to school. Mission schools were disrupted by things like throwing bags of ants into the school gate. Watson taught young mothers sewing, knitting, and other domestic skills. Reverend Njoroge's mother ran away from home in order to get education. The father beat her severely and tried to drag her out of school. Watson was one of the first opponents to female circumcision, and this made it very difficult for her to recruit girls. Watson retired in 1931 and died in 1949.

Another lady missionary was Marion Stevenson. Stevenson's emphasis was on communicating Christ in a way that the African women could relate to. She suggested that the best term to convey the Christian concept of God was *Mwene*, which means possessor or owner. She argued that this was a very useful term for a Kikuyu woman because they were owned by the father, the elder brother, and the husband. Kikuyu know that it is God who sends the rain and causes their food to grow without which they could not continue with life. God is the only owner of life who requires obedience.

In the 1930s, due to labour migration and other economic changes, men became more irresponsible. Women in Tumu-Tumu empowered themselves through the Woman's Guild and took over economic and leadership responsibility in their families and in the church. The Woman's Guild was founded in 1920 by seventeen women, most of them young wives of the early readers. The Woman's Guild took control of the sewing classes. Missionaries had thought that putting on clothes and sewing were a sign of Christianization. However, for the Tumu-Tumu women, it was also a means of socio-economic empowerment and a sign of class. Women therefore attended the sewing classes even when they did not understand the English of the instructor. They sewed bags, dresses, and book covers and then sold them for cash. In 1932, the Woman's Guild hired its own domestic instructor, Doris Nyambura.

They paid her one hundred and twenty shillings per year to teach classes in sewing and cooking at the Tumu-Tumu out-schools. Nyambura, who was also an evangelist in Nyeri area, was elected as president of the Woman's Guild. By 1933, she was drawing around one thousand women to the annual convention. In 1936, the Woman's Guild was sponsoring six sisters in education. The sewing classes brought revolution, and people discarded skins and were putting on clothes.

In 1936, many women had taken over responsibility in their families through applying the sewing and agriculture lessons they had learned in school. Mothers participated in trade and invested their profit from agriculture in their children's schooling. Mary Wa Miano sold beans in the market for successive days to raise sufficient funds for her children's schooling. Susan Kirigu Njebwara sent her son to school by selling the cabbages she had raised in her garden and purchased for him trousers. Women refused to be used as scapegoats by church leaders for the ills of the families and the society. In the 1937 convention – after a litany of lectures by the church leaders on the model of a God-fearing woman – the women passed resolutions to point out to the church leaders that undiscipline was men's problem. The women passed three resolutions:

1. There are some wrong things done by men, which should be looked into and corrected.
2. The elders who are family heads should meet and should be notified of their mistakes as they destroyed their families.
3. Women asked that:
   a. Their workload should be lessened.
   b. They should be allowed to travel to see the hospitality of other women.
   c. Cooking utensils and other cutlery should be looked into. Items such as these should be sufficient.

They concluded in their resolutions that the members of the church should look into these and set an example to others.[20] In 1939, Naomi Paulo in her sermon delivered to Kikuyu church leaders, focused on men's hypocrisy. Her

---

20. Derek Peterson, "Revivalism and Dissent in Colonial East Africa," in *The East African Revival History and Legacies,* eds. Kevin Ward and Emma Wild-wood (Kampala: Fountain Publishers, 2010), 114.

sermon was based on the story of the woman at the well. She underlined that Jesus revealed to the woman her sins and confronted church leaders to stop hiding sins.

Church Missionary Society

The Church Missionary Society moved to the interior in 1900, when Bishop Peel of the Diocese of Mombasa made two journeys to Nairobi, to get a place for the establishment of missions. The missionaries used education as the main tool of evangelism. The main aim was to teach literacy so that people could read the Bible. Education was also to train teacher-evangelists who would lead the churches. Ross McGregor arrived in Kabete in 1901, and in the same year was joined by Rev Harry Leakey and Mary Leakey. In 1902, Harry Leakey was in charge of the mission station, while Mary Leakey started girls' education. Mary Leakey was assisted by Alice Higginbotham. However, the Kikuyu in Kabete were reluctant to take girls to school as it would retard the production capacity of the household. Higginbotham observed that girls were only allowed to go to school after doing the day's work. The school was later developed into a girls' intermediate school. Women regarded the mission station as a refuge, and they ran to the missions to what they thought would be a freer society. Missionaries were viewed as liberators, who freed women from domestic oppression. Phyllis Wambui joined Harry Leakey at Kabete; her parents followed her and beat her to stop her from being a convert. They did not want her to become a Christian and abandon her culture. However, physical punishment did not stop girls from running away to missions in large numbers.[21] McGregor established a mission station in Muranga in 1903. In 1908, the first women converts, Sarah Ndutta, Sarah Wambui, Sarah Njeri, Martha Wa Nyaikama, Rebecca Wa Joshua, and Rahili Muere, were baptized. In 1911, a local committee was formed in Weithaga, which allowed the elders to run their own church. In 1919, Weithaga formed a pastorate and there were several women lay leaders in the parish, namely Elizabeth Mbatia, Esther Njeri, Esther Wangari, Edith Nyambura, Rosemary Wanjiru, Grace Njoki, Keziah Nyambura, and Nora Norman.[22]

---

21. Presley, *Kikuyu Women*, 82.

22. Keith Cole, *The Cross over Mount Kenya: A Short History of the Anglican Church in the Diocese of Mount Kenya (1900–1970)* (London: CMS, 1970), 38.

In 1906, Dr Thomas and Mrs May Crawford opened a dispensary in Kahuhia. In 1909, Rev Douglas Arthur Hooper took over and were later joined by their son Handley Hooper and his wife Cicely Hooper. In 1909, the girls' work began with the establishment of formal education. Kahuhia developed into a girls' boarding school headed by Mrs B. Brown. In 1910, the Crawfords arrived in Embu. Dr Crawford was in charge of medical work, while Mrs Crawford was in charge of education. In 1913, Rev John Comely took over the running of the mission station. In 1922, Miss M. Pethybridge assisted in the medical side of the missions. In 1910, Rev and Mrs Edward Crawford arrived in Kabare. In 1916, they established education for girls and the first girls to go to school were Mariamu Wangechi, Hannah Mukami, Sarah Wambura, Ruth Kethi, Esther Mutira, and Lizie Wagatu. In 1928, the Kabare Girls' Intermediate Boarding School was established.

Christianity was also viewed in the light of fighting for social justice. Chief Gutu was in conflict with the mission station in Kabare. First, Gutu was against mission education as he felt that it would undermine young people's loyalty to the chiefs and their parents. Second, school attendance hindered labour recruitment. Gutu wondered why female readers would not visit the camp like other girls. He was annoyed at Edward Crawford, the resident missionary's attempt to protect mission adherents from what was perceived as Gutu's persecution. Crawford reported Gutu and his subordinates to the District Commissioner. In 1915, Tabitha Karingo, one of the first converts to Christianity, lost her husband Mururia during her prime age and refused to be inherited by Mururia's brother. Karingo left her homestead and settled in Mutira mission to seek refuge from missionaries who were also opposed to the cultural practice and to strengthen her faith. Jesse Meero, the wife of Thomas Meero who had accompanied McGregor from Taita Taveta, also worked to liberate people from superstition, ignorance, disease, and poverty.[23]

One of the greatest advocates of women's empowerment was Cicely Hooper. Hooper arrived in Kenya in 1916 and was appalled by the position of women in African society. She published her view in a pamphlet entitled "Property in the Highlands of East Africa." Hooper set the picture of an

23. Julius Gathogo, *Mutira Mission: An African Church Comes of Age in Kirinyaga, Kenya* (Eldoret: Zapf Chancery, 2011), 144.

African woman as a piece of property. She denounced female circumcision as disgusting and pleaded with the Europeans to atone for their exploitation of Africa by working for the welfare of the African woman. Hooper was of the view that women's work should be focused on creating a system of boarding schools and dormitories culminating in an inter-mission college designed to produce teachers, nurses, and other trained women. Temporary immersion in such an institution she felt would give them something to take to their village that was not there before. In 1918, this proposal was made to the Alliance of Missions meeting in Kikuyu. Hooper took the lead in defending this idea but was not successful. The objection was that such schools would Europeanize African girls and destroy their families. The members argued that African men preferred village girls to dormitory girls. In reply, Hooper criticized men's training for not engendering an appreciation for educated girls. She wondered why the boys' boarding schools were not regarded as destructive to family life. Hooper underlined that the main aim was to Christianize the village, rather than Europeanize the girls.

The Establishment of Christianity in Western Kenya

The Establishment of Mission Work

In 1901, the American Friends established the Friends African Industrial Mission (FAIM). This was in response to the challenge by Willis Hotchkiss who had worked with the African Inland Mission in Kenya from 1895–1899. While serving in Ukambani, Hotchkiss had realized that Africans were living in an appalling condition. He observed that the worst affected were women and wrote: "A woman is practically a slave; a beast of burden, reckoned as just so much '*mali*' (property). Woman is still a slave, although slavery has ended in Africa. Womanhood is reduced to servitude, doomed to drudgery as mere beasts of burden. The women are a bulwark of superstition. Womanhood in Africa is womanhood without God."[24] Hotchkiss noted that Africans lacked adequate tools for agriculture. He concluded that Africans needed more than

---

24. Willis Hotchkiss, *Sketches from the Dark Continent* (London: Headley Brothers, 1945), 40.

the preaching of the gospel, hence the industrial missions. In 1902, three friends, Willis Hotchkiss, Arthur Chilson, and Edgar Mole established a centre in Kaimosi in Western Kenya. They were received by Charles Hobley, the District Commissioner. In 1904, they were joined by Emory and Deborah Gorman Rees who had been Quaker missionaries in South Africa. The two later moved to set up a mission station in Vihiga. The aim of the missions was to establish a self-supporting and self-propagating church.[25]

The first converts played a key role in evangelism and establishment of the church. One of the first converts was Maria Maraga. She came from Bumbo, a village adjacent to Kaimosi. In 1902, she came to the mission station – according to her testimony, she came to the mission station because she wanted to learn. Maraga worked as a house-girl for Edgar Hole, and in 1903, got married to David Lungaho. In 1905, Maraga and Lugaho were accepted into the membership of the church. Maraga was the first convert from Tiriki and the first woman convert to Quakerism in East Africa. Maraga served as an evangelist and Christian mother and cared both for her children and for orphans. Maria challenged cultural practices and led the women in Kaimosi to eat *engoko* (chicken), a taboo which supported and enforced their subordination.[26] Eating chicken was like competing with men.

Yohana Amugune and Rebeka Amagitsi established the Vihiga and Chavakali stations. Joseph Ngaira and Maria Maitsi set up Lugulu station. In the 1920s, Christians created their own villages referred to as "mission lines." The "mission lines" were Christian villages that assimilated Christianity and western culture. However, in 1933 the Local Native Councils abolished Christian villages.

Although the leadership of the Friend's Church was exclusively male, women played a key role in the establishment of the Church. The women were mainly involved in women's work and evangelism, occasionally preaching in the main service. Separate women meetings were established and referred to as Halhamisi and Ijumaa, according to the days of the meetings. Evangelists were in charge of preaching and Bible translation, as well as pastoral oversight and administration of the meetings. They taught reading

---

25. Mombo, "Position of Abaluhyia Women," 87.
26. Mombo, 180.

and writing to the young people, prepared converts for membership and did discipleship. Evangelists prepared people for marriage and counseled families facing difficult issues. They were the link between missionaries and converts.

The women converts challenged cultural injustices like prohibition of females from eating chicken and eggs, which was believed to cause infertility to women. Rebeka Amagitsu broke the taboo, after which she gave chicken to mission girls or avasomi. Despite the stir caused, most women broke the taboo as they became Christians. Rasoah Mutua, a leading evangelist interpreted this break in tradition as an opening for women to take an active role in the meetings, even if they were not allowed leadership positions in equality with men. Mutua was renowned as an evangelist, teacher, and preacher, who had become a Quaker after running away to the mission to escape forced marriage. Rasoah learned how to read and write and became a teacher of women and girls. She got married and after having four children, her husband died. Mutua decided not to remarry as was the custom and lived to serve the church. She was among the first students to train as a pastor at the Friends Bible College.[27]

Another prominent women's leader was Mugesia Enisi, born in Chandumba in 1912. She began school in 1924 and was accepted as an associate member of the Friends Church. In 1926, she went to school in Chavakali and was made a full member of the Quaker meeting. In 1927, she attended girls' boarding school at Kaimosi but left school in order to care for her widowed mother. Mugesia taught men and women in her village through preaching the word of God. In 1929, she married Ezekiel Mudegu, and they were blessed with five children, three of whom died as infants. The husband was a tailor and a clerk to Kengondu Friends Church. Mugesia continued as a preacher at Kegondi meeting after her marriage.

In 1940, Mugesia's husband died after a short illness leaving her with two small children. She lived as a widow for one year and after consultation between her family, the Church, and her husband's clan, it was agreed that she should return to her home clan. In 1943, Mugesia got married to a widower, Jeremiah Mkutu, in a church ceremony. Mugesia and Mkutu migrated to Kisii where she helped to found a meeting and served as a clerk

---

27. Mombo, 215.

and preacher to the women. She was actively involved in the formation of the Women's Yearly Meeting and attended most of the annual conferences. During one of the annual conferences in Budaywa in 1962, she was moved by a talk about Prisons Ministry. She felt called to care for the spiritual needs for those in prison and was appointed to the Prisons Ministry.[28]

The Friends emphasized a four-fold ministry: evangelism, education, industrial training, and medical work. The Friends used industrial training as a means of economic empowerment. The missionaries also believed that industrial training would help develop Christian character. It would also help to develop a positive work ethic, which was key for economic development. The converts were empowered with new agricultural techniques and grew new crops and fruits. The male missionaries introduced men to new farming methods such as the use of a plough. On the other hand, missionary wives stressed to the women the significance of having a garden in which to plant vegetables.

Education was used as a primary tool of evangelism. The focus of the curriculum was teaching the 3-Rs: reading, writing, and religion. They emphasized literacy so that people could read the Bible. Religion was at the heart of the curriculum, and the Bible was translated into Luragoli to act as the basic teaching text. Girls were encouraged to attend school from the beginning. In 1911, Deborah and Emory Rees underlined the need for girls' education and they called for the recruitment of single women missionaries. In 1913, Roxie Reeve came to Vihiga to give a hand to Deborah Rees with the work of girls and women. In 1915, Reeve started a class for women in Vihiga and among her students was Maria Atiamuga.

Atiamuga was one of the first girls to attend school. Atiamuga was born in 1903, in Vihiga, and the name Maria was given to her by Rees in 1920, when she was accepted as a full member of the Quaker Church. She went through the education system, which included reading, arithmetic and Bible knowledge. Atiamuga was appointed as prefect to the girls between 1919 and 1920, which involved teaching girls, but at a half salary. She was among the first teachers at the girls' intermediate school in Kaimosi. She also attended a course in Kericho and learned how to knit and spin. Maria therefore

---

28. Mombo, 215–216.

combined teaching, knitting, and farm work for income generation. During the annual gathering of Quaker women, she always talked about progress through farming skills. Priscilla Abwao, who was a social worker, recommended that she join a delegation of farmers who visited Central Province. In 1923, Atiamuga got married to Erasto Alenga in Kaimosi. Atiamuga was a prominent preacher and counsellor in the church. She served as a member of the permanent board of the East African Yearly Meeting (EAYM) after its inception. She rose to the position of Deputy Presiding Clerk in the EAYM in 1957 and 1960.[29]

Roxie Reeve was also very involved with starting education among girls in Maragoli. By 1915, she had started eight out-stations for girls' schools. In four of these out-stations, she had married women helping her to teach the girls, while she taught the girls at Vihiga, and Deborah Rees taught the women. Reeve also began a home for orphaned girls especially after the out-break of small pox in Maragoli. The orphanage moved to Liranda in 1917 to become a girls' school. The education of the girls included literacy, religion, and practical work. In 1921, Liranda became a boarding school, and in 1926, it moved to Kaimosi to become the Girls' Boarding School.[30] In 1927, Elizabeth Haviland took over as the headmistress of the Girls' Boarding School. By 1934, there were many girls in the school due to the presence of African women on the education board. These included Dinah Belimu, Rebbecca Mwanyi, and Miriam Nekesa. Salome Nolega became the first Abaluhyia woman to become headmistress of the Girls' Boarding School and also the first woman to become a principal of a teacher training college in Kenya.

Nolega was born in Kigama and was the daughter of David and Damari Mbarani. She studied in Kigama primary school and was admitted at Kaimosi Girls' Boarding School in 1946. In 1950, she was among the first girls to be admitted at Alliance Girls' High School.[31] Nolega did two years secondary school training at Alliance and qualified as an elementary (P.2) teacher in 1953. After Alliance, Nolega worked as a teacher and administrator at

---

29. Mombo, 235.

30. Mombo, 235.

31. Jacinta Kapiyo et al., *The Gift of a School: Alliance Girls' High School 1948–1998* (Nairobi: Christian Digest, 1998), 83.

Kaimosi Girls' Boarding School for seven years. In 1961, she received a scholarship and studied at Berea College, Kentucky, USA. In 1963, Nolega graduated with a bachelor of arts degree in domestic science. On her return to Kenya, she was appointed principal of Kaimosi Teachers College, the first woman to serve in that capacity in the Quaker Church.[32]

Salome also participated on wider issues to bring transformation to society. In 1978, she addressed the UN meeting on disarmament. She pointed out that while national security, which was used to justify an arms race, was important, and secure national boundaries and structures should be adhered to, it should not play down the security of persons. She pointed out that:

> Security of persons is threatened by hunger, population, disease and pollution, desertification, lack of pure water and lack of energy. To address these problems require equitable sharing of world resources and opportunities. The global economy should not be designed primarily to promote economic growth for the already affluent. Growth should be the goal and reality of the poor.[33]

Salome's identity with the poor made her to concern herself with the Maendeleo Ya Wanawake organization, a national movement of women of all walks of life. She was the chairperson of this movement in Western Kenya and mingled with women of all walks of life. Nolega encouraged them and contributed to their development in a society that marginalized them. Salome was a strong advocate for a proper position for women in both church and society. In a speech entitled "With a Bias to the Women," she pays tribute to the first girls to join the Quaker mission, arguing that women were involved in mission work from the inception of the church. Nolega was involved in the work of the EAYM and excelled in her work both as an educationist and as a church leader.

---

32. Mombo, "Position of Abaluhyia Women," 171.

33. Salome Nolega, "Disarmament: UN Calls for Universal Endevour," address to a special session of UN General Assembly, 12 June 1978, www.peaceworks.afsc.org/quaker-work-united-nations, 18–19.

The Establishment of the Church Missionary Society

In 1904, Bishop Alfred Tucker and John Jamieson Willis from Uganda visited Nyanza in order to find a suitable place for a mission station. Willis arrived in Nyanza in 1905, set up a mission station in Vihiga, Maragoli, before leaving for furlough. CMS later sold the mission station to the Quakers and established a mission station in Maseno. In January 1906, Henry Sarvile became the first missionary to take residence in Maseno. Sarvile was a nurse and was in charge of the dispensary. Sarvile left the mission to be a manager of the big estate owned by the East African Industries. CMS property was situated in the middle of this estate. The farm had been formed for the express purpose of supporting the missionary endeavor. The combination of mission and farm supplied the regular class of missionaries to teach by day. The farm and surrounding villages also provided the congregation for Sunday service. The little church was crowded, and the services had to be taken under the tree.

Willis returned and joined the Sarviles at Maseno in October 1906. In 1910, he was made the Archdeacon of Kavirondo. In 1907, Canon Pleydell, who had come to Uganda as a CMS missionary in 1904, joined Maseno to help in translation work. He took charge of the mission station when Archdeacon Willis became the Bishop of Uganda in 1912. Nyanza remained part of the church in Uganda until it was transferred to the Diocese of Mombasa in the Kenya Colony in 1921.

In 1912, CMS proposed the establishment of a mission station in Butere to focus on work among the Luhyia. Walter Chadwick was sent from Uganda to spearhead the work in Luhyia land. He brought with him lay evangelists from Uganda to help in the work. Chadwick learned the language and attempted the first Bible translation in Luhanga. The focus of the work in Butere was the use of education as a tool of evangelism. Church and schooling went together. Chadwick recruited boys for the school by giving them work in the mission station. He then invited them to come to school in the evening. Eventually the school focused on vocational training where the boys learned both the trade and the Bible. In 1913, Rev Alfred Leech joined Chadwick to work at Butere Mission station.

Evangelization and the establishment of the Anglican Church in Nyanza was mainly the work of lay evangelists. Luo evangelists had already evangelized and had established Christianity in Nyanza even before the establishment of the CMS mission stations. Even after the establishment of the mission stations, lay people played a central role in evangelism and in the establishment and leadership of the church. Bishop Alfred Tucker worked towards constituting a native Anglican Church in Uganda. The focus of Bishop Willis differed from that of Bishop Tucker. Willis felt that it was difficult to achieve a strong indigenous church under the leadership of local clergy. He pointed out that missionaries were appointed and answerable to CMS England. They were not directly answerable to the church in Uganda. Willis also asserted that the position of the missionary church was that of a leader. He believed the African church had to depend on the Europeans intellectually and felt that it was dangerous to leave Africans on their own. That would lead to the creation of an Ethiopian Church. Each mission station needed three Europeans: an evangelist, a schoolmaster, and a translator.[34] Walter Edwin Owen, who was posted in Nyanza as an Archdeacon in 1918, held views similar to Willis. It therefore took quite some time before teachers and clergy got trained in Nyanza.

However, Willis and all other missionaries affirmed that the establishment of the Anglican Church in Nyanza was mainly the work of the laity. Willis recognized that the Luo, whether trained or not, took the initiative to evangelize and form their own congregations. They would only involve a missionary after preparing candidates and were ready for baptism. The Christians made for themselves uniforms and were apportioned different ranks. The evangelists also made badges for their followers.[35] The Luo were appropriating the idea of *thuon,* or warrior, in Luo culture. Christians therefore visualized themselves as soldiers of Christ. This was in line with the prevailing situation of the First World War. Scripture also has constant use of soldier imagery.

Archdeacon Owen acknowledged that there was a great movement towards Christianity in Nyanza. Various classes for inquirers and catechumens were started and there was evidence of a movement of the Spirit in the hearts of the people. Many were responding to Christianity. All this was due to the

---

34. Willis, "Annual Letter," 1915. CMS, G3/A7/P3 01915.
35. Willis, "Annual Letter," 1916. CMS: G3/A7/P3 01916.

work of African teachers and evangelists. The teacher-evangelists had erected 225 schools or churches, and they were not just evangelists but pioneer educationists. Owen argued that both they and the evangelists recognized the importance of education in the establishment of the kingdom of God.

Wright, the missionary in charge of Kisumu town and the secretary of Kavirondo Missionary Council, also acknowledged the work done by Luo evangelists. They established churches in whichever part of the country they went. Wright cited the case of a young man he had baptized in 1914. In 1916, the man was placed in Tabora as a military transport porter. The man gathered together a congregation of his fellow porters and members of the Kings African Rifles. *Askaris* (soldiers) asked one of the military chaplains to visit and he baptized twenty converts. Another police corporal in Usain Gishu created a little congregation. Small parties of Luo Christians were meeting Sunday after Sunday under big trees or buildings they had been able to erect.[36] Wright was also a great supporter of the indigenization policy and observed that the native Christians were running their affairs well; they were financially independent and met for Sunday services in churches they had erected themselves.

Education was the backbone of mission work in Nyanza. The main aim of CMS was evangelism, which could only be achieved through the reading of Scripture. Reading and writing were the first major attractions to Christianity. The main focus of Maseno was evangelism through the school. Maseno School was established for the sons of the chiefs, who would act as leaders in both church and society. The school offered elementary education based on the 3-Rs. The students formed the nucleus of the church and were the first converts to be baptized in 1910. After completion they doubled as teachers and evangelists and are credited with founding the first churches in different parts of Nyanza. The aim of Maseno School was to provide an all-round training of body, mind, and soul. Around 1908, industrial training was introduced in Maseno to enhance the development of mission work. These included carpentry, joinery, brick-laying, mechanics and printing.

---

36. Willis, "Annual Letter," 1916. CMS: G3/A7/P3 01916.

Maseno graduates like Alfayo Odongo used brick-laying and building skills to build schools and churches and to expand the territory of the church.[37]

Agriculture was also very prominent in the curriculum of the school. Through agriculture lessons, missions taught new farming methods and introduced new varieties of crops. All the students had demonstration farms, and whenever they went back home their farms attracted many people. These gave them the opportunity for evangelism. The school boys also helped old women in their farms as a means of inviting them to attend the church services.[38] Maseno eventually became a normal school, whose major task was to train teachers for the out-schools. The out-schools, or bush schools, mainly focused on teaching catechetical classes.

CMS participation in the education of girls was mainly out of the concern that the Christian men should have Christian partners to marry. In 1909, at a conference of various missionary societies in Kenya, it was resolved that every effort should be made to give girls such an education that they may become intelligent companions to their husbands. By 1913, the backward-ness of women and girls in mission education was already disturbing the Luo Christians. Edith Hill recalled an incident when she spent some days with the Pleydells in Maseno on her way home from Uganda. She went to climb the hill to see the sunrise in the company of Yona Orao, one of the senior boys at Maseno School. Yona pointed to his home along the thickly populated ridge and said, "You English people are doing a very wrong thing. You are educating us and leading us to Christ, but you are doing nothing for our girls. In all that mass of huts is not one Christian girl whom I could marry. Are we only to be half Christians, what will our children be?"[39]

Edith Hill shared with Bishop Willis the idea of girls' education. She even volunteered her services. Hill therefore came to start some educational work among the girls in Maseno area. She started by learning the language and establishing a women's sewing class. Gradually, after mastering the language, it also became a Bible class. Luo women were keen to learn and encouraged

---

37. Cynthia Hoehler-Fatton, *Women of Fire and Spirit: History, Faith and Gender in Roho Religion in Western Kenya* (New York: Oxford University Press, 1996), 36.

38. Margaret Jean Hay, "Luo Women and Economic Change During the Colonial Period," in *Women in Africa: Studies in Social and Economic Change*, ed. by N. Hafkin and G. B. Edna (Stanford, CA: Stanford University Press), 100.

39. Richards, *Fifty Years in Nyanza*, 5.

Hill to visit their villages. She set out to recruit girls for a boarding school. She thought that most people would not be interested in the education of girls; however, she recruited a total of ten girls who became the nucleus of Maseno School. The school was however abandoned in 1920.

In 1916, CMS decided to focus on work among women and girls in Butere among the Luhyia. Jane Elizabeth Chadwick was sent from Uganda to establish education for girls in Butere. Chadwick was born in Belfast, Ireland in 1869. She was the daughter of George Alexander Chadwick, Bishop of Derry and Raphoe in Ireland. Jane Elizabeth was an older sister to Archdeacon Walter Chadwick. She first offered herself for CMS work in 1892 but was turned down because she was too young. She applied again in 1895 and was sent with four other women missionaries to Uganda. On arrival in Butere, the first classes were held only in the morning as the girls had to continue with farm and other household work. The focus of the curriculum was reading, writing, catechism, Bible lessons, and sewing. Sewing was the most popular subject. Chadwick secured a Muganda woman to assist her as a teacher. Lydia Kitandi and Mapesa were among the first women catechumens and students. They attracted many other girls to school. Eventually, Kitandi and Mapesa were appointed as teaching assistants.

The church also felt there was need for more focus on evangelism among Luo women and girls. Fanny Moller, a CMS missionary from Australia had come to Maseno in 1921 to work among Luo women and girls. In 1921, Owen who was the Archdeacon of Kavirondo, requested that Moller have a small class of women and girls at her Maseno home. Moller helped in preparing about nine girls for confirmation. Moller was not very fluent in the Luo language and so a lady called Louise, who was also part of the class, assisted her in both evangelism and teaching. Louise was the only Christian in the village and was trying to convert her younger sisters by having them read, but the father refused to let them go to school. Louise had decided to be a Christian after listening to the message preached in a nearby village. She wanted to be baptized and started to read with her little friends, but she fell ill, and the family thought she was dying. Her friends informed Pleydell, who had taken over from J. J. Willis, as the missionary in charge of Maseno, who came and baptized her. Louise was baptized; she recovered and remained true to her confession, and remained a Christian despite much opposition.

She refused an arranged marriage with a non-Christian who had offered her father a great number of cattle, but Louise refused to have anything to do with him. This required a lot of courage on the part of a Luo girl. She became the "right hand" of Moller, helping her in evangelism and later got married to a Christian man.[40]

Samuel Olaka, who was a teacher-evangelist trained at Maseno, preached to influential people who brought transformation to the Kowe village near Maseno. When he came from Maseno, one of his first converts was Yona Obara, son of Ogumbo, a lineage elder who was Kowe's most influential man. Obara established a day-school around his home and taught people reading, writing and the fundamentals of Christianity. Yona Obara preached to and converted his mother who was a very influential and famous woman among her people. Elizabeth Loye, the senior wife (*Mikayi*) of Ogumbo, was well-known for her wealth and skills as a dancer and a singer. People praised her as *Wuon Bel* (owner of sorghum) because her granaries were always full. The other women recall that Loye's home practically overflowed with sesame, ghee, and other signs of prosperity. She accumulated a large herd of cattle on her own through the sale of surplus crops.[41]

Elizabeth Loye converted to Christianity and burnt *chieno* (the tassel of sisal fibre around her waist which gave her status and identity in the society) and began to wear European cloth. This caused a major disruption within the home, and Ogumbo drove her from the house he built for her. He later sought help from various sorcerers to destroy Loye and her son. However, Loye persevered and enhanced her reputation even further. A skillful cultivator, she experimented with white maize, cassava, groundnuts, and other new crops. Through her, other women acquired seeds and learned how to work new crops into the agricultural circle. Loye was restored by Ogumbo due to her initiatives. Loye was the first woman in Kowe not to tear her clothes and wail at the death of her husband. She refused to be taken in leviratic marriage by one of his kinsmen.

After Ogumbo's death Loye succeeded him as *jagolpur*, or the one who begins cultivation for the family. These practices were deeply associated with

---

40. Fanny Moller, "Annual Letter," 1923. CMS Archives G3/AL/01923.
41. Hay, "Luo Women and Economic Change," 101.

the religious practices of the Luo because they involved rituals. Many people believed that Loye would encounter evil and not gain any harvest; however, she was a very successful farmer, and was eventually accepted in a position formerly reserved for men. Loye, using her Christian faith and space created for women by Luo culture, took initiative and assumed authority and remade gender relationships. Loye also used space created by Luo tradition that allowed a person to be independent in character to negotiate leadership. In Luo culture, those women who were deviants by taking initiative, were celebrated as heroes and classified as *Thuon* (Warriors), when they succeeded. This is evidenced in songs composed for Christian women who, during labour migration and the world wars, took the initiative and even built their homes: "Your mother built a home, your mother is extraordinary. Olango K'Obilo your mother built a home. She is wonderful, she is a warrior."[42]

The focus of the early Christian converts in Nyanza was not the church but the *dala* or the Christian home. The leadership structure and basis for authority was drawn from the Bible and from Luo ideas. Local indigenous Christianity was already established in Nyanza even before the coming of the missionaries. Luo migrants who had studied in Uganda established their own prayer houses when they returned home. They gathered Christian followers around them in the *dala*, or homestead. These homesteads were set up in Luo fashion.[43] These were autonomous Christian communities. From around 1910, migrant evangelists like Ezekiel Apindi who trained in Frere-town, Samuel Okoth who trained in Nairobi under Burns, and Alfayo Odongo Mango, set up Christian villages in different parts of Nyanza.[44] The Christian villages were established on the basis of Christian teaching and practices. The villages were established in discontinuity from some of the Luo cultural practices. The villages however also affirmed and reconstructed some of the Luo cultural value.

The Christian villages were referred to as *laini*, or lines. This was due to the fact that the homes in the Christian villages were rectangular as

---

42. Atieno-Odhiambo and Cohen, *Siaya: The Historical Anthropology*, 86.

43. Spear and Kimambo, eds., *East African Expressions*, 12.

44. Peter Indalo, "A Critical Study of the Contribution of Rev. Ezekiel Apindi to the Growth of the Church in Nyanza" (unpublished article, SPUTC Library, 1978); confirmed in interviews of Nyende, Omullo, and Okwirry with Crispin Onyango in 1967, SPA.

opposed to the traditional round huts. They were also built in a line. Some
of the leaders of the homes, such as Apindi and George Samuel Okoth,
had established homes as bachelors, which was a radical departure from the
Luo cultural practices. In the Christian homes, they observed both high
standards of hygiene and purity of life. The homes were supposed to be a
beacon to the community around. They were supposed to attract outsiders. The Christian villages developed strong Sunday schools and teachings
for young people. This was in continuation with the traditional system of
teaching the young people in the *siwindhe* and *simba,* that is the girls' and
the boys' dormitories respectively. These later formed part of the foundation
of schools. Catechetical classes were also established in the Christian villages,
teaching people how to read and preparing them for baptism. Strict prayer
schedules were observed in the Christian villages.[45]

The Christian villages did not allow practices like polygamy. They had
cemeteries for burying the dead – this was to avoid the customary rituals
done to dead bodies. Luo cultural practices, such as widow inheritance, were
also not allowed in the Christian villages. Instead, Christian festivals were
observed as opposed to the Luo traditional festivals. Most of the Christian
festivals incorporated ideas from Luo culture and religion. Christmas replaced *Uch,* the traditional harvest festival. *Uch* was celebrated twice a year,
with one of them nearly at the same time as Christmas. The festival was
marked by dances, games, and wrestling. Christmas was however marked
by concerts performed by the young people and a service. This service was
popular and widely attended by the unconverted. There were very lengthy
preparations for Christmas. Houses were renewed and compounds cleared.
The emphasis was on both receiving a guest and being renewed. These ideas
were prevalent both in Christianity and the Luo religion. Most people who
converted to Christianity did so during this week of Christmas.[46]

The Christians were making the church or the Christian village, rather
than the clan, their social focus. The new community therefore remained
separate from the day-to-day affairs of the older community. However, they
maintained close ties with their older homes.[47] There were even arranged

---

45. Julia Mbaka, interview with author, Usenge. May, 2004.
46. Indalo, "Critical Study," 5–9.
47. Bishop Jonathan Omollo, interview with author. March, 2002.

marriages in the Christian villages. The teacher-evangelists were the founders of these Christian villages or these new clans. They assumed leadership and were equivalent to clan elders. Most early Christian leaders were from a younger generation, who achieved credibility through appropriation of both Christian and Luo religious ideas.

All these early leaders were leaders in church and society and not just Christian leaders. This kind of authority was derived from the Luo religion, Christian religion, and even Western ideas. Most of the establishers of the first Christian villages had already acquired a Western education and were trained as teachers. They were agents of new ideas and change within their communities. Most of them used new farming methods, which produced a better yield. They taught people how to read and write, which was viewed as the new method of gaining power. This gave them credibility, but also put them at loggerheads with other leaders who saw them as a threat.

Alfayo used his knowledge as a builder and bricklayer to build schools and better houses for the community.[48] He also used skills acquired during his work on European farms. He modelled his farm on the European style to show the community that if farming was organized properly it would be greatly profitable. As people came to see his plot he had the opportunity of telling them about his faith. When Ezekiel Apindi started his evangelistic work, he immediately came into conflict with medicine men. They sought to kill him by placing witchcraft paraphernalia on his door. However, the witchcraft had no effect on him, but instead made him even more popular. People attributed this to supernatural powers and his close proximity to the white man.[49] The chiefs also attempted to sabotage the work of the first teacher-evangelists. The chiefs supported, but at the same time, undermined the work. They were suspicious that evangelists would inaugurate a force that would later overtake their own. This would deny their sons the right to succession.

In most parts of Nyanza the structure of the church was overshadowed by the power of the teacher-evangelists. In fact, one reason for disbanding the Christian villages was due to the fact that in places where the Christian

---

48. Samuel Ogacho, "The Participation of Africans in the Establishment of the Anglican Church in Nyanza, 1906–1955" (BD Thesis, SPUTC, Limuru, 1989).

49. Indalo, "Critical Study."

villages had gained a stronghold, it was rather difficult for missions to set up a church directly under mission control. Christianity as practiced in the Christian village laid an important foundation for women's empowerment and participation in leadership. First there was discontinuity with some of the Luo rituals which dis-empowered Luo women. These were practices like polygamy and widow inheritance. It also excluded death rituals and agricultural rituals, some of which were accompanied by sexual rituals and sexual cleansing. Most of the sexual rituals were deemed an assault to the dignity of women and to women economically. Christian villages also laid the foundation for Luo women participating in Christian leadership.

One of the greatest debates in mission work was generated as a result of the translation and interpretation of Scripture. This was because of striking similarities between some of the Luo narratives and the biblical narratives. Women had played key roles in some of the narratives, which were similar to the biblical narratives. There were also similarities between some of the Luo practices and Old Testament practices. This led to great fear, especially on the part of Archdeacon Owen, that if the Luo were exposed to the Old Testament, they would backslide into paganism. However, in contrast to this fear the Luo did not necessarily backslide into paganism. The Luo found it easy to identify with the biblical world. They saw themselves as part of the biblical narratives. The Bible also formed a very acceptable basis for radically challenging some of their cultural practices.

The main concern of Owen was that the Luo would be tempted to draw parallels between the Old Testament and their culture, which was pagan. There were similarities between some of the Luo narratives and the biblical narratives. *Simbi Nyaima* was a tale about a village that was submerged by a flood due to the villagers' refusal to heed to the advice of an elderly woman who was a *jabilo* or medicine woman. The Luo version of the narrative was meant to explain the origin of one of the hot springs in Nyanza and to explain why most of the Luo communities were not given skills to be rainmakers. However, the tale had some similarity with the story of the flood (Gen 6–8). The second parallel was between the tales of *Lwanda Magere*, the great warrior who was killed by enemies through his marriage to a foreign wife. The wife divulged his secrets to the enemies. The Luo saw some parallel between this tale and the story of Samson and Delilah (Judg

16–17). A third parallel was between the tale of *Podho and Arua*, the first siblings of the Luo community founders, *Ramogi* and *Nyipir*. Because of a family feud and the desire for revenge, their encounter ended in death and caused family separation. The Luo saw in this a parallel to the story of Cain and Abel (Gen 3). Lastly was the tale of *Nyamgondho* who was turned into a physical feature due to lack of gratitude. People saw in this a similarity to the story of Lot's wife (Gen 19).[50] In the oral transmission of the Old Testament, the Luo were already drawing parallels with some of their tales. Owen however felt there were no similarities between the Bible and the Luo background which was pagan.

Owen felt that the translation of the Old Testament into Luo would compel the missionaries to give definite teaching with regard to both Old and New Testaments. He however strongly felt that the time was not yet ripe for this. Owen argued that the publication of the Old Testament would make the Luo backslide, while consoling themselves that Luo culture was similar to the Old Testament. They would backslide to practices like polygamy of the surrounding society.[51] Owen argued that the majority of the Luo would read the Bible uncritically, while the CMS presented an interpretation of Christianity which did not exclude the broad discoveries of science. Owen felt that since the Luo had no sound sense of history, they would not be able to understand some passages of Scripture.

Luo Christian evangelists were however often very radical and used the Scriptures to oppose most Luo religious practices. This could especially be seen during the resurgence of Luo traditional religion through the Sumba cult and the Mumbo cult. The Sumba cult had arisen due to a widespread plague. People therefore sought healing from traditional medicine men and witchdoctors. The chief *Ajuoga*, or medicine man of the cult, was called Ongoro. He supplied people with *dawa*, or medicine, to heal, but he also supplied *nawi*,[52] which was used to kill enemies. People also offered sacrifices

---

50. Miruka, *Oral Literature of the Luo*.

51. Owen, "Annual Letter," 1943. CMS: G3/AL/01943.

52. *Nawi* was mixture of herbs and poison which was supplied by *Janawi* to kill enemies. *Janawi* was not a medicine man who healed but a witch doctor, or evil person, in the community.

and were given special herbs to tie in a goatskin by the roadside.[53] Most of the missionaries had dismissed witchcraft as non-existent; however, the evangelists rebuked the evil powers used by the witch doctors.

The Mumbo cult had arisen in Alego during the same period that Ezekiel Apindi and George Samuel Okoth were conducting extensive evangelistic work in the region. Mumboism was based on a vision from the Luo feminine ancestral spirit, *Nyangidi*. Mumboism had arisen in the context of famine and forced labour. In fact, there was a labour recruitment camp set up in Alego. It is within this context that it is said that Onyango Odunde of Seje in Alego was swallowed by a gigantic snake one evening as he sat in his hut. The snake was so big that as it stood on its end in the lake and its head reached the clouds. The snake then vomited Onyango back to his hut and said:

> I am the God of Mumbo, whose two homes are in the sun and in the lake. I have chosen you to be my mouthpiece, go out and tell Africans especially the people of Alego that from henceforth, I am their God. Those whom I chose personally and acknowledge me will live forever in plenty. Their crops will grow of themselves and there will be no more need to work. I will cause cattle, sheep and goats to come up out of the lake in great numbers, to those who believe in me, but all unbelievers and their families and cattle will die out. The Christian religion is rotten (*mbovu*), and so is its practice of making its believers wear clothes. My followers must make their hair grow never cutting it. Their clothes shall be skins of goats and cattle and they must never wash. All Europeans are enemies, but the time is shortly coming when they will all disappear from our country. Daily sacrifice preferably the males of cattle, sheep, goats and fowls shall be made to me. More especially, I prefer black bulls. Have no fear of sacrificing these, as I will cause unlimited black cattle to come to you from *lango* people (Masai, Nandi, and Lumbwa). Lastly, my followers must immediately slaughter all

---

53. District Commissioner's Report, Central Kavirondo, *Sumba Cult* in Central Kavirondo Political Records. November 23, 1923. KNA: DC/CN3/1/11.

their cattle, sheep and goats. When this is done, I will provide
them many more as they want from the Lake.[54]

Having said this, the snake disappeared back to the lake. The vision
echoed several ideas from Luo religion, like the lake and the sun, which
were sacred dwelling places of the divine among the Luo. Good harvest and
wealth were signs of blessing by ancestral spirits. In Luo narratives, spirits
could give people cattle, sheep and goats from the lake, as is especially seen
in the tale of *Nyamgondho*. The Luo myths also echoed the idea of para-
dise when people did not have to work, especially captured in the story of
Miaha. The vision also emphasized Luo sacrifice, and waged an attack on
the Christian religion being preached with its emphasis on hygiene. It also
waged an attack on white people.

The Mumbo cult must have been partly a response to the concerted
evangelistic work in the region. Ezekiel Apindi, who attended school in
Kijabe, and trained as a teacher at Frere-town was preaching at Ng'iya. He
was later joined by Shadrack Auma and Jeremiah Ndunga, who had studied
at Maseno. George Samuel Okoth, who trained as a teacher under Burns
in Nairobi, was doing evangelistic work at Hono and he was later joined by
James Lucas Oganga, who was also trained under Canon Burns in 1910.
Apindi had rebelled against tradition and set up for himself a home as a
bachelor. This was *kwero*, or taboo, and most of the medicine men and
elders had predicted that calamities would befall Apindi. However, when
no disaster befell him, people feared that he had some secret magic. Apindi
challenged the power of medicine men and preached against witchcraft. The
medicine men were annoyed by his ideas, and there were several attempts to
kill him. He always woke up to find witchcraft paraphernalia like dead rats,
nails and eggs in front of his house. The evangelists were introducing new
Christian and western ideas. They had introduced the observance of Sunday
as a sacred day of worship. Apindi set up a Christian worship place, on a
hilly spot, and built a church under the *ober* tree, which was a Luo sacred
place. They opposed the Luo sacrificial system.

---

54. Nyangweso, "The Cult of Mumbo in Central and South Kavirondo," n.d. KNA:
Mss/10/9/129.

Apindi and the other evangelists introduced new farming methods and new varieties of seed. Apindi cleared the forest and established a farm locally known as *kodundo*. He did gardening every morning, and visitors were taken round the farm. The plantation was used to instruct people in new farming methods, while providing seeds to the converts. Apindi emphasized hard work among Christians, especially on the farms. The evangelists had introduced Christian villages where high standards of hygiene and personal cleanliness were observed. Converts had to do away with their traditional attire and put on cotton clothes. Most of the people in the Alego region perceived evangelists, especially Apindi, as too strict against the Luo religion. So, against the view of the missionaries that the Luo would backslide into their traditional religion, the evangelists were very strict and had very strong engagement with their culture. Christians in Alego were agents of new ideas and change.[55]

The Establishment of Ng'iya Mission Station

Ng'iya was the second mission station in Nyanza established in 1919. The name Ng'iya or "observe me," was coined by Ezekiel Apindi who started work in Ng'iya around 1910. Apindi had set aside twelve acres of land in a hilly place visible from all directions.[56] He set up a Christian village and did evangelistic work. The Ng'iya Mission Station was unique because its main focus was on work among Luo women and girls.[57] Women played a dominant role in the establishment and development of the work at Ng'iya Mission Station. Women were central to evangelism, teaching, daily administration, and leadership of the mission. This was a great coincidence because Alego, in which Ng'iya was located traditionally, housed the shrine of the Luo feminine ancestral spirit, *Nyangidi*.

Luo women were among the early Christian leaders in the villages around Ng'iya even before the advent of the CMS mission station. Wives of migrant workers and Christian widows established themselves as teachers and workers in these new Christian homes. Women like Eba Aloo, Flora Awich, and

---

55. Indalo, "A Critical Study," 7.

56. In Luo traditional culture, shrines were always located on mountains or hilly places.

57. Moller, "Annual Letter," 1923. CMS: G3/AL/01923.

Sofia Oloo were some of the first converts. They set up Christian homes where children were baptized and taught to read and write.[58] Some of the women who were widowed, or whose husbands were migrant labourers, set up Christian homes alone. This was contrary to Luo cultural practices.[59] "Women also set up Christian schools in continuity with *siwindhe,* the girls dormitory tradition: The girls slept together in the same dormitory within the Christian villages. Focus shifted from just the teaching of Luo narratives, to include the Christian narratives. The girls were taught both Luo and Christian values. The Christian women teachers became the new *Pim.*"[60] Some of the Christian women therefore entrenched themselves as *pim,* teachers and counsellors within the Christian villages. The young girls who were products of *siwindhe* became evangelists and agents of Christianity. They took their faith with them wherever they got married. They were also agents of transformation wherever they went.[61]

Women within the Christian villages also established themselves as agents of new ideas and leaders within the church and society. The women opposed some of the cultural practices oppressive to women. Leah Ogony, later married to Rev George Samuel Okoth, was one of the first Luo women to discard the tradition of removing six lower teeth.[62] The removal of six lower teeth was an inititiation rite which gave Luo women identity. Women, like Sara Ongeche, were persecuted and ridiculed by others in society after discarding *chieno. Chieno,* the traditional cloth, was the status symbol for married women.[63] The women instead put on western cloth, which was the symbol of Christianity. Cloth also became the symbol of class and elitism. *Jonanga,* or people of cloth, was one of the new terms invented to describe the new class, which was both elite and urbanites.[64] The women led to the invention of a new status in Nyanza society. *Mond Anglikan,* or women of the Anglican Church, became a term used for these new deviants. The women developed

58. Atieno-Odhiambo and Cohen, *Siaya: The Historical Anthropology,* 114–115.

59. Bethseba Adikinyi, interview with Francis Otieno, Hawinga, May 2004.

60. Grace Owuor, interview with author, Ambira, May 2004.

61. Julia Mbaka, interview with author, Usenge, April 2004.

62. Jonathan Okwirry, interview with Crispin Onyango, 18 December 1967. SPA.

63. Sara Ongeche, interview with Tolo, December 1966. SPA.

64. Bishop Daniel Omollo, interview with author, Regea, March 2002; interview with Archdeacon Nyongo with the author, Seme, January 2003.

for themselves a new name of virtue *Angili Nyonyimbo Cha Chiewo Pamba Rachar.* This literally meant that the women were people of high taste like fresh milk and were as pure as cotton.[65]

Leadership of the Ng'iya Mission Station came from team work between the different missionaries in partnership with the Luo agents. Pleydell arrived in Ng'iya on 6 October 1921. He was warmly welcomed by Chief Ng'onga, elders, and hundreds of people who met him near the mission station. He addressed the people near the big tree, thanking them for their welcome and assistance in putting up a house. Savile had given a lot of input into the construction of the building.[66] Fanny Moller, the CMS missionary from Australia, did most of the routine work in the mission station. Moller had joined Maseno Mission Station in 1921 to work among Luo women and girls. She came to Ng'iya in 1923 to establish the girls' boarding school. Pleydell, who was in charge of the mission station, had to cover a wide area and rarely stayed at Ng'iya: "At the moment, I am in charge of Maseno, Kisumu and Ng'iya. Imagine Ng'iya is being held by two ladies alone. I am afraid the ladies will be on the verge of breaking due to stress of work, responsibility and loneliness."[67]

Moller took charge of the mission station when Pleydell was away on furlough. Moller raised funds and supervised the building of the church and school. Moller also doubled up as the principal of the school. She arranged all the church classes, took Sunday services, counselled and generally managed the mission.[68] Women were among some of the leading evangelists as Owen attested: "A number of refresher courses for Church leaders have been held. Courses for priests, deacons and leading evangelists have been held . . . The course was held at Regea (Padre Nyende's Pastorate). The course was attended by some thirty women who showed great enthusiasm and ability comparing quite favourably with that of men."[69]

One of the main issues with the coming of Christian missions was the appropriation of biblical teaching on being filled by the Holy Spirit, somehow

---

65. Rosa Okune, interview with author, December 2001.
66. Pleydell, "Annual Letter," 1921. CMS: G3/AL01921.
67. Pleydell, "Annual Letter," 1926. CMS: G3/AL/01926.
68. Moller, "Annual Letter," 1927–1928. CMS: G3/AL01927-28.
69. Owen, "Annual Letter," 1941. CMS: G3/AL/01941.

in line with the Luo concept of possession with *juogi*. The discussion on spirit possession at Ng'iya Mission Station was mainly related to issues of power and authority. Spirit possession was the most persistent manifestation of the supernatural among the Luo. The basic concept was the belief that the spirits of the ancestors could manifest themselves when they visited their descendants. They could enter the bodies of water snakes, lizards, old leopards, and pythons. These spirits were referred to as *juogi*. Possession by *juogi* was a pre-requisite for the post of religious leadership.[70] However, there were also other spirits like *sepe,* which were in most cases evil or wild spirits, which could torment people and bring diseases and other misfortunes.

Lawi, one of the teacher-evangelists working closely with Alfayo Odongo, was the leader of the Holy Spirit Movement, and Ng'iya was one of his major strongholds. There were several issues raised by the emergence of Lawi's Holy Spirit Movement. The main issue was that of authority. Most of the missionaries felt that Lawi had no authority to operate in the area: "It appears that an Old Maseno school boy, now about twenty-two or so (it is difficult to tell their ages) had entered Pleydell's district without seeking any recognition from Pleydell and had been holding 'Holy Ghost' revival and evangelistic meetings."[71] The concern was based on mission ideas of spheres of influence, through which they had absolute authority to preach in certain areas. Moller, the school teacher, confronted Lawi and demanded to see his permit authorizing travel and holding of public prayer sessions. Lawi responded that he did not need a piece of paper giving him permission because the Lord had authorized him. Moreover, he retorted, "You who came from your home-land, who gave you a permit?" Moller promptly reported to Bwana Leech that a witch doctor had come to his area and was casting spells on people.[72]

Owen was concerned by how some of the leaders were using religion as a stepping stone to power under the cloak of evangelism. He felt that like in the case at Ng'iya, Lawi was claiming healing power over the lads who were supposedly dead, mainly to enhance his prestige and power. Owen felt that

---

70. Onyango-Ogutu and Roscoe, *Keep My Words*, 16.
71. Owen's letter to Pitt-Pitts, 25 October 1933. CMS: G3/A5/0/1933.
72. Owen's letter to the District Commissioner, 1933. KNA: DC/NNO/1/1.

these actions gave people a wrong idea of the character of God and painted an incorrect way of approaching God and learning about him.

Owen and Pleydell therefore felt that they needed to inform the people that Lawi did not have authority. Owen went to the place of prayer and ordered the gathering to disperse. However, people questioned Owen why they were to disperse as they were worshipping God. To get people dispersed, Owen called the house to attention by saying, let us pray. He thought nobody would dare to challenge him. However, after Owen's prayer, Lawi took over and prayed, describing Owen as a persecutor of the gathering:

> My prestige was such that I thought that Lawi would find it difficult to openly rebel against a determined effort on my part, so I said that I wanted the gathering to disperse . . . I persisted. [I] quietly and finally took the bull by the horns and said with firmness "Let us pray." . . . Lawi couldn't give an order that people were not to pray . . . He said, "I will pray first and you will conclude." . . . Lawi poured out a very passionate rhapsody of prayer and went on to describe me as the persecutor of the gathering.[73]

Owen and Pleydell decided to use the colonial administration to assert their power, by reporting the matter to the ADC, the tax collecting agent, camping in the area: "Pleydell pointed out that Lawi belonged to North Kavirondo, and was operating in Central Kavirondo, and asked if it would not be possible to deport Lawi under the Native Authority Ordinance back to North Kavirondo. This the ADC said he thought could be done. Pleydell had written him his request first thing on the following morning."[74]

The next day, Owen and Pleydell went to the scene to convince the teachers and the elders that Lawi was a deceiver. They found the gathering of the church elders in progress. Lawi was devolving his authority to one of the elders who he referred to as "Elija" before he left. Owen felt that the elders were neither listening to him nor respecting his authority and therefore decided to teach them. He wrote the English words: hysteria, hypnotism, and saint vistas dance, and made the elders learn the words by heart. He told

---

73. Owen's letter to Pitt-Pitts, 25 October 1933. CMS: G3/A5/0/1933.
74. Owen's letter to Pitt-Pitts, 25 October 1933. CMS: G3/A5/0/1933.

them the history of these movements, describing their effects in Europe in by-gone days. Lawi ignored and continued to lay his hands on "Elija" giving him the gifts of the Holy Spirit. Pleydell tried to reason with the group, but the impression he left was that he was outside the movement, for he had not been baptized by the Holy Spirit so had no authority.

Second, the manifestation of spirit possession was a test to the missionaries' understanding of the Luo spiritual worldview, and their capacity to deal with the issues that arose. Owen described the movement as based on aspects of spirit possession among the Luo, which to him were deceptive. Owen felt the movement had the characteristics of *sepe*:

> Two youths lying in a huddled fashion apparently in deep sleep . . . Deep coma of two lads, extreme turning back of the eyes into the head . . . were told that the lads had been dead more than once . . . . The shaking and trembling and general St. Vitus dance business is identical to the so-called spirit possession (in which I heartily disbelieve). It is called among the Luo, *sepe*. They are always supposed to be dumb until the spirit moves them.[75]

Owen maintained that the movement was dangerous because, although it was done under the cloak of religion and evangelism, there was a conscious deception on the part of Lawi. He wanted to exalt his own prestige by claims that he could heal people. However, this remained a major problem for the church as the missionaries were not directly engaging the Luo spiritual worldview.

One major concern was that the majority of the people within the movement were women. Owen's perception of Luo women was that they were sexually deviant, feeble minded and emotional, and therefore they could be easily swayed. However, the main issue was that most of the men had been educated and trained and were the leaders in this movement, therefore they had power over the women. In traditional Luo society, training and opportunity for leadership was equally open to both men and women. Owen described the situation at the meeting: "The room was packed to suffocation with people, with the vast majority of women and girls . . . Moller had to

---

75. Owen's letter to Pitt-Pitts, 25 October 1933. CMS: G3/A5/0/1933.

come with us as some of her girls are deeply swayed by the movement and go to the village at about 9 p.m."[76]

In Owen's description, Lawi stopped and fixed his eyes on a decent-looking woman without saying a word for about three minutes; then the woman began to tremble and shake all over and set up a hysterical yell. Owen felt that the girls were easily misled due to lack of education:

> An outstanding lesson is the peril of leaving the girls uneducat-
> ed to an equal level with the boys; it is the girls, maturing and
> matured physically, and to a lesser degree the married women,
> who form the large bulk of the "converts" to the cult . . . I
> have recently said over and over again, in pressing the claims
> of the girls' education, that an unscrupulous Maseno school
> boy could twist girls round his fingers. I have pointed out the
> hopelessness of trying to cope with sex problems, if we have
> highly educated (comparatively) boys, whom girls put on the
> pedestal and uneducated girls.[77]

Owen also felt there were great sexual dangers to the girls: "Lads with their shoulders, pillowed on the willing laps of hefty wenches, when they come around would be able to twist those same wenches around their fingers. Sex passions must be aroused in these circumstances of darkness."[78] Owen claimed that he turned to the huddled figures of the youth in the laps of the wenches and said that the thing could not be of God. However, Luo women used spirit possession to try and claim for themselves authority in the church. They used hymns and poetic dances to critique what was happening in the society. When Owen intruded into the prayer meeting it is a woman who first confronted him:

> Whereupon a woman who had been trembling and shaking . . .
> Put her baby on the floor and executed a mad hysterical dance
> in front of me, raising her arms to heaven and behaving in a
> very strange and most embarrassing way. A hymn, strange to
> me and not in our collection, with very catchy rhythmical lilt

---

76. Owen's letter to Pitt-Pitts, 25 October 1933. CMS: G3/A5/0/1933.
77. Owen's letter to Pitt-Pitts, 25 October 1933. CMS: G3/A5/0/1933.
78. Owen's letter to Pitt-Pitts, 25 October 1933. CMS: G3/A5/0/1933.

was now begun and joined by all to the clapping of hands, a catchy thing seemed to get them worked up.[79]

The Luo Christians made a point to the missionaries that authority for ministry came through the Holy Spirit and not spheres of influence. There was also a major challenge because the missionaries did not understand the Luo worldview. There was also a clear need for proper training for women for church ministry.

The Establishment of the Women's Movement in the Church

Establishment of *Buch Mikayi* at Ng'iya Mission Station

Buch Mikayi, or the senior wife's forum, became the springboard for women's leadership in church and the society. It was also the forum for effective work among Luo women. *Buch Mikayi* was an initiative by Luo Christian women to recover the critical role played by *Mikayi* in leadership and in decision-making in Luo traditional society. The women believed that they had to play a central role in dealing with the issues affecting them.[80] The concern for recovering the critical role emerged because the Luo women had little space to make decisions in the newly established church structure. This is demonstrated in the decision not to have women representatives in the African church councils.

Owen had proposed at the Kikuyu Conference of Protestant Missionaries in 1918, that there should be a separate women's council to deal with their own issues; however, the main council, which was the men's council, had the final say. This led to a lament by Hooper that the male dominance of African society was matched by that of the CMS itself.[81] According to Ranger, the emergence of women's organizations was seen as a means of

---

79. Owen's letter to Pitt-Pitts, 25 October 1933. CMS: G3/A5/0/1933.

80. Grace Owuor, interview with author in Ambira, May 2004. Grace Owuor a former student of Ng'iya had been co-opted into *Buch Mikayi* as a helper while still a student. She was among the first women members of the Diocesan synod. Grace, Olyvia Agwa, and Mary Ochieng, all former students of Ng'iya, have become women canons in the Anglican Church in Nyanza.

81. Miss Hooper, to Mother, 11 August 1918, KNA: Mss.Afr.s. 1117 Box 3/2.

controlling women's sexuality. However, he argues that most of the organizations became an aggressive line for challenging male domination in the church. *Buch Mikayi* took this line and became a springboard for women's participation in decision making. Women discussed and made decisions on issues affecting them like polygamy and widowhood practices.

Pleydell joined her husband at Ng'iya in 1923, and in conjunction with Moller, formed an umbrella organization for women. This brought together the already existing women's groups within the churches to form a women's council. *Buch Mikayi* had always been organized at the local church level with the evangelist's wife being the leader.[82] Moller and Pleydell brought the church initiatives together to form the district meeting. Each district would have a monthly meeting. Two women representatives from every district would then gather for a quarterly meeting at Ng'iya. The main focus of the women's council was to teach and evangelize among women and girls. Moller was the first chair of the women's council, while Pleydell was the secretary.[83]

Moller and Pleydell organized the quarterly council around the policies of the Mothers' Union. CMS female missionaries working in East Africa had decided that the principles of the Mothers' Union in England had to be adapted to fit within the local context.[84] The female missionaries felt that women in East Africa were the greatest agents of moral and physical reform in the society. The prosperity of the nation would spring from the family life of the home. Family to them was the greatest institution in the world for the promotion of character in children. All of this depended on the married life of the parents. However, the female missionaries felt that in order to get to the bottom of the women's work, they needed durable structures. This could only be achieved through the establishment of day and boarding schools, and vocational training for girls:

> Schools for girls and infants must be arranged as part of women's work, superintended by senior lady missionaries. The priority is recruitment of trained women teachers to come and start educational work. The main task of the schools would be

---

82. Mildred Ololo, interview with author, May 2004.
83. Moller, "Annual Letter," 1924, CMS: G3/AL/01924.
84. Lady Missionaries Conference, July 7–8, 1908, KNA: G3/A7/01908/215.

to teach girls the beauty of Christian marriage. The schools would also train girls for vocations like nursing in European homes, nurses in women's wards and teachers in girls' school.[85]

The conference outlined the three-fold objective of the Mothers Union:

> First, to uphold the sanctity of marriage. Second, to awaken mothers of all classes to a sense of great responsibility to training their boys and girls as future fathers and mothers of the empire. Third, to organise in every place a band of mothers, who would unite in prayer and seek to lead their families by example in purity.[86]

The Mothers' Union emphasized the individual work of each member who was to carry the principles of the Mothers' Union in her home in the best way possible. The success of the mothers was supposed to result from the success of such individual work, rather than from the meetings, which as a rule, were only held quarterly. However, the Luo women had their own contextualized version of the Mothers' Union.

In 1934, Mrs Olive Owen joined the Ng'iya Mission Station and continued with the work of *Buch Mikayi*. Owen believed that, to a large extent, Luo women themselves had to work out a solution to the issues that affected them. Of the meetings, Owen's husband wrote in his annual letter:

> My wife's monthly meetings with women, which are held at centres all over Kavirondo and in the townships, have developed extensively. Between three and four thousand women attend these monthly gatherings. All kinds of subjects are discussed, a recent subject being the position of widows, especially the inheritance of widows. One of its objects is to get the public opinion among the women, especially with regard to features in African tribal life, which are a hindrance to a Christian life. A large measure of the salvation must come from women themselves.[87]

---

85. Weatherhead, "Educational Work," July 7–8, 1908, KNA: G3/A7/01908/215.
86. Weatherhead, "Mothers Union," July 7–8, 1908, KNA: G3/A7/01908/215.
87. Owen, "Annual Letter," 1939, G3/Ow/AL/1939.

The major emphasis of Olive Owen was on teaching and counselling senior girls at the boarding school. The senior girls were co-opted into *Buch Mikayi* as helpers. They were requested to assist in the writing of minutes. The main purpose of co-opting the girls was to mentor them into leadership.[88] Owen also emphasized the protection of girls from polygamous marriages and other related vices. They were to counsel and help young girls and women to make decisions about their lives. *Buch Mikayi* would help women to make decisions and guard against negative cultural practices that were felt to subdue women, like polygamy and widow inheritance. *Buch Mikayi* inspired and mentored young girls, giving them self-esteem. They discouraged them from early marriages and gave them sex-education in order to guard against pregnancy out of wedlock. They also encouraged the education of girls and talked to girls already in school to encourage other girls and later to pay for the education of their sisters.[89]

Buch Mikayi also acted as a pressure group to encourage disciplined families. They exerted pressure on people to respect the marriage institution.[90] The forum created space for women to deal with issues affecting them and suggested actions. These issues were brought to quarterly meetings that would then decide on disciplinary action. Women would make appeals if they felt that the decisions were unfair, and the women's council would then finally pass on the issues to the African Church Council.[91] Through this kind of channel, women participated in leadership of the church. Their decisions and actions had far-reaching consequences for church and the society. *Buch Mikayi* also focused on development issues. They contributed funds for charity both locally and internationally. During World War II, they contributed funds to women caught up in war in England and Malta through the East African Women's League.[92] *Buch Mikayi* therefore became the base of networking with other organizations.

Esta Lala was a full-time worker coordinating the women's work at Ng'iya. Lala chaired the meetings of the Ng'iya District Council. Each

88. Peresis Omollo, interview with author, March 2003.
89. Mildred Ololo, interview with author, Maranda, April 2004.
90. Mical Ogot, interview with Francis Otieno, Ng'iya, June 2004.
91. Owen, "Annual Letter," 1939, CMS: G3/AL/01939.
92. Owen, "Annual Letter," 1943, CMS: G3/AL/01943.

Saturday, she led women in groups of two or three in doing evangelistic work around the villages. Lala also worked in the Ng'iya Girls' Boarding School from the time of its inception. Women's work was an integral part of the school. Lala was widowed and experienced a lot of problems with her husband's relations. They wanted her to perform certain cultural practices that she was not prepared to perform.

As noted in an earlier chapter, according to Luo culture, when a man died, the woman had to remove *chieno*, the traditional cloth, and mourn naked. After burial, the woman had to observe several days of mourning. She was not supposed to take a shower, sweep her house, or interact with anybody. After about one week, a string referred to as *okola* would be tied to her waist symbolizing that she was unclean and was not supposed to interact with anybody. She was also not supposed to participate in any social and economic activities. This isolation would continue for one year, and the ban would only be lifted after the woman was re-married or inherited by the husband's relatives. Widow inheritance was therefore tied to participation in social issues and her status in the society. It was also tied to participation in economic issues and the inheritance of property. Lala defied these practices around widow inheritance and went to stay at the girls' school.[93]

Lala was employed as a teacher at the girls' school. Moller described her as "my right hand,"[94] and her official title at the mission station and school was *Bible Woman*. Lala was left in charge of the school in 1928 when Moller was taken ill. Her responsibilities included teaching handwork and machine sewing. Lala was in charge of the house-girls, who had come for teacher training. When Ng'iya developed a teacher-training branch, she was in charge of their hostel. Lala was also in charge of the class of the elderly women in the school. Lala taught both daily classes and women's church classes four times a week.[95] She also taught Sunday school, which consisted of a group of new converts who wanted to know more about the faith. She gave instruction to women who had just come forward to learn about Christ. Lala taught them catechism and Bible stories. The older women taught by Lala, in turn, taught others and discussed issues with them. Lala was again left in

---

93. Moller, "Annual Letter," 1924, CMS: G3/AL/01924.
94. Moller, "Annual Letter," 1928, CMS: G3/AL/01928.
95. Moller, "Annual Letter," 1933, CMS: G3/AL/01934.

charge of the institution when both Moller and Owen were away.[96] *Buch Mikayi*, therefore, became an effective forum where Luo women networked with the women missionaries to deal with issues affecting women and girls. *Buch Mikayi* was the new forum used for giving girls sex education. They mentored the girls and gave them leadership training. *Buch Mikayi* became the major springboard and advocate for girls' education in Nyanza.

Establishment of Mothers' Union in Kenya

The Mothers' Union was founded by Mary Sumner in Britain in 1846. The main focus of the Mothers' Union was to promote stable marriages, family life, and the protection of children. The Mothers' Union in Kenya became a significant avenue through which women take positions of leadership both at local and national levels in the church. This was the avenue through which the Christian woman could make her voice heard. The first branch of the Mothers' Union was established in Kenya in 1918, in Central Kenya, Diocese of Forthall by Mary Stewart Lawford. Lawford was the wife of the British District Commissioner. Initially, membership of the Mothers' Union was restricted to the white Anglican women. The Mothers' Union facilitated group social activities and weekly or bi-weekly meetings with focus on prayer, Christian fellowship and Bible study.

In the 1950s, the Mothers' Union was greatly influenced by Gladys Beecher. Beecher was born in 1901 and was the daughter of Harry and Mary Leakey, who came to Kenya as CMS Missionaries in 1902, and were stationed in Kabete. Beecher spoke fluent Kikuyu as a child, and she was also greatly influenced by Kikuyu culture. Her mother was in charge of the Girls' Boarding School in Kabete. She was married to the Anglican Bishop of Mombasa, Dr Leonard Beecher, and was one of the first women to be appointed national vice-president of the Young Women's Christian Association (YWCA).[97] She collaborated with her husband to write a Kikuyu-English dictionary. In 1955, Beecher founded the first multi-racial branch of Mothers' Union in Kenya, in conjunction with Lillian Karuiki. Karuiki was the wife of the first African Anglican bishop in Kenya, Obadiah

---

96. Moller, "Annual Letter," 1938, CMS: G3/AL/01934.

97. Eleanor Tiplady Higgs, "Mothers Union in Kenya 1955–2015," unpublished paper presented to Mothers Union in the Diocese of Carslie (London: SOAS, 2015), 3.

Karuiki. The Mothers' Union enrolled the first African members on 4 March 1956, under the leadership of Lillian. This was after a protest staged by six African women including Jemima Gecaga, Ruth Habwe, Mary Mugo and Muthoni Likimani. They protested against the domination of white women over African women. The Mothers' Union was therefore opened up to African membership in the context of change in the society and the awareness that colonial rule was coming to an end.

The focus of the Mothers' Union was to give guidance to Anglican church women groups, engaged in mutual support, prayer, and farming. The Mothers' Union took advantage of the widespread and semi-formal women's group and offered guidance and support to these groups. The focus was to help them to improve their communal work, cooperation, and leadership skills. Branches were soon established in all Anglican Dioceses, and they provided professional training for women in new skills such as bookkeeping and small-scale business management. They also gave the women improved skills in agriculture and vocational training for school drop-outs. By 1960, they had structured vocational training programs aimed at increasing self-reliance among women. A wide network of literacy and Bible classes were taught by educated members of the Mothers' Union, and also had a job-seeking service to assist unemployed members. The Mothers' Union worked on three levels: namely, the provision of educational and welfare services, personal improvement, and politics. The Mothers' Union conscientized women on issues affecting them and discussed possible solutions to the practical problems. They had a wide range of programs addressing issues of social justice. The first official function of the new Mothers' Union came in 1959, when a group of African Anglican women, paid a courtesy visit to Jomo Kenyatta in prison, where he was being held by the colonial government. The visit was made in the midst of public demand for the release of Kenyatta. Church members and clerics, including white clergy who were sympathetic with the fight for liberation, praised women for their involvement in the socio-political arena; however, they were criticized by most white church members and administrators for interfering in politics.[98]

---

98. Galia Sabar, *Church State and Society in Kenya: From Mediation to Opposition 1963–93* (London: Frank Cass, 2002), 56–57.

In the 1960s, the Mothers' Union focused on issues of community development, with the main focus on vocational training for those who had not completed their schooling. They offered literacy classes for adults who had not been to school and acted as an employment agency for girls in the city. By 1970, their main focus was to expand programs for girls at the local level. They provided women with opportunities for savings and loans, thereby addressing one of the ways through which women were trapped in poverty. This was through lack of access to commercial financial services. The Mothers' Union also focused on teaching nutrition to help prevent poor health. Women were taking formal employment in large numbers, therefore the Mothers' Union started organizing nursery schools, in most cases in the church premises, to help working mothers to care for their children while earning a wage.[99] In the 1980s, the Mothers' Union, like other religious spaces, created a space for integration and created solidarity among women in the dioceses, thus creating a space where women could meet and freely express their views.

The Mothers' Union also fulfilled the role of raising women's consciousness to issues within the society. The Mothers' Union meetings provided a unique space for women caught up in the struggle for survival; it was also a resistance movement. It became the basic unit for cottage industries integrating traditional handcrafts into the commercial market. In Mothers' Union meetings, women, regardless of their education, would gain information about political processes and learn their democratic rights and responsibilities.[100] In the 1990s, the Mothers' Union was the main instrument used to bridge social divisions between the members, especially class and ethnicity. Between 1993–2000s, the Mothers' Union in all the Anglican Dioceses mainly focused on dealing with the HIV/Aids pandemic, especially caring for the orphans, since HIV was a major threat to the families. The Mothers' Union, within the changing circumstances, focuses on working for a just and free society. They focus on working for social justice, especially as far as women and children are concerned.

99. Sabar, *Church State and Society*, 58.
100. Higgs, "Mothers Union in Kenya 1955–2015," 201.

CHAPTER 5

The Interaction between the Missions and African Culture

Female Circumcision

Female circumcision or clitoridectomy entailed either the excision of the clitoris or cutting away the surrounding tissues. This was a complex process of initiation which was done after a long process of education. Female circumcision was important because it defined individual rights and obligations and represented the initiate's transition from childhood to adulthood. It was a community activity and created cohesion among peers. Female circumcision was connected to issues of ethnic identity, gender, reproduction, land claims, morality, sexuality, patriarchal and state authority, and religion. Female circumcision gave the women opportunity for self-determination. It had a great impact on the social status of the initiate's mother. For example, among the Chuka and Mwimbi, a woman whose daughter had been circumcised passed from the stage of reproductive life to a stage where she could make decisions in the society. The missionaries' opposition to female circumcision was therefore a complete reorganization of the society.

The female circumcision controversy was sparked off when four girls were brought to Thogoto Central Mission on stretchers. They suffered from serious lacerations, and these lacerations turned septic. The missionaries were shocked at the method used for circumcision. Some of the old women used glass and blunt knives to make such operations and used scraps of dirty cloth to dry the blood. Initially, the missionaries thought that education in hygiene could solve the problem. In 1912, Church of Scotland mission doctors took some elderly women and trained them at Thogoto hospital. They mainly dealt with medical issues. The African women were supervised by missionary doctors and were convinced to reduce the amount of cutting. The experiment failed partly because the supervision was being done by male doctors. Dr John Arthur added female education in their curriculum in an attempt to counteract the native customs as they related to hygiene and initiation customs. Missionaries also maintained that the dances, songs and rituals accompanying circumcision were obscene and corrupting to the adult mind. In 1916, the Church of Scotland forbade its members from participating in the rite. However, the Catholic Church did not oppose circumcision, arguing that it was just a social event, which defined the initiate's position in their ethnic group, and did not have effects on any matters of faith and morality.

In 1918, the Alliance of Missions proposed that the government should be approached to legislate for the abolition of female circumcision. In 1919, the Methodist Church stood for the eradication of female circumcision but did not have an abolitionist stand. Rev Worthington of the United Methodist Church in Meru had written to the local DC that the church was offering a more sanitized form of female circumcision. This excluded all forms of rituals, which the missions considered immoral. European doctors at some of the mission hospitals were already performing the surgery.

In 1920, the Church of Scotland Mission led the attack on female circumcision. The church ruled that baptized church members undergoing the operation or allowing their daughters to do so would temporarily be suspended from church membership. The African Inland Mission and the Gospel Missionary Society (GMS) followed. The GMS indicated that any convert who allowed his daughter to be circumcised would be excommunicated for two years. Any girl convert who got circumcised would also be excommunicated for two years and would not be allowed a church wedding.[1] In 1922, the Alliance of Protestant Missions discouraged the practice among its members. They said that the rite was brutal and primitive, and a mutilation of the female body.

The African Christians in Kabete took a strong stance against female circumcision. This was attributed first to the neighboring CSM and AIM,

---

1. Wamagatta, "Presbyterian Church," 220.

and second, to the pioneering nature of the first Christian adherents. The Christians within the Anglican Church in Kamba also joined in the opposition of female circumcision. They felt it was their duty to take a stand to show that it was not just the Europeans who were making the law, but the Kikuyus themselves were convinced that female circumcision was wrong. In 1925, Wambugu, a member of the local native council asserted that Europeans had succeeded in imposing taxes and Africans heeded but warned that they would not heed to the issue of female circumcision.[2] The government recognized the harmful effect of female circumcision. However, they believed that such an ancient custom would disappear only through gradual education and campaigning for a return to the original less brutal form. In 1925, the government strongly condemned female circumcision and offered legal support for individuals who chose to refuse the operation. Native law and custom was not to override the individual decision taken by African Christians.

Women were active participants in this debate which led to women's agency. In 1926, Agnes Wairimu, a baptized Christian, met a group of girls who were her peers and friends in a circumcision procession. Wairimu decided to join the procession heading for circumcision. She had defied both the church and the customary law. Her uncle was disgusted by this action because according to customary law, she had to get permission from the maternal uncle before being circumcised. The uncle's wife was also to play the role of the sponsor, but instead Agnes got a sponsor on the scene. Wairimu also never underwent the preparation for circumcision as per the customary law. Agnes was suspended both from the church and Protestant school, but was however admitted in a Catholic school.[3]

There were women who strongly stood for female circumcision. Wanjiku despised those who did not undergo female circumcision underlining that anybody who did not undergo female circumcision could not abuse her. Wanjiku argued that from the ceremony she learned what it meant to be an intelligent adult, what it meant to be a pure Kikuyu, and had gained maturity. To her, female circumcision was like being awarded a degree for moving

2. Robert Strayer, *The Making of Mission Communities in East Africa* (London: Heinemann, 1978), 137.

3. Kanogo, *African Womanhood*, 76.

from childhood to adulthood. Uncircumcised girls were unmarriageable, but the moment they were circumcised, then no one could stand in their way.[4]

In 1927, Dr John Philip, the missionary doctor at Tumu-Tumu, shed tears after he performed an autoposy on a former student who died at childbirth. He reported that the cutting they had experienced had hardened the vaginal tissue, obstructed the urinary tract, and prolonged labour at childbirth. In response to this, the Tumu-Tumu Kirk session required all communicants to sign a pledge called *kiore*, promising not to allow circumcision of their daughters. The missionaries asked the LNC to help eliminate female circumcision on medical and moral grounds. The LNC did not eliminate it, but modified the operation amidst protest from most of the Kikuyu. First, only a small part of the clitoris was to be removed in an effort to prevent the scaring of the birth canal. Second, the women who did the operation had to be licensed by the government. Third, the girls were to be at least thirteen years old before the operation could be performed.[5] The LNCs in Central Province passed these by-laws. In 1928, the Kikuyu Central Association announced that they would contest the next elections of LNC by defending Kikuyu culture, including female circumcision.

In 1928, women at Tumu-Tumu Mission formed the "Shield of the Young Girls." They protected young girls who wanted to avoid female circumcision, and fended off fathers who wanted to reclaim their daughters from the boarding school. These women became objects of hostility and people sang *muthurigu* to them calling them servants of the whites. However, they responded that *kiore* made them more fertile than the circumcised women. At Mahiga in Othaya, people defected from the church and spread rumours that Marion Stevenson, the sewing teacher at Mahiga, was surveying land for the government. They spread fear that if anyone's daughter went to mission school and started wearing clothes, they would become prostitutes. The fathers therefore kept away their daughters from school. The women refused to carry Stevenson's luggage when she visited Mariga. Only three girls attended the sewing class, and they refused to keep the Scripture cards that Stevenson gave them.[6]

---

4. Peterson, "Revivalism and Dissent," 104.
5. Presley, *Kikuyu Women*, 92.
6. Peterson, "Revivalism and Dissent," 106.

In 1929, the United Native Conference held at Tumu-Tumu adopted a resolution that female circumcision was evil and should be abandoned by all Christians. They were in favor of enforcing church discipline on those who submitted to the rite. However, the CMS delegates from Kigari, Kahuhia, and Kabare dissented. In 1929, Arthur ordered elders in the congregation to sign an agreement denouncing female circumcision or face expulsion from the church. Arthur toured Central Kenya rallying support for his hardline position. He devised a paper in which all members of the church were to renounce female circumcision and KCA. This led to a big drop in church membership. In Kikuyu, all mission employees were expected to sign a vow against female circumcision.

In response, Ngendo a fifteen-year-old girl, and a GMS Kambui adherent, was forcibly subjected to a major operation in contravention to the by-law. When Knapp reported the matter to the Kiambu DC's court, two women circumcisers were fined thirty shillings each. The fine was not for forcibly circumcising the girl but for performing a major operation. The missionaries, annoyed at the light sentence, appealed. They felt that their converts had no protection against being forcibly circumcised. The missionaries felt that the girls in boarding schools like Kikuyu, Kabete, Kijabe, and Tumu-Tumu, who were determined not to be circumcised, were not safe. Arthur expressed his fears in a letter to the East African Standard of 10 August 1929. He pleaded for liberty of conscience for the African women. This sparked off a debate with the Kikuyu elders and the KCA arguing for the integrity of African culture. On 17 August the KCA responded by circulating a letter to all chiefs in Kikuyu country. They accused Arthur of issuing a law against circumcision and warned that if they were forced to comply, there would be a lot of trouble. Anonymous letters were also sent to Arthur, one of which warned him not to dictate to them as they had the right to do whatever they liked with their property. They argued that the daughters were like their "saving banks," but Arthur was causing confusion. Second, they warned Arthur to concentrate on preaching the word of God and not interfere with culture as he would make the gospel to be ill-spoken of.[7]

---

7. Strayer, *Making of Mission*, 139.

In September 1929, the missions petitioned the government to introduce legislation to protect Christian girls from being forcibly circumcised.
Missions wanted converts to sign, but this was hampered by the KCA
through propaganda. One rumour was that the petition would enable the
whites to marry uncircumcised girls and, in that way, seize their remain-
ing land. Another rumour was that the petition was meant to prevent the
return of Jomo Kenyatta, the secretary of KCA, from England. The mission
adherents were also deterred from signing through the *muthurigu* songs. One
song illustrated how the church was in league with the British government
to corrupt Kikuyu customs, to seduce women and take away their land. The
song claimed that the uncircumcised girls were being used to bribe the DC,
but such sexual disorder would not survive the return of Kenyatta and the
reinvigoration of the Kikuyu nation. They warned that all uncircumcised
girls would be circumcised and wondered with whom Arthur and Leakey
would have connection.

The mission adherents formed an alternative party, the Progressive Kikuyu
Party (PKP). This was led by Zachayo Muruwa Kagotho, one of the richest
men in Nyeri District. He was the first person to refuse to circumcise his
daughter. In 1929, he wrote a letter to the East African Standard stating that
he hated customs which bound the Kikuyu and prevented them from knowing true religion and moving forward in civilization. Zachayo asserted that
they wanted women to be whole in body, able to speak the truth, and give
evidence in their case. The PKP accused the KCA in front of the provincial
commissioner for blocking progress. They maintained that the Kikuyu must
change with the times. The Kikuyu had to leave the old barbaric customs if
they were to be regarded as civilized and capable of running Kenya.[8]

On 1 January 1930, Bishop Richard Heyhood wrote a pastoral letter to all
elders of CMS pastoral committees. The letter addressed the issue of female
circumcision and the crisis it was causing in the church. Bishop Heyhood
underlined that nobody wanted to destroy African customs, except such that
do not agree with the teaching of the gospel of Christ. Heyhood maintained
that female circumcision not only harms the body but is also against the

---

8. Peterson, "Revivalism and Dissent," 105.

teachings of Christ.[9] One cannot truly serve Christ if they desire to follow a custom which is not in agreement with what he would have done, he argued. Those who consented to their daughters being circumcised were deliberately exposing themselves to being disciplined by the church. The issues would have to be decided by the pastoral committee.

On the morning of 3 January 1930, sixty-four-year-old AIM missionary Hulda Stumpf was found murdered in her house in Kijabe. She was hard of hearing and lived alone. Stumpf, a lay missionary with AIM, was a trained stenographer and had served the mission for twenty-four years. Stumpf felt that lay missionaries, especially single women, were made to feel that they had no right in the missions except to do low-level work. She was the secretary to the general director of AIM and did most of the administrative work. However, her main role was in the women's ministry. Stumpf mainly worked with the girls in the mission station. She had questioned AIM's rigid perspective on African cultural practices, which were not necessarily unbiblical. However, she took a very firm stand against female circumcision. It was suspected that Stumpf was forcibly circumcised before being murdered. The London Times on 18 February 1930 reported that the medical evidence discounted any theory of rape. However, it inclined that certain unusual wounds were due to deliberate mutilation, such that might have been caused by the use of a knife, employed by the native in a form of tribal operation. Stumpf's death was very sorrowful to both the missionaries and the African converts, but also strengthened their resolve to fight against female circumcision.

The Anglican church encouraged an internal debate on female circumcision. In the southern area of Kabete, Yusuf Magu, an African pastor adopted an uncompromising attitude towards Kikuyu customs. He led the group of people who wanted female circumcision to be made a penal offence in the church. However, Samuel Nguru, placed in the Kiambaa area of Kabete, was more sympathetic to adherents who felt that mission Christianity had imposed on them difficult demands. He tolerated the educated Christians who allowed their daughters to be circumcised. For Nguru, Christianity was not an alternative to Kikuyu religion and culture but a means through

---

9. Strayer, *Making of Mission*, 146.

which he could realize his potentiality. Some of the church elders in the Kiambu out-station reacted very angrily to the bishop's letter, which they saw as interference with their culture. A group arranged for their daughters to be circumcised and reported their deed to Nguru so that he could excommunicate them. Nguru turned the whole issue into a joke and told the elders that he would not excommunicate them.

In Kigari, John Comely had an uncompromising attitude towards African customs and aspirations. He had excluded members of the KCA from the pastorate in Kigari. The elders who worked with him also lacked diplomacy. In 1931, knowing that elders were behind him, he announced that after prayers he was convinced that circumcision must be stopped. He decided that any communicant allowing female circumcision in their family would be excommunicated, and all candidates for baptism and confirmation must renounce the custom. Because of a lack of consultation, most of the out-schools were closed. The people demanded that missions leave and hand over schools to the local people. The church refused to comply and church services were disrupted, and those loyal to the church were abused. Comely's refusal to compromise led to a crisis. However, finally, at a meeting in December 1932, Comely concluded that people should give up female circumcision if God led them to do so and appealed to people to work in harmony.

In 1931, Rev Ramphley of Kabare convened a church meeting. The meeting allowed a moderate form of circumcision to be conducted under the auspices of the church. Two Christian women were chosen as operators: Miriam Daudi from Kabare and Naomi Ndito from Ngiriambu. The female circumcision of girls continued until the 1950s. No publicity was allowed, and the only people allowed to witness were those concerned. All repugnant customs associated with the rite were forbidden, except the payment of usual goats due to the uncle of the girl being initiated into womanhood.

However, in December 1931, addressing the LNC in South Nyeri, the "Shield of the Young Girls" maintained that female circumcision should be banned, and gave five reasons for the ban:

1. Men talk of female circumcision yet they do not give birth and feel the pain. Some women die and others become infertile, yet giving birth is the main reason for female circumcision.

2. Circumcision should not be forced. People are caught like

sheep, one should be allowed to find her own way either to be circumcised or not, without being dictated to about one's body.

3. Because among the Kikuyu, a girl who fails to give birth can be returned to her father even if she is circumcised. Where then is the profit of circumcision?

4. Because according to Gikuyu, women cannot give birth without being circumcised. However, Gikuyu women have given without being circumcised. What then is the reason for circumcision. We cannot see any reason!

5. Because Kikuyu men have more power than women, we ask the government to help in order to avoid oppression.

Bride-Wealth

Bride-wealth created conflict between the African colonial authorities and the missionaries. Argument over bride-wealth payment represented a struggle over the control of marriage and women's position in the family. It reflected generational authority and the power struggle between the elders, youth, and missions over access to and control over new forms of conceptualization for women. The debate over bride-wealth created new spaces for women,[10] and was also a result of women's agency. By women fleeing to the mission station and seeking help from European administrators, they created conflict which led to the shaping of attitudes.

Bride-wealth refers to goods and services that a bridegroom and his family transferred to the family of the bride. The missionaries and the colonial authorities used the term *dowry*. However, currently the term *dowry* refers to properties that a woman brings in marriage. Bride-wealth mostly entailed the delivery of livestock by a suitor to the prospective bride's home.

Bride-wealth was a complex practice. The payment of bride-wealth gave families credibility. It also gave women status, dignity, and a voice in society, and gave legal status to the children. The process of payment brought the families together, and since payment of bride-wealth was a life-long process, it facilitated life-long dialogue between two communities. This greatly helped in conflict resolution if there was an issue between the couple. Bride-wealth

---

10. Kanogo, *African Womanhood*, 11.

was also tied to the socio-economic structure of the family, which in some instances empowered women but in most instances disempowered them. In some communities, part of the bride-wealth was under the custody of the bride's mother. It therefore facilitated accumulation of wealth for the household headed by the woman. The bride-wealth was eventually used by the brothers to pay their own bride-wealth. By getting married, they were also further contributing to the economic empowerment of the household. In most cases therefore the girls' mother and brothers were at the forefront of dealing with bride-wealth issues. This can be clearly seen in the case of Rachel, a communicant from one of the districts. She had escaped to Ng'iya Mission Station from an arranged marriage. The family had received the bride-wealth. The brother, who claimed he was a Christian, followed her and claimed that the matter was already settled and the bride-wealth returned. After some discussion, Rachel agreed to go back home. However, this was just a plot and at night she heard the mother and the brother discussing how to take her by force to the man.

The colonial administration felt that bride-wealth was a mercantile trans-action. According to Ainsworth, a woman was a chattel, who never came of age. She was transferred from the custody of her father and guardians to some other man on payment of the marriage price. George W. Huttingford, a colonial officer, wrote that a cow was more valued than a wife for the Nandi. The daughter was viewed as valuable possession, as she would one day bring more cattle to the father. The missionaries were against the pay-ment of bride-wealth, as they felt that it was enslavement for women. In a resolution in 1907, they maintained that the practice should be discouraged among Christians as much as possible. However, the missionaries were not successful as Christians continued to give and receive bride-wealth. In 1912, Dr John Arthur objected to the custom of bride-wealth saying it was as if Christian boys were buying girls. Missionaries argued that their converts were finding it difficult to raise the high bride-wealth and were therefore tempted to elope. Missionaries even convinced some of the government officials that the exorbitant bride-wealth was inhibiting population growth and was therefore detrimental to the labour needs of the colony. On the other hand, missionaries like Herbert Downing, who was in charge of AIC in Kijabe in 1912, was in favor of payment of bride-wealth.

Both the missionaries and the colonial administrators felt that the ideal was to completely eliminate the practice as it was uncivilized. However, due to resistance they decided to restructure the institution of bride-wealth. First was to limit the bride-wealth by imposing a rate. This however reinforced the idea of women as property. Most of the elderly people did not support the idea of limitation of bride-wealth. Rev Eric B. Beavon, a missionary in Nyangori, was a major advocate of bride-wealth limitation. He focused on the dilemma of the mission boys. Rev Beavon felt that some of the girls were used by their parents to blackmail the boys. Beavon requested that the administration intervene to stop the exorbitant prices. At the same time, he cautioned against antagonizing potential fathers against mission people. Second, was the abolition of instalment in paying bride-wealth. This was meant to discourage girl or child pledging as the parents continued to pay the bride-wealth. In most cases this however led to forced marriages of either boys or girls. Owen also felt that paying bride-wealth by instalment encouraged Christian converts to continue negotiating with their non-Christian relatives. Third, the missionaries also wanted substitution of livestock for cash in the payment of bride-wealth. The colonial administration also restructured the process of dealing with cases of bride-wealth by establishing Native Tribunals, which were exclusively male.

In Kakamega, the first LNC meeting in 1925 made a resolution opposing bride-wealth limitation and argued that there should be no law on the standardization of bride-wealth. It should be left to each girl's parents. In 1927, Forthall LNC members maintained that there could be no fixed rate for bride-wealth. The financial worth of a girl was enhanced by industry among other factors. Also among the Kikuyu, a girl with a fair complexion fetched even more livestock. In some cases, the mission girls fetched much less because they had lost a lot of their lustre at the missions. Limitation of bride-wealth was also not acceptable as girls were perceived as investments whose dividends could be gleaned periodically. In 1927, John Mbuthia a LNC member at Forthall maintained that a daughter was like a bank, and it is only right that her father should be able to draw from her from time to time. However, the LNCs in Meru were against the commercialization of cultural institutions.[11] In 1928, Kiambu chiefs Koinange and Kenyajui argued that limitation of bride-wealth would be contrary to the inherent principle of bride-wealth payment, as the pattern of payment related to different stages of a woman. Second, marriage was an alliance of two clans and each stage was accompanied by various rituals. They argued that bride-wealth limitation also affected the litigation system.

Most young men however supported the limitation of bride-wealth. In 1926 at a public *baraza*, the Kisii young men argued that payment of bride-wealth in cash had led to the commercialization of bride-wealth. Many young people could not pay the bride-wealth expected in the girl's home. Second, there was growing individualism; hence the clan did not assist in the payment. This had led to young men taking girls by force as they looked for the money to pay gradually, but also led to stock theft. It also led to elopement or enticing suitors into marriage before the bride-wealth transaction was complete. Male wage earners also favoured limitation but preferred to pay by instalment. Wage employment afforded young people independence from the elders. They could raise their own money and buy the livestock to pay without relying on anyone.

However, some of the cases involving bride-wealth were very complex and therefore difficult to deal with. This is seen in the case of Salome, who had attempted to leave her polygamous husband after conversion to Christianity. The brother threatened to commit suicide because the issue was too complex to sort out. Salome and the brother were orphans and had been brought up under the custody of their uncle. The uncle had married his daughter to a man who paid fifty goats for her. His daughter however died without a child, and nothing to show for the fifty goats. He therefore went back to claim the fifty goats, but the uncle was too old. However, there was a liability on the whole family. The court of the whole village of elders decided that the claim for refund was right, so the sister (the dead girl's cousin) was to be given as a replacement. The man paid eight cows on top, which the brother of the girl used for payment of his own dowry. So if the girl had to return, the brother had to pay back fifty goats plus eight cows. This story highlights several issues relating to Luo culture which had to be dealt with,

---

11. Kanogo, *African Womanhood*, 115.

in this particular case the Luo custom of replacing the wife with a sister or a cousin. This case was made worse through lack of children in the union. One of the reasons for paying bride-wealth was to ensure legal ownership of the children by the man. In Salome's case, when this man decided to marry her, he decided to pay further bride-wealth of eight cows. Thus by Salome leaving her husband, the family had to deal with several complex issues.

Bride-wealth was also paid to families in exchange for the woman's productive and reproductive labour. It was seen as compensation to the family for the loss of labour. According to Luo customs, whenever a marriage did not work, the bride-wealth had to be repaid. However, repayment of bride-wealth was quite difficult because bride-wealth was not just paid to the girl's father. It was also a way of redistributing wealth, and various people like the uncles would receive some portion of the bride-wealth. Also, part of the bride-wealth paid was used within the marriage ceremony and was therefore very difficult to pay back. On the other hand, a father could not receive bride-wealth from another suitor unless the one from the former husband had been repaid. Parents therefore urged their daughters to stick to their marriages. This is illustrated in the case of Regina, who had been betrothed, and the father given bride-wealth without her consent. Although Regina did not like the man and the man was also not very keen on marrying her, the father forced her to stick to the marriage. Regina decided to appeal to Archdeacon Owen and told him her story and after confirmation; Owen took the girl to the father. They found the father sipping porridge outside his hut. On hearing the purpose of their visit, the father told one of the wives to bring a knife and demanded of the daughter that she should plunge it into his heart. Owen told him not to be silly, but he swore that he would commit suicide after they were gone. This was however an idle threat and had no effect on his daughter. He persisted that he would never give back the cattle that had been received for her and that she had to go back to her husband.[12]

The marriage ordinance led to further predicaments on bride-wealth. The ordinance required that both a man and a woman accept the Christian faith before they could have a Christian marriage. The missions had many boys,

---

12. Edwin Owen, "Annual Letter," 1939, CMS Archives: G3/AL/01939.

but only a few dozen girls, hence a shortage of prospective mission brides. The mission girl parents put up prices accordingly. In Kisii, the common price was five to ten head of cattle. When mission men failed to pay, the girls were dragged from the mission stations to marry "raw natives" who could pay the required sum. Inflated bride-wealth seemed to threaten the mission's ability to retain female students. Mission men were also forced to enter into marriage alliances with non-mission girls. Beavon argued that these kind of alliances turned African men into *shenzies*, or fools. He blamed the government for contributing to the "shenziation" of African males by supporting elders in not allowing girls to attend school. However, the marriage ordinance also gave the mission girls opportunity for agency work. The expectation that Christians marry Christians put a very high premium on the bride-wealth of mission girls. It also gave the girls a certain amount of leverage in dealing with husbands before and after marriage. Payment of bride-wealth in instalments resulted in blackmail (e.g. girls going back to their homes). Mission girls at other times agreed to marry boys who could not pay bride-wealth to the disappointment of their fathers. The girls' audacity to contract marriages against the wish of their parents was a sign of agency.

The African women however appealed to the missionaries or other European officials who would assist them to access the new justice system which applied the marriage ordinance. A case in point was that of a Christian girl who was forced to marry a lapsed teacher after the uncle was paid bride-wealth. The girl was already engaged to a school teacher. Owen took over the case, and it ended up in a court in Kisumu. The uncle had to repay the bride-wealth, and the girl was freed from the compulsion to marry. In 1943, another case was that of Anne who had been seized against her will by a polygamist and forced to be a fifth wife. She ran away nine times, and finally decided to appeal to Owen. She was a communicant member of the church, but the father had received a large sum of money for her, over three hundred shillings and five head of cattle and had dissipated the money. He did not consent to his daughter leaving the polygamist owing to his inability to refund the money paid to her. Owen held that paying a sum of money to the parent of a girl in order to obtain possession of her body was not a legal contract in any court in the British Empire, so placed her case in the hands of the local advocate to take action against those who had assisted in legally seizing her. Owen first proceeded against certain of the accomplices, leaving the principal to be proceeded against when they had got the preliminary cases out of the way. In December, at last a conviction was secured against one of the outstanding accomplices, who was sentenced for two months for seizing the girl and handing her over to the polygamist who had paid the father for her. The polygamist was also later on charged.

Forced Marriages

Forced marriages received a lot of attention both from missionaries and the colonial administration. There were different dimensions to what was referred to as forced marriages. First, there was bride capture (explained below), a cultural practice among several communities which missionaries misunderstood as forced marriages. Second, there were arranged marriages either for economic gain, political alliances, or to strengthen family friendships. In many instances the opinion of the young people was not sought in these arranged marriages. Third, there were instances when the bride-wealth had been paid and the father could not pay back, hence the women were required by their parents to stick to the marriages. During the colonial period, most of the girls escaped to the mission station in order to run away from arranged marriages. First courageous women used their Christian faith to liberate them from forced marriages. By women escaping to the mission station, they also caused conflicts and debates which led to a change of attitude. Women also escaped to the mission stations in order to access the new legal system, assisted either by missionaries or European officials.

Missionaries had in some instances misunderstood the African practice of bride capture. Bride capture was done after all the marriage procedures had taken place, and the marriage had been given the go-ahead. The girls' family would then organize "capture," which gave the girl the opportunity to communicate her final decision on marriage. If a girl had changed her mind, she would communicate this during the process by holding a stick from the euphorbia tree. She could also eat Sodom apples or climb the ant-hill.[13] Capture also gave girls the opportunity to deal with problematic situations without losing their social status. If a couple had something to

13. Ochola-Ayayo, *Traditional Ideology*, 140.

hide, they would organize an earlier capture to avoid public humiliation or embarrassment. However, most of the missionaries did not understand the custom; they felt that the girls were screaming because they were offended, while in reality they were staging a show. Missionaries therefore insisted that girls needed to give verbal consent, despite the explanation given by the evangelists. The missionaries insisted on hearing a verbal consent from the girls, to ensure girls were not being forced into marriage. They even appealed to the government for assistance, but they did not help. Hence the missionaries quarrelled with men for forcing girls into marriage. The administrators also regarded the process as a sign of oppression of women. They argued that "African customs apparently tend, perhaps even more than the other tribes, to regard women as chattels . . . there seems to be survival among the Luo certain custom associated to marriage by capture . . . a girl is dragged to her husband's home, she shows a sign of resistance."[14]

However, one type of forced marriage was the pawning of women. During famine, families could pledge or pawn young girls to more fortunate families in return for food and other resources including livestock. The girl would be sustained as she continued to grow within the adoptive family. Among the Kisii, the head of the adoptive household had the privilege of cohabiting with the girls as if they were his own wives. In many instances, the man would proceed and formalize the marriage. In most instances, the girls were not interested in such unions, but their views were not taken very seriously by the parents. Among the Kipsigis and the Kamba, it was hoped that when the situation of the parents changed they would redeem their daughter. However, in some cases, parents of the pawned girls failed in their efforts to redeem their daughters. There was also betrothal or pledging girls to old men during famine. Betrothal was accompanied by advance payment of bride-wealth. The girl would live with her parents until the day of initiation after which the marriage ceremony would begin. There were instances when the girls were not interested in marrying the old men but the parents of the girl would do all they could to prevail upon the girl to cooperate. In 1929, Nyeri LNC outlawed this practice, and parents who were caught could be tried. However, Muranga LNC did not see any problem in this. In Kapsabet,

---

14. Archdeacon Owen, report to Tribunal, 1944.

the missionaries had to come to the rescue of a Nandi woman who was given to the Luo during the great famine. The woman was taken to Kano plains, but when she got old and blind, she was neglected by the community.

The parents or foster parents in search of connection and wealth also arranged marriages for their daughters to wealthy and famous individuals without considering their daughters' wishes. In 1907, Chege made arrangements with a wealthy polygamist to marry his foster daughter. The arrangements were made behind Emily Mumbi's back. Mumbi questioned the motive of her foster father in making the arranged marriage. Mumbi ran away to seek refuge at the Kabete Mission station. She was against her foster father's perpetual exploitation as his only interest was good bride-wealth. Mumbi enrolled as an enquirer, and met Samuel Njunguna, who was a teacher at the CMS Kabete School. Njunguna paid bride-wealth to Chege, and this brought reconciliation between Mumbi and the foster father. They performed the first Christian wedding in Kabete in 1910.

Most of the girls ran to the mission station, and this brought conflict between missions, the colonial administration, and the Africans. In 1912, Downing, who was in charge of AIM in Kijabe, welcomed girls who sought refuge at the station to avoid forced marriages. This brought the mission into conflict with the government. The provincial commissioner wrote a letter to the mission superintendent that the government did not intend to interfere with native marriage laws. The provincial commissioner maintained that according to African law, a woman was first the property of her father then her husband, and the idea that a girl can dispose herself as she wishes cannot be entertained. According to the provincial commissioner, where there was misunderstanding, the district commissioner was to intervene and make a compromise. In 1913, Chief Gutu of Kabare was so interested in Gakunju, that he ordered one of the chiefs, Ireri, to send some men to seize her and drag her to the camp. However, Gakunju's relatives and friends fought the men, and prevented them from taking her. They reported the incident to the missionary in charge, Crawford, who informed the district commissioner. Gutu was severely reprimanded.

There was a sharp division of opinion as to what was native law and custom as regards marriages. One section held that the girls' consent was essential and that the father committed an offense if she married without obtaining it. Another section was of the opinion that freedom of choice in marriage as it was being expressed at present had come with the missionaries and was not part of native law. There was a growing trend where girls were either born into or grew within a marital arrangement largely out of their control. Bride-wealth in this case was paid during their infancy and additional funds paid periodically as the girl grew. At maturity, the girl was forced to marry the payer. In 1927 at the LNC meeting in Marenyo, Nyanza maintained that contracting immature girls to marriage was contrary to custom. They made a resolution that it was a punishable offence for a father to contract marriage for his daughter under the age of fifteen; he would be made to pay one hundred and fifty shillings. Nyeri LNC argued that such forced marriages were the exception in their area. A girl could not entirely be forced to marry any man. In case an arrangement was made and she refused, the bride-wealth had to be returned by the father, or if he could not repay, by the man that would eventually marry her.

Girls escaped to the mission stations in order to seek help from the European missionaries. In 1928, Regina had escaped to Ng'iya Mission station from an arranged marriage. One year later in January 1929, the family convinced her that the cattle had been given back, so she was free of the man. As soon as she was back home, the man secretly brought back the cattle for bride-wealth. One night, Regina's brother took her unaware and tied her with a rope and beat her badly, taking her by force. She was taken to an island, where she was left with the man and had no way of escaping. In April, the man was called back from the island after his mother had died. He brought Regina back with him, and she escaped back to Ng'iya. Archdeacon Owen had her case brought back the court in Kisumu, and the man was made to take back the cattle. Regina stayed at Ng'iya so that the issue might settle. Unfortunately, she fell sick and died on 18 July 1929.[15]

Another dimension to forced marriages was due to changes within the society. Many girls were escaping to the mission stations because the avenues of redress within African culture were no longer available. On 14 July 1939, Jane turned up at Owen's office asking for help. She had been a pupil at Ng'iya Girls' School until the time of her betrothal to a non-Christian.

---

15. Moller, "Annual Report," 1929, CMS Archives: G3/AL/01929.

She was then forced to stop attending the school. During the course of her betrothal, her suitor took another wife irregularly. Jane decided to break the engagement, but since bride-wealth had been paid, the father insisted that he had to go on with it. Soon afterwards she was dragged off unwillingly but could not stand it. So she did what girls in such a case would commonly do: she ran away to her lover who risked taking her in, gave her shelter, and made her temporarily his irregular wife. Jane was traced and taken back to the husband by the father and a tribal policeman. Jane then ran to her maternal uncle and was given shelter for a couple of months. Again she ran back to her lover and was again removed by her father and the tribal police and taken back to her "husband." Jane escaped again and sought help from Archdeacon Owen.[16]

In traditional Luo society, a girl could run to her maternal uncle's home to show that she disapproved of the marriage arrangement. When this happened, then the marriage arrangements were stopped, and the maternal uncle gave her protection. Another way of redressing forced marriage was through elopement. There were different reasons why the girls eloped; however, this was interpreted as cultural rebellion, and girls who eloped were stigmatized. This is captured in one of Luo sayings, *wangi tek ka nyar por*, meaning that you have a stubborn look like a lady who has eloped. However, such actions achieved justice for the leaders. A girl at times eloped when the boy could not pay bride-wealth, at times either due to poverty or other circumstances, but the man would later on pay by installment. Girls would also elope if there was pregnancy out of wedlock. If a girl eloped before the marriage process began, the girl would not be respected in her new home. Many girls eloped when the parents refused to grant permission on flimsy grounds like family background or that the two were distant relatives. This is illustrated in the case of one of the teachers at Ng'iya Girls' School who had an unhappy affair. They wanted to be engaged properly, but the parents could not give consent claiming that there was a distant relationship between the two. They had waited for a year hoping that the parents would consent, but they did not. Both of them were teachers, but the woman had to elope. The father later consented to take the cows, but it was too late for

---

16. Owen, "Annual Report," 1939, CMS Archives: G3/AL/01939.

her good name.[17] However, there is a great possibility that there was no relationship between the two as the father accepted the bride-wealth. What they needed was *jag am*, or a go-between, to deal with ideas of *jasem* who always acted out of envy.

Women went to the mission stations to access new avenues of justice. Jane had been unwillingly dragged to her "husband," and ran away twice. In both instances, she was beaten and taken back by a tribal policeman. The third time she ran away, her father took her to the blacksmith who hammered on her right-hand wrist a heavy twisted iron bracelet called *aminda*. This was supposed to be possessed with powerful witchcraft which would cause her ill fortune if she ran away again. It was also an outward and visible sign of her subjection for everyone to see. The girl was advised to appeal to Owen and therefore turned up in his office. Jane told Owen her story but omitted any reference to the *aminda* bracelet. Owen however noted that she wore a cloth around her right wrist. Owen got his car and first took her to the local evangelist who happened to be her relative. The evangelist confirmed the girl's story. Owen then took the girl to the father whom he described as a regular last-ditch pagan of the old school. The father insisted that he would never give back the cattle he had received for her, so she should go back to her husband. At this stage, Jane suddenly removed the cloth from her right wrist revealing for the first time the *aminda* witchcraft bracelet. She demanded to know with indignation why the father had submitted her to such indignity. As the law forbade the binding of the *aminda* bracelet, Owen took away the girl from the *kraal* and left the old father to his selfish reflections.

Next, Owen took Jane to her husband's *kraal*, but as he was away, the man came to see Owen in the evening. The man claimed that he no longer wanted Jane as he disliked her, but it was the old father who had insisted that he must take her as he would not repay the cattle given to him. Owen took the girl back to the office to record her story and take a photo of her so that he could highlight her plight. The girl begged Owen to remove the iron bracelet from her wrist. Owen was quite willing to do that, but he thought he had better consult the evangelists at Ng'iya. The evangelists advised against

---

17. Moller, "Annual Report," 1939, CMS Archives: G3/AL/01939.

it saying that Jane ought to be taken to a medicine man, one Otiato, who could be asked to remove it. Owen thought this was not wise and declined. The evangelist then advised Owen to take her to the district commissioner in Kisumu, forty-five miles away, and ask them to remove it. Owen also declined this suggestion. Owen hastily got together half a dozen members of the church council, all Africans and submitted the matter to them. They were unanimous that Owen yield to the girl's request, which Owen had decided all along to do. So with a hacksaw, Owen severed the heavy iron much to the joy of the girl. The next day Owen took her to Kisumu to complain of her treatment to the district commissioner.[18]

There was also the case of Mary who had been forced into marriage against her will. Mary had been most horribly and savagely beaten to force her into marriage with a polygamist. She ran away and was taken back, ran away and was again caught, and on the same day ran away at night. Mary was followed by her polygamist husband and beaten unmercifully. Mary was expecting a baby in a few months but the husband did not care. The husband inflicted injuries on her with a supple hippo-hide stick. Owen could not even take photos because most of the wounds were on her breasts and abdomen. Owen took her to the magistrate in Kisumu and showed the wounds to some of the leading European ladies in Kisumu. Her case was taken up by the court.[19]

The missionaries preferred to hand over the cases either to the district commissioner or to the courts. In 1942, a church leader, who had married his wife in church under the marriage ordinance, later married a young confirmed girl in church. He then also took other wives after he increased in wealth, one of them the sister of the young girl in question. Her father was dead, and the uncle accepted cattle for this lady. He seized her by force, which is not unusual, but her godfather, one of the padres, secured her release immediately before consummation could take place. Owen referred her case to the DC, who gave instructions that the uncle should return the cattle to the man, and the girl should be freed from compulsion to marry. The girl was engaged to a younger, better qualified aided school teacher. A few months

---

18. Owen, "Annual Report," 1939.
19. Owen, "Annual Report," 1939.

later, the man again seized her and attempted to rape her. She escaped and went to Owen who took the case to the DC's court. Rape was a matter of the Supreme Court, but the DC assisted with the preliminary enquiry.

The other issue of debate was on the authority of chiefs and tribunals versus the authority of the husbands in dealing with cases of runaway wives. In 1944 in Kisumu, the Supreme Court had upheld the decision of a resident magistrate in a case in which the native *askari* (process server) on the staff of the Central Kavirondo Appeal Tribunal had been convicted of assault and sentenced to two months imprisonment for forcibly seizing and detaining a girl with the object of returning her to the man, a relative of the accused, to whom she was alleged to have been married and from whom she had repeatedly run away. The authority of apprehending runaway wives had been given to the government officials. However, Jonathan Okwirry, at an LNC meeting, stated that he did not consider that the authority to apprehend the runaway wives be issued by the chief or the president of the tribunal on receipt of complaints from the grieved husband to be practicable. He felt that the power of the husbands to apprehend the runaway wives was being curtailed. According to Okwirry, the husband should be allowed to take whatever steps that seem practicable for him.[20]

Polygamy

The missionaries viewed polygamy as proof that African women were considered as mere chattels in their culture, the worth of many goats and cows. Missionaries were therefore forced to act on behalf of African women. Archdeacon Owen viewed emancipating African women from polygamy as his major calling. He maintained that he was determined to leave nothing undone to secure Christian girls freedom from being forced into marriage with polygamists, which they loathed. Owen made it clear to the girls that he would give them protection. On the other hand, some of the missionaries acted on polygamy due to the lack of wives for converted men. They regarded the backwardness of the girls as a serious danger to the church. This led to the establishment of girls' schools, which also acted as refuges for runaway

---

20. Minutes of LNC Meeting in Central Kavirondo, 1944, "Forced Marriage Debate."

girls. The missionaries were therefore determined to destroy polygamy in favour of monogamy.

The missionaries felt that one of the major factors that encouraged parents to consent to their daughter's marriage to polygamists was bride-wealth. Archdeacon Owen had observed that all the cases of forced marriages that he dealt with were related to marriage to polygamists. In all instances, the fathers had received bride-wealth, which they were unable to refund. On the other hand, the Gospel Missionary Society associated polygamy to sexual excesses. According to them, Africans always married for lust. Owen also described polygamy as a very selfish and anti-social custom. Men in their middle age took pride in marrying younger wives, which led to open competition with younger men. Polygamy created a class of bachelors, who had difficulty in getting wives. There were not enough women to allow every man to obtain a wife when he was reasonably young, and also supply the demand of the polygamists. This situation led to some of the young baptized men seeking out the young wives of the polygamists.

The missionaries also felt that having many wives was a source of wealth and pride among Africans. Pleydell maintained that men took pride in having many wives and numerous children to maintain their name and prestige, so that they were not ashamed to speak with enemies and friends at the gates or in the chief's *baraza*. There was an intense feeling that a man's name must not die out. This line of thought was also held by the GMS. They maintained that mission adherents found the temptation to marry more than one wife almost irresistible. They were contemptuously looked down upon and derided if they refused to be polygamists after they had sufficient property to marry.[21] The Church of Scotland mission was very concerned about Christians backsliding back to polygamy. In the CSM Chogoria mission, in Meru, one of the oldest teachers had taken a second wife. Dr M. Irvine concluded that polygamy did not arise from falling in love but meant a bigger harvest, bigger villages, more children, more prosperity and importance in the community. Polygamy facilitated increased production and the accumulation of wealth and therefore boosted the social status of the man. The AIM noted that Africans were tempted by the wages they earned to

---

21. Hearing and Doing (Church of Scotland Mission Doctrine Book) April–June 1906, 7.

marry other wives. In order to avoid such temptations, two AIM converts from Kijabe prevailed upon Charles Hulburt to abolish their stipend on the ground that wages tempted them with the thought of buying wives and other earthly entanglements, thus preventing whole-hearted service to God.[22]

Missionaries felt that women cooperated in the polygamous marriages. They accused women of being more interested in wealth than in the welfare of their children. Pleydell also observed that after childbearing age, marital relationships absolutely ceased among women. He argued that missionaries were thereby confronted with great difficulty in dealing with heredity, strong sexual desire and lack of mental development, which then influenced African men to take other wives.[23] Both GSM and Pleydell were agreed that a major factor which contributed to polygamy was for men to get a person to dig and cook. Missionaries felt that women never protested when their husbands drifted back to polygamy because they were overworked. Pleydell argued that there was less work for a woman under this system; in fact, she had more holidays and freedom. Second, Pleydell felt that the women preferred polygamy because with advancing age they would escape the heavy toll of cultivation. According to Owen, in Africa with no domestic servants, an overworked wife sometimes not only consented, but urged the man to take another wife.

Missionaries also maintained that polygamy was closely related to African attitudes towards single status. Owen had noted that Christian women who could not find baptized Christian husbands were caught up because there was no tradition of honourable singleness. Owen also noted that there was no economic opportunity for unmarried women to earn their living; hence, the practice of polygamy was inevitable. The GMS felt that women married polygamists to take away the stigma of being unmarried. Polygamy both encouraged self-indulgence and lowered the dignity of women. They concluded that polygamy was only advantageous to a woman of low culture, who had no real love for the husband and had no desire to remain faithful to him. In 1905, GMS taught that it was not right to buy more than one woman. Monogamy was therefore imposed as a condition of baptism. Men

---

22. Hearing and Doing (Church of Scotland Mission Doctrine Book), Jan–June 1908, 14.

23. Pleydell, "Annual Letter," 1931, CMS Archives: G3/AL/01931.

were required to get rid of all their wives except one, while a woman married to a polygamist could not be baptized unless she left her husband. Even non-Christians who wished to live on mission land had to conform to the monogamy rule; otherwise they were denied permission to settle there. Those already settled on mission land were evicted when they became polygamists.

The CMS was also against polygamy, and polygamists were denied baptism. Polygamy also resulted in being denied mission employment. Johana Muturi, one of the first three to be baptized at Weithaga, took a second wife. Both of them were forced to quit their mission employment. However, some of the missionaries felt the hard-line stand against polygamy was the cause of the slow growth of the mission communities. Many CMS missionaries were also genuinely concerned about the fate of those wives who had to be discarded when their husbands sought church membership. In 1907, some of the local CMS missionaries in Kenya formally indicated a desire to lobby the Lambeth Conference of Anglican Bishops to reconsider the whole question of polygamy. The mission conference expressed the view that baptism should not be denied to a man having more than one wife, though any church member subsequently taking a second or additional wife would be subjected to church discipline. However, the parent committee opposed any such move, indicating that allowing polygamists baptism would create great embarrassment. They were ordered to express no such opinion at Lambeth Conference. However, in 1909, CMS in Kenya was party to a Joint Protestant Resolution, which underlined that Africans should not be urged to put away their wives as a condition for baptism.

Owen however pointed out that cases of polygamy were complex and hence each case had to be dealt with individually. In most cases the missionaries were guided by the Native Marriage Ordinance. The ordinance made it an offence for a man who had contracted a monogamous marriage under the ordinance to take another wife by native custom during the lifetime of his wife. Also according to the ordinance, bride-wealth cattle would be confiscated in the case of those who lapsed into polygamy, because it was bride-wealth more than anything else that led the girl's parents to consent to such union.

Owen was convinced that some of the women in polygamous marriages were consenting parties and therefore were not deceived. He underlined that if a lapsed Christian with the consent of his legal wife persuaded some unfortunate girl to marry him by native custom, he regarded that on the same footing as a man taking a mistress in England, with the difference that the wife in England was not a consenting party. He concluded that in Africa, the wife not only consented but urged the husband to take another woman. In such a case no party was deceived. Owen gave the example of a woman who had been well-instructed and was well-read in the gospel. After examining her knowledge, Owen asked her whether she was married, and Owen was informed she was married to a polygamist, who had five other wives. Owen informed her that she could not be accepted as a catechumen because she had not given evidence that she was not in sympathy with polygamy, an anti-Christian system. The condition was that she had to satisfy Owen that she had made an earnest attempt to leave the man who had married her. Owen maintained that he had to be tough on lapsed Christians.

Missionaries however found it difficult to convince the Africans that polygamy was unscriptural. In 1906, the Kikuyu pointed out that opposition to polygamy was not about Scripture, but missionaries were out to destroy polygamy. The reason was to decrease their population, and eventually wipe them out of existence. Mission adherents who wanted to divorce their extra wives were threatened with dreaded traditional curses, and many opted to keep their extra wives in contravention of mission teaching. Paul Mboya, one of the Luo emerging elite pointed out there were several people in the Old Testament who were polygamous, so the idea that God wanted people to live with one wife was false. The missionaries dismissed Mboya as being uncooperative. Owen had even halted the translation of the Old Testament into Luo as he felt that translation would compel the missionaries to give definite teaching with regard to both the Old and New Testament. He however felt that the time was not yet ripe for this. Owen argued that publication of the Old Testament would make the Luo backslide to practices like polygamy, while consoling themselves that Luo culture was similar to the Old Testament. Owen argued that the majority of the Luo would read the Bible uncritically, while CMS presented an interpretation of Christianity which did not exclude the broad discoveries of science. Mboya maintained that the teaching on polygamy was most offensive because people were expected to discard their wives. Monogamy therefore introduced divorce, which did not exist among the Luo. Polygamy was also a symbol of wealth and status for the men.

Jonathan Okwirry maintained that polygamy resulted in great opposition to both Christianity and mission education. Monogamy caused a person to be despised by his others of his age. Okwirry argued that people hated the imposition of monogamy, especially in cases where a couple could not have children. He pointed out that many people backslid to polygamy after they got government jobs. Samuel Olaka, one of the converts, maintained that monogamy was the greatest stumbling block to the acceptance of Christianity. According to Olaka, the Luo were arguing that only wealth should restrict the number of wives a person was to have and not regulations. He maintained that monogamy was positive in the present time because maintaining many wives and children was expensive. In 1916, Kamba chiefs informed the Director of Education that they refused to send their children to mission schools on account of mission teaching on monogamy. This line of action was followed by Christian men who, in the 1920s, rebelled against the missions. One of the grievances of Kikuyu Native Association under Thakur was the effect of hut tax on the native customs. A polygamous man with three wives would have three separate huts for each of his wives as well as one for himself and in addition two separate for girls and boys.

According to Kenyatta, polygamy was ingrained in the social fabric; it carried prestige and was of great social significance in African society. The more male children a person had the stronger the society. It was also important to have several male children who could render assistance by cultivating land and looking after the general welfare of the tribe, while men were fighting to defend the homesteads. Society could not do without children because they were the salt of the earth. Only polygamy could meet all the demands, so when the missionaries demanded that Africans cast away their wives, they were demanding an impossibility. According to Kenyatta, if African men shunned polygamy, it meant shunning the responsibility they bore to their wives, children, community, and tribe. They would have lost their prestige, economy, and wealth – which they could not do and still belong to the tribe.[24]

---

24. A. J. Temu, *British Protestant Missions* (London: Longman, 1972), 108.

Women escaped to the mission station to challenge polygamous marriages. Women also sought help from both missionaries and European administrators in order to access the new legal system. Luo women escaping to the mission station were aspiring to be *mikayi*, the first and only wife. This was against the commonly held view that all women coming to the mission station were all cases of helpless victims, or that women accepted polygamous marriages because they were overworked. Being married as a second or third wife put a woman in a position of disadvantage both economically and in status. *Mikayi* in many ways controlled the other households and was a stepping stone to leadership. Luo women were therefore using the mission station as a way of regaining their dignity and status.

A case in point was that of Jane who wanted to break off after the suitor had taken somebody else as *mikayi*. This was a case where the parents of the two parties had organized the marriage of *nyar osiep,* or a friend's daughter. This was an arranged marriage between the parents of the boy and the girl. Parents would try to force their son to marry their friend's daughter. The boy could refuse to honor the parent's agreement, especially if he had another girlfriend. The parents would, however, find such an action degrading. The girlfriends of such girls therefore eloped to become *mikayi,* then the boy would marry *nyar osiep* as a second wife to satisfy the parents. Owen had narrated Jane's predicament, that during the course of her betrothal her suitor took another wife against tradition. This upset the young girl who told her people that the engagement must be broken off, as the suitor's action had put her to shame.[25]

The issue of polygamous marriage took a new turn due to the introduction of cash economy and labour migration. Lottie Extance, who was in charge of the teacher training at Ng'iya, told of the experience of one of the teachers. She said that the teacher had married a man who had several children from a deceased wife, and later on, a son was born to her. War took her husband away from home and he changed for the worse. On his return she was cruelly treated and another woman brought into the home. Then, while the Christian wife was in hospital bearing twins, the husband

---

25. Owen, "Annual Letter," 1931.

ran off with another woman again. This other woman had gone through the possessions of the Christian wife taking anything that appealed to her.[26]

Another issues that arose was that most of the labour migrants took new wives in the urban centres or just became unfaithful. Some of the men also took other wives who matched their newly acquired class and status and stayed in urban areas. Due to interaction with new cultures, there were also new standards of beauty, such as being slim like the women from Seychelles, or nice like the Arab women who were also admired for their hairstyles. The rural women referred to the new urbanite woman as *Amina nyar mji*, or Amina daughter of the town, because of their foreign identity. During this period, most of the mission-educated men reverted back to polygamy. This kind of polygamy gave low-social status to all women. The younger woman was viewed as generally benefitting from the work of the first wife. The revival women used locally made megaphones to remind the second wives that they were doomed. In their interpretation of Scripture, they used poetic language to censor wrong action in private and public. The East African revival women shaved the hair of the women who were born again. This was in protest of Swahili women's hairstyles, which was seen as the greatest attraction to men. Long or plaited hair therefore became synonymous with immorality.

Women also protested against this new shift in the practice of polygamy. Men moved to the urban areas and left their senior wives in charge of their homes. Some men neglected their rural wives and family in general. They sought to please their younger or newly acquired wives. According to Bethseba Adikinyi, this new kind of polygamy, the rural-urban polygamy, had to be fought under all circumstances. This kind of polygamy was one of the major marks of urbanization. Atieno-Odhiambo and Cohen observed that the town was disruptive to marital peace. The ultimate loser in the break-up of marriage was the husband's mother. This was due to the fact that the senior wife of the son was mostly left in the village as a helper to their parents in their old age. But marrying other wives in the urban area could lead to break-up in marriage. An admonishing song was composed

26. Lottie Extance, "Annual Letter," 1949, CMS Archives: G3/AL/01949.

in the 1940s, "Lo your mother may scream when your wife deserts you for hanging out with Amina, a town girl, who is . . . (Unmentionable)."[27]

The Christian women were very strong in their opposition to polygamy. They used their Christian faith along with poetic language from their culture to critique the new social evil. As Derek Peterson asserts, women of the revival used the language of conversion and damnation to argue about socio-economic and political issues.[28] They tried to recreate order in the home by criticizing the dissipation of their husbands. Alice Wanjeri was contemplating suicide after her husband married another woman; however, when she joined the revival she was able to deal with the husband's ill will. Through publicly speaking and debating, she distanced herself from the marital and social chaos. Abinija Wanjeke from Muranga joined the revival after her husband married a second wife and started treating her as a slave. She eventually settled with another revivalist family and was given a plot of land to farm.

Luo women in the East African revival used the Luo art of speech in their songs and testimonies to castigate the second wives. One of the passages used was Genesis 21, the story of Abraham having a son with Hagar. There is a perception that Hagar became very arrogant after having a son with Abraham. Women used poetic language to castigate Hagar. In the Luo language, *gar* literally means usurp or impose. The women said that *Hagar ogar e chuor Sarah*, literally meaning that Hagar has usurped or imposed herself on Sarah's husband. Agar was also used as a nickname for second wives. This was in line with the Luo idea of giving people nicknames to befit their character. The women used locally made megaphones to castigate the second wives plus their offending their husbands. They put the culprits on notice that they were doomed, and in song they reminded people of the coming judgment: "He will judge the world when He returns; all the dead and living will give an account of their lives. Second wives be wise and leave your sinful status, otherwise you will see . . . Be assured that you will see." The second wives left their polygamous marriages, and most of them gained economic independence.

---

27. Atieno-Odhiambo and Cohen, *Siaya: The Historical Anthropology*, 99.

28. Derek Peterson, *Creative Writing: Translation, Book-Keeping and Work of Imagination in Kenya* (Cambridge: GreenWood, 2004).

However, the greatest debate on polygamy in Nyanza was in the context of the effect of polygamy on other aspects of life. Ezekiel Apindi, one of the first African evangelists, maintained a very radical stand against polygamy. Apindi argued that it was a misconception that polygamy made men rich and powerful. He argued that through polygamy women became dominant figures and their voices were heard more than that of men. He maintained that in Luo tradition, polygamy was very acceptable. A man could not be buried in the second wife's house because that was not was his real wife. Even when a Luo prepared to build a new home, or plant his garden for the first time, he was not allowed to sleep in the second wife's house.

In 1942, Carey Francis, the Principal of Maseno, circulated a paper on polygamy to all missionaries to stimulate a discussion on the subject. The central issue raised in the paper was whether monogamy was essential for Christianity, or if it was just a factor of European civilization. Carey Francis advocated monogamy but insisted that polygamy should not be used to bar people from entering the church. He observed that not only were polygamists denied baptism, but also denied a means of livelihood working as teachers or even as personal servants. Carey Francis maintained that in many parts of Africa, polygamy was the custom and insistence on monogamy was one of the greatest factors preventing the entrance of men to the Christian church. Even within the church, there is great danger of serious hypocrisy in that professedly monogamous men could be secretly carrying an illicit affair. In some areas, men brought up as Christians reverted back to polygamy and other social customs, declaring this brought them no sense of guilt at all.[29]

According to Carey Francis, the great body of African Christians believed that monogamy was a European practice and not a Christian custom and had been wrongly made a necessary condition for official membership of the church of Christ. Francis himself felt that there was no scriptural basis for arguing against polygamy. The main passage used against polygamy was Matthew 19:5, "A man shall leave his father and mother and the two shall become one flesh." Francis maintained that Christ was not talking about polygamy in this case but was answering a question on divorce. However, Francis argued that the church should maintain its teaching on monogamy

---

29. Carey Francis, "Polygamy," unpublished manuscript, 1942.

because polygamy militated against the attainment of the fullness of life in Christ. Polygamy necessitated an inferior position to women. It was therefore not possible to have full development of personality within a polygamous relationship.

Francis maintained that the church should not advocate monogamy for its own sake but deal with the content of partnership. Francis felt that Luo women were almost slaves. He therefore argued that to have one slave was no more Christian and laudable than to have ten slaves. Francis felt that the African church found itself in a similar situation to that of the period of the Council of Jerusalem. He compared the practice of polygyny to that of slavery in the early church. The slaves were advised to give good services. However, slavery eventually died out. Francis argued that Africans would themselves abolish polygamy, especially after girls' education progressed. African wives would demand a new position and monogamy would be part of their program. Francis felt that the best the missionaries could do was to expose Africans to the Christian home, where the father and mother were partners and worked together to bring up their children and managed their home. True partnership also implied abandonment of some customs suitable only to polygamous conditions. This meant having help in the home through household servants. It also implied that the wife's loyalty was to the husband rather than the father, and the husband's duty was to the wife. Partnership even meant sharing of money.

Francis said that the debate on polygamy had to be extended to all related issues, like bride-wealth, sex problems, and childless marriages. He argued that bride-wealth was a major contributing factor to polygamous marriages. He felt that it was unfortunate because the Christian parents were the greediest when it came to bride-wealth. Francis also maintained that the church had to deal squarely with the issue of surplus women in the society. The Christian missions, according to Francis, should not only attack polygamy, but also deal with the attitude of the African Christian communities towards unmarried women. The church had to encourage the employment of girls. This also implied dealing with the issue of courtship between Christian boys and girls. Francis was worried that the practice at the moment was that any girl speaking to a boy would be summoned before the church council. They appeared before elders, who were both pharisaic and puritanical.[30]

The Luo had an elaborate procedure for sex education and courtship. Most of the sex education took place in the *swindle* and *simba* under the guardianship of *pim*. Traditionally, a Luo girl was free to develop friendships with several boys provided they were not from the same clan. Boys were free to invite girls to their dormitory whenever they pleased. This was done with the knowledge of *pim*. Such visits were called *wuowo* or *chode*. The Christians later translated *chode* as prostitution, an idea which was non-existent among the Luo. The aim of the visits was to help girls and boys achieve some level of closeness. However, there was a lot of discipline expected of the young people. Both Christian missions and administrators made a concerted effort to fight the tradition of *simba* and *siwindhe,* which were traditionally very important to all aspects of education. According to the administration, the custom of *simba* huts was to be made illegal. They argued that it induced infidelity and connected it to the spread of syphilis.[31] Administrators also argued that there should be legislation to prevent girls from being taken to *simba*. Girls should be prevented from wandering and getting into trouble.

Widowhood and Levirate Marriage

One of the main issues discussed by the missionaries and colonial authorities was the status of a married woman after her husband had died. Most African societies did not recognize any household that was not under male leadership. On the other hand, marriage was not just between two individuals, but an individual and the lineage or the clan. In this case, when a man died, his wife had to be placed under the guardianship of a male relative in the lineage. The brother or male relative of the husband had to act as a surrogate husband. Any children born out of this union remained the children of the deceased man. The widow could not therefore be a legal wife of somebody else. If the widow chose to leave the marriage, then bride-wealth had to be returned to the relatives of the man.

---

30. Francis, "Polygamy," 1942.

31. *Simba Huts* in minutes of LNC meeting, August 18–20, 1930, KNA: PC/NZA/4/11.

Among the Nandi if a man died, then his brother or close male relative would enter into a levirate relationship with his wife. The levir was to enter into a sexual relationship with her and give her children and had economic obligation to her. However, in most instances, widowhood gave women autonomy because they had their house property controlled solely by themselves. The widow had a personal choice on the person she wished to inherit her. Most of the Nandi widows resided in the compounds headed by their married sons. The society assigned responsibility to the youngest adult son to take care of the mother. The widow however conducted her affairs independently.

Among the Kikuyu, widow inheritance was the total transfer of a widow to another man and totally excluded any agency on the part of the woman. The widow required the intervention of elders for the acceptable functioning of their household. Widow inheritance was a way of securing the future of the deceased man's family. It provided social security for the woman and children. A woman who refused to be inherited was viewed as loose or as a prostitute. The levir was tasked with building for her a house and burying her when she died. Women were therefore considered as economic burdens. One of the colonial officials, Lambert, maintained that the only thing a Meru inherits is a burden as he cannot inherit a widow's property against her will. However, he must faithfully provide for her and her children and faithfully administer the brother's estate for their benefit and not his. Among the Kamba, a widow was married out cheaply to a non-kinsman to pass on responsibility, or alternatively mistreated so that they could flee.

Among the Luo and Luhya, the levir was a married man who lived in his own home and his responsibilities and interest were directed primarily to his wives and legal sons who could inherit from him and carry his name. The widow and the children sired by him belonged to the deceased husband's line, and they had to inherit property from there. To a large extent, the levir had no responsibility to support the widow as she had to work hard and support her children using her husband's estate. However, the levir was seen as a guardian for the woman, and they could not operate socially or economically without him. This is confirmed in the story of George Ogilo, a Kenyan Luo who was a civil service clerk in Tanganyika. He applied for leave stating that being the eldest son of his father he needed to be home for the mothers to be inherited, otherwise they would be in an awkward position. The father's wives had to be inherited on the first anniversary of his death. Among the Luo, the children could not benefit from the property of their father, unless the mother was around and had accepted the guardianship of the brother or male relative. The husband's brother was somehow seen as the guardian of some of the property like livestock, until the sons officially took over. Although the levir had no economic responsibility to the widow, he actually controlled the economic empowerment of the widow. Among the Luo, all agricultural seasons were controlled by sexual rituals. There had to be a sexual relationship between them before the onset of planting and harvesting season, hence if a woman has no husband, all agricultural activities were at a standstill. After the death of a man, the wives suspended all their social and economic activities for a year before they were inherited. Socially, a woman who had not been inherited was viewed as being loose or a prostitute.

The missionaries and colonial authorities were both opposed to leviratic marriage and the use of coercion in effecting women's guardianship. In the East African Marriage Ordinance of 1902, the widows were considered to have attained the status of freedom, and the senior commissioner for Kisumu observed that such widows were free to marry whom they pleased. The widows were considered to be of legal age and could not be forced to marry somebody against their will as this would be repugnant to justice and morality. The Native Christian Marriage and Divorce Ordinance provided that the widow was not bound to cohabit with the brother or any other relative of her deceased husband, or be at the disposal of any such relative. The widow had the right to support for herself and her children from the husband's estate even if she did not marry the relatives. Under the ordinance, a widow became the guardian of the children of the marriage until the children turned sixteen or were married. She was considered competent to dispose of such children in marriage, but in such an event, the customary bride-wealth should on demand be paid to such a person as was therefore entitled by the native law and custom.

However, the changes which accompanied the onset of the colonial period and the introduction of a cash economy led to the reinvention of the tradition of widow inheritance. The Luo acquired from their neighbours the idea of sexual cleansing of widows before they could be officially inherited by the brother or male relative. The person to perform the sexual cleansing was a foreigner of low social status. This had a very big impact on the dignity of the widows. The introduction of a cash economy led to the acquisition of other household properties by the couple. There was invention of a new custom that the levir and relatives controlled the deceased brother's property including livestock and household goods when he died. This brought a lot of conflict over the assets of the bereaved family. The economic impact of the husband's death was grave. The in-laws appropriated all kinds of assets in the widow's house. This is clearly illustrated in the case of Miriam Wambui's mother. Miriam Wambui was an only child and a female child at that. Wambuis's mother was very hardworking and kept her own goats. When Miriam's father died, they had sugarcane, banana plants, and other agricultural crops. The father's step-brothers took her mother's goats to pay their own bride-wealth. They also sold livestock and crops, which had been left for Wambui's mother. Wambui observed that her mother had been completely reduced to a slave.

Luo women told how the levirs had become an economic burden. Alice Auma said that the relationship with levirs had become too costly. They demanded good food and controlled most of the property, like livestock and household goods. They even took the late husband's clothing. They sold most of the things and used the money to educate their own children while the children of the deceased languished in poverty. The levirs gave no economic help to the widows, and their only role was to give the widow more children. The levirs were entitled to part of the bride-wealth. Rose Achieng's husband died and left her with young children. Her own mother had to assist in the education and upkeep of the children. Nobody in the husband's family helped, not even the levir. However, Rose had to keep and please the levir because she could not plough or harvest without him. She also needed the levir to lay the foundation of her new home after she had collected materials because her husband had died before establishing a home. Rose did not want to be viewed as a loose woman or a prostitute.

Despite the institution of the Marriage Ordinance, the women had to be courageous and take initiative in challenging the widowhood practices. In 1919, Elizabeth Loye Ogumbo, the first Christian convert in Kowe, refused to observe the Luo widowhood rituals. She refused to tear off her clothes, which was done to symbolize that the person who used to clothe her had died. During the funeral she also refused to wail and pour out her grain as expected by custom. Loye refused to be taken into leviratic marriage by the husband's kinsmen. She therefore succeeded her husband as *jagolpur*, or the one who begins the cultivating season, and controlled her own agricultural calendar. Her undisputed skills in agriculture won her acceptance in a position normally occupied by men.[32] In 1924, Esta Lala challenged the widowhood customs and went to live at Ng'iya Mission station after the death of her husband. She got employment as a teacher and was in charge of the women's work. In 1928, she was left in charge of Ng'iya Girl's School when Miss Moller was taken ill. In the women's meeting, they discussed how Christian women should respond to polygamy and widowhood rituals.

A case in point is that of of Jane who refused to be inherited according to Maasai customary laws. In 1929, Neso Arap Lesert went to the Supreme Court to recover the custody of his late brother Kemilil's widow, seven children and fifty herds of cattle. This was from Ibrahim who had remarried his brother's wife Jane. According to Maasai custom, if a man died leaving no son, then his brother was to take custody of his family and property. Kemilil had left three daughters and a son, Ndewa, who was to be in charge of the family after the father's death. However, Ndewa also died. Ibrahim, a Nubian, had married Jane and together they had three children. According to Maasai custom, all the children of the widow, even the ones obtained after the husband's death, belonged to the deceased men. Kemilil had died during the punitive action by the British and his widow had been awarded several heads of cattle as compensation.

Neso based his request for custody of the children and his brother Kemilil's property based on Maasai customary practice. The widow however flatly contradicted the story told by Kemilil's brother, denying that the deceased was her husband or that he was a Maasai, thereby denying the basis on which the plaintiff could justify his claims. The widow was thus denying her state of widowhood. Although the Chief Justice was of the opinion that the woman was lying, and although he held that the plaintiff as the brother

---

32. Hay, "Luo Women and Economic Change," 101.

of the deceased is entitled to the custody of the children and the cattle, his ruling did not give Ngeso the custody of the woman.[33]

Women used their new-found faith in the East African Revival to challenge the widowhood practices. They declared that Jesus was their husband and therefore did not need any man after the death of their earthly husbands. In 1948, Judith Aluoch lost her husband and refused to be taken into leviratic marriage. She used her skills in sewing and farming to become independent economically. Judith stayed in her husband's home and lived an irreproachable life and earned the respect of the whole community. In 1954, Trufosa Akoth mobilized the members of the church to establish a home for her after her husband's death instead of a levir. The women of the revival formed a song to castigate the levirs who were out to exploit widows. They put them on notice saying that they did not want to see men in "black jackets" slipping into their compounds at night. The revival women made for themselves white dresses, socks, and gloves and took control of the burial of their members to protest expectations from the culture.

Conclusion

The African cultural practices were complex systems. They defined the power structures, social relationships, individual rights and responsibilities. These cultural practices at times empowered women but most often disempowered women. Missionary activity, colonial administration and socio-economic changes had great impact on African culture. All this led to the redefining of power and social relationships. The roles of men and women were also changing in society.

The aim of the missionaries was to emancipate African women from oppressive cultural practices. However, some of them had a very simplistic understanding of African culture. Due to these misunderstandings they dismantled some of the structures which offered support systems for Africans. They also dismantled systems which provided economic empowerment for women.

The missionaries assisted in the liberation of African women from oppressive cultural practices. The missionaries assisted women to access new

---

33. Kanogo, *African Womanhood*, 154–155.

systems of justice especially through the courts. The mission stations became the new focus of women's empowerment as it gave women opportunity for education and gave some of them employment. The missionaries assisted the women in reclaiming their dignity in society. The Christian faith helped them to take the initiative to fight oppression and take up leadership roles.

CHAPTER 6

Mission Education for Girls: Case-Study of Ng'iya Girls' School

Aim of Education for Girls

As mentioned previously, the education of girls was mainly used by the early missionaries as a tool of evangelism. Girls were taught literacy so that they could learn how to read the Bible. Eventually, women were educated because they were viewed as a stumbling block to the conversion work. The main argument centred on the need for mission-educated men to have educated women to marry. In 1909, a joint mission's conference maintained that it was time to consider the education of girls. They decided that girls would be given an education so that they could become intelligent companions for their husbands.[1] This was a gender-biased policy because the main concern of missions was the men. In 1911, an education department was established in Kenya, with the aim of strengthening the education system. However, the education practice in the colony was along racial lines. The aim was to encourage settler farming as the backbone of the economy. The Asians formed the artisan class, while the Africans were mainly the source of cheap labour. In 1921, Kenya was declared a British colony. The educational policies were adapted and redefined to fit the prevailing circumstances. The policies were directed at addressing the economy and dealing with racial tensions.

However, after 1923 the colonial administration's policy on education was influenced by the recommendations of the Phelps-Stokes Commission. The

---

1. Report of United Missionary Conference, Nairobi, 1909, CMS: G3/A7/1909 155.

Phelps-Stokes Commission greatly borrowed from the Tuskegee philosophy of education. The underlying principle was the adaptation of educational activities, whether industrial or literary, to the needs of the community. According to Jesse Jones, the aim of education was to determine the real educational needs of the people and the extent to which educational work had been adapted to these needs. The education of Africans in this case had been limited to pressing needs like health, sanitation, health training, improved housing, and increased industrial and agricultural skills.[2]

Another urgent aim of education was to ease racial tensions through the appreciation of differences. This was by bringing a brake to the unrealistic ambition of the African races' pursuit of academic education, which would de-Africanise them and alienate them from their people. Second, the aim of this kind of education was to stimulate the white man's concern for African races. Both the government and the missions had to start from the grass-roots and give priority to village schools. The missions and the government worked together to achieve the aim of Phelps-Stokes Commission which was "to form men and women, healthy in body and growing in all qualities, which belong to the true manhood and womanhood, able to control their environment and contribute to human welfare, capable of enjoying and making use of their hours of leisure, fitted to be makers of home in which children of each succeeding generation will be guarded from hurtful influence and will learn to love what is pure, good, and beautiful."[3] The policy emphasized the development of character, and religion was considered as a valuable and even necessary means of attaining this result. Moral health and physical health were also an indispensable aspect of this. According to the Phelps-Stokes Commission, the education of women and girls was an integral part of the education system. However, even after the Commission, the education of girls was solely carried out by the mission societies. The emphasis of the missions was on vocational training for women. They had to be trained as teachers, mid-wives, or nurses. However, most girls did not

---

2. K. J. King, *Pan Africanism and Education: A Study of Race, Philanthropy and Education in Southern States of America and East Africa* (Oxford: Clarendon, 1971), 28.

3. J. H. Oldham, "The Christian Opportunity in Africa: Some Reflections on the Report of the Phelps-Stokes Commission," *International Review of Missions* 14, no. 2 (April 1925): 176.

train as nurses because they did not reach a high enough standard of literacy. According to Owen, the CMS in Nyanza mainly focused on the training of female teachers, who would then marry teacher-evangelists. The priority of CMS was therefore to establish a boarding school that would train teachers to marry outstanding Christians.

In 1937, a joint lady missionaries' conference met in Tumu Tumu to discuss the education of African girls.[4] The Africans presented their views to the conference through the Kikuyu African members of the native council, which had from time to time shown that Africans in Kenya desired proper education for their women by voting for money to be utilized for this purpose. They argued that women needed proper education because women played a very important role in African society; "Not only did she provide the future progeny of the race, but also concerned herself with the social and economic welfare of the society. She looked after her husband and children, she grew crops, cooked, swept the home and in a word, she did all the household duties, so the educability of the African girl could not be disputed."[5]

The Africans emphasized the importance of both literacy and vocational training for girls. Girls needed very good literary grounding if they were to benefit from their vocational courses such as hospital nursing, domestic science, and teaching. They emphasized that without proper grounding of these subjects, the future of the girls as well as that of the race was crippled. On the other hand, if girls were well taught, it would raise the Africans to a higher stage of civilization and mental development by improving the homes. It would also improve the physical and hygienic conditions of African life in Kenya. They also emphasized the importance of vocational training, especially the need of women teachers.

Finally, one of the major recommendations of the conference was the focus on the training of female teachers, which was done at two levels. First was elementary teacher training, in which attendance at normal school was not compulsory. However, an examination was to be taken after two years

---

4. Conference of Lady Missionaries on the Education Girls in Kenya, Kenya Missionary Council Report, August 23–28, 1937, KNA: MSS/61/443 Education Conference.

5. "Katu's View on African Education," Lady Missionaries Conference, August 23–28, 1937, KNA: MSS/61/443 Education Conference.

of practical teaching, with training in method, under close supervision of a European. Second was the preliminary examination level. This was to be done by the majority of the schools who did not qualify for elementary teacher training. Local arrangements had to be made for a preliminary teachers' certificate. The candidates had to finish standard 3, and had to have one year subsequent teaching experience under European supervision. Female teachers had to be examined at their own station. The conference however recommended that the curriculum in Nyanza had to be referred to the local bodies. They also recommended preliminary examination as suitable for backward places like Nyanza and parts of the coast.

The conference re-emphasized the centrality of character formation to the curriculum. They outlined the components of character building as religious education, and religious life of the school, discipline, hygiene including sex education and extra class activities. They emphasized that it was important to create a general atmosphere in the school that would make it easy for girls to grow in grace. The religious life of the school was important, especially Christian worship and fellowship. The girls had to be encouraged to work, play, pray and eat together. Discipline was also central to character formation. The role of the principal and the assistants was to control the school. The principal had to delegate authority to the school council and prefects, however the principal was the final court of appeal. It was also important for the corporate life of the school to create in the pupils a desire to do right, which would offer invaluable training for leadership.

The conference also maintained that hygiene practice in the general running of the school would give pupils a taste for cleanliness and the right way of living. They maintained that questions of sex hygiene or sex education were much bigger in view of the changing circumstances. It was unlikely that the parents were teaching their children frankly and fully. The conference emphasized the teaching of facts on sex physiology, which had to be given before puberty. They emphasized extra-curricular activities as important avenues for emotional outlets of energy, and opportunities for self-display. Drama, hobbies, and expression work were valuable and most important. It was also important to introduce healthy relationships between boys and girls.

Case-Study of Ng'iya Girls' School

Establishment of Ng'iya Girls' School

Education work along European lines had already been going on among Luo girls since 1910, even before the official establishment of the girls' school. This was done by migrant evangelists, Ezekiel Apindi and George Samuel Okoth, who both concentrated their work around Ng'iya. Apindi's emphasis on the education of girls was within the context of fighting for the rights of the girls. He fought practices like early marriage of girls, polygamy, and widow inheritance. He challenged the cultural practice that girls should not consume poultry and poultry products, which was a symbol of women's inferiority. A song was composed in his honor: "My hen, my hen will know me, the chick will enter my throat / and my daughter will eat with me, Apindi husband of husbands / is the only one in the village."[6] Initially, Apindi and Okoth influenced the chiefs to use force so that girls could attend classes. Most of the Luo did not want their daughters to go to school because they felt that girls who went to school would not get married and bring wealth. Rumours also went around that when girls went to school they would also refuse to marry men chosen for them. This position was perceived as an alternative to prostitution, as most of Luo closely related the idea of a working woman with prostitution. Most of the parents also perceived the education of girls as a loss, as they argued that the girl would eventually get married.[7]

The Luo also felt that girls who went to school would be too radical and would challenge both the authority of the elders and cultural practices. However, the migrant evangelists used their influence to promote the education of girls. This kind of education emphasized literacy, as they were given reading skills to be able to read the Bible. The education originally took place in the catechetical classes, which later turned to normal classrooms. Girls who were converted to Christianity were also taught in girls' dormitories, a common sleeping place developed for girls in the Christian villages. They were taught by Christian women who had been converted to the faith. The

---

6. Emily Onyango, *For God and Humanity: One Hundred Years of St. Paul's United Theological College* (Eldoret: Zapf Chancery, 2003), 95.

7. Bishop Omollo, interview with author, Regea, March 2003.

church buildings were used to impart the gospel and other kinds of knowledge during the weekdays.

Fanny Moller, the CMS missionary from Australia, arrived in Ng'iya from Maseno on 5 October 1923 to establish a girls' school. Moller, who was later nicknamed *Mismula* by the community, literally meaning "Miss Gold," was first principal of Ng'iya from 1923–1952. Ng'iya Girls' School was situated in the centre of the Luo reserve, so communication was easy. The school was established in response to CMS's concern for having organized work among Luo women and girls. The Kavirondo Missionary Council pointed out that there was no serious education work among Luo girls. There were no native women teachers, and so the Christian men were forced to marry non-Christians, which greatly affected the morals of the society. The Missionary Council had also noted that Luo women themselves took initiative in the pursuit of baptism and instruction, and that Luo women were very independent in character and had great influence in society.

Ng'iya was established as a centre for literacy work, with a girl's school. It was also developed into a centre for teacher training, baptism and catechumen classes, and other forms of continuous education. Ng'iya was also the centre for all women's work; it held classes for old women, and hosted the women's council offices, as well as being the place for the protection of girls. Ng'iya was established on a plot of about seven acres of land. The school was further allocated five acres of land. The elders had pressurized the local native council to provide more land for girl's education. When Moller arrived, she concentrated on learning the language and helped in teaching the sewing class. Later she was assigned the task of preparing women and girls for baptism and confirmation.[8]

On the first day of school on 6 October 1923, about two hundred students turned up, aged from five years to very old women. They were all at different levels of literacy, and Moller had first to sort them into classes. The school was conducted in the afternoon when most of the women had finished their daily chores. The average attendance was about one hundred women per day. By 1925, there was a great go-to-school movement, and there was an average attendance of one hundred and fifty per day. The main

---

8. Moller, "Annual Letter," 1922, G3/AL01922/Moller.

focus was to teach the girls to read and write. Literacy was basic to attending baptism and confirmation classes. Those people who were aspiring for baptism were therefore very keen to go to school.

Most of the Luo parents were also becoming more positive towards girls' education. This was mainly due to the influence by Dr Aggrey of the Phelps-Stokes Commission, who had visited Nyanza in 1923. Dr Aggrey, an African from the Gold Coast on the Commission urged the Luo that the only way towards achieving progress was through education. He maintained that "if you educate a man you educate an individual, but if you educate a woman you educate the whole community."[9] The local Christian leaders also played a major role in encouraging girls' education. After his ordination in 1924, Rev George Samuel Booth went around the district and used the influence of the head-men and chiefs to encourage the parents to send their daughters to school.[10]

Clergy, such as Simeon Nyende, pushed for the education of girls through the local Native Councils. The LNC even agreed to include estimates in their budgets to fund the education of girls.[11] Parents also changed from their conservative stance after seeing the fruit of the education of girls. The girls who had gone to school and were employed, built for their parents corrugated iron-sheet houses, which was a symbol of status and social mobility in the society. The girls also paid fees for their younger sisters and brothers. Some even paid taxes for their parents. Parents and even spouses were very proud to be associated with girls and women who had acquired the skills of reading and writing. This gave them power, because, apart from writing their own letters, they would read and write letters for other people in society.[12] The educated girls were also revolutionaries, which was, as earlier described, a virtue in Luo society; they became known as *thuon*. The school developed very fast, and there was a growing need for another female missionary. The Kavirondo Missionary Council proposed that the missionary appointed should be highly qualified but also must have had instructions on managing a home and sex education.

---

9. Bishop Omollo, interview with author, Regea, May 2002.

10. Moller, "Annual Letter," 1924, G3/AL01924/Moller.

11. LNC Minutes, 1928, KNA: PC/NZA3/33/8/27.

12. Peresis Omollo, interview with author, Regea, May 2002.

There were different categories of girls who came to the school. The first group were enquirers, those who were basically seeking to learn about the Christian faith. Most of them were just given reading skills, so that they could read the Gospels.[13] The second group were those who came to seek protection from persecution because of their faith and from forced marriages. The third group were daughters of chiefs and evangelists. This formed the nucleus of the boarding school. Moller had requested evangelists to select outstanding girls and send them to the school. Eventually, the boarding school was attended by the sisters of the Luo elite who had studied in Maseno. This was due to the fact that they could afford the fees. Later most of the girls who had gone through Ng'iya paid for their younger sisters to go through the school.

Ng'iya girls' school was progressively developed into a boarding school. The concept of boarding schools had already existed among the Luo partially through *siwindhe,* or the girls' dormitory. Daughters of Christian converts continued with this tradition by having a girls' dormitory in the Christian villages.[14] All the girls slept in the dormitory where they were taught Christian narratives and the narratives of the Luo but with emphasis on Christian moral teaching. They were taught by Christian women converts. Eventually the Luo Christian parents and church elders felt that there was an urgent need for establishing a boarding school for Christian girls. This was to help them escape the negative influences of their surroundings and establish a Christian culture.

Boarding schools were also in line with the general focus of missions on girls' education. The missions held that the main purpose of Christian education was to help build up Christian character. Boarding schools also offered an opportunity for girls to live in a Christian atmosphere, where they were mentored through interaction with teachers and other students. Character building was also achieved through discipline. The head of the school offered discipline through direct control, and through the delegation of authority to school prefects. Peer influence was important for instilling discipline as students would motivate each other to do good through a cooperate

---

13. Moller, "Annual Letter," 1924, G3/AL01924 Moller.

14. Grace Owuor, interview with author, Ambira, May 2004.

life.[15] The Phelps-Stokes Commission had also reiterated the importance of boarding schools in non-Christian surroundings. Boarding schools were important because they provided a program for moral education, closely related to social education. They were important for mentoring and family.[16]

By 1928, Moller felt that there was an urgent need for a girls' hostel. This would encourage proper mentoring as the girls would live in the school and receive training. The school would also be able to admit girls who came from a distance as Moller maintained, "There is a need for a girls' hostel at Ng'iya, we would bring girls from the district, train them as teachers, and then send them out to the districts again, in the district schools."[17] The girls' boarding school was officially established in 1932, after the completion of the hostel. The boarding section was opened officially with about four girls in September. However, growth was slow in the boarding school, due to the high fees charged for girls' education. The boarders initially paid sixty shillings per year, while CMS paid the teachers and contributed towards the development of the school. Later the government paid forty shillings in grants-in-aid for each student and paid the teachers. The girls paid forty shillings on top of the grants. Boarding school education was therefore for the elite. By January 1933, eleven girls were in the boarding section, and Moller pushed for a second female missionary at Ng'iya, owing to the increased work. Lottie Extance from England joined the school in 1933. She was nicknamed *Oiro Nyandesa*, due to what her students referred to as her beautiful quick steps. Despite the establishment of the formal boarding school, the missionaries felt that the house-girls who doubled up as trainee teachers received the better training. Apart from the training, they received a wage and were being directly mentored by the missionaries.

Bible, Bath, Broom: The Curriculum at Ng'iya Girls' School

The main aim of setting up Ng'iya Girls' School was to deal with marriage related issues. The Kavirondo Missionary Council, therefore, in putting up

---

15. "Minutes of Lady Missionaries Conference in Tumu-Tumu," 1937, KNA: Mss/61/433 Education Conference.

16. P. Bovet, "Education as Viewed by the Phelps-Stokes Commission," *International Review of Mission* 15, no. 3 (1926): 484.

17. Moller, "Annual Letter," 1928, CMS: G3/AL/01928.

the qualities of the teacher they were looking for, underlined two major factors. First, she should be more anxious to teach 3-Bs – Bible, Bath, and Broom, rather than the 3-Rs – Reading, Writing, and Arithmetic. Second, she should be keen to demonstrate new ideas of womanhood and Christian ideals of marriage. The main aim of the education of girls, for all the parties involved, was ultimately marriage. The Phelps-Stokes Commission emphasized the education of girls in relation to their responsibilities as women in society. According to the commission, it was important to meet the African girl or woman at her starting point in the social order. They argued that education would lead into a new life, opening the door for fuller partnership in marriage. Education would add to the woman's privilege, but would also add responsibility and heavy strain. Monogamy was viewed as one of the major areas of challenge, as it would greatly increase the duties of the wife and deprive her of fellow workers in the field and garden. The woman would have a larger dwelling place and additional clothing, which would involve sewing, washing, and mending. There would be better food and higher standards of moral training of children. All these responsibilities required social adjustment according to Phelps-Stokes. This had to be addressed through education.

The main aim of mission education was also to prepare girls for marriage. This was in line with the CMS policy for Africa. The major task of the CMS was that of evangelism, and the Christian home was a focal point. The Christian home had therefore to be addressed through the education policy. Education needed a comprehensive and religious setting for the cultivation of deeper qualities of character, which would result in a sense of vocation to serve others. The aim was for the students to get to know Christ, whether they were going for secular jobs or jobs in the church. The aim of education was fulfilled in the homes, which brought wives into focus. Archdeacon Owen also emphasized the need for the education of girls in Nyanza. The girls were to be trained as teachers so that they would marry outstanding Christians. The curriculum of the school was tailored towards this end. Moller maintained that the girls had to be kept at school for as long as possible until they reached marital age. At this point they would have achieved healthier domesticity. The centrality of marriage to the school is depicted in the inspection reports, the annual letters, and even in the press and rumours[18] which were going around at that time. Olive Owen spent most of her time in counselling the senior girls. She also taught sex hygiene, which was a kind of sex education.

Education practice at Ng'iya was a blend of the requirements of CMS policy and the recommendations of the Phelps-Stokes Commission. Phelps-Stokes had evaluated the conditions under which women lived in Africa and took into consideration their responsibilities. There was an appalling death rate of infants, and ignorance of women was a major contributing factor. The death of infants had staggering economic consequences in a continent where labour was of vital importance, but also led to human suffering. According to the evaluation of the Commission, African women had three concrete areas of responsibility. The first was in the supply and preparation of food, which included gardening. The Commission was however of the opinion that gardening, especially the production of cash-crops, should be taken over by African men. The second responsibility had to do with habitation. Women cared for the decencies and comforts, guaranteeing proper facilities for refreshing sleep. The third had to do with clothing. The CMS policy on education was also in line with the above-mentioned responsibilities of women.

The curriculum at Ng'iya therefore emphasized the teaching of domestic science, handwork, sewing, hygiene, and related subjects. The emphasis of the curriculum was on a practical approach to most subjects. This was mainly to ensure that the students were not de-tribalized but thoroughly rooted in their communities. The school sessions at Ng'iya were only in the afternoons. In the mornings the girls were supposed to get in touch with home life and do manual work as required by native custom. Moller reiterated that the afternoon classes were adequate for them to learn all that was helpful for married life.

---

18. In interviews with the Luo who had contact with Ng'iya between 1930–1945, they all have similar tales about the school. The former students of Ng'iya tell similar stories, and some of the stories have been enshrined in Luo oral literature, song, or dramatized in the annual music and drama festivals. Rumour is a very important tool of censor in Luo society. Although the contents of the rumour might not be absolutely true, they always give evidence to events and ideas of a particular time. These rumours are qualified through letters written to the press and some of the annual reports. There are also songs and riddles of this period which confirm the same ideas.

Handwork was prominent in the curriculum. The girls had to make pots, native mats, coiled basketry, attractively coloured trays, and sisal strings. Knitting and spinning were very prominent. The girls made socks out of the wool spun at the school. Those doing teacher training had to make drill apparatus and were required to submit handwork for the final exams. Domestic science occupied a large part of the curriculum. The girls at Ng'iya gained a lot of practical knowledge in cookery because they did their own cooking in the school. Child welfare and "house-wifery" was also part of the curriculum. The students did exams on this aspect of the course for two days. Sewing was also very prominent in the curriculum. It was allocated several lessons a week, and included both machine-sewing and hand-sewing. They made their own school uniform and Sunday dress. The school uniform was made of khaki material and was done by machine. The girls also mended torn blankets and sheets. The girl teachers also took sewing lessons and sat a sewing exam.

The school put an emphasis on manual work. Hygiene was taught as a practical rather than as a theoretical subject. The idea was that in the general running of the school the girls were given a taste of cleanliness and a right way of living. At Ng'iya the girls had to do the cleaning every morning between 5:30 and 6:30 a.m., and at the weekends they did a thorough cleaning. Miss Lottie Extance did rounds of inspection three times a week without prior notice. One of the parents had presented a trophy to the school and there was competition between houses on cleanliness.

Practical gardening was also part of the school curriculum. Gardens occupied a considerable portion of the land, the students looked after them, and a large amount of produce was used by the kitchen. Garden work was done daily before the prayers. The inspector of schools even complained about the fact that gardening took the place of physical training in the timetable. He argued that games were important for growth and more space covered by the gardens should be covered by grass. The inspector also emphasized that time allocated for games in the timetable should be respected. Despite the position of Phelps-Stokes that agriculture be transferred from women to men, it was one of the most popular lessons. Dorcas Nyongo and Judith Ochieng felt that this was one of the activities of the school which was most beneficial later in life.[19] However, academic subjects like geography, history, and general knowledge were not prominent in the curriculum. They were each only given one hour per week, while arithmetic was given four hours.

Luo Language and Vernacular in the Curriculum

In Ng'iya most of the teaching was done in the vernacular. This was in line with CMS's policy, the colonial administration's policy, and recommendations by the Phelps-Stokes Commission. There was a big issue in Kenya over the appropriate language to use in schools. This arose out of tensions between the different races, and the colonial policy. One of the great concerns of the colonial administrators and settlers was which language was appropriate in controlling and containing Africans. The settler community viewed the teaching of English to the Africans as subversive. They felt that teaching in the vernacular would help in keeping the social distance between master and subject. Colonial policy in Kenya was also aimed at regulating language so that the people were not politicized. The colonial administration also encouraged an education policy which would deal with racial problems. The Dual Mandate advocated that the British had to facilitate civilization while at the same time safe-guarding the integrity of local culture. English was therefore to be provided in a regulated manner.

The Phelps-Stokes Commission on the other hand emphasized the importance of the vernacular for community rooting. The Commission maintained that Africans had an inherent and invaluable right to their mother tongue. They emphasized that the use of the vernacular in education had to be studied. At the international level, missionaries felt that the vernacular was important for understanding the worldview of the people.[20] At local level, CMS emphasized the use of local language in their work.

In Ng'iya, the vernacular was given seven hours out of a total of nineteen hours a week. On top of that, most of the other subjects were also taught in the vernacular. There were already a variety of texts translated and used in teaching. Texts from Scripture formed some classic texts. In Ng'iya, the Bible was the major literary and oral text. However, there was also other

---

19. Dorcas Nyongo, interview with author, May 2003.

20. D. Westermann, "The Place and Function of Vernacular in African Education," *International Review of Mission* 14, no. 1 (1925): 35.

material already translated into the vernacular. In Nyanza local narratives had been written and were used as texts in the schools. Paul Mboya, and Zablon Okola and Michael Were had compiled books on Luo culture and history. The missionaries in Nyanza were happy for these narratives to be included in the curriculum. They argued that it was important for young people to learn about their heritage. Mboya, in the preface to his book, maintained that no people could develop if they discarded their culture. Each group of people had to lay a foundation on their positive cultural practices.[21] Then on the basis of this foundation, they would accept positive practices from interaction with others.[22] Mayor, one of the educational missionaries, published narratives of Luo heroes in the vernacular. This was to be used as a reader in Class 3; however, in the preface to the book he maintained that there were several ideas in the book about witchcraft, medicine men, and other ideas Christians could not accept. Every culture had such stories, but the content of most of the Luo narratives was not true, but they had to read them for fun and to know what the Luo thought in the past.[23] Lottie Extance also translated some of the English fairy tales into Luo. She published a text book which was used as a reader to train teachers. Teaching in the vernacular also ensured that Luo communication methods were used like poetry, narratives, songs, and even proverbs.[24]

Centrality of Religion in the Curriculum

Religion was the most central subject in the curriculum of Ng'iya Girls' School. One of the main reasons for the establishment of Ng'iya was to help build Christian character. The missionary council maintained that the standard of Christian morals and ethics had been kept low by neglecting the education of girls who were the most influential section of African society.[25] The Phelps-Stokes Commission also maintained the centrality of moral education in the curriculum. Character development had to be removed from the abstract realm of ethics and related to the concrete conditions

---

21. Okola and Were, *Weche Moko Mag Luo.*

22. Mboya, *Luo Kitgi Gi Timbegi*, 1.

23. Mayor, *Thuondi Luo.*

24. Lottie Extance, *Sigendni Magosoji* (Maseno: CMS, 1938).

25. Wright, "Annual Letter," 1925. G3/AL/ 1918–1922.

and daily experiences of life. The Commission felt that it was important to reveal the practical values, virtues, and ideals. This would stimulate students to perceive the character needs in the community, so that they could consciously develop them.[26]

Religion was also central to the education policy of missions. According to Oldham, the teaching of religion was essential, because contact with education and civilization had the tendency to weaken tribal authority and sanctions of existing beliefs. Education would erode the prevailing belief in the supernatural which affected the whole life of an African. It was therefore essential that what was good in the old belief be strengthened, but what was defective be replaced.[27] Oldham also viewed religion as important in the issue of a strong and disciplined character. The aim of education was not only an enlightened head, but also a changed heart. This was to be based on routine and industrious habits which were the foundations of a good character.[28] Both the colonial administration and the missions had placed great emphasis on the centrality of teaching religion. Fraser, the Department of Education adviser, had in 1911 asserted that education of any kind had to be provided with the cooperation of missionaries. The missions were central in imparting morals. In 1918, the Sir Charles Bowring Commission recommended that missions had to continue running most of the schools. He believed that the teaching of religion was central to building character. The report asserted that for the moral development of the natives there was no influence equal to that of religious belief, which was one of the most important influences of Christianity. Regular moral and religious instructions had therefore to be given in schools.

Religion cut across all subjects in the curriculum of Ng'iya Girls' School. Every school session, both in the morning and afternoon, started with half an hour of prayer and religious instruction. The largest number of lessons within the week was assigned to religious instruction. Church classes were fixed in the timetable every Thursday afternoon. The whole school was divided

---

26. L. J. Lewis, *Phelps-Stokes Reports on Education in Africa* (London: Oxford University Press, 1962), 191.

27. J. H. Oldham, "Educational Policy of the British Government in Africa," *International Review of Missions* 14, no. 55 (1925): 425.

28. Oldham, "Christian Opportunity," 179.

according to their respective church classes. The church classes ranged from children coming to kindergarten and being introduced to Christianity to higher classes with girls who were already confirmed. The senior class was given instruction by Olive Owen, who mainly concentrated on sex hygiene, or sex education. Sex education was viewed as very important to the girls by the missionaries. They felt that the Christian parents were not teaching children frankly or fully on issues related to sexuality and sex physiology.[29]

The teaching of sex education was also viewed as another important dimension of character building. This aspect was therefore undertaken also at other religious forums, like the holiday camp. The camps were conducted during the Easter week. The main aim of the camp was an indepth teaching of the Bible. The girls participated in the leadership of the camps as a way of influencing their peers. The main method of teaching religion was through recounting biblical narratives. Any other narrative used in teaching had to be related to Scripture. The translation of some of the English stories had a series of religious questions to be discussed at the end of the story. The interaction between Christian narratives, Western narratives, and Luo narratives helped in transforming the ethos and values of the girls.

Teacher Training at Ng'iya

Moller started training of teachers at Ng'iya right from its inception. She had to devise a practical system that would deal with the rising number of African children interested in education. Older Christian women were taught in the morning, while the young girls were taught in the afternoons. Moller started the first teacher training among the older girls. She would give them instructions in the morning, and then they would assist her in training the younger girls in the afternoon. Among the first group of teachers was Norah (who was married to Luka), Rhoda Agutu (wife of the catechist), and Sarah.[30] The first two years at Ng'iya was devoted solely to literacy training. This was followed by a three-year course in both literacy and technical training. The skills taught included carpentry, tailoring, agriculture, and clerical work. After this, the girls would be allowed to teach in the lower school.

---

29. "Lady Missionaries Conference," 1936, KNA: MSS/61/433 Edu.

30. Barasa Samson Omachar, "The Contribution of the Church Missionary Society to the Development of Education: A Case Study of Ng'iya Girls' School of Siaya County of Kenya 1923–1967," (Med. Thesis, Moi University, 2014), 26.

By 1928, Moller already had an agenda of bringing girls from the district to train them as teachers and then send them out in the districts again in the district school.[31] They would act as both teachers and evangelists to fulfil the CMS policy. Second, the training was in line with the policy of the department of education. They maintained that there was already a need to support African teachers' education. The education report stated that the principal need in African education was properly trained teachers. However, in order to secure this end, candidates who must have good personal qualities should first pass through a sound school tradition and about three years of general professional.[32]

In order to achieve the dream of systematic teacher training, Moller needed to put up hostels for the girls. However, it was impossible to put up a hostel immediately because of lack of funds. Moller therefore decided to employ a few girls as house girls and at the same time train them as teachers. By 1929, four of the girls sat for elementary "B" (training in vernacular) vernacular exams. Two of them, Salome and Leah, passed their exams and left to teach at the village school. In 1930, seven girls were enrolled for teacher training among them the daughter of the chief. Moller later focused on teacher training for bright girls who would become teachers in the bush school and local village schools. In Ng'iya such teachers included Hilda Mbala, Zeruya Adhiambo, Esther Awino, Miriam Atieno, Zipora Agawa, and Beatrice Nyaguta. In 1931, Abishage Opiyo passed the elementary teachers examination, being the first Ng'iya girl to do so. The teacher training brought total transformation to the school.

In 1932, after the building of the hostel, teacher training was strengthened at Ng'iya. Most of the girls at Ng'iya sat for a preliminary exam, which was a diocesan exam. The subjects examined included blackboard work, drill, practical hygiene, and handwork, class teaching of arithmetic, reading, writing, and sewing.[33] In 1941, a decision was made to separate the class for teachers under the care of one European. In previous years, the teachers

---

31. Barasa Samson Omachar, "Forgotten Educators in Colonial Kenya: An Australian Fanny Moller and Canon Pleydell Educational Mission 1923–1952," *International Journal of Education and Research* 3, no. 7 (July 2015): 379.

32. Education Department Annual Report 1928 (Kenya National Archives).

33. Lady Missionaries Conference, 1937, KNA: Mss/61/433 Edu.

had only had separate and concentrated attention in the mornings. The rest of the week they worked together with teachers, except for when they were doing teaching practice. The teacher trainees were in two categories, those following the usual teachers' course and those specializing in domestic science, who usually ended up as domestic workers in European homes. By 1941, Ng'iya Girls' School provided employment to the young teachers, who later graduated to the teacher training centre. The students of Ng'iya also excelled in the elementary teachers examination. This is confirmed in Moller's Report:

> Native girl teachers are effective and efficient and they did excellent work and can be relied on to take responsibilities when necessary. The inspector of schools for Nyanza visited us during the year of inspection and examined the teacher trainees for elementary teacher certificate on December 9th and 10th, where all candidates passed, of the girl teachers who passed the teacher certificate will be on the staff at Ng'iya school, but the other eight will be taken to other sector schools. One in South Kavirondo, one in North Kavirondo and the others in different schools in Central Kavirondo.[34]

Female teacher training met with a lot of challenges. The major challenge was low salary and poor standards of female teachers. Luo men had raised the need for immediate action. They argued that until there were sufficient female teachers, the education of girls would suffer. They pointed out that the conditions in Africa were changing rapidly, and the standard of living was rising every day. There was need for change in the social conditions in the villages so that the female teachers could stay longer in village schools. Another problem was that most of the teachers received preliminary or diocesan certificates, and there was a need for the Department of Education to recognize the certificates. Another challenge was the frequent marriages of the trainees and the teachers. However, from the point of view of the school administration, the marriage of the teachers was not a loss. Girls who were married to Christian wmenay and kept good Christian homes would give great publicity to the school. This was confirmed by the positive

---

34. Mollers Annual Report 1942, KNA/MSS/61/1443/120.

report given of two teachers, one married to the principal of Amira and the other married to a master in Alliance High School. The other cases cited in the report were teachers married around Eldoret and Kitale Districts.[35] Another cause of pride for the school was one of the girls who was engaged to a doctor while undergoing training. The teachers, Extance and Moller, hoped that nothing would happen to break the engagement. The teachers spent a lot of time counselling girls on marriage issues and even at times engaged in matchmaking. The main problem was girls who eloped or got married according to native custom.

Generally, the female teachers were paid less because it was assumed that they were on their way to marriage. At the diocesan level, this trend was worrying and discussion was in process on how the issue could be dealt with. The girls however were under a lot of pressure to marry. This was the CMS mission ideal, plus they had also pressure to marry from their parents and guardians. Most of the Luo men did not like their wives to work on account of their egos. Archdeacon Nyongo asserted that the major question among the men was: who was the boss? The headmaster or the husband?

The school also conducted one-week annual refresher courses for former students of Ng'iya. The refresher courses were not only meant to be an opportunity for reunion, but also to deal with aspects of the curriculum in detail. An example was in 1941, when Mr R. L. Hull gave a lecture on the history of the Luo. Mrs Hull, on the other hand, helped the teachers in the art of sewing, especially of African designs. She showed them how to introduce the same in their embroidery in preference to copying English designs. However, it took a very long time before the Luo girls could attain the Lower Primary Teachers (LPT) course. Mary Oloo had to go to the Quaker school in Kaimosi, a Bantu-speaking area for her LPT in 1943.

Moller was not impressed when the government proposed that Ng'iya become a teacher training institution for both Luo men and women. A primary school would consequently be introduced at the boys' school. The girls would then attend primary classes with boys in the morning session and attend domestic science at the girls section in the afternoon. Moller was against any kind of co-education, arguing that it was neither suitable nor

---

35. Extance, "Annual Letter," 1941, CMS: G3/AL 01941/Extance.

helpful for Africa. She cited an experiment which she claimed was done by educationists working in America. They had proved that co-education was a big failure. Moller also felt that there wasn't enough land in Ng'iya. She stated that having a lower primary teacher training centre and a primary school would alter the working plan of the institution. Moller was also not very keen on the idea of men being in close contact with her girls at Ng'iya as this would create a difficulties.

The setting up of the Ng'iya Teacher Training Centre came in reality in 1957, when the District Commissioner, Central Nyanza, wrote to the provincial commissioner, Nyanza Province, expressing the need to publish the establishment of the Ng'iya Teachers Training Centre in the government gazette of 10 August 1957. At this time the principal of Ng'iya was Ms Churchill who served until 1969. The teacher training included the training of male teachers from Ng'iya Boys' School. Ng'iya Teachers College solved the shortage of teachers both at Ng'iya and the bush schools around. The teachers' training also provided Africans with an opportunity to start independent schools, which offered Africans relevant educational needs and played a critical role in the rise of African nationalism. There was a three-level teacher training: first, Elementary Teacher Training, supported by missionaries through grants-in-aid from the government and they received, an Elementary Teachers Certificate. Second, the Lower Primary Teacher (LPT) Training Colleges, which lasted two years, undertaken both by the government and the mission station. This led to the acquisition of a LPT certificate. Third, Primary Teacher Training colleges controlled by the government after 1943. The teacher education existed until 1968, when it was eventually phased out to pave for the creation of Ng'iya Girls High School, due to the ever-increasing demand for secondary education. The teachers' training was transferred to Siriba College in Maseno.[36]

Interaction with the Wider Society

Ng'iya school was of great interest to the Luo community. One of the major subjects of speculation was the marriage of girls from Ng'iya which generated

---

36. Omachar, "Contribution of Church," 85–87.

a lot of rumours,[37] debates, riddles, songs, and even press reports. The girls attending the school were generally perceived as deviants in the public perception of the community.[38] Ng'iya girls were perceived as people who had turned their backs on the community's system of education. It was therefore felt that they would easily become victims of pregnancy out of wedlock. Among the Luo, if a girl got pregnant out of wedlock they would become junior wives of very elderly men. This implied that they could not rise to any leadership position. They were also disadvantaged in property ownership and had very low social status. One of the popular songs composed for the school girls in the 1940s was:

> The school girl has gotten pregnant out of wedlock!
> All the old men in the village are very excited.
> Each one of them is scrambling for her hand in marriage!
> Each one of them saying, leave her for me!
> Leave her for me!
> Cha cha cha [adds to the rhythm].[39]

There were also rumours going round about girls who went to school at Ng'iya. One such rumour was that girls who had gone to Ng'iya could not cook good Luo millet bread or *kuon*. They were therefore in the habit of writing a note to their husbands and stuck it at the bottom of the plate. The note read, "Sorry darling the food is not well cooked." This established that they were agents of foreign ideas, but at the same time painted them as lacking in basic skills needed for Luo marriage. New statements like, *amwom nyar skul*, literally translated "the school girl who lacks precaution," were coined

---

37. Community-wide rumours are common among the Luo as a way of discussing issues which affect community values. Girls' education, especially Ng'iya, was the subject of one such rumours, and rumours about school girls have been enshrined in oral traditions of Luo. Another community rumour was over *Anyango Nyar Loka* or Anyango from south-Nyanza, which was a figure coined to castigate prostitution by young girls prevalent in the society. Another rumour was that of *Maro oketho Ugunja*, or mother-in-law who had defiled ugunja (in Ugenya), by being immoral with her son in law, who paradoxically had come to the vicinity to pay bridewealth for the woman's daughter. This was in castigation of immorality among older women (Onyango-Ogutu and Roscoe, *Keep My Words*, 148–151).

38. Deviants, or *Thuo*, among the Luo were courageous people who could take risks. This terminology was generally used for warriors, or for people who could take a stand against the general tide of the society. *Thuon* were therefore daring people who brought changes in society.

39. Joyce Odundo, interview with author, Maranda, May 2004.

during this period. This was both descriptive of the prevailing situation but also used as a term of censure for those people who lacked precaution.

Another problem the society had with Ng'iya Girls' School was the slow progress due to the lack of professional opportunities for girls. On the other hand, the slow progress of the school also meant there were very few girl teachers at the village schools, so the girls did not have mentors or role models. From the point of view of the Africans, low wages was a major stumbling block to girls taking up teaching jobs. Teaching was the main profession opened to girls, and the girl teachers from Nyanza were among the most low paid. The Lady Missionaries Conference, which Moller failed to attend, proposed an increment on the elementary teachers' salary. There was to be an increment of 1.50 shillings per month. However, Moller maintained that this could not be implemented in Nyanza. She argued that there was not only difficulty in sourcing the funds, but also maintained that the girl teachers were already well paid. Moller maintained that additional pay would spoil them and make them go wrong. She argued that several girl teachers had savings in the bank; they also had a lot of clothes and could pay their fathers' hut tax.

The other issue was that the government policy, whose major emphasis was the production of clerks, artisans and labourers, did not have room for the education of girls. The government also did not offer employment opportunities for girls. Most of the education and employment was therefore done by missions, who mainly employed girls as nurses and teachers. The major qualification for this was good character. Some of the girls got married and never pursued any career after completion of school. The report from Ng'iya confirmed that their graduates were scattered all over the country, either married or working as teachers, nurses, or domestic workers in European houses. Originally, most of the girls who went for hospital training were admitted to the maternity hospital at Maseno. The original aim of Maseno was to provide for the teaching of native midwives to deal with native maternity cases and child welfare.[40] However, in time the graduates of Ng'iya extended their training to other institutions. In 1943, Moller stated eight of their girls were in hospital training, two at Pumwani Maternity Hospital,

---

40. Nyanza Provincial Commissioners Report, 1938, KNA: PC/NZA 3/33/8/25.

one at Kaloleni and several at Maseno. Girls going for a nursing course were expected to have completed standard 3; those below that, and the older ladies, would train as midwives. The African men, however, raised a concern that even the professional training needed good grounding in literacy. They felt that literacy of girls needed to be on the same level as that of the boys if they had to benefit from vocational training like domestic science, teaching, or nursing. The men felt that the education of an African woman was important because she played an important role in the society and the home.

There was also a complaint from the inspector of schools that Ng'iya was not achieving maximum results, compared to the number of years it had existed. The inspector of schools observed laxity, especially on the issue of afternoon school. The inspector felt the girls should be allowed to attend school both in the morning and in the afternoon. He also felt that the girls should also be allowed to take examinations and proceed to primary school. Another issue at Ng'iya was the issue of academic standards. The girls felt that the fees charged were too high while most of the time was spent on manual work. This led to a strike in Ng'iya on 10 July 1941. Bishop Peresis Omollo maintained that the girls were not getting value for the high fees charged by the school. They wanted a more academic education – the girls therefore organized a riot and sang resistance songs demanding better quality education.[41] According to Aluoch, the girls felt that there was an over-protective attitude which would not allow Luo women to progress. Moller however linked the episode to one which had earlier taken place in Maseno. There was a general dissatisfaction with what the Africans viewed as sub-standard education offered by the missions. Moller therefore felt it was the Maseno boys influencing the girls at Ng'iya. After the riot, Moller called the prefects to list the complaints. The main complaint listed to the administration was the need for blankets, mattresses, and petticoats. Moller concluded that these were complaints against the parents and not against the school. The happenings at Ng'iya Girls' School had a great impact on the Luo community. Moller had a very strong character and managed to weather the storms as a leader. Although people did not like her policies, she clearly won herself a place as *thong* in the community, and her ideas

---

41. Peresis Omollo, interview with author, Regea, March 2003.

brought change. The girls who went to school during this period still refer to themselves as *nyi Miss Moller,* or daughters of Miss Moller, in line with Luo practice of virtue boasting.

Developments Between 1946–1960

Education practice in Ng'iya during this period could be understood within the context of the CMS policy, government policy, and the Beecher Report on African education. The Beecher report was produced after the colonial government appointed a commission to look again at the education policy. This commission was chaired by Archdeacon Beecher. From 1946, CMS had no clear plans for Ng'iya. This was due to several internal and external factors. One of the main factors was the transfer of Archdeacon Owen, and his subsequent death in 1946. Archdeacon Walter Owen and Olive Owen had made the work among Luo women and girls the major focus of their ministry. This was clear in the sense of loss expressed at his transfer and subsequent death. Ng'iya had been developed as a centre for work among Luo women but after Owen, there was no encouragement from a pastoral worker. In her annual letter, Moller lamented that there was drastic change and lack of support.

According to Moller, the people of Ng'iya were specifically affected as the Owens were like dear parents to them. This sentiment was also echoed by most of the Luo people. According to Bishop Omollo, it had to take somebody of the calibre and courage of Archdeacon Owen to put forward the issues of women to both the church establishment and the government leaders.[42] According to Omollo, Olive Owen was popularly referred to by the Luo community as *Mikayi* and was one of the main inspirations to girls' education. She could call the girls individually and ask them to influence other girls to come to school. Olive maintained that going to school was the greatest liberation for women. Olive also mentored girls into leadership by inviting them to attend the women's meetings and take minutes. Girls were therefore enrolled in the Mothers' Union as helpers. Olive regarded the school as integral to evangelism. However, after her departure, no European pastoral worker felt called to champion the cause of education and ministry among Luo girls.

---

42. Bishop Omollo, interview with author, Regea, January 2003.

Another major factor which affected the education practice at Ng'iya was the CMS re-organisation policy. In 1945, CMS held a conference to look at CMS policy on education in Eastern Africa in view of the changing circumstances. The greatest priority of missions was to demonstrate the highest technical proficiency in each institution they ran. The CMS made a resolution to run fewer institutions and staff them better. Max Warren, the CMS General Secretary, observed that the greatest challenge for CMS was not the lack of recruits, but proper distribution of the available staff. CMS had to regroup the institutions with a view to maintaining, within the education system, centres in which the Christian view could be demonstrated, and from which they could influence the wider society. In response to the re-organization policy, the CMS executive board resolved that all teacher training was to be done at the government institution in Vihiga. They needed two primary boarding schools in Nyanza, one among the Bantu and another among the Luo. Each school had to be run by Europeans assisted by Africans. It was preferable to have two Europeans on the staff. However, due to shortage of Europeans, one European could run the institution assisted by Africans. In the second instance, there must be European companionship on the mission station. Since Owen left Ng'iya, there had been no European companionship at the mission station. The CMS therefore decided to take a drastic decision to move the school from Ng'iya, since European companionship was only available at Maseno and Butere. They felt that although the decision was bound to cause pain and disappointment to those who had helped build up the tradition of the particular station, the decision was inevitable.

The decision to close the school was made while both Moller and Extance, who were actually doing the work at the school, were away on furlough. The school was being run by African staff under the occasional supervision of Reverend Stanway. Rosa Achola, one of the teachers trained at Ng'iya, was in charge of the boarding section. Ng'iya was eventually allowed to continue for a while because there was some sort of European companionship. An anthropologist had been allowed to occupy a house which had earlier been occupied by Archdeacon Owen. However, even after he left, Moller and Extance continued with the school at Ng'iya. Eventually, the school's emphasis was teacher training. The decision to close down the school brought about broken trust between the missions and the community. The missions had struggled all along to control the education process. The Luo elite had suggested that the government put up a girls' school, but the missions had insisted on providing their education. In Nyanza, the government officials eventually supported the missions in offering girls education. The government had therefore resolved to assist the missions through grants in aid in order to provide education for girls. The missions, however, found themselves in a fix, because the Department of Education had no clear action plan for the development of a school for Luo girls.[43]

The action taken by the missions on Ng'iya also put the government on the spot. The government had misallocated funds raised by the Luo for the development of Ng'iya school. The African District Council had voted for money to develop the school, but there was a lot of foot dragging. By the end of 1958, the future of Ng'iya was still being discussed. In 1959, there was a massive complaint that the colonial administration had used the money collected by the Luo people for building a secondary school in Ng'iya to erect intermediate schools.[44] This was even echoed as a priority by the government officials. Most of them felt that in line with the Beecher Report, the greatest need in Nyanza was intermediate schools apart from Ng'iya. The government plan was therefore to introduce girls' intermediate schools, especially in the townships.[45] The District Education Officer even claimed that girls lacked interest in higher education. Most of the Luo read ethnicity in the whole process. The Luo had a feeling that right from the beginning most of the missionaries had preferred the Lydia to the Luo, because of the tendency of the Luo to react against domination.[46]

Another twist to the lack of development at Ng'iya Girls' School was the struggle between the missionary society and the diocese. Through the process of "diocesanization," CMS in Salisbury Square had devolved authority to the local church, or the diocese, and to the relevant education committees. However, the educational missionaries wanted to be independent of local boards and the local church. Therefore, conflicts between expatriates working for the church and those working for missions made it impossible for girls

43. Smith to Hooper, July 5, 1946, CMS: AF/35/49 Ag E4.

44. ADC Minutes 1959, KNA DC/KSM/1959.

45. Education Department Report, 1953, KNA/EDU/I/GEN/297.

46. FocusGroup interview, by author in Maranda, 2004.

to receive proper education. The women educational missionaries demanded the right to form an advisory board to work with the African Education Board. In response, Carey stated the missionaries should work through the African councils of which they were members.

Another controversy between the missionaries and the diocese, which affected the progress of education of the girls, was over the implementation of the Beecher Report. Both the mission and the diocese felt that they should have control of the recruitment of staff. The diocese felt that it should have a say over the people who were coming to work because eventually their salaries would be subsidized by the government from African taxes. The recruits should at least be answerable to the African church. Beecher and the other church officials felt that the church could use this opportunity in East Africa to further its evangelistic task. They felt it was a chance to participate officially in African educational development. Beecher felt that both missions and the church would work hand in hand with the African Education Board to recruit.[47]

CMS missionaries, on the other hand, wanted to recruit without interference and have control over the institutions. CMS London, however, had gone ahead and had advertised for a missionary recruit without any reference or consultation with the African Education Board. The CMS had also given preference to Butere as a girls' high school, as opposed to Ng'iya or Kahuhia, without any local consultation. This was in conflict with the discussions which were already taking place between Bishop Beecher and the African Education Board. CMS were perceived as subverting the provisions of the Beecher Report, which did not provide for a high school, but for standard 5 and 6, and junior secondary school. This was also the official government policy. They felt this would be a stimulus to a more general expansion of education in other centres, when trained African specialists would eventually be available. CMS on the other hand, was more concerned over the recruitment process in England and was not apologetic.

Moller and Extance continued at Ng'iya despite the decision to close down the school. However the main focus of the school with the reorganization policy was now teacher training. This was mainly due to the fact that

---

47. Diocesan Records (Mombasa Diocese) 1951, KNA MSS/61/125 DOC/ED/2 1951.

the teacher played a central role in the Luo community. The teacher was the greatest agent of change. In 1947 Engmann, the educational adviser to CMS, had observed that there was great evidence of the influence of the teacher in Africa. The teacher had great responsibility and sacred trust within the community. This was evidenced by the respect given to the teacher. The scariest threat to a student was, "I will tell your teacher," and the teacher always had the final say. Esther Wakio narrates her experience after completing intermediate school at Ng'iya. Her dream was to be a nurse as she hated teaching with passion. However, the teachers at Ng'iya felt that she would make a good teacher due to her involvement with Sunday school. Although she was called for a nursing course, the teachers at Ng'iya insisted that she had to go back for teacher training. Finally, the father made the verdict, the teachers had said, so she had no alternative but to train as a teacher.

The job of a teacher was also permanent; even after retirement and resignation, the term teacher was still attached to a person's name. The teacher was a leader in society, a friend, and a peer to the chief and elders. The teacher was also the custodian of values in the society. Teachers were noticed everywhere and all their actions were observed. Teaching was a high status job. Nearly all the teachers were mission teachers. The mission teacher was exposed and was a great influence in the society.

The emphasis of the Beecher Report was also in training elementary school teachers as opposed to setting up secondary schools for girls. The immediate aim of the government was to encourage a greater proportion of the girls to train as primary teachers. When each primary day-school was provided with women teachers, this would help to provide a more balanced education. It would also provide a proper outlook for girls. Girls needed to emulate their teachers, so there was a need for educated women in the reserves. However the number of educated women in the reserves was currently too small to provide for the need.[48] In the report, it had been acknowledged that most of the girls that were trained never ended up as teachers because of two main factors. First, the salary of the teachers was not very attractive, and second, the educated girls were on high demand as housewives for the educated men. However the Beecher Commission did

---

48. Education Report, 1953, KNA ED/CN/GEN/30/109/1953.

not see this as a set-back, as women did not end their careers of usefulness even when marriage took them out of school. Many of them remained progressive and an educative force to the rural life when they returned. The report however maintained that if girls were taken to secondary school, they would turn out to be girls of a higher academic standard, but would not become women trained to pass on what they had learned. Training girls as elementary teachers, on the other hand, was important because they were better able to handle junior classes in the school. It was also essential that each intermediate school had a domestic science and physical training mistress. The report also recommended that girls' boarding schools should have a staff almost entirely composed of women.

The period from 1939–1945 was marked by a big debate on the future of Ng'iya Girls' School. The school management was not very keen on Ng'iya moving to primary school or having a joint teacher training. By 1940, the local community was very keen on Ng'iya being developed as a girls' primary school. Moller however felt that Ng'iya was better off as a normal school, as the girls were better equipped for home life. By 1942, there was a lot of agitation to have a girls' primary school in Nyanza. The leaders in Nyanza had earlier put forward the case at the Local Native Council Meetings.[49] The community had even requested the governor to give facilities for girls' education on his visit to Nyanza. The governor pointed out that there was already a girls' school in Ng'iya which would be developed. Moller however pointed out that the department of education had just appointed a lady supervisor to be in charge of all girls' education. Moller therefore maintained that it would be best to wait and see what she would advise.

The CMS conference however decided that Ng'iya should proceed to primary 4. Five girls passed their exams and were admitted to primary 4. Moller however placed them in the same class with the trainee teachers because Extance was on leave. Moller later maintained that the girls should continue with the teacher training or hospital course because that was what was best for them. Moller was perceived to be very high-handed by both the community and the department of education. The CMS and the department of education both felt that the institution should be run by the most

---

49. LNC Meeting, 1939, KNA: PC/NZA/2/11/19.

qualified educationalist. Moller had entrenched herself as the head of the school, despite the fact that Extance was more qualified and getting a higher salary. Moller chose to ignore some of the instructions from the CMS office, which seemed to have recognized Extance as the school's principal.

Women's Negotiation of Mission Education: Gender and Development

Recapturing Dignity through Sewing and Domestic Science Skills

The missions focused on educating women for marriage; however, most of them used mission education for their socio-economic empowerment. Women used sewing and domestic science skills to recapture their dignity. In Luo traditional culture, being creative enhanced a person's dignity. God was seen as a creator, and some of the symbols used for God were the creator as a potter and a weaver. These were feminine activities among the Luo. The dress code also inspired great debate among the Luo. This was an entry point for discussing power arrangements in the society. The women were central in transforming the society.

The main aim of teaching sewing and domestic science in the schools was to enhance the domestic role of women in society. Sewing and cookery skills were meant to make them better wives in the home. However, sewing, dressing, and cookery were used by women in unintended ways. The sewing lessons proved to be one of the most effective ways of transcending cultural, language, and age barriers. When Moller arrived in 1922, her first assignment was in the sewing class. Sewing could be effectively taught even without adequate knowledge of the language. Sewing proved a very important method of building relationships and creating confidence. Moller eventually established several classes in the village where women of different ages learned to sew. Eventually, these became religious instruction classes.[50] Esta Lala, the Christian widow, left her husband's family after his death to avoid negative cultural practices like sexual cleansing and widow inheritance. This however meant that she also lost her property rights. Lala was given

---

50. Moller, "Annual Letter," 1922, CMS: G3/AL/O1922 Moller.

a job at the girls' school to teach sewing both by both hand and machine to women of different ages. Through her sewing skills, she could get some income and achieve economic independence. Lala therefore used the sewing skills as a means of transcending the cultural taboos imposed on Luo widows.

Sewing and the dress code became a major springboard for discussing very pertinent issues within the society. The dress code of the school girls created contradictions which resulted in debates. It also became an important avenue of discussion and the interaction between Luo and Western cultures. Dressing, or clothes, was also a pointer to the deeper issue of power within the society. In traditional Luo society, a person's attire symbolized their age and status. People also dressed to suit the occasion. Girls wore *asemba*, or a skirt made out of sisal fibres. They were knitted and dyed beautifully using colours obtained from the barks and leaves of trees. Women wore *chieno* which were skirts similar to the girls, except that theirs were made of skin. The first *chieno* was tied to the bride in a ceremony performed by a religious leader. *Chieno* symbolized the woman's new status in society and confirmed that she had accepted marriage.[51] She was under the authority of her newly married husband and his community. The man had symbolically clothed her, covered her nakedness. When the man died the woman had to tear off *chieno* and mourn naked because the person who clothed her had died. She would tie *okola*, a special kind of leaf round her waist during the mourning period. This would last for about one year, and would be removed after re-marriage when another man would clothe her. A woman who had *okola* was not supposed to interact with anybody in the society. She was also banned from participating in any economic activity.

The art of sewing and the introduction of a new dress code in mission schools were used by the girls as avenues of change and transformation in society. The mission girls were viewed as agents of new ideas and change. According to Ana Aluoch, who went to Ng'iya in 1927, the major attraction to the school was the type of clothes worn by the school girls. She would acquire new skills, but clothes were also a symbol of status. Aluoch emphasized the creative skills in sewing and handwork, maintaining *nahero bedo jachuech*, literally translated, "I enjoyed creating."

---

51. John Ndisi, *A Study of the Economic and Social Life of the Luo in Kenya* (Lund: Upsalla University Press, 1974), 69.

Decent clothing was one of the main reasons that Christian parents used to request a girls' boarding school. This was symbolic of their new values and a new view of life. The missionaries claimed the parents wanted their daughters to rise above the naked appearance of their neighbours. The Luo had used the term "darkness and naked," figuratively and symbolically. Samuel Okoth, one of the early evangelists described Alego at the time of the coming of the missionaries that "there was darkness and everybody was naked."[52] "Darkness and nakedness" in this context implied being powerless or helpless. The Luo metaphor *piny otimo mudho* (literally, "the world is engulfed in darkness") was used in instances when people felt powerless. The term naked was also used for lack of authority. The Christian girls who had discarded *chieno* were described by the society as naked. According to Sarah Ongeche, people claimed that due to Christianity and education women were discarding *chieno*. Women like Ongeche were cooking for their husbands – naked. She had removed *chieno* and had therefore discarded authority. The husband would die because she had discarded *chieno* unlawfully.

The dress code or clothing therefore embodied a wider discussion on the new power arrangements in the society. Bethseba Adikinyi argued that women became *jonanga* and *thuondi*, with reference to the new power arrangements.[53] According to Samuel Alaka, the newly appointed chiefs in the colonial administration were given a red piece of cloth as a symbol of office. In the 1940s, new terminologies were developed in Nyanza to describe the new scenes. The new term *jonanga* (literally "people of the cloth") was invented to describe a new class of the elite. These were people employed outside the village who would bring back gifts of clothes for the people.[54] The type of clothes a person put on also gave evidence of their status. This was evident in a popular song sung by school girls in 1950 depicting the school girls' attitude to marrying agricultural officers: "The *magenge (Ondoro)* girls sang another song which mocked the clothing typically worn by agricultural workers in Kenya. In a song competition in 1953, Jennifer's Liganua

---

52. Document written by Rev George Samuel Okoth, handed over by Grace Leah Ogony, wife of Rev Okoth to Rev John Nyesi, on December 27, 1966.

53. Bethseba Adikinyi, interview with Francis Otieno, Hawinga, June 2004.

54. Atieno-Odhiambo and Cohen, *Siaya: The Historical Anthropology*, 111.

Ondoro team sang, 'the boys who purchase blue-striped shirts, the boys who purchase blue-striped shirts those we despise.'"[55]

Mission-educated girls used their knowledge from domestic science classes to bring change and transformation to society. In the cookery class, the girls were taught new methods of cooking different foods. They learned the importance of including chicken and eggs in the diet for proper nutrition. The women used this as a springboard to challenge food taboos, most of which were tied to power relationships. Women started to eat poultry, normally the preserve of men. Eating poultry symbolized male authority and not femininity. The community composed songs to censure them for breaking taboos: "Nyakota composed a song about them that was sung widely in Alego, Gem and Ugenya in 1930s and 1940s, 'the educated girl, see how she behaves, she consumes chicken, calling the intestines "beads," see how she dashes off with chicken's legs.'"[56] The girls would retort back singing resistance songs and praising the first Christian evangelists as being an eye opener:

> Yes, I am eating chicken, and my daughter will eat with me.
> My hen, My hen will know me
> the chick will enter my throat, and my daughter will
> eat with me
> Apindi husband of husbands is the only one in our village.[57]

Julia Mbaka argues that by eating chicken, women became *chuo*, or male, referring to power.[58] According to Reuben Omullo, the mission-educated women introduced better nutrition to the women. This was especially in the case of expectant mothers who needed a lot of protein. To achieve this, they needed the courage to challenge deeply engrained societal beliefs. Omullo maintains that as the women ate the new variety of food they sang a line to provoke others: "My chicken, now you are tasty, my chicken." The actions

---

55. Atieno-Odhiambo and Cohen, 98.

56. Atieno-Odhiambo and Cohen, 95–96; this song was confirmed in an interview with Julia Mbaka, by author in Usenge, May 2004.

57. Indalo, "Critical Study," 8; also confirmed in an interview with Rosa Okune, Kokise, April 2003.

58. Julia Mbaka, interview with author, Usenge, May 2004; *chuo,* or male, was the traditional Luo term for power.

of these mission-educated girls created contradictions in the society which was helpful for redefining gender relationships.

Sewing, as an artistic piece of work, was looked upon by Luo women as enhancing women's dignity as opposed to the generally held idea of domestication. Sewing, both by machine and hand, brought out the creative gifts of women. According to Bethseba Adikinyi, they enjoyed *chuecho*, or being creative, as it gave them a sense of self-worth and confidence. Eventually, mission-educated women used their sewing and embroidery skills as an entry point to trade and business careers. Peresis Omollo perfected her sewing skills and became a very prosperous tailor and cloth merchant in Kisumu town. Later she perfected her sewing skills to specialize in making clergy robes. Omollo maintained that the sewing and embroidery classes at Ng'iya were a major fascination to her. Although she trained as a teacher, she resigned in order to expand her cloth business, which was a great economic empowerment. Peresis later developed a tailoring training school as part of her business. She also developed a wholesale and retail shop.

Challenging Negative Cultural Practices Related to Luo Marriages

Mission education enabled Luo women to challenge some of the widowhood practices imposed on them. Luo women had to undergo all the mourning rituals, most of which were dehumanizing. The women had to be remarried to one of the husband's relatives. All these were tied in with the property rights of the widows. When Moller arrived in Ng'iya, she observed that the position of Christian widows was particularly difficult. Moller became aware that the chains of custom and marriage laws were too strong and difficult to break and thought that women were still counted as their husband's property even after his death.[59] From Moller, we learn of the Christian widow, Lala, who had taken a bold step and broken from the web of widowhood practices. She was employed as a teacher at Ng'iya in 1924. Lala relocated to the mission station after the death of her husband. Moller described Lala, who was one of the women leaders, as "my right hand."[60]

---

59. Moller, "Annual Letter," 1924, CMS G3/AL/01924 Moller.
60. Moller, "Annual Letter," 1928, CMS G3/AL/01928 Moller.

Joyce Molo Mitula, who lost her husband only three years after marriage, maintained that the education she received at Ng'iya was quite helpful in her later life. Joyce completed her teacher training and immediately got married to Naftaly Mitula. The husband, who was also a teacher, died leaving her with two young children. Mitula then felt that the period in the boarding school gave her a good foundation and strength of character. Mitula had the courage to make difficult decisions, and was happy that character formation was at the core of the curriculum. She argues that she could overcome the pressure to remarry because she was employed and had a source of income. Mitula was not bound by the cultural practices because she did not entirely depend on the property she was to get from the husband's family; she could also relocate and rebuild her life. When her husband died, she was teaching at Ng'iya which was near their marital home. In 1963, after the funeral, she decided to ask for a transfer to Kisumu and was determined to give her children a secure future.

Mitula maintained that although girls were given education only at primary level, this acted as a springboard for further training. She made use of her posting to the urban area as an opportunity to progress professionally. She finally did her ordinary level exams in 1970 and had several promotions. This gave her financial stability. In 1972, Mitual was promoted to head Kisumu Union Primary School. She was remarried in 1977, after educating her children. She maintains that most of the Luo widows are helpless and are caught up in negative cultural practices due to both lack of knowledge and economic empowerment. Women do not know their rights as entailed in the law, and even Luo culture is not well defined. Women also have to undergo all the cultural rituals because they need economic support. Mitual got a lot of support from the Mothers' Union, and from the church where she was a lay-reader.

Justice Joyce Aluoch, a former student of Ng'iya, in her address to the 1982 Maseno South Diocesan Synod, challenged the church to be at the forefront of empowering women. Aluoch was one of the first women to be appointed a high court judge and the first Kenyan judge to be appointed at the International Criminal Court. She argued that it was important for women to know their rights and gain access to relevant information. Women have to know their property rights and where to seek help when they were being denied those rights. She urged the church to be at the forefront of fighting for the Affiliation Act to be passed so that people in positions of responsibility do not use girls and dump them. The debate on the Affiliation Act had become greatly politicized, with most of the male politicians arguing that it was a colonial imposition and completely unAfrican.[61] Women, who were part of the synod, the majority of whom were graduates of Ng'iya, decided to take up the challenge.

The mission-educated girls used both the Mothers' Union and *Maendeleo ya Wanawake* as a springboard for empowering women. At an Archdeaconry Mothers' Union meeting in Bondoc Diocese,[62] their major emphasis was to enlighten women over their property rights. They felt the lack of property was a major factor in the predicament of widows. Sylvia Achieng, who studied in Ng'iya in 1946, narrated her own experience. Her father, who was an evangelist, encouraged the education of girls, and by 1950, her father had already allocated her a piece of land. This was the greatest Christian witness to the surrounding community. The mothers maintained that it was urgent that children be given equal opportunity in education and property rights. Joyce Odundo, in her sermon, maintained that even in Luo traditional society ladies had basic property rights. Odundo maintained that due to changes in the society there was a more urgent need to include girls in the property inheritance. Many ladies remained single or married into struggling families and therefore deserved support.[63] Mildred Ololo, the chairperson of the Mothers' Union in Bondo Diocese, emphasized the importance of literacy in curbing some of the cultural practices related to widowhood. Mildred used her position, both as a community leader and in the Mothers' Union, to encourage basic literacy among women. This enabled women to read documents and follow up issues related to title deeds and bank accounts. Most of the women, due to illiteracy, were not aware of the husband's benefits at their work place. Ololo argued that the basic literacy girls had received at

---

61. L. M. Thomas, *Politics of the Womb: Women, Reproduction and State in Kenya* (Berkeley: University of California Press, 2003), 178.

62. The Archdeaconry Meeting, Maranda, May 2004; the four top officials were former students of Ng'iya, they organized the meeting.

63. Joyce Odundo, sermon at Mothers' Union Archdeaconary Meeting, Maranda, 14 May 2004.

Ng'iya made a huge difference. The Mothers' Union, therefore, had a special responsibility to look into the education of girls.

Socio-Economic Empowerment

Women used the basic education they received through missions, that is gardening skills, teacher training, and nurses training, to better the economic status of their families. They also enhanced their social status within the community. During the colonial period, Africans did not have many opportunities for economic advancement. This was due to government policies, natural calamities, and depression at the international level. Luo women were the worst hit due to their traditional connection with agriculture. The government policy encouraged settler farming at the expense of local farming. Mission and government education policies did not include the teaching of agriculture in girls' schools. Although men were taught agriculture in schools, most of them left the reserves due to labour migration. Women, however, had to continue with farming in their gardens to meet the basic needs of their families. Mission-educated girls used the gardening skills they had acquired in schools to excel as farmers. They used new agricultural techniques, new seeds, and new technology as a means of improving the economic status of their families.

After World War I, several factors discouraged African productivity in the agricultural sector. Britain had lost its position as the most industrialized nation in the west. British policy was to strengthen its own industries and trades. The aim was to control the source of raw material, and control avenues for trade and markets for export. The economic policy was to encourage forms of production which would not compete with British manufactured goods. In Kenya, only tropical and semi-tropical raw material was to be produced. Settlers were therefore encouraged to grow coffee, cotton, sisal, wheat, and maize. They were assisted by commercial banks in new investments in order to achieve reconstruction. Africans were not allowed to grow cash-crops.

The period from 1920–1949 was generally not very good for agriculture; the prices of agricultural products fell. To encourage farmers' recovery, the colonial administration encouraged the farmers to grow maize. There was a foreign market for it from which they would get a small but regular profit. The settlers would buy maize from African farmers at throw-away prices and sell it in the foreign market. From 1927–1931, the New York stock exchange had collapsed leading to economic depression. At the local level, there was an invasion of locusts which destroyed the crops and led to an economic depression.

In an attempt to boost African production, the teaching of agriculture was encouraged in boys' schools. Cotton was introduced in Nyanza, and cotton gins were erected in Kibosh, Acerbo, and Ndere, but this project failed due to lack of seeds and labour migration by the men. Women who were participating in agriculture were not well empowered for the task; however, they used their gardening skills to entrench themselves as farmers. Practical agriculture was a major part of manual work undertaken daily at Ng'iya. Gardening was emphasized so much that gardens took over most of the school compound: "Gardens occupy considerable portion of the land. The students look after them and a large amount of the produce is used by the school kitchen. Most of the school is planted with maize; garden work is done daily before prayers."[64]

Dorcas Nyongo found gardening one of her most inspiring activities during her period as a student at Ng'iya. After her marriage to Archdeacon Nyongo, she resigned from her work and spent more time farming. Dorcas, with the encouragement of her family, bought a farm in Muhoroni. Dorcas developed a sugarcane plantation as a cash crop and also continued with food-crop farming.[65]

Judith Ochieng, a former student of Ng'iya, introduced new farming methods in her village in Gem. Instead of planting by the traditional method of scattering seeds, she planted the seeds in rows for maximum yield. She did not observe the clan agricultural rituals, which were a major stumbling block to most women. Ochieng did inter-cropping, farming crops like maize, groundnuts, sesame, beans, and millets. During the short rainy season, she planted crops like sweet potatoes, and also planted cassava, which was a drought-resistant crop. Ochieng counteracted the newly constructed taboos which discouraged women from participation in horticulture, and part of her farm was planted with *sukumawiki* (kale) and tomatoes as a cash-crop,

---

64. Ng'iya School Inspection Report, 1942, KNA/DC/KSM/1/10/39.
65. Dorcas Nyongo, interview with author, Seme, May 2003.

which was against the prevailing attitudes: "Women are not supposed to plant kales and tomatoes or any vegetable crops, if women of child-bearing age walk in the plantation when they are in their monthly period, the crops would wither, horticulture for cash-crops is therefore the preserve of men and women should not interfere."[66]

Ochieng went against the culture by establishing a fruit orchard which was a taboo for Luo women. Ochieng was quite innovative; farmers went to her for different kinds of seeds, and during a good harvest, she exchanged her produce for livestock. Later, she used her savings to buy an ox-plough, which she used as a source of income by ploughing for people. During the harvest season, Ochieng bought beans, seasame, green grams, and maize, (which were being sold cheaply), and later sold the items for a profit when there was greater demand. When she became widowed, Ochieng used her income to educate her children; later, she educated her grandchildren after the death of her son. Ochieng therefore established herself both as a prosperous farmer and as a trader and was referred to in the village as *Okebe*.[67]

Joyce Achieng, a graduate of Ng'iya, was employed as a teacher in her family home in Sawagongo. Achieng doubled up as a farmer and kept poultry and dairy cows, and supplied the community with milk and eggs. Many people also came to learn farming techniques from her. Achieng's position, both as a teacher and a farmer, entrenched her as one of the community leaders. Women used the education they received at Ng'iya to transcend some of the stumbling blocks created by government policies.[68] In 1954, the government implemented the Swynnerton Plan. The Swynnerton Plan took advantage of the emergency to use the special powers available to enforce measures of land consolidation and the issuing of title deeds. This was to improve agricultural production by enabling people to use their title deeds to access loans. However, the Swynnerton Plan greatly disempowered women. In traditional society, ownership of land was communal. All members of the society were entitled to use land for economic improvement. However, in the new arrangement it was men who were issued with title deeds. It is therefore

---

66. Judith Ochieng, interview by author, Gem, March 2002.

67. Okebe among the Luo was a person who established themselves as leaders due to their hard work and wealth.

68. Ana Aluoch, interview with author, Sinaga, April 2003.

men who had access to bank loans and other means of economic improvement. Some of the former students at Ng'iya bought land in Muhoroni and
in Songhor and established themselves as cash-crop farmers.

Women in Church Leadership

Luo women used mission education to entrench themselves as leaders in the
church. Leadership in the Anglican Church in Nyanza was mainly offered
by the teacher evangelists. The clergy was in charge of very large districts
and rarely got to visit the individual churches. Most of the clergy would occasionally visit a group of four or five churches for communion and baptism
services. The teacher-evangelists were in charge of the day-to-day running of
the churches. The evangelists also did most of the preaching on Sunday. They
were central in shaping people's ideas and attitudes. The main focus of CMS
was to train teachers who would also double as church leaders. In Nyanza,
male teachers were trained at Maseno, while women trained at Ng'iya.
Due to labour migration, women played a very important role as village
evangelists. This is confirmed in Owen's report, when he acknowledges that
most of the people attending the evangelists training were women. Owen
also maintained that the churches in Nyanza had to rely on the financial
contribution of women for its daily running.[69]

Most of the girls were mentored into leadership during their training at
Ng'iya. The girls participated in the teaching of Sunday school. The girls
also participated in the leadership of camps during vacations. They were also
mentored in church leadership by being given the opportunity to assist in
communion. Despite active participation in church leadership, women were
not formally recognized as church leaders during the colonial period. The
women however officially participated in leadership through the Mothers'
Union and the Revival Movement. Mrs Appendi, one of the teachers at
Ng'iya and a Mothers' Union leader, mentored most of the young people.
Rebekah Agola was also a Mothers' Union leader and was one of the early
mentors of girls in the Christian village at Ng'iya.[70] Her husband, Evans
Agola, was one of the teachers at Ng'iya.

---

69. Owen, "Annual Report," 1923, CMS: G3/AL/01923 Owen.
70. Damaris Ochieng, interview with Francis Otieno, Ng'iya, May 2004.

Rebekah and other women in the Mothers' Union wrote protest letters to the colonial administration on several issues in society. They protested against forced labour and forced marriages. Evans Agola was elected a bishop in 1966 and worked in Nyanza, and Rebekah became the patron of the Mothers' Union in the diocese. Her major focus was on teaching women to uphold the dignity of Christian marriage. She maintained that a good family was the foundation for a progressive society; at the same time, she encouraged mothers to take their role of mentoring girls seriously. The Mothers' Union, in conjunction with the secondary schools, organized holiday camps for girls. These provided opportunities for discussion on the different challenges the girls faced in society. The Mothers' Union therefore continued with the tradition of *siwindhe*.[71]

Abishage Ogot made a great impact on the church, both as a teacher and as a member of the revival movement. Ogot was a product of the early Christian village in Ng'iya. She was one of the girls who volunteered to teach in the afternoons when Moller established the school. Ogot later worked both as matron and teacher at Ng'iya. She was later employed as a teacher at Kisumu Union School, one of the first mission schools to be established in the urban centre. Ogot was one of the early members and leader of the revival movement. She became a member of the Nyanza team and later the Kenya team, which were the top leadership organs of the revival movement. She believed that Christianity was countercultural, and so was opposed to most of the cultural practices. She maintained that the practices were not biblical and a stumbling block to development. According to Ogot, Christian repentance meant a complete turn from the past. A person could not be a Christian and retain negative cultural practices. She maintained that times had changed, so people had to move from their past ideas.

Ogot led other revival members and the Luo in Kisumu in the process of peacebuilding during the ethnic tensions in 1969. The situation had been triggered off by the assassination of Tom Mboya in July 1969. This was followed by a political crisis in the country and oath taking in Central Province. Kikuyu adult males were forced to swear in mass oath-taking ceremonies at Gatundu. This was on pain of death in order to keep the presidency in the

---

71. Mildred Ololo, interview with author, Yimbo, May 2004.

house of Mumbi. Refusal to participate was seen as disloyalty to the state. Most of the Christians who refused to participate suffered violence. The ethnic tensions had been heightened by the massacre of people in Nyanza on 25 October 1969. President Kenyatta had come to officially open the provincial hospital in Nyanza. There were still tensions caused by the death of Mboya, which was viewed as a state-instigated murder. There was open opposition and booing as the president spoke. Some people were chanting *dume*, which was an opposition slogan. Kenyatta felt provoked and said:

> *Dume*! . . . I have given my orders right now, those creeping insects are to be crushed like flour. They are chanting *dume*, *dume*, *dume* (bull, bull, bull . . .), your mother's cunts, and this *dume*! *Dume*! have to be crushed like flour if they play with us. You over there do not make noise; I will come and crush you myself.[72]

At this point, Kenyatta's guard shot at the crowd, killing at least one hundred people.

The opposition party Kenya Peoples Union was banned, and Luo members of parliament were detained. There was a backlash, and most of the Kikuyu staying in Kisumu were beaten and some were killed. People were even drowned in the lake. A state of emergency was declared in Kisumu, and the General Service Unit police were sent to deal with the situation. Ogot led other members of the revival in a movement of peacebuilding and reconciliation.[73] Ogot maintained that Christianity transcended ethnic barriers and that people were supposed to discuss issues and not fight their innocent neighbours. She insisted that most of the Kikuyu were her brothers and sisters in Christ. The brethren in Central province were equally suffering, due to their refusal to take oaths. Again, Ogot argued that from her time as a student at Ng'iya she had learned to live in a multi-cultural society and maintained that Christ transcended all barriers.[74]

---

72. Anonymous transcription, Yale University, dated 1986.

73. Ogot's son was one of the political detainees.

74. Author, Participant Observer, in a discussion with members of Revival at Lundha in April 2004

In 1974, Henry Okullu was elected the bishop of Maseno south (Nyanza Province). One of his main priorities was to encourage the participation of women in the official leadership of the church. In 1975, he appointed Grace Aloo Owuor, a former student at Ng'iya, to the Diocesan Synod. Owuor was in later years elected to the Synod by her local parish. Her major focus was to challenge the church to participate in community development. Owuor, a trained teacher and social worker, maintained that the church was uniquely placed to be part of the solution to problems in society. Owuor maintained that Christ had engaged in holistic ministry, and that this was in line with the mission policies in operation at Ng'iya. She also maintained that religion engaging in issues of society is also in line with Luo culture. In 1997, Owuor was appointed lay canon of the Diocese of Maseno West. According to Owuor, poverty in Nyanza was mainly due to illiteracy and repugnant cultural practices. She therefore advocated that the church must strengthen its Christian education programs.[75]

Sylvia Ochieng, a former graduate of Ng'iya, was a lay reader and evangelist in the church. Ochieng felt called to church leadership during the course of her studies at Ng'iya. Her father was one of the first African evangelists. Ochieng was brought up in the Christian faith and mentored into leadership from home. She assisted Mr Arthur W. Mayor in organizing church services, as well as being a Sunday school teacher. Sylvia Ochieng was posted to Egerton primary school in Njoro to join her husband who was a lecturer at the university. She did ordinary- and advanced-level examinations privately and was promoted to Head of Egerton Primary School. During her period at Egerton, Ochieng served as a lay reader and evangelist in the church at Njoro. She had been greatly influenced by the youth camp tradition at Ng'iya, so her major focus was Christian education in the church. The church had pastoral charge over the institutions around Njoro. After her retirement, Ochieng was appointed an evangelist and lay reader in Maranda where she did evangelism and planted three churches. Ochieng's major focus in Bondo was community development and mission to widows and orphans. The community had been devastated by HIV/AIDS. According to Ochieng, her major focus was to address poverty and lack of proper education among

---

75. Grace Owuor, interview with author, Ambira, May, 2004.

women. Through the Mothers' Union, they tried to educate the orphans, especially the girls. The orphans stayed with different church members.[76]

Mildred Ololo, chairperson of the Mothers' Union in Bondo Diocese, was also trained as a teacher in Ng'iya. Her husband, Archdeacon Ololo was the vicar general of the Diocese, and their major focus was to mentor young people. Mildred derived this from the Easter camp tradition of Ng'iya and the mentoring she received through *Buch Mikayi* as a student. Mildred viewed the Mothers' Union as an important instrument, both for the spiritual and economic empowerment of women. The focus of the organization in Bondo Diocese was on offering training to women. The aim was to provide them with basic budgeting, accounting, and leadership skills. This enhanced the administrative skills of the women both in the churches and empowered them as individuals. Mildred's focus was also the mentoring of girls in the schools.[77]

Olyvia Agwa, a former student of Ng'iya, became the first woman coordinator of the Diocesan Christian Community services in the Diocese of Maseno South (Nyanza) in 1985. Agwa, a trained teacher and a social worker, was already in the book of *Who's Who* in Kenya in 1966. According to Agwa, the way forward for development in Nyanza was education and the inculcation of Christian values. Her major focus as a development coordinator was to empower women both economically and with knowledge. Knowledge was important so that women would be able to access relevant information. Knowledge makes a person independent. When women were independent economically then they would free themselves from negative cultural practices.[78]

Women's Leadership in Society

Women made use of mission education to negotiate leadership at different levels of society. Women used their positions as teachers and nurses, traditional positions of influence in the community, as a stepping stone to leadership. Most of the female nurses and midwives were given a lot of respect in society. This was partly due to traditional respect accorded to medicine

---

76. Focus group interview with author, Maranda, 14 May 2004.
77. Mildred Ololo, interview with author, Yimbo, May 2004.
78. Olyvia Agwa, discussion with author, Homabay, April 2003.

men and healers. Their influence was enhanced by the fact that they were accessible to ordinary people. They developed a trust with the people and could influence their ideas and attitudes. Apart from their influence, they were also viewed as the village elite.

The mission-educated girls used their salaries to create for themselves a socio-economic base. Most of the female teachers established themselves as responsible bread-winners. They took on the role traditionally preserved for the first-born sons. The girls paid for their parents' hut tax. Many of the female teachers built corrugated iron-sheet houses for their parents. This was a sign of social mobility. They elevated their parents to a different class. Bishop Daniel Omolo maintained that most fathers felt encouraged to educate their daughters because apart from paying their taxes and building houses, the educated daughters also earned them good bride-wealth. Most of the girls proved themselves as good teachers and later became community leaders. Trufosa Anyango became one of the community leaders in Mombasa. Anyango had been educated at Ng'iya from Kindergarten to Form 1. She did her teacher training at Ng'iya and graduated as a grade 3 teacher, which was a grade higher than the elementary teacher. In 1948, Anyango was employed as a teacher at Ng'iya.

Mary Oloo, a former student of Ng'iya, was one of the first Kenyan women to study at Makerere University. Oloo, who did her elementary teachers course at Ng'iya, went on to do further training at the Friends Mission Kaimosi. Oloo's parents could not pay her fees, so she had to work for Mrs Brown during the holidays. Oloo also paid her younger sister's fees at Ng'iya and her brother's fees at Maseno. In 1947, Oloo came back to teach in Ng'iya.[79] Both Oloo and Anyango used their influence as teachers as a springboard for initiating community development. Trufosa Anyango later used her position as a teacher as a springboard to vie for the position of a councillor. Women felt that due to her literacy skills and experience in the community she could effectively represent their views. Anyango could effectively help to frame better policies for women.[80]

---

79. Moller, "Annual Letter," 1949, CMS: G3/AL/01949 Moller.
80. Ana Aluoch, interview with author, Sinaga, March 2002.

Women negotiated mission education to empower them to be decision makers over their lives, their homes, and in society. Education and literacy were important tools to help them understand the changing circumstances. They were able to create awareness in others and also to make use of the available opportunities. Esther Wakio Ochieng remembers the injunction of their teachers, especially Reuben Oyamo. They were told to take their education seriously as knowledge would enable them to be independent and access leadership positions. Wakio maintained that education and literacy empowered women and were a means of accessing information. She narrates how, when her husband had an accident, she could adequately deal with the insurance agencies and her husband's employer. She used her skills to empower other women in the society by informing them about their rights.

Canon Jean Mary Ochieng maintained that one of the major contributions of mission education was to empower women to make a difference to the policies in education. Many of the former Ng'iya Girl's School teachers have been elected as board members in girls' secondary schools, which is an important way of influencing policies in education. Canon Ochieng emphasized the importance of instilling Christian values, which was important in helping girls to be responsible leaders in future society. She maintained that the best way of achieving change in young people was through peer influence.[81] Herine Owuor, a former student at Ng'iya, was long-time headmistress and later appointed education officer. Owuor emphasized character formation as an important aspect of education. The priority was to encourage the school heads in instilling a sense of confidence and self-worth in the school.[82]

Grace Aloo Owuor was trained at Ng'iya from 1946–1947. In 1953 she went for further training as a teacher at Jeannes School, Kabete; and two years later, she went to Kisumu for domestic science training. Aloo Owuor was posted back to her home area in Ambira where, apart from teaching, she served in community development work. In 1957, she became the leader of the local *Maendeleo Ya Wanawake*, a women's community development group. The aim of the organization was to help women attain basic literacy.

---

81. Mary Ochieng, interview with Francis Otieno, Siaya, May 2004.

82. Informal discussion at Mothers' Union Conference, Maseno-West Diocese, December 14–19, 2004.

In addition to literacy, they taught sewing as an income generating project. In 1966, Aloo Owuor trained as a community development assistant, and in 1970 undertook further training at Nairobi University in adult education and as a family field educator. Aloo Owuor acknowledged that the greatest stumbling block in Nyanza was negative cultural practices like the sexual cleansing of widows. The greatest need was community education, so that women would say no to such practices. This needs a lot of conscientization and the empowerment of women.[83]

Mildred Ololo was a member of the District Development Committee and an official of *Maendeleo ya Wanawake*. Ololo introduced a village bank, as women needed a place where they could save their money and get small loans without interest. Women needed economic empowerment but they could not compete within the existing structures. Ololo's major focus at the local level was the education of orphans, especially girls. The girls rarely received education and care after the death of their parents. There was a lot of bureaucracy in the government and non-governmental organizations (NGOs). Ololo's major focus was to conscientize the people to help orphans with their limited resources. She believed that orphans were best cared for within the family set-up.

According to Ololo, many widows in Bondo District were victims of HIV and other poverty-related problems. In Nyanza Province, a major issue was the rising level of poverty and abuse of human rights. Part of the problem was the heightened emphasis on negative cultural practices, most of which were recent inventions. Most of the practices targeted women, and the worst were related to widow inheritance. Widow inheritance was closely tied to issues like property rights, sexual cleansing of widows, and non-participation in agriculture or any other income generating projects. Most of the women were not aware of what the true Luo cultural practices were, nor were they aware of their rights within the laws of the country.[84]

In Maranda parish, some former students of Ng'iya used their leadership position within the Mothers' Union and in the community to respond to the issues. They maintained that women were affected by poverty and HIV

---

83. Grace Owuor, interview with author, Ambira, May 2004.
84. Mildred Ololo, interview with author, Yimbo, May 2004.

due to low self-esteem and lack of knowledge. The female leaders helped women to reclaim their dignity through weekly Bible studies in their home groups. They also mentored girls and addressed the growing sexual abuse of girls. They sensitized the community, both men and women, on community challenges. They addressed injustices within the community.[85]

Grace Onyango and Grace Ogot, both alumni of Ng'iya, maintained that there was a need to get to the root of the problems in Nyanza. In a forum discussing the HIV/AIDS pandemic they maintained that most of the NGOs and government bodies had over-emphasized the cultural practices as the major cause of the pandemic. They felt that this diverted people's attention from some of the most pertinent issues like poverty, some of which had to deal with national and international policies. At a recent Mothers' Union conference, it was also agreed that women have to address systems of justice. Women's liberation will come only when they are aware of what is the real cause of their predicament and can also take decisions over their lives.[86]

Most of the female leaders trained at Ng'iya tried their best to achieve economic empowerment for women. Some of the missionaries had discouraged education for women due to a fear of materialism and urbanization. However, the women maintained that not only urbanization, but also globalization, was a reality. Therefore Christian women had to deal with the issues and not run from them. The economic empowerment of women was essential if societies were to survive. One of the major areas addressed by Ololo was the area of trade. Luo women had to engage in all levels of trade for empowerment. However, the greatest problem in Nyanza was unfair trade and lack of opportunity. Women in Bondo were involved in the fish trade, due to their proximity to Lake Victoria.

Women however could not adequately compete due to the presence of middle-men. The middle-men, who are mainly people from outside, put on a lot of restrictions. Women also did not have access to funding to establish a trade. The Mothers' Union tried to have a revolving fund from which they could loan women money to start a business. Women in the Lake Region however could not compete in the business. Rich people owned most of the

---

85. Jenipha Anyango, interview with author, Maranda, May 2003.

86. Discussion raised by Peres Odhiambo, Mothers' Union Conference, Ambira, December 14–19, 2004.

boats, and the ordinary fishermen did not get any fish. The government put a lot of restrictions in the way of poor people, and women had to undergo a lot of indignity to purchase fish for sale.

Ololo maintains that since mission-educated girls had challenged oppressive practices in colonial Nyanza, Christian women should also bring social transformation today. Women must challenge the cultural practices which discourage Luo women from participating in the fish trade. Women must also confront injustice related to the fish trade. Most children in Nyanza suffer from malnutrition because their parents cannot afford fish. Local traders, who are a bit better off, have to travel to Kisumu to buy *mgongo wasi*, or fish bones, which remain after fillets are removed for hotels and for export. This is transported back and sold to people around the lake as this is what they can afford. The local people die, while the lake continues to benefit the middle class and the export traders. The web of poverty and oppression of women is therefore very complex.[87]

Women's Negotiation of Mission Education: Case Study, Lucia Okuthe (1919–1989)

Lucia Auma was born on 25 December 1919 in Manyatta, Kisumu District. She was therefore nicknamed *Sikuku* (Christmas). Auma was born to Ephraim Ochieng and Lina Awuor of Gem, and received her basic education in Pumwani in Nairobi. Between 1934–1938, she joined Ng'iya boarding school where she was trained as a teacher. She proceeded to work in Ng'iya as a teacher in charge of the kindergarten class. She also taught in the Sunday school and helped in the annual camps. Auma was described by Moller in her annual letters as a trusted teacher, a sweet girl, who was loved by all the little ones. Auma later went to train as a nurse at Kisumu Medical School. Auma therefore, through mission education, acquired for herself two very influential roles in Luo pre-colonial society, that of a teacher and medical worker.

In 1941, Auma married Charles Okuthe of Ugenya and became Lucia Okuthe. She worked as a midwife at Kakamega Hospital and Vihiga Health Centre, as well as teaching at Vihiga Teachers College. Grace Onyango

---

87. Mildred Ololo, interview with author, Yimbo, May 2004.

and Julia Ojiambo, the first women Members of Parliament in Kenya, were among her students. Onyango later taught at Ng'iya Girls' school. Okuthe worked as a matron and a cateress at Siriba Teachers College in Maseno. Okuthe received the motivation for continuous education at Ng'iya. Although the missionaries were not directly encouraging higher training for girls, they saw their teachers, especially Moller and Extance, as role models, and felt that education was the only way for progress. Okuthe underwent theological training at St Philips Bible College in Maseno from 1973–1976. She was a classmate of the late Bishop Muge and Ven Okeno Moyi, the Vicar General of the Diocese of Maseno West. According to Moyi, Okuthe was already viewed as a pastor by people at the college and several people around Maseno. Okuthe was a very gifted person, and several people went to her for counselling. She was a prayerful and a gifted teacher of the word of God.

Okuthe was made a deaconess in 1976 and assigned to do chaplaincy work at Siriba College and Maseno Hospital, and did pastoral work in the churches. Meanwhile, there was still great controversy over the ordination of women in Kenya. In 1978, after the Lambeth Conference, the Standing Committee of the Provincial Synod passed a resolution allowing women's ordination in principle. Talking to Target Newspaper, Archbishop Mannases Kuria of the Anglican church declared that the Anglican Church of Kenya had accepted in principle to ordain women, but women would not be pushed into it. When women were ready they would be processed through proper channels of training, and each bishop would decide whether to ordain them or not – it was up to women to initiate it.

After consultation within the Diocese of Maseno South, Okuthe commonly referred to as *Jaduong*[88] by her parishioners, was ordained deacon in July 1980. This led to a lot of controversy in the Anglican Church of Kenya. The archbishop maintained that the ordination of Okuthe was not in order. He maintained that all women who wanted to undergo training had to pass through the Kenya Anglican Council of Training Ordained Ministers (KACTOM).[89] After training, the archbishop's opinion had to be

---

88. *Jaduong*, term used by Luo for elders, especially men, but comes from root word *duong* or senior.

89. KACTOM had been set up especially to interview Anglican students who were undergoing training at St Paul's, which was a United Theological college. All the students

sought before ordination. The archbishop maintained that the ordination of Okuthe was not procedurally correct because even the Church of England had not yet ordained women. The archbishop maintained that although the bishops had power to ordain without consulting the archbishop, it was not so for the ordination of a woman. In April 1982, the Diocese of Maseno-South unanimously agreed to proceed with the ordination of Okuthe to the priesthood. However in November 1982, the Provincial Synod reversed their earlier decision on the ordination of women. They maintained that although the ordination of women was accepted in principle by the Province, many Christians did not fully understand the implications. It was therefore recommended that all Diocesan Synods communicate their votes *for* and *against*.[90]

In January 1983, Okuthe was ordained the first woman priest in the Anglican Church of Kenya. This generated a lot of controversy. Most of the opponents of women's ordination argued that although there was no scriptural or theological problem, it was not yet time to ordain women. The main opponents argued that there were more pertinent issues in the church, especially on issues of the relationship between church and state. Okuthe however maintained that women's empowerment was the main issue in the church. She said that there was no need for the church to tell the state about issues of justice, human dignity, and rights, while the church did not observe the same. In his sermon during the ordination of Okuthe, Bishop Okullu maintained that it would be a betrayal of his theological conviction to deny Okuthe the right to serve in her capacity as a minister in the church. Several churches in the Anglican Communion had ordained women to be clergy. The bishop maintained that he did not want to be a stumbling block to Okuthe's call – God had called her and she had also met all the requirements as per the synod. Bishop Okullu maintained that he was sure that if Jesus came today, he would appoint women to serve him.

The bishop maintained that the time had come for women to take greater responsibility in the church. He cited that Lucia had devotedly served the church for many years. Despite the raging controversy among the hierarchy of the church, Okuthe did her work with confidence. She maintained that

being trained at the diocesan theological colleges never went through KACTOM.

90. Provincial Unit of Research, *From Rabai to Mumias* (Nairobi: Uzima, 1994), 170.

when Christ called an individual, it was important to obey the call. Okuthe argued that the church preached equality between people, so it was important for the church to practice their teaching. Okuthe was alarmed at the citing of the authority of African culture to bar women from ordination. She pointed out that the women held leadership positions in pre-colonial Luo society. She felt that culture had been used selectively to oppress women in Africa. Okuthe maintained that it was important to retain aspects of culture which enhanced human dignity, but on the other hand, Christians must be in the forefront in criticizing aspects of culture which dehumanize women. Okuthe maintained that the gospel was above any culture and that church leadership had a tendency to spend more time in board meetings at the expense of fulfilling the mission of Christ. Okuthe must have had a lot of influence from the emphasis on the use of vernacular at Ng'iya, and translation of Scripture. This resulted in a creative interaction between the Bible and Luo culture.

Most of the parishioners welcomed the ordination of Okuthe. One of the journalists from her parish pointed out that the ordination was a historical event of which they were proud. It was met with unanimous applause, particularly from the parishioners in Muhoroni. The Christians felt that the ordination was a challenge to women who still did not realize that the long-debated equality was not just an ideal but a reality. It presented an opportunity for women to show their gifting. The journalists asserted that during the period Okuthe had served in the Songhor parish as a deacon, her congregation was always thrilled with her services. They were often left inquisitive by some of the remarks she had made.[91]

Okuthe, who was widowed early in marriage, was one of the first women to buy a farm and establish her home in a cosmopolitan place at Muhoroni Settlement Scheme, which was viewed as going against Luo culture. Okuthe acted as a voice for Luo widows within the Anglican church. Many widows looked up to her for advice and inspiration. This must have been the strong influence of Ng'iya, which focused on women's issues, among them issues surrounding widowhood. Okuthe was a farmer and felt that she needed to approach her ministry differently. She maintained that most of the male

---

91. Partrick Omondi, "Woman Ordained," *Daily Nation*, January 27, 1983.

clergy were served and given gifts by women when they were performing their pastoral work. However, for her, the priority was to meet the basic needs of the poor where possible. She maintained that the poor should not be struggling to give her what they could not afford. Okuthe therefore kept a vegetable garden from which people who visited her could get provision.

Okuthe had established an orchard farm from which members of the community got provisions. The members of the community referred to her as *Okebe*, a wealthy leader whose home was a refuge place for many. Matthew Onyango, one the Diocesan drivers, confirmed that Okuthe's home was a bee-hive of activity. There were different groups, especially young people and women, who came to consult her over different issues. Okuthe's ministry was quite challenging because most of the time the parish could not pay her dues. However, she was worried because as a farmer and could meet her own basic needs. One of the activities she enjoyed most at Ng'iya was gardening, from where she learned new farming methods. Okuthe mainly felt called to a prayer ministry. She had a special focus on the widows and the sick, and she also mentored young girls.

Okuthe died in 1989, and at her funeral, Bishop Okullu maintained that he had lost a prayer partner. Okuthe would go to his office and pray with him over different aspects of the ministry of the diocese. By the time of her death, she had officially retired but was still visiting the sick in hospitals. Okuthe could be classified as *thuon* among the Luo because of her courage; she opened the door for women's ordination in the church. Her action generated a lot of controversy and debates on issues such as the role of women in the church, the nature of ministry, issues of power and authority in church, the relationship between Christianity and culture, and the place of traditional culture in a changing society. Okuthe believed that her Christian faith and education gave her the capacity to weather the storm.

Women's Negotiation of Mission Education: Case Study, Grace Onyango (1931–Present)

Grace Onyango was born as Grace Monica Aketch in 1931 at Goibei, Bondo, in Nyanza Province. Onyango studied at Ng'iya Girls' School and became a teacher in the same school. She later proceeded to further her training as a teacher at Vichuga Teachers College, where she graduated in 1951. She was again posted to teach at Ng'iya. In 1954, she was appointed principal of Ng'iya Teachers' College, where she worked for ten years. Onyango married Onyango Baradi who was a teacher who later joined the Kenya News Agency as a journalist, and they had six children. Between 1951 and 1964, Onyango was also the girl-guide assistant commissioner in Kisumu District as well as the chair of the Kisumu branch of the Child Welfare Society.

Onyango was very concerned about the gender imbalance within the Kisumu Municipal Council. She and a group of women formed the Gill Women Group, and the chair was Mrs Shabir, the mother of Shakel Shabir, who was elected mayor of Kisumu in 2000. The group served as a meeting place and problem-solving arena for its members. Onyango recalls that at this point there was no woman at the Municipal Council even as a sweeper. The women found this untenable and organized a demonstration in the streets of Kisumu to call for representation in the municipal council. In 1963, Onyango and Marcella Osir were nominated to run for one of the municipal council seats. Most of the men opposed their nomination and argued that the council was no place for women. The opposition was so immense that Osir opted to step down from the race.[92]

In 1964, Onyango contested a council seat at Kaloleni Ward and emerged the victor. Onyango continued with her work as a teacher at Kisumu Union School. She was also appointed as the chair of the Education Committee in the municipal council due to her training in education. In January 1965, she was appointed to act as the deputy mayor of Kisumu for three months. In April 1965, she was elected as the mayor of Kisumu, the third largest urban centre in Kenya. Her major concern was the provision of adequate housing in the rapidly growing town. Her major project in her Kaloleni Ward was a slum clearance project, whereby they would provide alternative and affordable accommodation for Kaloleni residence.[93] Onyango focused on road construction, provision of water, and construction of houses, which were basic to people's livelihood.

---

92. Musandu, "Daughter of Odoro," 46.
93. Municipal Council of Kisumu, "Annual Report," 1965, KNA.

Onyango showed courageous leadership and was also a mediator during the volatile period in Kenyan politics between 1966 and 1969. In 1966, Oginga Odinga, who was the vice-president, resigned from the Kenyan African National Union (KANU) and was kicked out of the ruling party. He formed the Kenya Peoples Union (KPU) and was followed by many people in Nyanza to the new party. Onyango remained the mayor of Kisumu and had to constantly mediate between KPU and KANU members who brought their political battles to the Kisumu Municipal Hall. Onyango was a courageous fighter and rose to the occasion when one of the most eloquent politicians challenged her. Tom Mboya, the Minister of Economic Planning and Development, who was also the KANU Secretary General, claimed that Onyango's loyalty to the party was questionable and that he wold install a KANU mayor in Kisumu.[94] Mboya opened a campaign office at Kaloleni the mayors' ward. Onyango was undaunted and challenged Mboya, who was famous for his oratory skills, to a public debate that would settle the issue of popularity as a leader of the town. Mboya said no to the debate. The group finally disqualified Onyango alongside other KPU candidates from Kisumu. Mboya intensified his attack on Onyango and even used the gender card. He claimed, "Mrs Onyango is reaping the fruits she herself had sown, if she is asking for sympathy as a woman she should leave politics alone."[95]

Mboya was addressing potential Luo voters, whom he hoped would buy into his verbal portrayal of the mayor. Mboya was implying that Onyango was going against Luo-ethnic norms that frown on women using their sex as ground for preferential treatment. Onyango, however, kept her sex out of the campaign rhetoric. She managed to finish her term as mayor despite the campaign rhetoric. This was due to her cooperation with members of both sides of the political divide in the local politics. She pointed out her development record since her appointment as a mayor. In 1969, Kenya was declared a single party state, and anybody who wanted to remain a politician had to do so on a KANU ticket. Onyango used her development track record in the council to take her political career to the national level, a move that saw her easily win a seat as the Member of Parliament for

94. Nation Reporter, "Mrs. Onyango Attacked on Loyalty," *Daily Nation*, July 13, 1968.
95. Nation Reporter, "Mrs. Onyango's Challenge, Mboya's No to Debate in Kisumu," *Daily Nation*, August 9, 1968.

Kisumu Town Constituency. Onyango emerged the first woman Member of Parliament in Kenya.

Onyango chose to view the electoral contests as political battles and not referendums on gender. She was comfortable in using society's structures to navigate her career and chose to de-emphasize the role of sex in the fashioning of her political platform. On 21 December 1969, Onyango surprised people on the way she responded to questions that were addressed to her as a woman:

> **Q:** Do you think that you have something special to do for the people of Kisumu, which another elected member would not be capable of doing?
> **A:** Well it is the representative's duty to see that things are done according to the wishes of the people.
>
> **Q:** Do you have any plans of what you propose to do for the people of your constituency once you become a Member of Parliament?
> **A:** I think it is for the people to tell me what they want done.
>
> **Q:** As one of the pioneer women in Kenyan politics, what are your views on the role of women both in political life of a nation and in national building?
> **A:** As an elected representative of both men and women, I will not represent women only . . . because it is not only women who elected me.[96]

Further, in her response to the recent abolition of the Affiliation Act and claims that a woman's presence would have prevented or at least have it amended or abolished, Onyango still maintained that she had been elected by a community and was going to serve as an MP for everybody, male and female, and would not confine her career to gender issues. She maintained that if people felt that it was necessary for a woman to represent women's interests solely, then elected members must ask the president to kindly elect a lady for this purpose. Onyango's attitude towards gender issues could be

---

96. Enid Da Silva "Place of Women in Kenya Politics," *Sunday Nation*, December 21, 1969.

understood within her ethnic context, where team work with others was greatly valued.[97]

In 1969, the executive committee of Luo Union East Africa unanimously elected Onyango to act as Secretary General of the organization, before the elections scheduled for that year. The election of a female to serve in such a prestigious position was a testament to the presence of non-gendered Luo-leadership ideologies. Onyango fought for justice and equal treatment of all people, some relating to women. On 6 November 1970, Onyango raised question No. 815 on Paid Maternity Leave.[98] Onyango asked the minister if he would tell the house whether he would consider awarding employed married women leave, when the the issue of maternity leave arose, since it was a time when financial aid was greatly needed. The assistant minister, Peter Kibisu, responded that since African women at the time were calling for equal pay for equal work, to grant full pay for women during maternity leave would render women more expensive to employ. He added that some unions had made considerable progress in winning for women partial payment during maternity leave, and the industrial court had been supportive to women in this respect. The minister then concluded that the matter is best left to unions to negotiate with individual employers. Onyango was not pleased with this response and persisted that in most cases women can only be paid while on maternity leave if the doctor indicated that they were sick. The minister responded that maternity was not strictly speaking an illness but a natural hazard. Another issue raised by Onyango in parliament was on "civil service terms of employment for married women."[99]

Onyango asked the Minister of State in the President's office to explain why, despite the fact that the government advocated for equal treatment of their citizens, this did not include women. Onyango specifically cited married women not being eligible for appointments on pensionable terms; pensionable women officers were required to resign when they got married.

97. Grace Onyango, Interview with author May, 2004

98. Republic of Kenya, "The National Assembly Official Report, First Session (Cont.) Tuesday 22 September 1970 to Friday 6 November 1970." (Nairobi, Kenya National Assembly Library.)

99. Question no. 783, Republic of Kenya, "The National Assembly Official Report, First Session (Cont.) Tuesday 22 September 1970 to Friday 6 November 1970." (Nairobi, Kenya National Assembly Library.)

Adverts for jobs offered permanent terms for men but not for women. When women were employed, it was done on a temporary contract. Although these issues only affected women, Onyango brought them up as issues for all of society. She argued that in the context of African culture, gender issues required the participation of the whole community, and she believed that if women were part of the problem, they must be part of the solution.[100]

Women's Negotiation of Mission Education: Case Study, Grace Ogot (1930–2015)

Grace Emily Akinyi Ogot was referred to by her peers as *unbwogable,* a corrupted Luo word meaning a tough person who cannot be easily intimidated. She was referred to by journalists as "the politician with a motherly presence." Her constituents and the general public referred to her as mama or mother. Ogot was born on 15 May 1930 to Joseph Nyanduga and Rahel Kogori. She was born into a Christian family; her father was initially a teacher, and her mother a leader in the Anglican church. Ogot was born and partly brought up in her rural home in Asembo, Nyanza, before the family moved to Mombasa. However, she kept very close ties with her grandmother, a strong Christian, whom she referred to as the main inspiration of her life. At the age of ten, Ogot went to stay with her older sister and attended Maseno Junior School.

Ogot attended Ng'iya Girl's Intermediate School between 1942 and 1945. This was possible due to the support of her parents. She had attended boarding school at a time when her mother was ill, prompting her father to do house chores so that Ogot might remain in school. One of the main reasons for setting up Ng'iya School was due to the demand by Christian parents that their daughters get Christian education. Ogot was described by her fellow students as a hardworking and disciplined student, a natural born leader. She studied in Ng'iya at a period when there was a demand for better education for girls by the Luo community. There was a great demand and pressure that Ng'iya should be developed into an upper primary school for girls in Nyanza. The CMS was however not very keen as there were plans to move the girls' school to Butere, due to lack of resources to run two

---

100. Musandu, "Daughter of Odoro," 62.

girls' schools. Moller on the other hand felt that the major emphasis of the school should be to prepare girls for marriage and not for higher education. Moller's priority was therefore community rooting for the girls.[101] However, the girls held discussions among themselves and staged a demonstration against the low standard of education among other things. This meant that it had to take a strong will for Luo girls to pursue further education beyond intermediate school.

After Ng'iya, Ogot proceeded to Butere from 1946–1949, and later joined a secondary school in Uganda as a private candidate. In 1953, she did a nursing course in midwifery. On her return to Kenya, Ogot secured a job as a sister in charge of the maternity section at Maseno Hospital, responsible for the training of nurses. These two roles of teacher and medical practitioner were positions of respect and influence in Luo pre-colonial society. She used her position as a midwife to her advantage. In 1955, when she won a scholarship to study in England, but her community were reluctant to let her go. They took issue with the impact of girls' education on marriage, wondering when she would go to the husband's house. The Luo community was ridiculing mission-educated girls for postponing marriage, and there were all sorts of stories about Ng'iya. Marriage was central in Luo pre-colonial society because it was the stepping stone to leadership and also social and economic empowerment. However, in the new landscape there were new sources of empowerment.

In the course of the discussion on whether Ogot should be allowed to go for further studies or not, some villagers came to seek her expertise on delivering a baby. A woman had been in labour for six hours; it was a case of breech delivery in which the baby was trying to come out legs first. The local birth attendants had failed to correct the situation. Within an hour, Ogot had manipulated the foetus to the correct position and helped the woman to deliver successfully. The family therefore accompanied Ogot to help plead her case to her relatives. They urged the family to let her go and study as she had saved both the mother and the child. Her position as a medical worker was parallel to that of *jayath,* a healer, which was a position of seniority. Ogot therefore proceeded to further training in the area of midwifery. She

---

101. Moller, letter to Smith, "Protest Against Male Teacher Training at Ng'iya," June 10, 1940, KNA: Mss/61/443.

also gained further training at St Thomas Hospital in London and became the first Kenyan to qualify as a state qualified midwife.

In 1959, Grace married Bethwell Allan Ogot, and accompanied her husband back to London, where he was doing a PhD. During this time, Grace secured a job with the British Broadcasting Corporation as a news broadcaster for East and Central Africa. On returning home in 1961, she took up an appointment as a District Community Development Officer, and the headmistress of Kisumu Training Centre. These positions strengthened her role as a teacher, which was a position of influence in Luo society. Ng'iya had put an emphasis on training women teachers with a view of empowering opinion leaders in the villages. Ogot was nominated the first woman councillor in Kisumu, which marked the beginning of her involvement with politics. In 1983, she was nominated as a member of parliament, and two years later, was elected a member of parliament for Gem Constituency. Ogot was also appointed as the second female member of the cabinet, as an Assistant Minister for Culture and Social Services.

As a politician, Ogot emphasized the centrality of family life to progressive and stable societies. This was in line with both her faith and the emphasis at Ng'iya of the importance of marriage for a progressive society. This was also in line with Luo pre-colonial society, where the family was central for social and economic progress. Ogot believed that the education she received had greatly helped her work for the transformation of lives and societies. Ogot viewed her political position as an opportunity to participate in the transformation of society. Her main agenda as a politician was welfare and economic development, and in order to achieve this, education was top of her priorities. Ogot built secondary schools and established an education bursary fund. Her focus was on the education of young people and girls, as she believed that it is only through education that women will be liberated from oppression. This echoes the main aim for the establishment of Ng'iya Girls' School. The Luo were convinced that if you educate a man, you educate an individual; however, when you educate a woman you educate a community. Although the curriculum emphasized marriage, Luo women in pre-colonial society achieved economic independence through marriage. Luo women had therefore negotiated many aspects of the curriculum to achieve economic independence in the new landscape. Ogot was very popular in

Gem for starting the *mabati* (corrugated iron sheets) women group, a housing project for rural women. Through this group, women saved money among themselves, and each individual was given the money in turn to help them buy corrugated iron sheets. The aim was to have decent housing for every woman. As a member of parliament, she also established several health centres at the local level. Ogot also developed both rural electrification and infrastructure development as a way of encouraging trade. She was also an established business person and established the Anyange Press in Kisumu. Besides employment, Ogot served several other organizations in official capacities. She was the founding member of the Kenya Writers' Association, and the chairman at its inception. Ogot was a member of the Kenyan delegation to the UN assembly in 1975, and a delegate to the General Conference of UNESCO in 1976. In August 1983, she was the first woman to be appointed to the chair of the teachers' tribunal.

Ogot presented most of her ideas and thoughts through her writings. She maintains that her greatest mentor and inspiration was her grandmother. She says, "My grandmother was a great storyteller and I was always moved by the stories and I had always wanted to share them with people who did not know my culture."[102] Ogot had a good understanding of the traditional techniques of storytelling, and believed that a well-told story is indispensable today as the community is getting busier. Ogot's interest in storytelling must have been greatly sharpened during her period at Ng'iya as storytelling was one of the main methods of teaching. Ogot's major focus was writing stories, which she did both in English and in her mother-tongue. Her main purpose in writing in the Luo language was to provide those who go through adult education with reading material in their own language. Interaction between Luo culture and modernity is central to both the writings of Ogot and her general engagement in society. According to Ogot,

> I delve into the past with a view of demonstrating to Europeans that when they came here, people had a culture and civilisation of their own. I also tend to emphasise Luo culture and it takes centre stage in all my works. This is for the simple reason that

102. Reporter, "Grace Ogot," *Weekly Review*, 21 October 1983.

> I am a Luo and therefore I understand my culture and my
> community better than others.[103]

Ogot disagreed with those who claim that the theme of cultural heritage has been overtaken by events. Ogot maintained that some external factors, like education and urbanization, weaken aspects of cultural heritage. However, there are certain aspects they cannot destroy like some of the marriage and funeral rites. Cultural change and conflict between rural and urban life has led to a deterioration of morals and ethics in the society. Urbanization has disrupted the cultural heritage, which formed the basis of African life. Ogot maintained that change was inevitable, and even the Luo forefathers believed that change comes with every successive generation. It is important to manage change, so that people do not lose their identity. The synthesis of the rural and the urban may eventually remove ethnic differences but should not remove identity. Ogot advocated for changes in some of the out-moded Luo traditions, especially the ones surrounding death and widowhood. Ogot challenged the Luo to have a cosmopolitan outlook and change from their conservative view of life to inspire economic development.

---

103. *Sunday Standard Reporter*, "Interview with Grace Ogot," November 3, 2002.

CHAPTER 7

Mission Education: Case Study of Alliance Girls' High School

Aim of Education

After World War II, the missions realized the need to rethink their education policies. There was need for an education which would facilitate change in the society. In 1945, Max Warren, the CMS general secretary, felt that the changing circumstances called for a rethink of the strategies. The missions and churches needed to discard their nineteenth-century ideas and think of new ways of doing missions. They had to work in partnership with the local Christians. Warren felt that although leadership was rapidly changing hands, there was no evidence that the new leaders had any new ideas. Education should help people reap for themselves the advantages which the changing conditions might offer.

Margaret Wrong, a mission educationist, maintained that missions should give an education which would lead to social, political, and economic advance. Education should empower women so that they could cope with changes in the society. She advocated for literacy among women so that they could read and be knowledgeable not only on local issues but also those of wider importance. Due to rapid change, it was imperative to give people every possible means of understanding and controlling what was happening among them. Wrong felt that women also needed to know how to budget and keep accounts[1] The missions also needed to fight injustice and the use of human beings as a source of cheap labour. The missions would only do this by raising competent leaders and teachers, who would in turn establish a firm foundation for mission and church. They would make Christian education an integral part of the leaders' lives.

Wrong emphasized the need for study and research into the African communities. This would aid missions in understanding the context in which they were working. The research would also help to draw up relevant education policies. Wrong emphasized the need to have joint training at a professional level for Africans and Europeans, which would encourage joint and equal leadership. Africans would then eventually take over most of the responsibilities. Wrong also felt that missions had to share ideas with local people through joint consultation and planning.[2]

According to Andrew Doig, the aim of education was to prepare Africans for leadership into the future. This involved preparation in all spheres of life. There was a need to give Africans the opportunity to develop their skills, thus education was important for both personal and community development. Doig maintained that the greatest challenge was education for leadership, with an emphasis on decision making. There was value for Christian discipline, which was essential for Christian faith and creativity in a Christian community. Doig also emphasized the need of education for girls. He argued that the new African community required women with a new outlook to life. He recalled the words of Aggrey of the Phelps-Stoke's Commission: "Win a man and you win an individual, win a woman and you win a family."[3] The best foundation for Africans within the changing circumstances was a Christian home. There was therefore need to educate women, so he proposed the involvement of women missionaries and evangelists on girls' education.[4]

1. Margaret Wrong, "Literacy and Literature for African Peoples," *International Review of Missions* 33, no. 130 (1944): 193.

2. Margaret Wrong, "The Church's Task in Africa South of the Sahara," *International Review of Missions* 36, no. 142 (1946): 222–231.

3. Bishop Omollo, interview with author, in Regea, May 2002

4. Andrew Doig, "The Christian Church and Demobilization in Africa," *International Review of Missions* 35, no. 138 (1946): 181.

Another major change after World War II was the interest of the colonial government on African education and the decline of the mission's capacity to exclusively offer education. The government therefore cooperated with the missions on offering education. In 1945, Warren pointed out that earlier the church had virtual monopoly over education with unrestricted scope for experiment. However, at present because of lack of resources, the church could only offer education on a small scale. On the other hand, the state had started to take education seriously. This had come first through the states newly developed sense of responsibility. Second, it was the duty of the state to satisfy the wider conscience of the world community. Third, it was the state's awareness of the importance of education as a medium of instilling ideas that are judged most useful. The missions share in education in the territories was therefore becoming that of a junior partner. However, Warren challenged the government because they had no clearly articulated policy on education.

By 1947, the British government was also keen on creating a more progressive situation in the colony. Education was not just for imparting skills but to develop a sense of public responsibility and encourage students to examine problems with tolerance and responsibility. This led to the formulation of a Memorandum of Education for Citizenship, which stated that literacy and technical skills were not enough in a rapidly changing world. Education had to help develop a sense of public responsibility – democracy was not just something for the classroom.[5] The memorandum advocated education for leadership and self-government. This was a gender-biased policy, because women were not viewed as potential leaders.

In 1947, the British government became serious about both African and girl's education in Kenya. The government appointed an advisory council for the development of African education, and Miss Janiseh Gwilliam was appointed as an Assistant Education Advisor. The council made a recommendation to discuss the whole issue of education of African girls. They appointed a sub-committee to look into the possibility of the immediate establishment of a girls' secondary school, since the social progress being planned would depend on a higher standard of education among women.

---

5. Colonial (Government Report), 1947, 216 (Kenya National Archives).

The appointment of Gwilliam led to the calling of a colony-wide conference for girl's and women's education. Gwilliam was the principal speaker at the conference, and the discussion was around the topic, "Education, to What End." The assistant director of education, Miss Janiseh Gwilliam, gave a review of the plans on education. The ten-year development plan on education stated that the focus of African education would be on teacher training and secondary education.

In 1949, the Colonial Administration appointed a commission under the chairmanship of Archdeacon Leonard Beecher to look into African education. The Beecher Commission was appointed to articulate education policies within the changing circumstances. The Beecher Commission proposed a restructuring of the education system. The primary school was to concentrate on literacy and vernacular, simple arithmetic, elementary practical skills, and fundamental discipline. Intermediate school on the other hand concentrated on English and elementary mathematics, with an appropriate combination of practical subjects.

The Beecher Report, however, had contradictory ideas over girls' education. On one hand, the report maintained that it was fundamental that girls' and boys' education be placed side by side and principles applied with equal force to both. On the other hand, the report did not have any hope for the education of girls due to what they termed as the negative attitude of the tribes. They argued that there were fundamental sociological considerations arising from the traditional attitude on the place of women in the tribe, whose rate of change would not be affected by educational planning alone. The Beecher Commission also evaluated African opinion on the education of girls. However, they felt that the education of girls was for the self-interest of the parents. Parents tended to regard fees paid for their children as an investment through which they accepted a cash return. Education was also viewed as a means of enhanced bride-price in marriage. Parents expected ready employment and a high salary. These led to feelings of great frustration if the school leavers failed to get a highly remunerative, non-manual employment.[6]

---

6. Beecher, Commission Education Report, 1949, 31.

The Beecher Report did not recommend high academic achievement for girls. The commission planned for only two secondary schools for girls within the next ten years. The Beecher Report maintained that the greatest demand on the part of girls was teacher training. The immediate aim of government was to encourage a greater proportion of girls to train as primary teachers, as this would provide a more balanced education. It would also provide a proper outlook for the girls. Girls needed to emulate their teachers, so there was a need for educated women in the reserves.[7] However, the number of educated women in the reserves was currently too small to provide for the need.[8] They also maintained that the improvement in teacher training would improve the quality of teaching in primary school.

In the report, it was acknowledged that most of the girls who trained never ended up as teachers because of two main factors. First, the salary of teachers was not very attractive, and second, the educated girls were in high demand as housewives to educated men. However, the Beecher Commission did not see this as a setback. Women did not end their career of usefulness as teachers even when marriage took them out of school. Many of them remained progressive and were an educative force to the rural life to which they would return. The Beecher Report however maintained that if girls were taken to secondary school, they would turn out to be girls of a higher academic standard, but would not produce women trained to pass on what they had learned. Training girls as elementary teachers on the other hand was important because they were better able to handle junior classes in the school. It was also important that each intermediate school had a domestic science and physical training mistress. The report also recommended that girls' boarding schools should have staff entirely composed of women.

The Beecher Report had also highlighted that due to social changes in Africa, there was a breakdown in moral values. The teaching of Christian religion was therefore important for the foundation of morals. Character became inbuilt through the schools implanting moral principles. Teaching Christian principles was just as specialist as teaching other subjects. Hence, there was a great need for cooperation between the government and Christians, because

---

7. Beecher Report, 73.
8. Education Report, 1953, KNA: ED/CN/GEN/30/109/1953.

secular education alone was not helpful. The Beecher Report laid the task of education as improving what was sound in indigenous tradition. What was good in the old beliefs and sanctions would be strengthened, and what was defective would be replaced. The greatest importance on religious teaching had to be related to the conditions of daily life and experiences of the people. It had to inculcate habits of discipline. Education had to strengthen a sense of responsibility to the community and strengthen the will power.[9]

Most of the witnesses appearing before the Beecher Commission stressed the importance of character training. Most of them emphasized that the churches and missions had a strong role to play in building the character of the youth. The Beecher Commission felt that this contribution could be made through the training of teachers. The Beecher Report recommended that churches and missionary societies be encouraged to take a full share in the training of teachers and be afforded necessary grants in aid to enable them to do so.[10]

In the 1950s, the colonial government emphasized the need to speed up the output of high-level African manpower, by expanding higher and secondary education. This was to provide trained manpower to run the economy and eradicate illiteracy. Binn's commission proposed a radical change in the education system. Binn's report was based on a thorough survey of the colonial territories. This culminated in the Cambridge Conference on 8–20 September 1952 under the chairmanship of Sir Philip Morris. It was sponsored by the Nuffield Foundation and the colonial office. Binn was the chair of the African study group focusing on East and Central Africa. He was accompanied by Prof John Fletcher, the director of the Institute of Education, and Gwilliam, the Assistant Education Advisor to the secretary of state.

Binn's report presented the Kenyan situation in the context of a rapidly changing continent as opposed to the Beecher Report. He proposed the expansion of secondary education to Form 6. The students would sit for both the African Secondary Education Certificate and Cambridge School Certificate. He also recommended the strengthening of teacher training as

---

9. Beecher Report, 246.
10. Beecher Report, 63

a way of improving the quality of education. Binn also discussed the language policy in education. They advocated for the preservation of selected vernaculars for cultural value. However, they proposed replacing Swahili with English. Binn's Commission maintained that using Swahili as the lingua franca impeded the learning of both vernacular and English. They also emphasized that religion had to be the basis of education. They argued that intellectual advancement as evidenced by examination results achieved at the expense of sound moral and cultural growth did not suffice. The need for religious education was based on the fact that traditional morals were disintegrating.[11] Binn's Commission encouraged the partnership between the church and the state in school governance. The schools had to be run through a board of governors.

In the late 1950s, the education policies were greatly influenced by the winds of change in the colonial territories. This was as a result of the growth of nationalism and the reality of independence. There was the reality of political independence passing to the hands of the Africans. Hence, there was need for schooling in order to Africanize civil service posts. There was need for skilled manpower; hence the priority was secondary and higher education. The emphasis was on academic reform of the curriculum. Another focus was the need to achieve national unity. Education was no longer just a social service but a national investment.

Alliance Girls' High School

Background

Before 1945, missions offered the only secondary education in Kenya. However, there was no secondary school for girls. The education department maintained that the lack of secondary education was mainly due to la ack of qualified candidates. The remedy to the situation was through enlarging the pool of students in the upper stage of primary school and improving the standard of teaching in those classes. The immediate focus was to be on teacher training and particularly expanding and improving the training

---

11. J. R. Sheffield, *Education in Kenya: A Historical Study* (New York: Teachers College Press, 1973), 46.

of teachers in the two upper categories.[12] In 1945, the first government African-women teacher training was established at the Church of Scotland Mission. They enrolled twenty-one girls drawn from five tribes and eight schools from Nyanza, Central, and the Coast. The education was offered through cooperation between the government and missions. The curriculum focused on home-skills, physical training, short courses on citizenship, agriculture, and blackboard work. Initially the parents were worried about sending their daughters to the out-skirts of Nairobi.

The government also appointed an advisory council for the development of African education. Among the first issues to be discussed was the language policy. They adopted Beecher's Report on the use of vernacular in the first four years of school. However, English was to take the place of Swahili as the lingua franca. The council made a recommendation to call a conference to discuss the whole issue of education of African girls. They appointed a sub-committee to look into the possibility of the immediate establishment of a girls' secondary school and make recommendation of its constitution. Fifty-five students had enrolled for primary school examinations, and seven had qualified for secondary school. The social progress being planned would depend on a higher standard of education among women.

In 1948, the Director of Education, Miss Janiseh Gwilliam gave a review of the education plan. The ten-year development plan on African education would be teacher training and secondary education. The secondary education was divided into two: the first was Forms 1 and 2, which were the seventh and eighth year of education. This was referred to as Junior Secondary Course, and at the end of this course, the Kenya African Preliminary Education was taken. The results were used to select students to the Senior Secondary School, a four-year course, Forms 3 to 6, leading to a certificate examination. The Kenya African Secondary Education was taken at the end of Form 4. This offered further opportunity of selecting the best candidates for the final two years of secondary education. The syllabus of the Junior Secondary School was based on teaching manual skills, while the syllabus for secondary school was based on the Cambridge School Certificate.[13]

---

12. Department of Education, "Annual Report," 1946.
13. Department of Education, "Annual Report," 1948.

Establishment of Alliance Girls' High School

In 1948, in line with the newly developed government policy, the emphasis was on education to train men and women upon whom progress of the colony would depend. The first high school for African girls was established at Kikuyu, the African Girls' High school later on referred to as Alliance Girls' High School (AGHS). AGHS was founded in Kikuyu, west of Nairobi city. The school was established on a seventy-acre piece of land donated by the Church of Scotland Mission. The girls' senior secondary school was first located in a temporary building at Thogoto, next to Watson Memorial Church, built in memory of Rev Thomas Watson. The first and oldest dormitory was named after Minnie Watson, who was among the first women missionaries in the area.

The focus of AGHS was both on academics and education for life. Education was seen as a life-long process that developed human virtues to prepare individuals for a fuller life for the benefit of the individual and society at large. The aim of education was to give a meaningful balance between knowledge, skills, and attitudes.[14] The focus of the school was on instilling Christian faith and character formation. All the students were drawn from Christian-sponsored primary schools and Christian homes. The majority of the teachers were missionaries, and the core of the curriculum was instilling Christian values such as the fear of God, humility, reliability, and social conscience. Right from the beginning, AGHS was looked upon as a centre of excellence in both academic and extra-curricular activities. The students were drawn from all parts of Kenya and from all walks of life. The school is referred to as Alliance High School as it was based on the ideals of the Alliance of Missions. Alliance of Missions brought together the Christian missions working in Kenya with a view of working together on common areas like education and social work. The school's motto, "Walk in the Light," was adopted during the spiritual awakenings in the 1940s with the climax in 1948, at the mission grounds in Thogoto. This happened when the Gospel Missionary Society was celebrating its fiftieth anniversary. There was a move towards revival or reawakening in the church and the lives of Christians especially through the East African Revival Movement. Emphasis

---

14. Kapiyo et al., *Gift of School*, 7.

was given to living right or walking in the light of the Lord Jesus. Through revival, God was purifying the church by the blood of his son Jesus and the power of the Holy Spirit. God was giving new life to his drowning children. Fellowship meetings were characterized by public confession of sins and the request to walk in the light. The climax of the revival was between 1948 and 1950 in Kabete and was very significant to the girls' secondary school.[15]

The first group of girls to get secondary school education was admitted to Alliance Boys' High School in 1938. Mr George Arthur Grieve the first head teacher of Alliance Boys' High school admitted Zibia Wangari Ngatho of Thogoto and Lois Njeri Koinange of Banana Hill to the boys' high school. Later, Margaret Kenyatta and Joan Gitau joined them. Gitau, later referred as Joan Githaka, was the daughter of Musa Gitau, a school master at Thogoto and later a pastor of a Presbyterian church. Musa Gitau had advocated for the education of girls. John Arthur, who was the head of the mission station, was trying to persuade a nearby chief to encourage girls to go school. The chief, Kinyanjui, retorted that a woman's work was to attend to her husband, to cultivate his garden, cook his food, carry his water, and care for his children, and therefore she didn't need to learn to read and write. However, Kinyajui was fighting a losing battle, and Musa Gitau continued to encourage girls to go to school.

In 1940, Carey Francis succeeded Grieves as the head teacher of Alliance Boys' High School. Francis had occupied a central position in Kenya African Education. Francis served as a CMS missionary in Kenya, and served as headmaster of two African boys' secondary schools, namely Maseno School (1928–1940) and Alliance High School (1940–1962). Francis stood for an elitist education (i.e. education offered to a few while holding a relatively high standard). The few would then blossom and give seed to many. Alliance School was built in an English style of the grammar school. They admitted the best students who excelled in Kenya African primary education, drawn from all parts of the country. The students studied and sat for both the Kenyan African Secondary School Examination and the Cambridge School Certificate Examination. Francis emphasized both scholarship and the development of character and Christian values. The curriculum followed that

---

15. Kapiyo et al., 10.

of the English public school. The emphasis was on mathematics, geography, chemistry, music, physics, biology, French, art, woodwork, domestic science, religious education, physical education, Swahili, and English.[16]

Francis was reluctant to have co-education and advocated for having separate secondary schools for girls. Francis viewed girls as inferior and stated that he was inadequate to offer education for girls. He suspected that if girls were given academic education, they would rebel against their husbands. Francis wanted a girls' school built very far from the boys. He believed that the girls would pollute the boys and kept on commenting that if the girls were not there, the boys would have done better in exams. Francis argued that the admission of girls to the school even affected the staffing system. The first female teacher, Miss Rosie Freedman, took care of the girls who were accommodated near her house; however, she left to work in Israel.

In 1944, a committee was appointed consisting of Francis, Greaves, Blaike, and Warobi to work in consultation with the Director of Education and Miriam Janish, Assistant Director for Girls' Education. They were tasked to make a proposal for further development of girls' education. They recommended the establishment of a separate school for girls but with continued liaison between the proposed girls' school and Alliance Boys' School. In 1948, in line with this vision, the Alliance of Missions founded the first African Girls' Secondary School, referred to as the Girls' Senior Secondary School. Rev Robert M. Calderhood, the head of the Church of Scotland Mission, provided the premises for the new school. They first built a hut on the grounds of the then intermediate school at Thogoto, which became the home for the first girls' secondary school. The first headmistress of the secondary school was Jean Ewan. Ewan, later on Jean Wilkinson, had a bachelor of science degree and a diploma in education from Edinburgh University. She had taught in secondary schools in Scotland. Wilkinson was then appointed to head Tumu-Tumu Girls' Primary School for one year. She came to Kikuyu in January 1948 and laid the foundation for AGHS. In May 1948 she wrote, "It is everyone's hope that if this is a successful experiment, a full and fine Christian Girls' Secondary School will grow from these small

---

16. Benjamin Kipkorir, "Carey Francis at Alliance High School, Kikuyu 1940–1962," in *Biographical Essays in Imperialism and Collaboration in Colonial Kenya* (Nairobi: KLB, 1980), 130.

beginnings, which I have been privileged to help." Wilkinson's major task was to set up the necessary facilities for the school, and she and her team of three teachers worked tirelessly to build the school.[17]

Wilkinson was assisted by three staff members, namely Crispus Kiongo (later Rev Kiongo) who taught Swahili, Joan Gitau who taught history, geography, English, and science, and Miss F. L. Brownie who was in charge of the girls' boarding school and taught domestic science. Gitau had just acquired her Cambridge School Certificate at Alliance High School. Wilkinson taught the other subjects including English, mathematics, Scriptures, singing, and PE. The girls went to Alliance Boys' School for science as there was no laboratory in the girls' school. The first ten girls were representatives from five Kenyan communities drawn from all over the country on the basis of their performance. The first ten girls were:

1. Abigael Kageha – Friends African Mission, Kaimosi
2. Dorcas Aleyo – Friends African Mission, Kaimosi
3. Edith Ukima – Church of Scotland Mission, Chogoria
4. Hannah Jerono – African Inland Mission, Kericho
5. Jane Wacera – Church Missionary Society, Kahuhia
6. Jedidah Kivali – Friends African Mission, Kaimosi
7. Keziah Wangui – Church of Scotland Mission, Tumu-Tumu
8. Miriam Nyathogora – Church of Scotland Mission, Tumu-Tumu
9. Perpetua Wamuyu – Church of Scotland Mission, Tumu-Tumu
10. Lornah Omollo – Church Missionary Society, Ng'iya

In 1949, the government decided to offer teacher training for girls at Alliance Girls' School. Later, the teacher training was transferred to Siriba in Maseno and Machakos. After two years of the secondary course, six of the girls entered the teacher training course in 1950 and left in 1951 as grade 2 teachers. Alliance Girls' High School gave opportunity for girls from different backgrounds to study together.

In 1949, plans were made to acquire more land a mile away where construction was started. The girls participated in clearing the compound. In November 1950, the new school was officially opened by the governor of Kenya, Sir Philip Mitchell, and his wife, Lady Magery. The headmistress

---

17. Kapiyo et al., *Gift of a School*, 54.

was Jean Mckillop, who had succeeded Jean Wilkinson. Wilkinson had to leave for Chogoria Hospital to join her husband, Dr John Wilkinson, a medical doctor. Mckillop was also a graduate from Edinburgh, who was seconded to the school from the government education department. The new school was opened in line with the newly developed government policy on education. This was the 1949 Beecher Report, which reaffirmed the action of the missionaries by proposing the establishment of two secondary schools for girls, one for Protestants and another for Catholics. The Protestant school was established as an independent school, run by a board of governors drawn from the government, the missions, and the African people. The missions were represented by the Church of Scotland Mission and the Christian Council of Kenya. The Christian Council of Kenya was a body which brought together all the mission societies and churches in Kenya. The girls were to take a four-year course leading to a certificate. The first girls in this class were selected representing different parts of the country. Among the first girls in this group was Eddah Waceke (later Gachukia) and Julia Auma (later Ojiambo). Between 1953–1962, there was a general change in the curriculum. General home skills now covered areas like hygiene and nutrition, and child-welfare replaced needlework, as it was felt this was a practical subject and relevant to the girls as mothers. The school offered English, arithmetic, religious studies, history, general science, geography, biology, art, and domestic science. In 1960, general science became physics and chemistry. In the first few years, both teacher training and secondary school went hand in hand. McKillop was in charge of the teacher training. Between 1953 and 1954, Miss H. M. Turner became the headmistress of the school. The purpose of the curriculum was to offer holistic education so that the girls could grow mentally, socially, and spiritually. Apart from academic work, the students also participated in extra-curricular activities. The girls were supplied with wool and needles and had to make their own cardigans. They also decorated their own bedcovers and blankets. The training was to make them hard-working and self-reliant. On 20 October 1952, a State of Emergency was declared in Kenya after Kenyans started fighting to regain their land and it mainly affected Central Kenya. This led to a lot of tension and unrest and therefore the security at Alliance Girls' School was compromised as it was under the missions. The girls' school had therefore to be evacuated and relocated to Machakos Girls' Intermediate School. In 1953, the secondary school students came back, while the teacher trainees remained at Machakos.

At Alliance, the girls came up with a routine, which has remained as part of their tradition. The aim of the routine or schedule of events was to balance school activities and to ensure that each activity was attended to at the right time. They would wake up at 6:00, take care of their personal hygiene which included taking a bath and dressing, and then they would go for breakfast at 7:00. After breakfast, they would do general cleaning, including scrubbing dormitories and classrooms, and collecting litter in the compound. Some of the girls helped in the preparation of food, like sorting out rice. All students had to be in the chapel at 7:55 and lessons would begin at 8:15. Each lesson lasted for forty minutes, and there were nine lessons per day, which ended at 16:00. After classes, the students went for extra-curricular activities to refresh their minds and their bodies. These would enable them to socialize with others and acquire skills and talents. The students participated in games and different clubs like choir, drama, and debate. The girls would go for supper at 18:00, and after there would be voluntary prayers in the chapel. The private studies in the evening began at 19:00 ending at 20:30 for Form 1 and 2, and at 20:45 for the rest of the school. After prep, everybody went into the dining hall for cocoa followed by lock up at 21:30 conducted by the teacher on duty, who ensured that all the girls were in bed. The weekends were more relaxed. On Saturdays, the girls woke up and did their normal cleaning and then went for prep between 9:00 and 11:00. Then there was a tea break, and at 11:30 they did community work. In the afternoon, they were free to walk around Kikuyu or receive visitors. Roll call was taken at 18:00 after which the girls went for supper and then entertainment. On Sundays, the girls went to a service at 9:30 and after the service, they were free.

A lot of changes took place in the school during this period. First, there was change in the administration with the appointment of a new head-mistress. In 1955, Mary Bryson Bruce (1955–1968) was appointed as the headmistress. Bruce was born in Northern Scotland in 1908. She studied at Edinburgh University and on completion took a teaching job in central Scotland as an English teacher. This exposed her to the impoverished conditions brought forth by the depression in the 1930s. Bruce, therefore, saw the need of education to be related to the needs of the community and to develop the growth of Christian values. The publications of the Institute of Christian Education influenced her interest in Africa. Therefore, after the death of her mother in 1954, she decided to enquire from the overseas appointment bureau about employment abroad. Bruce applied for a position in Kikuyu and was interviewed in London and offered an appointment as the headmistress of AGHS. Bruce arrived in Kikuyu on 19 January 1955 before the new term began, and welcomed the girls who were very eager to learn. Bruce laid a strong and stable foundation for the present day AGHS. Her greatest responsibility was to build the infrastructure of the school, and therefore she initiated the building of new classes and dormitories through appeals to friends and former students. Bruce's vision of education was an education that was linked to the needs of the society from which students were drawn and into which they would go back. Bruce was always on call to respond to the expanding demands of the school. She did the work with a lot of energy and was nicknamed by her students as "galloping horse." Her student Asenath Odaga described her as a firm administrator but loving and motherly and having a personal concern for the girls. Bruce was also a person of uncompromising integrity.

Bruce was humble when dealing with people of all walks of life in and around the AGHS community. She dressed simply and smartly and lived a simple life, which became a model for both her students and the staff. Education at AGHS was offered at its best without unnecessary luxuries of expensive diet, clothing, or much pocket money. Bruce ensured that high academic standards were maintained at AGHS. She took personal interest in students as individuals, right from the beginning of their association with AGHS. Before admissions, Bruce would go to several schools all over the country to conduct personal interviews with pupils who were considered brilliant, in order to give the school a national outlook. Apart from good performance in the primary leaving school examination results that ensured the top places at AGHS, Bruce embarked on offering fairer chances to those whose background in school or teaching were a handicap to attaining entry requirement to AGHS through interviews. Bruce also gave the report cards personally, keenly paying attention to the teacher's comments. She strongly believed that academic progress or change was possible if faults were recognized and tackled honestly with the available resources. She therefore took the chance to discuss personal issues with individuals; hence, the quality of education that she introduced was unequalled. Bruce also introduced a scholarship fund for needy students and raised these funds until the time of her death. She tried to understand the circumstances of her students by visiting them at home, in order to know their families and the conditions under which they live. Bruce retired in 1968 after an outstanding and dedicated service and was awarded an Order of the British Empire by the queen. At her death, the president of Kenya, Daniel Arap Moi, eulogized her as a leader in the development of education for girls and stated that many families had benefitted from instilling of discipline and sound education.[18]

By the early 1960s, there was a great need for higher certificates for the girls. There was also pressure by the African nationalists for higher education, since the country was moving towards independence. In 1962, the Lancaster Conference negotiated for independence in Kenya. Makerere University could also only admit those who sat for higher school certificates. In line with this demand, some of the boys' schools including Alliance Boys' High School began their Form 5. The AGHS was only offering Form 4 certificate at the time, and the greatest challenge was where the girls would go after completing their fourth form. Madeleine Micere (now Micere Mugo) was admitted to Limuru Girls' School, a European school, after obtaining good results. In 1961, a science student, Eunice Wagga, had to join Kenya High School to pursue science, and later joined Makerere to study medicine. In 1962, the school started Form 5 in arts. The admissions was nationally based; however, the majority came from AGHS. In the first class, six students were admitted from AGHS and seven from Butere. The first Form 5 (A Level) offered the following Cambridge Higher School Certificate subjects: English, history, and geography with subsidiaries in maths, Scripture, and general studies. In 1964, they started Form-5 work in science offering botany, zoology, and chemistry with subsidiary in maths. For the first two terms, girls taking chemistry were taught at Alliance Boys' until the arrival of a chemistry teacher. Miss A. Philips was eventually posted in the school

---

18. Kapiyo et al., *Gift of a School*, 57.

to teach chemistry, and Alliance became a fully fledged high school teaching both science and arts.

Joan Waithaka was appointed as the headmistress from 1969–1984. Waithaka was the daughter of Musa Gitau, a school teacher and a great advocate of African education, who encouraged girls to go to school amidst great opposition. Waithaka was therefore among the first African girls to fully complete the primary education course in 1943. In 1944, she joined Alliance Boys' High School for the school certificate course. In 1944, she emerged as the first and only girl to pass with division 1 and proceeded for a higher school certificate. In 1948, when the girls' school was started, she assisted Wilkinson and taught history and geography. At the end of 1948, she joined Makerere for a diploma course in teaching which she completed in 1951. Waithaka was posted to teach in Machakos Boys from 1957–1958 and when the teacher training college began in Machakos in 1958, she joined as a teacher trainer. In 1960, she moved to Thogoto College and later to Highridge and then to Nairobi Girls', where she was headmistress until 1969. In 1969, she took over from Jessie Cousins (1968–1969) as headmistress of AGHS. Waithaka had been a member of the Board of Governors in Alliance for several years even before taking over as the headmistress. She was therefore was not a stranger to the school and was able to build on the foundation laid by her predecessors. Waithaka was a great mentor to the students because of her great intellectual talents, coupled with her simplicity and humility. She was a strict disciplinarian but treated the students in a humane way. She assisted most of the teachers to develop in their careers, helping them to draw their schemes and teaching methods in order to maintain high standards. She believed in hard work and was highly committed to the building of her students' character and Christian values. Her focus was on holistic education and encouraged the students to develop all their talents. Waithaka is described by her former students as a charismatic leader and powerful administrator, who instilled absolute discipline at AGHS. She came to office when the focus of the nation was on development. She launched international fundraising to expand the infrastructure of the school. Apart from the infrastructure, she introduced several programs in the school. She was also a good administrator and tightened the budget and worked with a lot of transparence and accountability. Waithaka's contribution was notable as she was the first Kenyan born headmistress; however, she continued with the traditions of the school, which included Christian service with virtues of simplicity and integrity.

The Women's Movement

The Establishment of the Women's Movement

The education of girls at a higher level led to the establishment of the women's movement in Kenya, part of the bigger international movement. The women's movement in Kenya was built on the foundations laid by women in African traditional society, by the international movement for women's empowerment, and by African women's struggle against colonialism. In most African societies, women mobilized themselves in groups for social welfare activities, and later some of these groups pushed for the need for women to be integrated in the political and decision-making processes. The women's movement brings women together to attain their common purpose, especially in instances when their interests are not adequately addressed in society. Through the women's movement, women have re-examined their position in society and have questioned and challenged society's values and the structures. Women have also formulated strategies to improve their overall status. This was done through the formation of women's clubs and voluntary women's associations. This was done through dialogue, rebellion, and mass movement. They agitated for the abolition of discriminatory laws against women and advocated for the incorporation of women in decision making.[19] A common feature of the traditional African economic system was the grouping and mobilization among women to assist each other during cultivation, weeding, harvesting, and occasions such as birth.[20] Women from traditional societies used artistic means, especially songs, to struggle against oppression and gender-based violence. An example is that of a Maasai singer:

---

19. W. A. Oduol, "Kenyan Women's Movement and Women's Political Participation," in *The Women's Movement in Kenya*, eds. S. A. Khasiani and E. I. Njiro (Nairobi: AAWord, 1993), 21–22.

20. Patricia Kameri-Mbote, Wambui Kiai and S. A. Khasiani, "The Women's Movement in Kenya," in *The Women's Movement in Kenya*, eds. S. A. Khasiani and E. I. Njiro (Nairobi: AAWord, 1993), 10.

My father, why do you send me to Ole Kareso, why do you
send me to such an old man?
Ole Kareso has eleven wives, Ole Kareso cannot look af-
ter himself.
You say Ole Kareso can look after me, but Ole Kareso cannot
look after himself.
He is too old!
Father, why do you send me to Ole Kareso?[21]

The women's movement in the West was formed by the middle class
(1865–1915). The first phase of the movement was within the context of
both industrialization and urbanization. The family within this context was
defined as the nuclear family. There was a new workload in middle-class
homes as more clothes needed to be kept clean and ironed. There was also
more sophistication in food, and therefore domestic servants were sought.
Childcare was studied by scholars and medical doctors – hence there was
expert opinion on childcare. There was also emphasis on moral training and
character formation and a network of mothers' clubs. In 1900, middle- and
upper-class women and their ideas were part of the political mainstream.
Their focus was on creating a better society with better sanitation, health
care – basic health knowledge began to improve. They advocated for regulating the amount of hours women worked for better homecare and family
care. Club women were educated in the new colleges and became motivators
for change. Women also took outside work like teaching in primary school,
which became the domain of women. The development of the typewriter led
to girls being employed as secretaries in offices, as most of them were also
taught to spell and punctuate correctly in secondary school. Women were
also employed as school workers and nutritionists, but they were paid low
wages. There were several factors which were important to bringing change
in society: first, sexuality and birth control through spacing of children and
legalization of contraceptives; second, the new role of families as there was
more contribution by women both economically and psychologically; third,
educated women had the opportunity to participate significantly in society

---

21. Mukabi Kabira Wanjiku and Elizabeth Akinyi Nzioki, *Celebrating Women's
Resistance* (Nairobi: New Era Publications, 1994), 27.

and in business. However, despite women's participation, there were still many barriers (i.e. relatively few women became decision makers and most areas of their decisions were confined to the women's spheres of childcare, elementary education, nursing, social work, and other areas related to women). On the other hand, the women who became great achievers, doctors and lawyers for example, rarely got married. Phase two of the women's movement focused on liberation as women started to question the focus on women as housemakers. There was a major push for the education of women and girls as educated women greatly influenced the development of their societies. Women also wanted legal reform, especially the right to control their own earnings. In the Equal Rights Movement, educated urban women rejected traditional gender roles as women fought for equal responsibilities and equal opportunities. They did not want to be tied to domestic roles and therefore championed the empowerment of women. The women also campaigned for political office as a platform for fighting for women's rights.

The women's movement in Kenya was also established within the context of colonialism. The main agenda of the colonial government was to rule but get money for running the country from the Africans. This was done through imposition of taxes, which was to be paid in the form of cash. The men were therefore obliged to leave their homes and procure jobs in settler farms, where they could be paid in cash. Due to labour migration, women had to take the workload that was previously the preserve of men. The African woman became a beast of burden which is well captured in Okot "P" Bteks' poem:

> Woman of Africa, Sweeper
> Smearing floors and walls with cow-dung and black soil
> Cook, Ayah, baby on your back
> Washer of dishes, planting, weeding, harvesting
> Store-keeper, builder, runner of errands
> Cart, Lorry, Donkey . . .
> Woman of Africa, what are you not.[22]

This also generated conflict between the genders because as men came back home, women were managing without them.

---

22. Okot p'Bitek, *Song of Lawino and Song of Ocol* (Nairobi: Heinemann, 1972), 33.

Maendeleo Ya Wanawake

One of the main bodies used as a springboard for development by the women educated at Alliance Girls' High School was Maendeleo Ya Wanawake. The Maendeleo ya Wanawake Organization (MYWO) (literally translated "development of women") was formed in 1952 by a group of women under the auspices of the colonial government's department for community development. Their main focus was to promote the advancement of African women and raise their living standards. Their main focus was to improve the living standard of women in the rural areas through self-help. MYWO was also greatly influenced by the post-World War II development policies. This was based on the resolutions of the Cambridge Council of 1948, whose main focus was to encourage initiative in African societies. The Cambridge Conference mainly emphasized community development. The Secretary of State for the colonies adopted the recommendations of the conference for use in the British colonies. The Cambridge Conference defined development as a movement designed to promote better living in the whole community, with the active participation and initiative from the community.[23] Their focus was on social development, especially helping people to adjust to changing conditions and cushion the effects of progress. They had to take steps so that development schemes did not aggravate the social norms and bring too much distruption. The aim was to enlighten people on the changes that were taking place and the reasons for them. People were to be encouraged to play an active part in development projects, especially focusing on group action.

In line with the Cambridge policy, Maendeleo Ya Wanawake was formed under the auspices of the colonial government's department under the Ministry of Community Development and Rehabilitation. The movement came under the direction of Nancy Shepherd, an Assistant Commissioner for Women and Girls, in the department. Shepherd was the daughter of Archdeacon Binn, the CMS missionary who worked in Mombasa. She was at first the principal of Jeanes School, a government training centre, currently the Kenya Institute of Administration, and a supervisor of the MYWO activities. Shepherd was appointed Assistant Minister for Women

---

23. Anne Nasimiyu, "The History of Maendeleo Ya Wanawake Movement in Kenya," *The Women's Movement in Kenya*, eds. S. A. Khasiani and E. I. Njiro (Nairobi: AA Word, 1993), 95.

and Girls and later Assistant Minister for Community Development and Rehabilitation. Jeanes School was the main training center for MYWO leaders and the springboard for the clubs. The curriculum at Jeanes School mainly focused on cooking, sewing, child welfare, and hygiene. Shepherd became the first president of Maendeleo Ya Wanawake. It is claimed that the aim of MYWO was to curtail women's participation in Mau-Mau and the liberation movements.

Shepherd began to organize the women's clubs with the aid of volunteers. The women's clubs were in line with the women's movement in the United Kingdom and were organized at branch level. From the beginning, Maendeleo came under the patronage of the upper-class colonial women. They were led by Lady Baring, the governor's wife, and Mrs Gladys Beecher, who was the wife to the Anglican Bishop Beecher. The women were members of the East African Women's League, a European Voluntary Association formed in 1917 for the advancement of women. Lady Baring underlined dedication to community service and was devoted to social justice and humanity without regard to politics, race, or religion.[24] The volunteers in the MYWO were mainly wives of colonial administrators and settlers, while the professional leadership was supplied by the community development personnel. African assistants were trained so that in time the branches could function under their leadership. The movement joined the Federation of Social Services in Kenya in October 1954. Twelve Europeans and two African women home-craft officers were in charge of the clubs. The European women mainly did supervisory work in MYWO clubs, while the African women were on the committee but with no leadership role. The main aim was to prepare African women to take positions of leadership in the movement. The main principle was to have cooperative efforts and group work in the rural areas legitimized. Institutionalization of women's work came through MYWO. The Secretary of State of the colony formed a subcommittee to review the special needs of women and girls and the contribution they make to social development in the colony. He made recommendations on ways in which various contacts could be made between the voluntary organization and various resources in the United Kingdom. He argued that if the

---

24. Anne Nasimiyu, *History of Maendeleo*, 100

relationships were established, they could stimulate and sustain progress and work among women in the colonial society.

Mandeleo clubs gave women opportunity to come together, exchange experiences, acquire new information and skills, and cooperate to promote their common interests. By 1954, there were more than 508 clubs and a membership of 37,000 people, and most of the officials worked voluntarily. The approach of the Europeans was to do things for the African women and children (i.e. care for the "backward" people). The activities of Maendeleo Ya Wanawake included teaching farming methods, child care, nutrition, and hygiene. They held baby shows where prizes were given to the cleanest and healthiest babies. They also encouraged traditional handwork, for example, basketwork, pottery, traditional dancing, and singing competitions. Home-craft centers were built, and literacy classes were held. They visited clubs of different areas, and sports were organized between neighboring clubs.

The rural women groups provided the basis for the MYW movement in Kenya. The Mandeleo Self-Help Organization was concerned with change at the most fundamental level – in the home. The colonial office suggested that the Kenyan government give attention, first to the clubs, especially to home hygiene and child welfare, rather than art and craft, although the economic value of the latter was appreciated. They argued that efforts were to be made to overcome resistance to individual latrines. There was need for a bold plan to deal with homeless and abandoned children and the possibility of training local women to take part in the work. Although the colonial office was interested in hygiene, women were more interested in arts and crafts, which would lead to their economic empowerment. The establishment of women's clubs was very rapid, and the main focus of government was on leadership training for the leaders. Each member of MYW paid a subscription fee of two shillings a year and received a membership card. The subscription fee however eliminated several rural women, introducing class differentiation. But the broad basis of the movement was with progressive rural women who were traders, leaders of community clubs, members of marketing cooperatives, or simply mothers saving for school fees.[25] In the rural areas, male out-migration was high, yet production of cash crops

---

25. Nasimiyu, "History of Maendeleo," 107.

continued to increase. Women responded enthusiastically to the formalization of informal women groups.

Eventually, African women trained at Jeanes School, who had earlier taken lower positions in the movement, overturned the system from within and focused on the development of African leadership. In 1961, at the annual general meeting, they voted out British leadership policies and changed for the benefit of African members. The MYWO converted to an indigenous organization not only concerned with domestic issues but the overall welfare of the Kenyan women. They decided to break away from government control, and when it became clear that they could not be controlled by the government, they were kicked out of government premises. MYWO was declared a non-governmental organization after dissociating from the state. They did not have funds, but the women worked on a voluntary basis and used their personal finances. MYWO survived due to the determination of African women leaders and the assistance of African nationalists. Foreign donors also provided financial and technical assistance. There were two types of leaders in the women's movement, namely, the patrons and the militants. The patrons were content with pouring tea, opening exhibitions, and attending fundraising and social events. The militants on the other hand advocated for a change in the women's role in the society.

In 1961, Phoebe Asiyo was elected as the first African president of Maendeleo Ya Wanawake. Asiyo was supported by the expatriates during the transition. She appreciated that European women were sympathetic and concerned, but they did not understand the needs of the African women. Asiyo had joined MYWO in 1956. She was born in 1935 on the shores of Lake Victoria and was one of the first girls to attend Gendia Primary Mission School in Karachuonyo. Education at that point mainly consisted of home economics and farming. After her time at Gendia, she took correspondence courses and then proceeded to study at Embu Teachers College. During this period, the only professions opened to women were teaching and nursing. Asiyo considered her training as a teacher as simply a stepping stone to her future career. She later did a degree in Britain in community development, focusing on hygiene, childcare, and gardening for women's empowerment. After teaching for a short time, Asiyo was recruited to work with the prisons. The prisons at this time were male dominated, but she managed to rise through the ranks to become senior superintendent in charge of a women's prison. Her main focus was to design a rehabilitation program for the women's prison. In this capacity, Asiyo managed to establish separate prisons for women across Kenya. She also got involved in collecting children whisked to the prisons, and helped to develop Child Welfare of Kenya with laws to care for and facilitate the adoption of children. As the chair of MYWO, Asiyo participated in the liberation movement of Kenya. She organized visits to Jomo Kenyatta in detention in Lodwar, although the British government demonized Kenyatta. They discussed with Kenyatta about the inclusion of women in the government after independence.

Due to her experience at MYWO, she realized that most politicians were male chauvinists and did not support women's empowerment. Asiyo realized that the women's organization did not offer a good platform for effecting change; she decided to stand for a political seat so as to discuss the issues of women's rights, gender equality, and education, especially of girls. Phoebe contested and was elected as a Member of Parliament for Karachuonyo and held the seat for two five-year terms. Her major focus was to fight for women's rights and their full participation in decision making. The most important motion she brought to parliament was on Affirmative Action, whose main aim was to give women, who had been marginalized, equal opportunity with men. In 1963, Asiyo resigned, and Jael Mbogo took over as the chairperson.

From 1967–1968, Elizabeth Mwenda was the chairperson of MYWO. In 1968, Ruth Habwe was appointed to chair MYWO. Habwe was the daughter of Archdeacon Canon Esau Ywaya and was one of the first girls to be sent to school. She was one of the first women admitted to Kabete Teachers Training College and attended Jeanes School. In 1962, she received a grant from the Israeli government to set up the Rural Social Workers School at Machakos. In 1963, she attended leadership training in New York City sponsored by the African American Institute. Habwe worked as a volunteer in a Nairobi clinic working with children with disabilities. She became one of the leading feminists in Kenya and also a leading figure in the women's movement. During the tenure of Habwe as a chairperson, she focused on creating more groups, and MYWO started to function as political pressure group. In the 1968 AGM, there were several resolutions concerning the rights and demands of women. First, was equal-employment terms with men in the public and private sector, and second, an increase in the number of female students at the University of Nairobi. They formed several groups, for example the *Mabati* Women's Group, whose major aim was to do away with grass-thatched houses to corrugated iron-sheet houses.

Habwe ran unsuccessfully for parliament in 1974, and after that she wrote: "I am aware of the difficulties that men face when they consider the possibilities of women getting positions of influence. They habour the inevitable fear that men being superior to women, if women reached the same level, they would fall far from the exalted stature that they have exploited for so long."[26] One male parliamentarian advised her to go back to the kitchen and cook for her children and Mr Habwe. In her tenure as the chairperson of MYWO, she was greatly frustrated with the lack of action to back the rhetoric on gender equality. Habwe, in addressing a Maasai men's meeting at Gong, said it was time for men to start taking better care of their wives, not treating them as slaves. African women are beasts of burden, carrying loads from early childhood until they are old; women need new roles in society as the days of being beasts of burden are over. Habwe said that the aim of women was to fight for equal rights and equal treatment. The role of women in Kenya is undermined, although there is a claim that they play an important role. Women have to throw off a heritage that has allocated them a position subordinate to men in a number of areas. Polygamous marriages lead to authoritarian family structure, with preferential treatment for men. Wealth and power in society is in the hands of men.[27] Habwe resigned from being chair of MYWO in 1971.

From 1971–1984, Jane Kiano was the MYWO chairperson. Kiano is always viewed as one of the most dynamic leaders of MYWO. However, she was criticized by intellectuals and other women organizations for being compromised, although she had the potential of being more radical. Kiano enjoyed the support of the state, built the Maendeleo House, and the Maendeleo Handcraft Shop was converted into a successful cooperative and business, assisted through funding by donors. Kiano's success was mainly

---

26. A. Wipper, "The Politics of Sex," *African Studies Review* 14, no. 3 (December 1971): 465.

27. Wipper, "Equal Rights for Women," 434.

due to her personal style of leadership, home-making ideology, diverse economic and political alliances, and the capacity to deliver goods and services.
Through endorsement and participation in *harambees*, she was high profile
in women's affairs internationally. Women's groups became development
engines. She had connections with individuals working with the state, and
she used her personal relationships with Kenyatta to raise MYWO issues. She
was conservative – she did not challenge Kikuyu patriarchy and did not make
radical demands for women's rights. She concentrated on non-threatening
feminine home-making roles. Even when vocal on trending issues like rising
food prices and women's house allowance, she was non-aggressive, unchal-
lenging, and soft. Kiano did not disturb the gendered sphere of power.
Kiano believed in building alliances both with the government and with
donors. She led delegates to the Women's Conference in Mexico in 1975 and
Copenhagen in 1980. During her term, the focus of Mandela changed from
teaching mothers about nutrition and sanitation to engaging in income-
generating projects. The national office employed female experts from various
fields to help uplift the standard of women. The women's clubs and women's
group had projects such as beekeeping, fishing, and brickmaking. They also
focused on home improvement and raised funds so that they change former
grass-thatched houses to permanent houses using corrugated iron sheet. The
groups came together to buy water tanks for preserving water, to build flour
mills for milling maize, to give adult and literacy classes in dress making and
cookery, and to provide maternal health care.

Jael Mbogo

Jael Ogombe Akinyi was born to Fanuel Akech and Dorsilla Awiti, who were
settlers in a European farm in Eldama Ravine in the Rift Valley. When she
was eleven years old, they relocated from the Rift Valley and she went to
study at Ng'iya Girls' School and was taught by Grace Onyango. In 1953,
she entered Alliance Girls' High School, where she was greatly influenced by
Masinde Muliro and Bernard Mate, who were her teachers. Both Muliro and
Mate were elected as members of the Legislative Council in 1957. In 1956,
Akinyi sat for her Cambridge Overseas Certificate. In 1957, she trained as a
secretary stenographer, and got married to Shadrack Mbogo. On completion
of her course, she was employed at the Nairobi City Council personnel department. In 1958, she was nominated a councillor of the Eastland's area of

Nairobi and was the only woman nominated councillor. She later proceeded for further studies, but in 1961 cut short her studies and came back home when she got information that her husband was sick in Tabor, Tanzania. In Tanzania, she was employed by TANU to be the secretary of Nyerere, who became the first Prime Minister of Tanzania in July 1961.

In 1963, Akinyi was elected as president of Maendeleo Ya Wanawake and was one of the most dynamic leaders of the women's movement. She worked voluntarily at Maendeleo, while getting her salary from her employment at Freedom from Hunger organization, where she was the secretary of Bruce Mackenzie, Minister for Agriculture, and later, Andrew Slade. One of the major debates, which Akinyi contributed to while at Maendeleo Ya Wanawake, was on the changing gender relations and women's status before the law through the repeal of the Affiliation Act of 1969. The Affiliation Act was a law that granted all single women the right to sue the fathers of their children for paternity support. This law was passed by the colonial legislative council on 28 April 1959, and a successful affiliation suit meant that a single mother maintained the custody of her child and could receive up to two hundred Kenyan shillings (approx. $28) per month to support the child up to sixteen years.[28] The women organizations hailed this act as it would protect the women from irresponsible men. However, most politicians claimed that it was a foreign imposition that made men the slaves of women and encouraged female promiscuity and prostitution.

In 1969, the Affiliation Act became the subject of debate in the context of a perceived gender crisis, and the all-male National Assembly repealed the act. Those who had supported the Affiliation Act felt that it was the promotion of modern laws, aimed at elevating women's status. The Affiliation Act differed from the existing customary law on pregnancy compensation. According to this law, in case a woman got pregnant out of wedlock, the woman's father would be paid a sizeable amount in cash or in livestock, and later the man would take custody of the child. However, the Affiliation Act designated the woman rather than the father as the wronged party. It uniformly granted the single mothers custody of their children. The Affiliation Act mainly applied in urban areas, while the customary law of pregnancy

28. Affiliation Act Ordinance, 1960: 107–113.

applied in the rural areas. In May 1969, the government introduced a bill in the national assembly to repeal the act. The bill was introduced, first, because the Affiliation Act was being brought against members of parliament. Second, the politicians had the desire to portray the ruling party as a champion of nationalist ideals, as a strategy to assist the Kenyatta government to recapture their political high ground. The critics believed the Affiliation Act encouraged girls to have children in order to buy things and make themselves beautiful. They argued that the act encouraged promiscuity and discouraged marriage by providing single women with comfortable income, with which to purchase wigs, cosmetics, and fancy clothes. The other argument was that the act fundamentally contradicted the African tribal customs by granting custody to the mothers rather than to the fathers.

One of the parliamentarians, John Khaoya, made a personal attack on Margaret Kenyatta, whom he dismissed as having personal interest in the whole act. Kenyatta was the daughter of President Kenyatta and was among the first female students at Alliance High School. She was elected as the first female mayor of Nairobi City. Kenyatta, who was the chairperson of the NCWK, had personally placed the letters addressed to the Members of Parliament about the Proposed Act of Affiliation in the pigeon holes. For Khaoya, Kenyatta's position as a prominent member of the nation's family and a single mother was a proof of the very dangerous situation that the Affiliation Act was encouraging. Philip Ochieng, a prominent journalist, sought to discredit the women's organizations that defended the Affiliation Act. He claimed that they were mainly western-oriented and out of tune with the African way of thinking out issues. Most of the opponents felt that the leaders of Kenya's women and welfare organizations represented the country's political elite, and they were posing a political challenge when they stepped beyond their prescribed role as tea-party hostesses and charity patrons to criticize the state policies.

On 10 June 1969, Charles Njonjo introduced a motion to repeal the Affiliation Act. Khaoya supported the repeal motion claiming that prostitutes had taken advantage of the act to enrich themselves and create a lot of havoc among the male population by using promiscuity for profit. Another Member of Parliament, Justus Nguku Munyi, claimed that the repeal would bring the prostitution industry to an end, while Aggrey Ochwada stated that it would force women to be "closing the door of their houses and not leaving it open, as if they were toilets." Wasonga Sijeyo said women were hunting for men with big money in mind, while according to Martin Shikuku, women had taken men to different courts for the same pregnancy. The parliamentary opponents accused women of misusing affiliation payments. They used the cash not to provide for children, but instead buy wigs, mini-skirts, and the skin-enlightener, *Ambi*, that enabled them to attract new boyfriends. African women wearing western clothes and using cosmetics became the central subject of the debate. They claimed that the women were not proud of being Africans and were ashamed of their skins. They used money from the Affiliation Act to purchase clothes and cosmetics to enable them appear Western and white. Women were portrayed as selfish and betrayers of African culture. Martin Shikuku and Mark Mwithaga further argued that the greatest affront to African tradition was its definition of children as belonging to mothers rather than fathers.

Other leaders who supported the Affiliation Act explained that although the act had been abused by some people making a trade out of it, repealing it would lead to an increase in illegal abortion and cases of destitution and neglect of young children. The National Council of Churches in Kenya (NCCK) and the National Council of Women in Kenya (NCWK) declared their opposition to the acts' repeal and wrote letters stating their annoyance that they were not consulted. They both argued that parliament should have dealt with the abuses by reforming rather than repealing the act. Maendeleo Ya Wanawake expressed their surprise at the opposition of the act. Jael Mbogo, who was the president of MYWO, described the repeal bill as the latest move to show up how badly represented women are in Kenya. Mbogo argued that the Affiliation Act played a crucial role in providing for children born out of wedlock and protecting girls and women from men who feel that they can do as they please.

The focus of Mbogo was on the liberation of women, and she had her eyes on politics. This did not sit very well with most people in government. However, Slade was very supportive, and encouraged her that it was not mandatory for her to resign before contesting a Parliamentary seat. By 1973, when Mbogo resigned, the MYWO had grown, and she left 85,000 members and over 5,000 clubs spread across the country. Mbogo used the support base that she had built in the women's movement to plunge into politics. She was a regular writer in the Nation Newspaper, where she articulated issues related to the Women's Liberation Movement. In 1969, she stood for parliamentary seat in Bahati, and this was in the context of ethnic tensions after the assassination of Tom Mboya. Mbogo stood against Mwai Kibaki, a very powerful minister in Jomo Kenyatta's government. She was requested by the powers that be to stand down or lose her position at MYWO. Mbogo believes she won the elections hand down; however, she was chased out of the counting hall and beaten. It is believed that this defeat led Kibaki to relocate to his rural constituency in the next elections. In 1974, she again stood in Bahati, this time against Fred Omido and Muthoni Likimani; hence, women's votes were divided between Muthoni and Mbogo, while the western Kenyan votes were divided between Omido and Mbogo. Finally, Mruiki emerged as the winner.

Case Studies

Margaret Kenyatta

Margaret Wambui Kenyatta was born in 1928 to Johnstone Kenyatta and Grace Wahu. Her father, who later changed his name to Jomo Kenyatta, became the first president of the Republic of Kenya. Margaret was raised up in the Dagorretti area of Nairobi and attended Ruthimitu Primary School and the Church of Scotland Mission School in Kikuyu. She was raised in a fairly well-off family as her father was a meter reader in Nairobi. In 1944, she was one of the first students to be admitted to Alliance Boys' High School before the establishment of the Girls' School. Kenyatta received an elite education offered to the cream of the society.

In 1948, Kenyatta went to teach at Githinguri Teachers' College. This was an independent school, started by her father Jomo Kenyatta, and Mbiyu Koinange, to spearhead nationalism in Central Kenya. In 1952, after a state of emergency was declared in Kenya, Githinguri was closed, and Jomo was detained. Kenyatta joined the other nationalists to mobilize people in order to keep the spirit of nationalism burning. During this period, she focused on doing social work as she worked for her father's release from prison.

In 1960, Kenyatta ventured into politics and was nominated as a councillor in Kiambu County Council representing Dagorretti. In 1963, at independence, she was elected as one of the councillors in Nairobi City Council. In 1970, she was elected as the mayor of the city of Nairobi. Kenyatta became the first African woman to become a mayor in a major city in Africa.

During Kenyatta's tenor as mayor, she greatly contributed to the development of the city of Nairobi. This was mainly due to her inclusive style of leadership. There was rapid expansion in the city, which included building low-income housing in Dandora and Eastleigh. She built roads which led to the industrial area of the city. Nairobi developed into a financial hub in East Africa and also the international headquarters of UN-Habitat and United Nations Environmental Program (UNEP). During Kenyatta's tenure in the office, the Kenyatta International Conference Centre (KICC) was completed. This was one of the most brilliant architectural works in East Africa. The completion of the centre led to Kenya hosting the joint World Bank and World Trade Organization meeting.

In 1976, Kenyatta was appointed as Kenya's permanent representative to UNEP, which was the most senior position held by a woman in the Kenyan government. Margaret was one of the main leaders of the Maendeleo Ya Wanawake Organization. She was also one of the leading lights of the National Council of Women of Kenya (NCWK). This was an umbrella body that brought together all women's organizations. In her capacity as a leader in NCWK, she advocated for the passing of the Affiliation Act. Kenyatta was an advocate of women's rights and one of the founders of women's movement in Kenya.

In 1984, UNEP initiated a program to enhance women's participation in environmental management and subsequently established the Senior Women's Advisory Group on sustainable development. This was mainly comprised of senior specialists interested in environmental issues. Margaret was appointed as a member of this group. The group structured the input on environment and sustainable development within the 1985 UN Conference on Women and Development. They were to propose the adoption of key paragraphs in the final conference document. Women and the environment became a major part of the agenda. They recognized women as legitimate and necessary environmental decision makers. Women's gender-based activities involved the use of the environment. They highlighted that women's knowledge of environmental conservation and protection was marginalized and distorted. Kenyatta was one of the leading delegates to the UN Women's Conference in Nairobi in 1985.

Julia Ojiambo

Julia Auma Ojiambo was born on 29 November 1936 in Busia. Her early primary school education was at Sigalame School, and she later proceeded to Butere, an Anglican Mission School from 1947–1950. Ojiambo was among the first class at the new site Alliance Girls' High School in 1951. In 1954, she joined Royal Technical College (University of Nairobi) and graduated in 1957 with a diploma in education. In 1961, Ojiambo got married to Professor Hilary Ojiambo, Kenya's first cardiologist, and they were blessed with four children. In 1965, she received a post-graduate diploma in applied human nutrition from London University. From 1965–1968, Ojiambo was the first African female warden of the University of Nairobi women's hostels of residence. In 1969, she got the opportunity to study for a master's of science in public health and nutrition from Harvard University. She went with her three-week-old son, and when she visited the High Commission, the High Commissioner asked her why she came with the child, because it would be impossible to concentrate. However, she had grabbed the opportunity to show that this was possible. In 1973, she received a PhD in human nutrition in a joint program by the University of Nairobi and McGill University in Canada. She became the first African woman lecturer at the University of Nairobi.

Academics. Professor Julia Ojiambo is an established academic with her area of study being nutrition. In the 1960s, while working as a research assistant at Mulago Teaching Hospital in Kampala, Ojiambo along with other researchers, developed a protein-rich biscuit that was used in the treatment of *kwashiorkor* in the Infantile Malnutrition Unit at the hospital and other hospitals in East Africa.[29] She has received several awards for the contribution in the field of nutrition. Between 1966 and 1968, she received

---

29. *Kwashiorkor* is a form of serious protein malnutrition. There is sufficient calorie intake, but with insufficient protein consumption. *Kwashiorkor* cases occur in areas of famine or poor food supply, but cases in the developed world are rare.

the Dean's Research Grant Award at the University of Nairobi for research in nutrition status of pregnant and lactating mothers. In 1976, the Food and Agriculture Organization (FAO) named her Ceres Gold Medal winner for distinguished service in rural programs and in the advancement of women. Ojiambo is the founding chairperson of the Kenya Nutritionists and Dieticians Institute (KNDI), a statutory regulatory body created by an act of parliament in Kenya in 2007. The aim of the body was to deal with nutrition and dietetics matters in Kenya. The focus was on implementation of laws relating to quality assurance, as well as training, registration and licensing of institutions, and qualified personal in nutrition and dietetics.

The KNDI came up with a core curriculum, which the institutions awarded interim license must use to train people in nutrition and dietetics. This includes the idea that all dietetic students must go for a one-year internship after graduation, which would turn them into professionals. The institute also produced guidelines against which the student's performance is judged while on internship. The internship builds the student's competencies in preparation for practice in four main areas, namely Public Health Nutrition, Community Nutrition, Clinical Dietetics, and Food Service Diet Therapy.[30] In 2007, the Kenya Coalition for Action in Nutrition (KCAN) named Ojiambo as the nutritionist of the year. She also served as the executive director for the International Centre for Health Development and Research (ICHDR) and also a Commissioner of the Higher Education Board. She has written over a hundred publications on nutrition.

Politics. In 1970, Ojiambo became a Kenyan African National Union (KANU) party youth representative, which roused her interest in politics. KANU was the ruling party at that time and being a youth winger brought her the opportunity to lead delegations to international meetings. In May 1974, Ojiambo resigned from her position as an Associate Professor at the University in order to vie for a political seat. She challenged a seasoned politician for the Funyula Parliamentary seat. She emerged the winner, after an election campaign marred with gender violence, to become the second female member of parliament in Kenya. In parliament, the women were described as prostitutes who left their husbands to join politics. Ojiambo's

---

30. Esther Kiragu, "Prof. Julia Ojiambo: A Lifetime of Service to Kenya," *Parents*, no. 354, January 2016, 30.

major agenda as a member of parliament was to raise the living standards of her constituents. Her major focus was on education as she believed that education is the backbone of development. She started an Adult Education Program and put up several primary and secondary schools. She also put up bore holes for her constituents with the assistance of the Danish Government to make water accessible at the domestic level. She also introduced a goat milk project in Funyula, which was replicated in other parts of Kenya. The Ministry of Livestock introduced it at their dairy farms at Naivasha, Baringo, and Kibwezi. In addition, she initiated handicraft, poultry, and fishing projects to empower her constituents economically. She also ensured that her constituents could access affordable healthcare through the construction of several health centres and dispensaries among many other projects. She also helped to construct the Odiado Rehabilitation Center for people living with disability. In recognition of her work with people living with disability, she was given state recognition by President Uhuru Kenyatta in December 2015.

From 1974–1979, President Jomo Kenyatta had appointed Ojiambo as an Assistant Minister for Housing and Social Services. She became the first woman to hold a cabinet position in Kenya. Ojiambo retained her seat in the 1979 elections and was appointed as an Assistant Minister for Education. In 1980, she negotiated for the establishment of the Kenya Institute of Special Education (KISE) with the support of the Danish government. However, most of the men were very skeptical of women holding cabinet positions arguing that the environment in cabinet meetings is not for women.

Ojiambo also participated in party politics. In 1977, she was appointed the vice-chairperson of the KANU sub-branch in Busia. In 1988, she was elected as KANU Director of Youth and Women Affairs. But in 1982, there was an attempted coup in Kenya, which led to the calling of snap general elections and Ojiambo did not manage to recapture her Funyula Parliamentary Seat. In 2003, as part of the democratization process, she teamed up with other politicians to form the National Alliance Rainbow Coalition (NARC), the party that trounced KANU from power after forty years of dominance. In 2003, she was nominated as a Member of Parliament by the NARC government. She was also appointed to the Public Accounts Committee, which kept the government in check. She excelled in her continuous contribution to the legislative process through initiating parliamentary bills. She also made contributions as a member of the Kenya Women Parliamentary Association.

In 2005, Ojiambo founded the Labor Party of Kenya. The focus of Labor Party was to champion the rights of the less fortunate and empower the next generation of leaders. This is seen in her work with people living with disability. She championed the rights of the people living with disability and was elected to the board of the National Fund for Disabled of Kenya. This board offered support services to those living with disability. In 2007, she joined hands with the Orange Democratic Movement (ODM) party and was a member of the summit, which was the leadership team. She later defected to Stephen Kalonzo's ODM Kenya and was appointed as the deputy leader of the party. She was later appointed as Kalonzo's running mate in the presidential elections. However, she left the party, when due to her gender, she failed to be nominated as a member of parliament. Ojiambo decided to concentrate on building her Labor Party of Kenya.

Women's Movement. Ojiambo has greatly contributed to the women's movement in Kenya and generally to women's empowerment. She maintains that women should not play second fiddle to men, but in order to achieve this they have to be empowered through education. Her major focus was to empower girls through education, so that they could be mainstreamed in the life of the society. Imparting skills to the girls would help them to survive in male-dominated careers like medicine, engineering, aerospace, and architect. Ojiambo argued that the journey for the emancipation of women has not succeeded. This is mainly due to the failure of the post-independent governments to mainstream gender. She argued that the government should focus on issues that hinder women from participating in political governance. She strongly participated in the journey to women's emancipation in Kenya by greatly contributing in most of the international women's conferences.

In 1975, Ojiambo was picked by the government to run with the preparation for the Women's Conference in Mexico. The Mexico Conference, organized by the United Nations, was a reminder to the international community that discrimination against women continued to be a persistent problem in many countries, both developing and developed. The UN was devoted to intensified action to promote equality between men and women. They wanted to ensure full integration of women in the development process and increase women's contribution to the strengthening of world peace. The conference coincided with the launch of the UN Decade for Women 1976–1985. This marked a new era of global effort to promote the advancement of women and opened a worldwide dialogue of gender equality. This era also marked the beginning of a process of learning, involving deliberate negotiations, setting objectives, identifying obstacles, and renewing the progress made. The UN conference in Mexico identified three objectives to work on behalf of women. The main areas were gender equality, development, and world peace.[31] Ojiambo ran with this agenda and led the Kenyan team to the conference. She did a country analysis and put up a report in which she highlighted the plight of Kenyan women on the global map. She underlined that the needs of women in Africa are very different from the needs of women in the West. One major realization in the analysis was that women in Africa were disadvantaged; they needed first to deal with issues of want before they clamored for emancipation.

Ojiambo also participated in the Second UN Women's Conference in Denmark, Copenhagen in 1980. The conference realized that there was disparity between women's guaranteed rights and their capacity to exercise them. They identified three spheres in which equality, development, and peace was needed. These were equal access to education, employment opportunities, and adequate health care services. In order to achieve this, there was a need to eliminate the structural imbalance that compounded and perpetuated women's disadvantage in society. They emphasized that equality is not just legal equality, but also equality of rights and responsibilities and opportunity for the participation of women in development both as agents and beneficiaries. However, the resolutions did not take into account the socio-economic context of the people from the developing world. The women from the developing world therefore decided to invite the women from the developed world to a conference in Africa so that they could have a feel for the situation. According to Jamabo, inviting the conference to Africa was like a fist fight, but the African women wanted them to feel development in a different context and understand the situation of the continent. However, despite campaigning hard, Ojiambo states that it was difficult to convince

31. Hilka Pietilä, *Engendering the Global Agenda: The Story of Women and the United Nations* (New York: NGLS, 2002), 34.

them to come to Nairobi. They argued that Africa had no home, no good venue, and no human capital to host a conference of that level. However, finally the 1985 UN Women's Conference was brought to Nairobi. Although Ojiambo was no longer a member of parliament, the government asked her to lead the government delegation. Having the conference in Africa was a great eye-opener both to the nation and to Kenyan women, and exposed the need for women to participate in the management of public affairs. It also opened the nation's eyes to the need for equality between men and women. At the Nairobi meeting, the gender language was born, and it was indicated that this was very important. Ojiambo felt fantastic about it because since then women have not just gone up the corporate ladder, but women groups have changed from their pitiable sight of hand-outs. However, she regrets that despite the level of advancement, there are still issues with religion, family, attitudes, and politics which create an impression that women cannot rise to the occasion. A major step forward in the UN Decade for Women was that the very concept of development came under scrutiny from the point of view of women. A pre-conference meeting produced an alternative report by Development Alternatives with Women in a New Era (DAWN). The focus of this report was that development was not serving the needs of women and does not correspond with women's values and aspirations. The report brought the role of women in development into focus in the 1985 meeting. In 1985, the UN Assembly endorsed the Nairobi Forward Looking Strategies for the Advancement of Women (NFLS). Even though the objectives of the UN Decade for Women were not achieved, the NFLS document included new improved strategies for the attainment of the goals of the UN Decade by the year 2000.

Eddah Gachukia

Eddah Waceke was born on 13 July 1936. Her greatest inspiration was her father who was keen on seeing his children, including the girls, going to school. Waceke's mother, Judith Wanjiku, taught her how to read and write, made clothes for her and generally disciplined her. Her mother died when Waceke was six years old, and she and her sister went to her maternal grandmother's home until her father remarried. Waceke's father helped her in doing her homework whenever he came home from Nairobi, where he was working. She was always compared to a boy because of her prowess in maths and sciences. One day her father, who always fondly called her my in-law because she was named after her maternal grandmother, told her, "Waceke you know you can get so much education that one day you can be referred to as Dr Nelson." Waceke performed well, and at Primary 5 she went to Loreto Girls, a well-regarded Catholic boarding school. In 1951, she was admitted at the African Girls' High School, later renamed Alliance Girls' High School. At Alliance, she was greatly influenced by Mrs Mary Welch, an English teacher who encouraged the girls to read widely. In 1954, four girls from the senior class were admitted to Makerere, one of the top universities in East Africa. Waceke escorted them to the railway station bare-footed, which was a memorable experience. She also determined to study at Makerere University. During this period at Alliance, she became politically motivated, as it was the time of trial of Jomo Kenyatta, and she read a lot of information relating to this trial. Waceke was inspired to start the Kiambu Youth Association (KYA), but this did not go very far, as life was very difficult during the Emergency Period declared by the colonial government. After Alliance, Waceke was admitted to Makerere University for a diploma in education. Waceke married a fellow educationist, Dr Dan Gachukia.

Eddah Gachukia, a veteran educationist, started off her teaching career at Thika High School, before she left for further studies in the United Kingdom. It was during this period as a teacher that she started her fight for justice. Although Thika was a missionary school, races were still separated, and there was a demarcation where Europeans lived and where Africans lived. The school was allocated money by the government to put up two staff houses, one for Europeans and another for Africans. The designs of the houses were totally different, and she challenged this at a staff meeting. One day, teachers of a visiting school and their headmaster visited her house for tea. In her house, there was only one socket – in the sitting room where the visitors were sitting. Gachukia took the electric kettle to the sitting room and asked one of the visitors to move so as to plug in the kettle. Later the headmaster asked why she had to boil water in the sitting room. She responded that this was the only socket in the house, as opposed to the European houses, which had several sockets including a hot-water system for baths and shower. This kind of defiant act won the family the kind of house that they preferred. Later she took on many other issues of racism – she was convinced that struggle pays.

From 1963–1964, Gachukia received the opportunity to further her studies at Leeds University. She returned home immediately after independence in the middle of the government's education reform, whose aim was to make education more relevant to the needs of the new nation. She went on to complete her BA, MA, and PhD at the University of Nairobi, and her major areas of focus were literature and curriculum development. From 1973–1987, she was a lecturer at the University of Nairobi, and left the university to become the national advisor of UNESCO on population, information, and development communication for Kenya. She was nominated by the president to be a member of parliament for ten years (1974–1984), and while in parliament she mainly focused on women's and children's issues. Gachukia, who is a career educationist, also served as the chairperson of Uchumi Supermarkets, director of the Institute for Policy Analysis and Research, Kenya Airways, and *Nation* newspaper. She was also a trustee of the Young Women's Christian Association (YWCA) and board member of United States International University (USIU). She was the first woman Chancellor of Moi University (2003–2006). Gachukia and her husband established the Riana Group of Schools, starting from kindergarten to university-level. The aim of the schools is to achieve best education outcomes by focusing on a holistic philosophy of education.

Gachukia has made an indelible mark in education development, gender, and women's rights, championing the cause of girls' access to education and leadership. She has dedicated four decades of her life to education and the development of women's welfare both in Kenya and the continent as a whole. In 1962, she attended the East African Women's Seminar, where she was greatly influenced by the articulation of women's issues by both Margaret Kenyatta and Tom Mboya. Kenyatta was one of the first students at Alliance and became the first female mayor of the city of Nairobi, while Tom Mboya was a renowned trade unionist and politician. While studying at University of Leeds (1963–1964), Gachukia got an opportunity to address an international meeting on issues relating to women's development in Kenya and Africa. By 1965, she had developed a sound perspective of what could be done to address the women's cause, especially in education.

In 1966, Maendeleo Ya Wanawake elected her as chairperson in absentia. From 1976–1979, she was the chairperson of the National Council for Women in Kenya (NCWK). NCWK is an umbrella body for all women's organizations, whose agenda is to help remove obstacles to the advancement of women by urging the abolition of traditional norms that discriminate against women and by trying to change men's negative attitude to women.

Gachukia has been involved in most of the world's women conferences with special focus on the UN Decade of Women (1975–1985). The Decade of Women started with the first Women's Conference in Mexico. The Mexico Conference further enlightened her on women's issues, and she became a civil society activist. However, at this first meeting she could not pursue the main issues; she had to talk very carefully on issues affecting women because she did not want to jeopardize the position of women. She had to put the agenda of women and children in such a way that she did not threaten the male politicians. However, in the sidelines of the meeting she decided to have her own women's network with a clear agenda on peace and development. Prior to the Mexico meeting, women's bureaus in Kenya had researched and prioritized the development needs of women. Hence, despite the raging debate within the global women's movement trying to adopt the agenda of equality, the African women underlined development. They argued that if one wanted to develop society, they should develop women. The women argued that if you wanted children in school, educate women as the households are changed by mothers. Gachukia also focused on women's health with a big focus on family planning.

She was also part of the government delegation to the second Women's Conference in Copenhagen; however, she sneaked into the NGO forum so that she could experience the real issues in the women's movement. This is when she learned what the Women's Decade was all about. One of the greatest debates by the northern feminists was female circumcision, and they accused the African women of being complacent. However, the African women retorted that their children are malnourished, many mothers die at childbirth, yet the West choose to go under their skirts to identify their problems. The African women argued that banning female circumcision at that point would force it underground, and the government would not be able to effectively stop it. They maintained that they did not want babies and girls circumcized, but there was need for a different approach. They wanted sensitization and educational campaigns in communities, where this was happening. The northern women disagreed with them as they preferred militarization, an issue which continued to be divisive in the movement for many years.

In the UN Assembly of 1983, the Kenya government won the bid to host the Third World Conference on Women in Nairobi in July 1985. Kenya was also to host the NGO forum, which was parallel to the assembly. The NGO committee was convened, and Gachukia was elected as the chairperson of the NGO committee. Gachukia mobilized the women and took the leadership role and shaped the African women's priorities based on their encounter with women at the grass root. Gachukia called a Regional Preparatory Conference on Women in Arusha in October 1984. Their main focus was that Africa should develop its own forward-looking agenda, up to and beyond the year 2000. The women decided to use Women's Empowerment Framework as opposed to focusing on Women in Development. In preparation for the women's meeting in Nairobi, Gachukia also worked closely with Dame Nita Barrow. Barrow, an Afro-Caribbean woman from Barbados, who was a former president of the Young Women's Christian Association (YWCA), had been asked by the UN to chair the NGO Forum 85 Planning Committee. Gachukia believed that Barrow's NGO forum-planning committee based in New York held a privileged and powerful position in determining the 1985 forum program. She was concerned that the less privileged African women's voices, and their alternate definition of women's interest and needs, would not be heard by the forum planners. In her many communications with Barrow, Gachukia stressed repeatedly that according to the African women's perspective, economic development was key to women's liberation. In a pre-conference consultation held in Vienna, she asserted that, given the urgent situation, Kenya hoped that famine and drought in Africa would take precedence over controversy, that there would be more constructive dialogue, and that Nairobi would be the venue where third world women would be taken more seriously. The controversy she referred to were global conflicts that had raged throughout the Decade for Women and impacted the conference and forum proceedings.

Gachukia also attended the Women's Conference in Beijing, where there was consensus on twelve critical areas of action, namely poverty, education and training, health, violence against women, armed conflicts, economy, power and decision making, institutional mechanisms, human rights, the media, the environment, and the girl child. The focus of Gachukia was on the global NGO forum at the sides of Beijing. The African women came up with an analysis of the constraints that have hindered the achievement of development goals. These included: gender inequality, poverty, structural adjustment programs, militarization, deforestation, damping of toxic waste and pesticides that destroy the environment, high population growth, poor governance, indifference of donors to gender, biased use of resources, language barriers, and the exclusion of young people from leadership.

African women development and communication network (FEMNET). FEMNET was conceived out of the African NGO Regional Preparatory Conference on Women in Arusha, 1984. Women had been sent to Arusha by interested development agencies, with the main aim of preparing an African position for the Third World Conference on Women in Nairobi, 1985. Gachukia was part of the government delegation from Kenya, but she was also the chairperson for the NGO forum-organizing committee. The main focus was that Africa should develop its own forward-looking strategies for the advancement of women up to and beyond 2000. However, at the plenary meeting, they realized that there were no machineries or structures that could implement their ideas. The women therefore formed a caucus of an African women's task force with Gachukia as the chairperson. The terms of reference for the task force was, among other things, to create a long-term machinery for coordinating African women's development, communication, and solidarity beyond the Third World Women's Conference. FEMNET was finally founded in April 1988 at the UN complex in Nairobi; about fifty women from ten African countries attended the meeting. The keynote speaker was Sarah Longwe, who introduced one of the most radical frameworks at that time: empowerment. The aim of empowerment was to remove all obstacles to women's active participation in all spheres of private and public life, through a full and equal share in economic, social, cultural, and political decision making. In the 1980s, it was referred to as the Women's Status Criteria as the term empowerment brought jitters to believers in women's development at both the government and civil level. At the meeting, the way forward was to come up with a constitution and develop the first program. Gachukia was elected as founding chairperson, while Njoki Wainaina was elected as the coordinator with the headquarters in Nairobi. However, the registration of FEMNET was a major challenge as there were undercurrents suggesting that the women's activities were subversive. According to Gachukia, this was a backlash after the 1985 conference, when the patriarchal political system realized that if women united around a cause, they would change the world. The political forces therefore deliberately fractured, quenched, and destroyed the women's movement. Government agents were used to frustrate every effort for women to regroup. In 1990, Gachukia came up with a plan, and registered FEMNET as a women's group in Westlands, Kenya, which gave them legitimacy to open a bank account and operate according to the regulations of the Department of Social Services. Two years later, with the onset of the multi-party era, FEMNET was registered as a regional NGO.

In 1991, FEMNET did an assessment survey which provided the basis to develop its programs by promoting the concept of networking among African women, recruiting national umbrella organizations to become FEMNET focal points. The survey revealed that the socio-economic, political, and legal situation of women had not changed much since the 1985 Nairobi Conference. There was still constraint in key areas of education, health, economic, legal, cultural and political status. Ambiguous legal status of women, discrimination, unequal treatment, dubious interpretation of customary law and non-recognition of domestic labour all remained key constraints in most countries. Though the NGOs were well grounded, they were dogged with many problems, including weak grassroot reach, uncertainty in mobilizing resources, poor relationship with government, unwillingness to work with other NGOs, withholding information, inefficient operations, and confusion in mandate as a result of pressure from government and donor partners; hence the awakening was on the need for empowerment of women and establishment of new NGOs that were focused on higher goals of empowerment and professionalism. The needs assessment identified priority areas for FEMNET and formed the basis for discussion of the first FEMNET programming conference in October 1992.

The first FEMNET Programming Conference was attended by ninety-six participants from fifteen countries. Their main focus was on gender equality, involving African women in the transformation of African societies and embracing the principle of gender equality and respect for the human rights of women. They identified eight priority areas of need that would be addressed by the program (1993–1998). These included women's empowerment, legal rights of women, evolution of a new concept of development, management skills, NGO coordination and collaboration, relationship with government and donors, research documentation, and dissemination and representation of women. The conference tackled themes of gender empowerment, democratization, health, environment and food production, women's agenda for peace, information, communication, networking, and research. They elaborated on the legal rights of women and international conventions. Thematic priorities like motherhood, including maternal, mental, and other health concerns, were discussed. The thematic area of the girl child was introduced and discussed in the context of education, health, nutrition, and child labour. Recommendations were made to remove disparities between the male and female child. They underlined the vital role of information sharing, communication, networking, and research. FEMNET also monitored the implementation of the Nairobi forward-looking strategies, reviewing what has been achieved and looking for new strategies. They also spearheaded the process of preparation for the Beijing Conference.

FEMNET also established the *African Women's Journal*, featuring analytical and well-researched articles from the members and partners across Africa on diverse issues related to the promotion of gender equality and women's empowerment. FEMNET gender programs focused on gender and development approach. Gender is about women and men and so most of their programs included men. The FEMNET board decided that the gender programs needed to raise their funding locally and become an autonomous Kenyan organization, and it was constituted into the Collaborative Centre for Gender and Development as an autonomous entity. FEMNET remained the gender resource center and developed a gender analysis tool known as the ABC of gender used by teachers, writers, scholars, artists, the media, and others to asses the gender responsiveness of the learning material and program. FEMNET together with UNICEF initiated an eight-country study on the situation of the girl child and produced a synthesis of the study which attempted to distinguish trends and patterns in education systems and in the wider society, which militated against effective education of women and girls. Another major partner of FEMNET was AAWORD, African Association of Women Research and Development. The girl child initiative became the most unique area of African success, especially the inclusion of the girl child as proposed by the African regions as one of the critical areas of action at Beijing.

Forum for African Women Educationalists (FAWE). Gachukia was the founder and first executive director of the Forum for African Women Educationalists (FAWE). FAWE was founded out of the concern to promote girls' education in Africa. Fay Chungu, the Zimbabwean Minister for Education, mobilized other female Ministers of Education to form a network to promote girls education. The first meeting was held in 1992, and brought together about sixty influential women, mainly current and former Ministers of Education and Vice-Chancellors of universities, researchers and activists. Gachukia was requested to present a concept paper, which would form the basis for discussion. In her paper, she underlined that girls and women are the intellectual resource in Africa that will contribute to the crucial change that the continent is looking for. Girls must not only be educated but must be accorded the opportunity to use their education and their skills to make decisions about, and be participants in, development in Africa. Gachukia argued that lack of resources was always cited as the reason for lack of girls' education. However, Africa has resources and only needs to manage them properly for the benefit of everybody. The first executive committee meeting was held at Bellagio Conference Center courtesy of the Rockefeller Foundation. At this meeting, Gachukia was appointed as the Executive Director, and they proposed that FAWE be registered as a pan-African NGO. FAWE was therefore registered in June 1993, with the headquarters in Nairobi, Kenya. Gachukia's first task was to establish a physical infrastructure for FAWE, especially office space, equipment, and personnel. Then she had to link FAWE with donors interested in girls' education and also develop a clear mandate and framework.

Gachukia's focus was to work so that the dream of girls' education is adopted by the African governments through networking with both donors and governments. She decided to adopt a scientific strategy using statistics on girls' education to convince even the male ministers that girl's education was vital for development. Strategy was key to success. Gachukia convinced governments to internally review their education policies for gender responsiveness and empowered both male and female ministers for education as well as NGOs to lobby for girls' education. FAWE members were encouraged to initiate creation of national chapters as a way of translating regional agenda for girls' education to unique activities and programs at the country level. The goal of FAWE was to offer mutual support, assistance, and collaboration in developing national capability to accelerate the participation of girls in education at all levels in line with Education For All (EFA) goals. The focus was on creating positive societal attitudes, policies, and practices that promote equity for girls in terms of access to, retention, performance, and a good quality education. The vision was educated women engaged in the public life of Africa. FAWE's major concern was on influencing the transformation of education systems to achieve gender equity through four main strategic objectives:

1. Influencing policy formulation, planning and implementation in favor of increasing access, improving retention and performance of girls;
2. Building public awareness and consensus on social and economic advantages of girls' education;
3. Demonstration through intervention on the ground, how to achieve increased access, improved retention and better performance
4. Influencing replication and mainstreaming of best practices from demonstrative interventions into broader education policy and practice.

In 1994, citing research findings, FAWE successfully lobbied the ministers of education in several African countries to change policies that excluded pregnant girls from entering school. Their message was that education is the right of every child, even the girl who becomes pregnant, and not a privilege for those who do not become pregnant. The FAWE National Chapter supports grassroot efforts with grants and awards to individuals and institutions that have found cost-effective, innovative, and replicable ways of promoting girls' education and gender equity in education.

Conclusion

Women played a key role in leadership and development in the pre-colonial period. This was mainly due to their empowerment through education, African religion, and culture. Although most of the societies were patriarchal, women still had opportunity for leadership. In some communities, they were even part of the council of elders. Since most of the communities were patriarchal, power was a male attribute. However, women could be "male" after menopause, when they were finished with their reproductive role.

In pre-colonial Kenya, women to some extent had property rights. Property mainly consisted of land and livestock. In most Kenyan communities, there was no idea of individual ownership of land. Ownership of land had to do with allocative use, decision of what to plant, and control of production. Land was allocated property of both husband and wife. Distribution of property was done through the household, whose head was the woman. Livestock was the major form of investment and some women could own livestock. Women were also traders in traditional society, and they also controlled industries like basketry and pottery.

However, despite opportunities for empowerment, some of the cultures greatly disempowered women. Some of the myths depicted women as the cause of sin, the reason for hard labour, and even being autocratic leaders. There were rituals like sexual cleansing of widows and widow inheritance, which gave women low dignity in society. Some of the agricultural rituals economically disempowered women, for example, before the onset of the ploughing and planting season there was need for sexual rituals. This meant that without a man, a woman could not participate in agriculture. This was greatly manifested in the fact that widows could not participate in economic activities, unless they had been inherited by a man.

The colonial period was a watershed for African women. Colonial administration set up new methods and new structures for leadership. The centralized administration led to authoritarian leadership. There was no consultation or consensus, which was integral to African leadership styles. This style of leadership side-lined women. The colonial administration evolved separate structures for administration and the judiciary. Education was a prerequisite for participation within these new leadership structures. Women were however excluded due to lack of education and skills necessary for such leadership. A new political class also emerged through the elite who had access to education and other instruments of power. This group was nurtured to leadership through participation in local native councils. They were also mentored by missionaries like Owen who was patron of the Kavirondo Tax-Payers Association. They had grass-root support by having influential positions like teachers and chiefs. They also had education and an economic base, which later acted as a springboard for participation in nationalist political movements. However, women did not have the opportunities that men had.

Complex changes during the colonial period also had a negative effect on the social and economic status of women. Agriculture became the main economic activity within the new context; however, due to several complex factors women were eventually side-lined from participation in agriculture as an economic activity. Colonial policies like punitive actions and taxation were a major blow to women in the agricultural industry. Male dominance in agriculture as an economic activity started with the onset of cattle rinderpest. Men had to participate in agriculture to rebuild their herds. Later the colonial policies favoured male participation in agriculture. Men were taught new methods of agricultural production and had access to new seeds. Men also had access to new technology. Another factor which affected women's participation in agricultural activity was African culture. According to African rituals, men were the ritual leaders and had to declare the onset of the agricultural season; however, due to labour migration, men were never available at the right time. This had a negative impact on agricultural production.

Labour policies and taxation policies had a negative effect on both the social and economic status of women. African women became beasts of burden. Due to the labour migration, there was a change in gender roles in most of the families. Women in most cases became the head of families. Women had also to perform male roles like clearing of the field and looking after cattle. This was on top of their daily chores of food production and looking after their families. Women had a major set-back because their food production was at times sold due to lack of payment of tax. They also had to use their own resources to entertain the administrators who came to collect taxes. Women were forced to work on the roads and at the chief's camp. There was also an evolution of a new concept of work. Men were perceived as wage earners with a higher social status. Women on the other hand did a lot of work, but no economic value was attached to it.

Colonial policies had a negative impact on the dignity of the Africans and on the moral values and social fabric of society. Men were dehumanized and mistreated at their place of work. This had a negative impact both on their families and on them. Luo men were forced to carry the missionaries and administrators on their backs. This was very demoralizing because it was done in front of their wives and children. The workers were not given enough food, had poor accommodation, and were beaten. Most of the African men were referred to as "boys" by the colonial masters. Separation of families also led to men keeping concubines, which was very different from the traditional practice of polygamy. There was a development of the new concept of *ochot*,[1] or prostitutes, for the new wives acquired in the urban areas. The separation of families also ushered in a new trend where some men just chose to neglect families. There was no system to hold men accountable. Therefore women had to run their families without any assistance. The colonial policies also encouraged men to be the emerging elite, by empowering men through education. The policies also supported men, while alienating women from economic activities like trade. Eventually, through the Swynertton plan, men were given title deeds, and as land owners, they had access to loans which were key to economic development. However, some of the women used resources from their culture to participate both in leadership and economic activities.

---

1. *Chot* was Luo word for lover, which was quite acceptable for young people; however, *ochot* was now given a new meaning. It referred to concubine or prostitute, which were foreign ideas to the Luo.

Kenyan women recovered their dignity and power through the establishment of Christian missions. First, this was through the interaction between Christianity and the African worldview. There was continuity between Christianity and some aspects of the African worldview. This is evident in some of the African tales that were similar to the Old Testament stories, like the story of the floods and of Lot's wife. However, in the African version of the stories, women played a very positive and critical role. There was also discontinuity with some of the negative African cultural practices. Women therefore used their faith to challenge the practices, which had disempowered them.

Second, the establishment of Christianity offered an opportunity for women's agency. Missionaries' wives, women missionaries, and African women agents had opportunity for leadership. Most of the women missionaries were teachers and medical workers, which were influential positions in African traditional societies. In the coastal region, the wives of Bombay Africans who had vocational training, held very influential positions in the mission station. During the establishment of the Christian faith, the focus was on the Christian village and not on a church structure. The focus of the Christian village was lay leadership. Women were leaders in several of the villages because the men were absent due to labour migration.

Most of the Christian missions contributed to community development through their focus on holistic mission. Missionaries did relief work during the periods of famine and other calamities. Missions set up schools, hospitals, and orphanages in response to the needs of the people. The missions also focused on gender issues. A major focus of their work was to liberate African women from oppressive cultural practices. They did advocacy work by highlighting the plight of women. Missions offered protection for women, and several girls sought refuge in the mission stations. The missionaries fought for justice for the African women.

The Christian missions were also avenues for economic empowerment of women. The missions offered literacy and vocational training for girls, which led to economic empowerment. Missions were also one of the chief employers for the girls and women. The establishment of Christianity was also the springboard for the women's movement in the church. The women's movement gave women the opportunity to participate in church leadership and decision making. It was also an avenue for challenging male domination in both the church and society. The women's movement was the springboard of girls' education, especially the establishment of boarding schools. The women's movement became the place for addressing gender issues in both church and society. It also laid the foundation for women's socio-economic empowerment.

The aim of both the CMS and the colonial administration was to give vocational training for the girls. The Luo requested literacy or intellectual training to accompany vocational training so that the girls would be grounded in their fields. The curriculum used at Ng'iya did not stress on intellectual knowledge. The school however used both Luo language and traditional methods of communication, which put emphasis on the intellectual Luo concept of *rieko,* which included both intellectual and practical skills. The missionaries emphasized literacy as a means of reading the Bible, but it became the springboard of interacting with new ideas. The Ng'iya Girls' School therefore set a good foundation, but most of the girls did not end their learning at Ng'iya; they had been motivated to take further training.

The curriculum of school focused on language, religion, and preparing girls for marriage. Vernacular was important as it encompassed the worldview and philosophy of a people. Adapting education to vernacular helped the creative interaction between Luo and western ideas. The emphasis of religion in the curriculum was very useful in maintaining values, which are very important for any society. Through emphasis on character formation and mentoring of girls, the schools produced girls of high Christian discipline, which was important for leadership in church and society. By focusing the curriculum on marriage, the education system was in actual fact addressing itself to political and socio-economic issues in society.

Education and exposure were very important tools of empowerment. The women used education in ways neither intended nor imagined by the authorities. The women were not coming to the mission schools as empty slates but already had education from Luo society. Luo women used resources from both Christianity and Luo culture to transform society. The main focus of mission education was evangelism. Character formation eventually proved very useful in terms of creating discipline and enhancing the women's capacity to make decisions. Women emerged as agents of new ideas and transformation. They took what was relevant for them both in traditional and modern society. The women defined what was good for them, and they went for it. These women empowered by education, initiated transformation in their lives and society. Women used education to live within the context of a multicultural society. They used the literacy they received at school as the foundation and springboard for seeking further information. Access to information enabled them to transcend barriers and build relationships. The focus of mission education was to train teachers and midwives; however, in Luo traditional society, these were positions of influence and power and were marks of seniority. Women therefore used these positions as stepping stones for economic empowerment and leadership positions.

The focus of education at the Alliance Girls' High School was education for change and transformation. The aim of education was to achieve liberation and socio-economic empowerment. This would lead to both personal and community development. Religious studies were central in the curriculum, so that the girls could develop Christian values and ethics. The focus was both on academics and education for life. Education was key to liberation and development of the society.

Higher education for girls led to the establishment of the women's movement in Kenya. The women's movement was based on both African traditional ideals and the international movement. The movement became the springboard for both empowerment and fighting for justice. Women were included in political and other decision-making processes. They became professionals and renowned academics. Maendeleo Ya Wanawake at first focused on community development, especially in the rural areas. Eventually, it became a platform for leadership and decision making. The individual girls who studied at Alliance played a key role in women's empowerment both locally and internationally. They helped in mainstreaming the African women's agenda, especially at the international level; they all underlined the importance of education for girls.

Glossary

ajuoga – diviner, medicine-man, who had both mystic power and knowledge

Angili Nyo Nyimbo Cha Chiewo Pamba Rachar – women from the Anglican church, are of high taste, like fresh milk, and as pure as cotton

apamo – cattle rinderpest

Amina Nyar Mji – Amina, "the lady from the city"; a term used for a foreign woman

aminda – bracelet

asemba – girl's skirt

askari – police

baraza – meeting

bilo – medicine

bondo – euphorbia tree

Buch Mikayi – women's council

Buch Piny – territorial council

chi liel – widow

chieno – married woman's clothing

chira – violation of certain rules, and the misfortune which results from such acts

chode – courting; in later usage, prostitution

chodo okola – ritual cleansing done through sexual intercourse

chola – ritually unclean

chot – lover

chuny – spiritual heart; site of deep intellect; ethical emotions and wisdom

chuny motegno – strong heart

dala – home, enclosure

gagi – jingles

harambees – Kiswahili term for fundraising

huwege – songs composed to uphold debate or discussion within community, or songs composed to ridicule a certain situation

jaber – beautiful one

jabilo – diviner, prophet, priest, community leader, war leader

Jachuech – Creator, moulder

jadolo – priest

jagam – go-between in marriage

jagolpur – agricultural ritual leader

janawi – witch-doctor who administered *nawi* which was a mixture of herbs and poison to kill enemies

jater – widow inheritor; caretaker who inherits his relative's wife

jodak – tenants

Jok – Supreme Spiritual Power, Powerful Spirit Force

jomemorandum – people who issue memorandums; a nickname given to elites in Nyanza during the colonial period

jonanga – people of cloth; one of the new terms invented to describe the new class, which was both elite and urbanites

josepe – people who manifested power at the particular time of possession by Spirits

juogi – spirits; collective term for spiritual world

juok – totality of spirits characterized by accumulation of knowledge and wisdom, one with highest power and was therefore source of supernatural power to human beings

juok – witchcraft

kar buch tong – war time meeting place

Kit Mikayi – group of three rocks placed on top of each other and one small one by their sides located in Seme; was one of the shrines in Luo land

kode – a kind of leaf or *okola*, tied by widows after the death of their husbands

kodundo – Odundo's place; also referring to something small

Kraal – father's home

kwaro – grandfather

kwer – prohibitions or taboos

Lango – Masai, Kalenjin, Nandi and Lumbwa sub-tribes

liswa – sacrifice

lowo – land, soil

luth – leadership stick

lwanda – rock or boulder

mabati – corrugated iron sheet

Maendeleo ya Wanawake – women's movement

mbovu – foolish

miaha – a newly married wife

mikayi – first wife, or the senior wife in a marriage relationship. *Mikayi* was a position of seniority, and therefore position of authority in society. It was a stepping stone to leadership positions and economic empowerment.

Mismula – Miss Gold; Moller's nickname

misumba – an unmarried land tenant, servant

Mond Anglikan – women from the Anglican church

mondo – saving or investment

nawi – mixture of herbs and poison supplied by Janawi to kill enemies

Ngeche – Proverbs

nyaduse – humble or graceful

Nyakalaga – one of God's titles; describes attributes of God as one who is everywhere flowing in and through people

nyar oda – daughter of my house; also a term used by *Mikayi*, for the other women in the marriage

nyar osiep – daughter of a friend, always used in the context of an arranged marriage

nyar yimbo – special high quality hoe

nyarombo – lamb; also a title used for Christ

nyasache – his or her God; but traditionally also used for womb

Nyasaye – God; literally meaning to adore or to go on one knees

nyiego – jealousy or competition

nyieka – co-wife, a relationship characterized by competition; also terminology used by grandmothers for their granddaughters

nying juok – ancestral name

ober – tree

obwombe – a type of creeper plant

obwongo – brain

ochot – prostitute

ogaye – peace maker

Oiro Nyandesa – the one with beautiful steps; a nickname for Miss Extance

okebe – a highly respected person whose home lacks nothing in terms of cattle, grains and poultry, this wealth brought other status symbols

okola – a kind of leaf, tied by widows for about one year after the death of the husband *orengo* – flywhisk

ot – household

otange – sodom apples

pakruok – publicly naming both inwardly and outwardly oriented conceptions of
	virtue; virtue functioned as the main feature of right conduct; virtues were
	tied to thoughts, feelings, beliefs, intentions and attitudes

pim – an elderly woman, a grandmother, who is widely knowledgeable, with a
	task of teaching, nurturing and mentoring young people

pinje – territories

piny – land

Piny Owacho – the title given to the meeting held at Lundha in Gem to resist
	white domination; the literal meaning is "the world asserts," or people's voice

podho – to fall; also root word for land

por – elopement

puodho – land, cultivated field

rateng – black; used symbolically for courage

rieko – an expansive term which referred to knowledge, intelligence, being
	skilled, wisdom, experience and exposure; the older a person becomes, the
	more *rieko* he or she acquires

"Rieko lo teko." – "Knowledge is mightier than strength."

riso – final marriage ceremony

ruodhi – chiefs

ruoth – chief; also term for Lord

sepe – spirits

sem – to discourage or dissuade

silual – brown; also symbolizes decency

simba – boys' dormitory

siwindhe – girls' dormitory; also forum for girls' education

ter – widow inheritance; act of being a care-taker of a kinsman wife

thuon – courageous person, hero, war leader

thuondi – courageous people, heroes, war leaders

tieko kwer – removing certain prohibitions; make possible transition to a
	new situation which puts an end to an old one in which certain deeds
	were prohibited

uch – harvest festival

unbwogable – corrupted word for tough person, not easily scared

"Wangi tek ka nyar por." – "You have a stubborn look like a girl who has eloped."

wende juogi – songs of spirit

wuon dala – the head of a compound or a home

wuon lowo – land owner; person with birthright; person having the right to allocate land

wuon puodho – owner of field; cultivated land

wuoro – father

wuowo – seduce

Bibliography

Archival Sources

Rhodes House

British Parliamentary Papers Uganda: Colonies Africa 70 Sessions. 1892–1899. Mss. Brit. Emp.s., 27.7 C.9 RH

East Africa and Labour Matters. 1932–1937. Mss.Afr.s., 1117. Box 3.

John Ainsworth, Reminiscences of East Africa. 1930s–1940s. Mss. Afr.s., 380–381.

Louis Leakey, "Southern Kikuyu before 1903." 1929. Mss.Afr.S., 1117 RH

Memoirs of J. J. Willis: Reflections of Uganda. 1872–1954. Mss.Afr.s., 1296. Box 5/14.

Memoranda on Forced Labour. 1930–1935. Mss.Afr.s., 1427. Box 3/1.

Memoranda & Reports by Orde Browne on Labour Matters. 1929–1945. Mss. Afr.s., 1117. Box 2.

Papers of C.E.V. Buxton. 1921–1964. Mss.Brit.Emp.s., 390.
: "Kenya," 1921–1964. Box 1–1A.
: "East Africa," 1909–1964. Box 7.

Papers of Charles Roden Buxton. 1908–1944. Mss.Brit.Emp.s., 405.
: "East Africa," 1930–1937. Box 6/5.
: "Colonial Pamphlets," 1917–1947. Box 6/7.

Papers of Sir Granville Orde Browne. 1913–1946. Mss.Afr.s., 1117. Box 1.

Papers of C. M. Dobbs: Correspondence/Reports. 1908–1930. Mss.Afr.s., Box 665/1.

Papers of C. W. Hobley. 1890–1960s. Mss.Afr.s., 143–148.

Papers of J. J. Willis. 1900–1902. Mss.Afr.s., 1296.

Seminar and Conference Papers Historical Association of Kenya. 1968–1981. Mss.Afr.s., 1792. Box 7/33–40.

Church Missionary Society Archives: Birmingham

Archdeacon Owen's Annual Letters. G3/AL, 1918–1944.
Education Policy. G3/X ED, 1927–1934.
Fanny Moller's Annual Letters. G3/AL, 1921–1948.
Lottie Extance Annual Letters. G3/AL, 1934–1948.
Original Letters, Uganda Mission. G3/A7/0, 1906–1921.
Original Letters, Kenya Mission. G3/A5/0, 1921–1949.
Pleydell's Annual Letters. G3/AL, 1918–1932.
Willis Annual Letters. G3/AL, 1906–1920.
Wright's Annual Letters. G3/AL, 1918–1923.

Kenya National Archives

African District Council Minutes, 1931–1951, PC/NZA 2/11/19.
African District Council Meetings, 1958–1960, DC/KSM/1/2/1 Box 18.
African Education (Beecher Report), 1950–1954, DC/KSM/1/10/2.
Anglican Church Council Kavirondo, 1934–1940, MSS/61/104.
Church Missionary Society-Schools, 1930–1960, DC/KSM/1/10/39 Box 49.
Domestic Training, 1950–1953, DC/KSM/1/1/255 Box 17.
Education of Girls, 1953, E/EDU/1/GEN 297.
The Legislative Council Ordinance, 1925–1927, PC/NZA 3/1/8 Box 3.
The Legislative Council Ordinance, 1927–30, PC/NZA 3/1/9 Box 3.
Local Native Councils, 1931–1934, DC/KSM/1/1/119 Box7.
Local Native Councils, 1934–1936, DC/KSM/1/118 Box 7.
Missions: CMS Ng'iya, 1937–1939, PC/NZA 2/11/25 Box 32.
Ng'iya Girls' School Inspection Reports, 1937–1940, MSS/61/443.
Ng'iya Girls' School Inspection Reports, 1941–1943, MSS/61/444.
Nyanza Provincial Annual Report, 1906–1943, PC/NZA/1/2-41 Box 1 & 2.
Religions, 1942–1954, DC/KSM/1/1/126 Box 7.
Schools in Luo-Land, 1956–1958, PC/NZA 3/60 Box 45.

Transcripts of Interviews, housed at St. Paul's United Theological College, Limuru, (SPA), on Colonial Period and Establishment of the Church in Nyanza

Alaka, Samuel (Church Teacher), Interview with Crispin Onyango, Seme, 16 December 1967.
Mboya, Paul (Pastor, Secretary LNC, Politician), Interview with Crispin Onyango, Karachuonyo, 21 December 1967.

Musiga, Isaiah (Anglican Church Priest), Interview with Tolo, Ugenya, December 1966.

Obando, Nelson (Evangelist), Interview with John Nyesi, 14 December 1966.

Odidi, William (Revival Member, Farmer & Businessman), Interview with Crispin Onyango, Karachuonyo, 21 December 1967.

Ogony, Grace Leah (Wife of G. Samuel Okoth, Evangelist & Priest), Interview with John Nyesi, Ng'iya, 27 December 1966.

Oguma, Joshua (SDA Pastor), Interview with Crispin Onyango, Oyugis, 21 December 1967.

Ogutu, Hezkiah (Farm Laborer), Interview with Onyango, Karachuonyo, 23 December 1967.

Ogutu, Manas (Evangelist), Interview with Tolo, Ng'iya, December 1966.

Okeyo, Isaac (County Council Member/Rtd SDA Pastor), Interview with Onyango, Karachuonyo, 21 December 1967.

Okwirry, Jonathan (Former Senior Chief), Interview with Crispin Onyango, Yuma, 18 December 1967.

Omullo, Reuben Crispin (Evangelist, Headmaster, Priest), Interview with Crispin Onyango, Gem, 15 December 1967.

Ongeche, Sarah (Wife of Evangelist), Interview with Walter Tolo, Ambira, December 1966.

Oywaya, Canon Esau (Priest), Interview with John Nyesi, 14 December 1966.

Oyigo, Jeremiah (SDA Pastor), Interview with Crispin Onyango, Uyoma, 24 December 1967.

Songa, Daniel (AIM Pastor), Interview with Onyango, Kisumu, 19 December 1967.

Transcripts on *Piny Owacho*, housed at St. Pauls' United Theological College, Limuru, (SPA), Signed by Okaro-Ojwang, n.d.

Nyende, Simeon. Teacher at Maseno, Priest in Anglican Church, 70 years.

Okaka, Jeremiah. Elder at Lundha, 99 years.

Okello Mariko, Ramula. Teacher at Maseno, 99 years.

Okwirry, Jonathan. Teacher at Maseno, Senior Chief, years.

Omullo, Reuben. Evangelist, Teacher at Maseno, Priest.

Otako, Rosebella. Wife to sub-chief in whose home the meeting took place in Lundha-Gem.

Owuor, Benajmin. PC's Office, Teacher at Maseno, 69 years.

Oral Sources

Interview with Former Students of Ng'iya Girls' Mission School

Achieng, Sylvia, student, 1950–1953, in Maranda (May 2004). Teacher.

Aching, Judith, student, 1933–1936, in Gem (March 2002). Housewife, self-employed farmer/business.

Aching, Mary Jean, student, 1959–1960, in Siaya (May 2004). Headmistress, teacher-evangelist, CCS worker, lay canon.

Acholi, Rosa, student, 1927–1929, in Kisumu (March 2002). Teacher.

Adhiambo, Dorcas, student, 1934–1938, in Yimbo (April 2001). Teacher.

Adhiambo, Mary, student, 1930–1933, in Chianda (April 2003). Housewife.

Adikinyi, Bathsheba, student, 1934–1938, in Ng'iya (June 2004). Teacher.

Agwa, Olivia, student, 1941–1944, in Homabay (April 2004). Social-worker, director of CCS in Diocese of Maseno South, Lay Canon Southern Nyanza.

Aluoch, Ana, student, 1927–1928, in Sinaga (March 2002; April 2000). Teacher, farmer.

Anyang, Ethel, student, 1938–1940, in Maseno (May 2004). Teacher-evangelist.

Anyango, Jenipha, student, 1933–1936, in Lweya, (May 2003). Housewife/business.

Awando, Dina, student, 1946–1948, in Lweya (May 2003). Housewife, teacher-evangelist/ KANU party grass-root chairperson.

Awuor, Meresia, student, 1951–1954, in Maranda (May 2004). Teacher.

Mbaka, Julia, student, 1926–1929, in Usenge (May 2004). Housewife.

Nihongo, Dorcas, student, 1934–1936, in Seme (May 2003). Housewife, farmer.

Ochieng, Damiris, student, 1938–1940, in Ng'iya (May 2004). Housewife.

Ochieng, Esther, student, 1956–1958, in Maranda (May 2004). Teacher.

Ochieng, Joyce, student, 1955–1957, in Maranda (May 2004). Headmistress, teacher-evangelist.

Ochieng, Truphosa, student, 1936–1940, in Kisumu (April 2001). Teacher, councillor.

Odundo, Joyce, student, 1955–1957, in Maranda (May 2004). Headmistress, MU chairperson.

Okine, Grace, student, 1945–1949, in Nyakongo (May 2003). Teacher, teacher-evangelist.

Okuthe, Lucia, student, 1930–1933, teacher in Muhoroni (January 1983; May 1985). Deaconess, priest.

Ololo, Mildred Apondi, student, 1946–1947, in Yimbo (May 2004). Teacher, Mothers' Union chairperson, Bondo Diocese.

Olweny, Monica, student, 1928–1930, in Ramba (April 2003). Housewife, self-employed farmer.

Omach, Sarah, student, 1931–1933, in Ramba (April 2003). Housewife.

Omollo, Peresis, student, 1943–1946, in Regea (May 2002, March 2003). Business person, MU patron, Diocese of Maseno West 1985–1992.

Onyango, Grace, teacher, 1957–1960, in Nairobi & Kisumu (May 2004). Teacher, Mayor of Kisumu, member of parliament, deputy speaker, chairperson KICOMI, member *Katia* Watch, Synod member, Diocese of Maseno South and the provincial Synod.

Onyango, Mikal, student, 1959–1960, in Ng'iya (May 2004). Teacher.

Ougo, Alice, student, 1938–1942, in Mahaya (May 2003). Teacher, Synod member.

Owino, Zilpa, student, 1948–1950, in Ambira (December 2004). Teacher, MU chairperson.

Owok, Sophia, student, 1939–1941, in Ng'iya (May 2004). Teacher, teacher-evangelist.

Owuor, Grace, student, 1938–1940, in Ambira (May 2004). Social worker, Maendeleo Ya Wanawake chairperson, Synod member, lay canon.

Other Interviews

Aduogo, Hezron. Clergy, Maseno-South, in Kisumu (April 2002).

Ajuoga, Matthew. Archbishop, Church of Christ in Africa, in Kisumu (January 2001).

Amollo, Samson. Clergy, Southern Nyanza, in Homabay (April 2001).

Angela, Johannes. Bishop of Bondoc Diocese, in Bondo (April 2002).

Fred, F. F. Former Inspector of schools, in Kisumu (May 2000).

Nyang, Haggia. Retired Bishop, Southern Nyanza, in Homabay (April 2001).

Nyang, Nereah. Retired Mothers Union Patron, in Homabay (April 2001).

Nyongo, Hebron. Canon & Archdeacon, Maseno-South, in Seem (March 2003).

Ochieng, Judith. Mothers' Union Leader/Evangelist, in Nyakongo (December 2002).

Odamna, Conslate. Development Worker, in Ambira (December 2004).

Odhiambo, Peres. Mothers' Union Leader, in Ambira (2004).

Ogot, Mical. Former Health Co-coordinator Maseno-West, in Hono (May 2004).

Oigo, Phelgona. Evangelist, in Nyakongo (December 2002).

Okeno-Moyi, Henry. Clergy, Maseno-West, in Maliera (April 2002).

Okune, Rosa. Church Member, in Kokise (April 2003).

Omollo, Daniel. Retired Bishop of Maseno West, in Regea (January 2003; April 2004).

Owing, Jael. Former NCCK Co-coordinator, Western Kenya in Amira (December 2004).

Wasonga, Joseph. Bishop of Maseno-West, in Ng'iya (January 2003).

Wasonga, Jenipha. Chairperson, MU Maseno-west Diocese, in Ambira (December 2004).

Group Interviews

Sylvia Aching, Esther Wakio Ochieng, Meresia Owuor, Joyce Odundo, Dan Ochieng (male teacher trained at Ng'iya) – All former teacher trainees at Ng'iya, Interview at Maranda Church, on 14 May 2004.

Participation in Group Discussions:
1. Mothers' Union Conference, Bondo Diocese, Nyakongo December 2002
2. Mothers' Union Conference, Maseno-West Diocese, 14–19 December 2004.

Books, Chapters in Books, and Journal Articles

Abreu, Elsa. *The Role of Self-Help in the Development of Education 1900–1973.* Nairobi: KLB, 1982.

Abwo, Priscilla. "Memorandum on Behalf of African Women to Kenyan Constitution." Conference in London, 1962.

Acholonu, C. O. *Motherism: The Afrocentric Alternative to Feminism.* Owerri: AFA Publications, 1995.

Adegbola, A. E. A. *Traditional Religion in West Africa.* Ibadan: Daystar Press, 1983.

Adeyemo, T. *Salvation in African Tradition.* Nairobi: Evangel Publishing House, 1997.

Agesa, J., and R. U. Agesa. "Gender Differences in the Incidence of Rural to Urban Migration: Evidence from Kenya." *Journal of Development Studies* 35, no. 6 (1999): 36–58.

Ajulu, Deborah. *Holism in Development: An African Perspective.* Monrovia, CA: MARC, 2001.

Altbach, P. G., and G. P. Kelly. *Education and Colonialism.* London: Longman, 1978.

Alberti, J. *Gender and the Historian.* London: Longman, 2002.

Allen, Tim. "Understanding Alice: Uganda's Holy Spirit in Context." *Africa* 61, no. 3 (1991): 370–399.

Amadiume, I. *Male Daughters and Female Husbands: Gender and Sex in African Society.* London: Zed Books, 1987.

———. *Reinventing Africa: Matriarchy, Religion and Culture.* London: Zed Books, 1997.

Anderson, David. *Eroding the Commons: The Politics of Ecology in Baringo, Kenya 1890–1968*. Oxford: James Currey, 2002.

———. *Histories of the Hanged*. London: Weidenfield & Nicolson, 2005.

———. "Master and Servant in Colonial Kenya 1895–1939." *Journal of African History* 41, no. 3 (2000): 459–485.

Anderson, G. *Biographical Dictionary of Christian Missions*. New York: Macmillan, 1998.

Anderson, J. *The Struggle for the School*. Nairobi: Longman, 1970

Anderson, W. B. *The Church in East Africa 1840–1974*. Dodoma: CTP, 1977.

Ansu, D. *Education and Society: A Sociology of Education*. London: Macmillan, 1984.

Assie-Lumumba, T. "Educating Africa's Girls and Women: A Conceptual and Historical Analysis of Gender and Inequality." In *Engendering African Social Sciences*, edited by A. Imam, A. Mama, and F. Sow, 297–316. Dakar: CODESRIA, 1997.

Atieno-Odhiambo, E. S. "Ethnic Cleansing and Civil Society in Kenya 1969–1992." *Journal of Contemporary African Studies* 22, no. 1 (2004): 29–42.

———. "Hegemonic Enterprises and Instrumentalities of Survival: Ethnicity and Democracy in Kenya." *African Studies* 61, no. 2 (2002): 223–249.

———. "Hegemonic Enterprises and Instrumentalities of Survival." In *Ethnicity and Democracy in Africa*, edited by B. Berman, D. Eyoh, and W. Kymlica, 167–181. Oxford: James Currey, 2004.

———. "The Movement of Ideas: A Case-Study of Intellectual Responses to Colonialism among Liganua Peasants." In *History and Social Change in East Africa*, edited by Bethwell A. Ogot, 165–185. Nairobi, EAPH, 1976.

———. "A Note of Chronology of African Traditional Religion in Western Kenya." *Journal of East African Religious Development* 5, no. 2 (1975): 119–122.

———. *The Paradox of Collaboration and Other Essays*. Nairobi: EALB, 1974.

Atieno-Odhiambo, E. S., and D. W. Cohen. *Burying SM: The Politics of Knowledge and Sociology of Power in Black Africa*. Portsmouth, NH: Heinemann, 1992.

———. "Synthesising Kenyan History in African Thought and Practice." *Journal of the Philosophical Association of Kenya* 1, no. 1 (1974): 37–42.

———. "Seek Ye First the Economic Kingdom: A History of Luo Thrift and Trading Corporation (LUTATCO), 1945–56." In *Hadith 5: Economic and History of East Africa*, edited by Bethwell A. Ogot, 218–256. Nairobi: KLB, 1975.

———. *Siaya: The Historical Anthropology of an African Landscape*. London: James Currey; Athens: Ohio University Press, 1989.

Atieno-Odhiambo, E. S., and J. Lonsdale. *Mau-Mau and Nationhood: Arms, Authority & Nationhood.* Oxford: James Currey, 2003.

Ayany, Samuel. *Kar Chakruok Mar Luo.* Kisumu Equatorial Publishers, 1947.

———. *Kar Chakruok Mar Luo,* 2nd edition. Kisumu: Equatorial Publishers, 1951.

Ayot, Henry. *A History of Luo Abasuba of Western Kenya from 1760–1940.* Nairobi: KLB, 1979.

———. *History Texts of the Lake Region in East Africa.* Nairobi: KLB, 1977.

Bahemuka, Judith. "Social Changes and Women's Attitudes towards Marriages in East Africa." In *The Will to Arise: Women Tradition, and the Church in Africa,* edited by Mercy A. Oduyoye and Musimbi R. A. Kanyoro, 119–134. Maryknoll, NY: Orbis, 1992.

Banks, O. *Faces of Feminism.* London: Basil Blackwell, 1986.

Barber, K. "Interpreting Oriki as History and as Literature." In *Discourse and Its Disguises: The Interpretation of African Oral Texts,* edited by K. Barber and P. Demorges, 13–21. Birmingham: Centre of West African Studies, 1989.

Barrett, David. *Schism and Renewal in Africa.* Nairobi: Oxford University Press, 1968.

Baumann and C. Briggs. "Poetics and Performances as Critical Perspective on Languages and Social Life." *Annual Review of Anthropology* 19 (1990): 59–88.

Bay, Edna. *Women and Work in Africa.* Boulder, CO: Westview Press, 1982.

Bedeck, Gillian. *Primal Religion and the Bible.* London: Sheffield Academic Press, 1997.

Bediako, Kwame. *Christianity in Africa: The Renewal of a Non-Western Religion.* Maryknoll, NY: Orbis Books, 1995.

———. *Jesus in Africa: The Christian Gospel in African History and Experience.* Akropong: Regnum Africa, 2000.

———. *Theology and Identity: The Impact of Culture on Christian Thought in Second Century and Modern Africa.* Carlisle: Regnum Books, 1999.

Behrend, H. *Alice Lakwena and the Holy Spirit 1985–92.* Oxford: James Currey, 1999.

Behrend, H., and U. Luig, eds. *Spirit Possession, Modernity and Power in Africa.* London: James Currey, 1999.

Bennet, G. *Kenya: A Political History of the Colonial Period.* Oxford: Oxford University Press, 1963.

Berger, I. "Rebels or Status Seekers? Women as Spirit Mediums in East Africa." In *Women in Africa: Studies in Social and Economic Change,* edited by Nancy J. Hafkin and Edna G. Bay. Stanford, CA: Stanford University Press, 1976.

Berger, I., and Clare Robertson. "Introduction: Analysing Class and Gender in African Perspectives." In *Women and Class in Africa*, 3–26. London: Africana Publishing Company, 1986.

Berger, I., and Frances White. *Women in Sub-Saharan Africa: Restoring Women to History*. Bloomington: Indiana University Press, 1999.

Berman, B. *Control and Crisis in Colonial Kenya*. London: James Curry, 1990.

Berman, B., D. Eyoh, and W. Kymlicka. *Ethnicity and Democracy in Africa*. Oxford: James Curry, 2004.

Bell, Judith. *Doing Your Research Project*. Buckingham: Open University Press, 1993.

Black, Jeremy, and Donald MacRaild. *Studying History*. New York: Palgrave, 2000.

Blakely, D. T., W. E. VanBeek, and D. L. Thomson, eds. *Religion in Africa*. London: James Currey, 1994.

Blumberg, R. L. "Women's Rights, Land Rights: Dilemmas in East Africa." *Journal of Development Alternatives and Area Studies* 23, no. 3/4 (September/December 2004): 17–33.

Boahen, A., ed. *General History of Africa, Vol. 7: Africa under Colonial Domination 1880–1935*. London: James Currey, 1992.

Boko, S. H., M. Baliamoune-Lutz, and S. R. Kimuna. *Women in African Development: The Challenges of Globalization and Liberalization in the 21ˢᵗ Century*. Trenton, NJ: Africa World Press, 2005.

Bovet, P. "Education as Viewed by the Phelps-Stokes Commission." *International Review of Missions* 15, no. 3 (1926): 483–491.

Bowie, Fiona. *The Anthropology of Religion: An Introduction*. Oxford: Blackwell, 2002.

———. "The Elusive Christian Family: Missionary Attempts to Define Women's Roles: Case-Studies from Cameroon." In *Women and Missions: Past and Present*, edited by F. Bowie, D. Kirkwood, and S. Ardener, 145–164. Oxford: Berg Publishers, 1993.

———. "Reclaiming Women's Presence." In *Women and Missions: Past and Present*, edited by F. Bowie, D. Kirkwood, and S. Ardener, 1–22. Oxford: Berg Publishers, 1993.

Bozzoli, B. "Marxism, Feminism and South African Studies." *Journal of Southern African Studies* 9, no. 2 (1983): 139–171.

———. *Women of Phokeng: Consciousness, Life Strategy, and Migrancy in South Africa 1900–1983*. London: James Currey, 1992.

Brantley, Cynthia. *The Giriama and the Colonial Resistance in Kenya 1800–1920*. Berkley: University of California Press, 1981.

Brenner, L. "Histories of Religion." *Journal of Religion in Africa* 30, no. 2 (2000): 143–167.

Britton, J. "The Missionary Task in Kenya." *International Review of Missions* 12, no. 47 (1923): 412–420.

Brown, D., ed. *Oral Literature and Performance in Southern Africa.* Oxford: James Currey, 1999.

Brown, S. "Theorising Kenya's Protracted Transition to Democracy." *Journal of Contemporary African Studies* 22, no. 3 (2004): 325–342.

Bruke, Mary. *Preaching for Justice: The Women's Movement.* Washington, DC: Center for Concern, 1980.

Bundy, C. "Continuing a Conversation: Prospects for African Studies in the 21st Century." *African Affairs* 101, no. 402 (January 2002): 61–73.

Burton, D., ed. *Research Training and Social Scientists.* London: Sage Publications, 2000.

Carey, W. *Crisis in Kenya.* London: Mowbray & Co, 1952.

Cheru, F. *African Renaissance: Road Map to the Challenge of Globalisation.* London: Zed Books, 2002.

Chukwudi, E. E., ed. *African Philosophy: An Anthology.* Cambridge, MA: Blackwell, 1998.

———. *Post-Colonial African Philosophy: A Critical Reader.* Oxford: Blackwell, 1997.

Clark, K. D., and R. V. Rakestraw. *Readings in Christian Ethics Vol.1: Theory and Method.* Grand Rapids, MI: Baker Book House, 2002.

Clayton, Anthony, and D. C. Savage. *Government and Labour Policies in Kenya 1895–1963.* London: Frank Cass Publishers, 1974.

Clifford, A. M. *Introducing Feminist Theology.* New York: Orbis, 2001.

CMS. *The Centenary Volume of Church Missionary Society for Africa and the East 1799–1899.* London: CMS, 1902.

———. "The Specific Task of CMS in Africa." *International Review of Missions* 15, no. 59 (1926): 12.

Cohen, David. *British Policy in Changing Africa.* Evanston, IL: NorthWestern University Press, 1959.

———. "Doing Social History from Pins Doorway." In *Reliving the Past: Worlds of Social History,* edited by O. Zunz, 191–198. Chapel Hill: University of North Carolina Press, 1985.

———. "The River-Lake Nilotic from the Fifteenth Century to the Nineteenth Century." In *Zamani: A Survey of East African History,* edited by B. A. Ogot, 136–149. Nairobi: EAPH, 1974.

Cohen, D. W., F. S. Miescher, and L. White, eds. *African Words and African Voices: Critical Practices in Oral History.* Indianapolis: Indiana University Press, 2001.

Cole, Keith. *The Cross over Mount Kenya: A Short History of the Anglican Churches in the Diocese of Mount Kenya (1900–1970).* London: CMS, 1970.

Collin, R. *Real World Research: A Resource for Social Scientists and Practitioner Research.* Oxford: Blackwell, 1993.

Comaroff, John, and Jean Comaroff. *Ethnography and Historical Imagination.* Chicago: University Press, 1992.

———. *Of Revolution and Revelation.* Chicago: Chicago University Press, 1997.

Connolly, P., ed. *Approaches to the Study of Religion.* London: Continuum Books, 2002.

Cooper, B. "Reflections on Slavery, Seclusion and Female Labour in the Maradi Region of Niger in the Nineteenth and Twentieth Centuries." *Journal of African History* 35, no. 1 (1994): 61–78.

Cooper, F. "What Is the Concept of Globalisation Good For? An African Historian's Perspective." *African Affairs* 100, no. 399 (2001): 189–213.

Cornwall, A. *Readings in Gender in Africa.* Oxford: James Curry, 2005.

Cox, J. L. *Rational Ancestors: Scientific Rationality and African Indigenous Religions.* Cardiff: Cardiff Academic Press, 1998.

Crazzolara, J. P. *The Lwoo.* Verona: Ngirizia Press, 1954.

Cruz-Doña, R. D., and A. Martina. "Some Links between Education, Household Well-Being and Credit Markets: Evidence from Rural Philippines." *Oxford Development Studies* 28, no. 3 (2000): 289–308.

Cutrufelli, M. R. *Women of Africa: Roots of Oppression.* London: Zed Books, 1984.

Datta, A. *Education and Society: A Sociology of African Education.* Nairobi: Macmillan, 1984.

Davidson, J. "History, Identity, Ethnicity." In *Making History: An Introduction to the History and Practices of the Discipline*, edited by P. Schofield and P. Lambert, 1–6. London: Routledge, 2004.

Dawson, E. C. *Missionary Heroines in Many Lands: True Stories of the Intrepid Bravery and Patient Endurance of Missionaries in Their Encounter with Uncivilized Man, Wild Beasts and Forces of Nature in All Parts of the World.* London: CMS, 1924.

Doig, Andrew. "The Christian Church and Demobilization in Africa." *International Review of Missions* 35, no. 138 (1946): 174–182.

Dougal, J. W. C. *Christianity and the Sex-Education of the African.* London: SPCK, 1937.

———. "Education and Evangelism." *International Review of Missions* 36, no. 143 (1947): 313–323.

———. *Missionary Education in Kenya and Uganda: A Study in Co-operation.* London: Edinburgh House Press, 1936.

———. "The Relationship of Church and School in Africa." *International Review of Missions* 26, no. 102 (1937): 204–214.

———. "Religious Education." *International Review of Missions* 15, no. 59 (1926): 493–505.

———. "Thomas Jesse Jones: Crusader for Africa." *International Review of Missions* (1950): 139–155.

Doyle, Shane. *Crisis and Decline in Bunyoro: Population and Environment in Western Uganda: 1860–1955*. Oxford: James Currey, 2006.

Dube, Musa, ed. *HIV/AIDS and the Curriculum: Methods of Integrating HIV/AIDS in Theological Programs*. Geneva: WCC Publications, 2003.

———. *Other Ways of Reading: African Women and the Bible*. Geneva: WCC Publications, 2001.

Edet, N. R. "Christianity and African Women's Rituals." In *The Will to Arise: Women, Tradition and the Church in Africa*, edited by Mercy A. Oduyoye and Musimbi R. A. Kanyoro, 25–39. New York: Orbis, 1992.

Eliot, S. C. *The East African Protectorate*. London: Edward Arnold, 1905.

Elkins, C. *Britain's Gulag: The Brutal End of Empire*. London: Jonathan Cape, 2005.

———. "Detention, Rehabilitation & the Destruction of Kikuyu Society." In *Mau-Mau and Nationhood*, edited by J. Lonsdale and E. S. Atieno-Odhiambo, 191–227. Oxford: James Currey, 2003.

Ellen, R. F., ed. *Ethnographic Research: A Guide to General Conduct*. London: Academic Press, 1984.

Ellis, S. "Writing Histories of Contemporary Africa." *Journal of African History* 43, no. 1 (2002): 1–26.

Emecheta, Buchi. *The Joys of Motherhood: A Novel*. London: Heinemann, 1988.

Engmann, E. A. W. "The Work of a Teacher in Africa." *International Review of Missions* 36, no. 43 (1947): 324–327.

Etienne, M., and M. Leacock., eds. *Women and Colonization: Anthropological Perspectives*. New York: Praeger, 1980.

Enid Da Silva. " Place of Women in Kenya Politics." *Sunday Nation*, 21 December 1969.

Evans-Pritchard, E. E. "Luo Tribes and Clans." *Rhodes-Livingstone Journal* 7 (1949): 24–40.

———. "Marriage Customs of the Luo in Kenya." *Africa* 20, no. 2 (1950): 132–142.

———. *Nuer Religion*. Oxford: Oxford University Press, 1956.

Extance, Lottie. *Sigendni Magosoji*. Maseno: CMS, 1938.

Fafunwa, A., and J. Aisiku, eds. *Education in Africa*. London: George Allen & Unwin, 1982.

Fanusie, L. "Sexuality and Women in African Culture." In *The Will to Arise: Women, Tradition and the Church in Africa*, edited by Mercy A. Oduyoye and Musimbi R. A. Kanyoro, 135–154. New York: Orbis, 1992.

Fearn, Hugh. *An African Economy: A Study of the Economic Development of Nyanza Province 1903–1955*. London: Oxford University Press, 1956.

Fiorina, E. S. *In Memory of Her: A Feminist Theological Reconstruction of Christian Origins*. London: SCM Press, 1998.

Francis-Dehqani, G. E. *Religious Feminism in an Age of Empire: CMS Women in Iran 1869–1934*. Bristol: Centre for Comparative Studies in Religion and Gender, 2000.

Fraser, A. G. "Aims of African Education." *International Review of Missions* 14, no. 56 (1925): 514–522.

———. "The Place of Education in Spreading Knowledge of Health and Hygiene in Village Life." *International Review of Missions* 14, no. 75 (1930): 377–387.

Fraser, D. "The Evangelistic Approach to the African." *International Review of Missions* 15, no. 3 (1926): 438–449.

Friedman, J. *Cultural Identity and Global Processes*. London: Sage Publications, 1994.

Friere, P. *Pedagogy of the Oppressed*. London: Penguin, 1993.

———. *The Politics of Education*. London: Penguin, 1985.

Friere, P., and A. Faundez. *Learning to Question*. Geneva: WCC, 1993.

Gaidzanwa, Rudo. "Burgeosis Theories of Gender and Feminism and Their Shortcomings with Reference to Southern African Countries." In *Gender in Southern Africa: Conceptual and Theoretical Issues*, edited by Ruth Meena, 92–125. Harare: SAPES, 1982.

Gaiha, R. "Are Millennium Goals of Poverty Reduction Useful?" *Oxford Development Studies* 31, no. 1 (2003): 59–84.

Gaitskell, Deborah. "Crossing Boundaries and Building Bridges: The Anglican Women's Fellowship in Post-Apartheid South Africa." *Journal of Religion in Africa* 34, no. 3 (2004): 266–297.

———. "Devout Domesticity? A Century of African Women's Christianity in South Africa." In *Readings in Gender in Africa*, edited by A. Cornwall, 177–187. Oxford: James Currey, 2005.

———. "Hot Meetings and Hard Kraals: African Bible Women in Transvaal Methodism 1924–60." *Journal of Religion in Africa* 30, no. 3 (2000): 277–309.

———. "House-Wives, Maids and Mothers: Some Contradictions of Domesticity." *Journal of African History* 24 (1983): 241–256.

———. "Interpreting Contemporary Christianity, Global Processes and Local Identities." *Journal of African Religion in Africa* 34, no. 3 (2002): 266–297.

———. "Ploughs and Needles: State and Missions Approaches to African Education in South Africa." In *Christian Missionaries and State in the Third*

World, edited by H. B. Hansen and M. Twaddle, 98–120. Oxford: James Currey, 2002.

Garfield, Williams. "Relations with Government on Education: British Colonies in Tropical Africa." *International Review of Missions* 14, no. 53 (1925): 3–24.

Gatheru, M. R. *Kenya: From Colonization to Independence 1888–1970*. Jefferson, NC: McFarland & Co., 2005.

Gathogo, Julius. *Mutira Mission: An African Church Comes of Age in Kirinyaga, Kenya*. Eldoret: Zapf Chancery, 2011.

Geiger, Susan, Nakanyike Musisi, and Jean Marie Allman, eds. *Women in African Colonial Histories*. Bloomington: Indiana University Press, 2002.

Geissler, P. W., and R. J. Prince. "Shared Lives: Exploring Practices of Amity between Grandmothers and Grandchildren in Western Kenya." *Africa* 14, no. 1 (2004): 95–119.

Geller, S. "The Colonial Era." In *Africa*, edited by P. O'Meara and P. Martin, 25–36. London: James Currey, 1995.

Getui, M., and E. A. Obeng, eds. *Theology of Reconciliation: Explanatory Essays*. Nairobi: Acton Publishers, 1999.

Githiga, G. G. *The Church as a Bulwark against Authoritarianism*. Oxford: Regnum, 2001.

Goddard, L. B., ed. *The Encyclopaedia of Christian Missions*. London: Thomas Nelson & Sons, 1967.

Goldin, I., and K. Reinert. *Globalization for Development: Trade, Finance, Aid, Migration and Policy*. Washington, DC: World Bank and Palgrave Macmillan, 2006.

Good, K. "Democracy and the Control of Elites." *Journal of Contemporary African Studies* 21, no. 2 (2003): 155–172.

Gorringe, T. J. *Furthering Humanity: A Theology of Culture*. Aldershot, UK: Ashgate, 2004.

Government Publishers. "Education for Citizenship." *Colonial 1947 African Education in Kenya (Beecher Report)*. Nairobi: GP, 1949.

Greaves, L. B. "African Education: A Commentary on Cambridge Conference, September 1952." *International Review of Missions* 42, no. 3 (1953): 318–331.

———. "Educational Advisorship in East Africa." *International Review of Missions* 42, no. 167 (1947): 329–337.

Gross, Susan, and Majorie Bingham. *Women in Africa of the Sub-Sahara*. Hudson, WI: GEM Publications, 1982.

Gyekye, K. *An Essay on African Philosophical Thought: The Akan Conceptual Scheme*. Cambridge: Cambridge University Press, 1995.

Hafkin, N., and G. B. Edna, eds. *Women in Africa: Studies on Social and Economic Change*. Stanford, CA: Stanford University Press, 1976.

Hansen, H. B., and M. Twaddle, eds. *Christian Missionaries in the Third World*. Oxford: James Currey, 2002.

———. *Religion and Politics in East Africa*. London: James Currey, 1995.

Hansen, K. T., ed. *African Encounters with Domesticity*. New Brunswick, NJ: Rutgers University Press, 1992.

———. *A Short History of African Philosophy*. Indianapolis: Indiana University Press, 2002.

Harcourt, W. "Millennium Development of Goals." *Development* 48, no.1 (2005): 36–52.

Harlow, V., and A. Smith, eds. *A History of East Africa, Vol.1*. Oxford: Clarendon Press, 1965.

Harries, Lyndon. "Linguistics Research in the Church in Africa." *International Review of Missions* 36, no. 142 (April 19467): 258–262.

Hartman, H. "Some Customs of the Luwo (or Nilotic Kavirondo), Living in South Kavirondo." *Anthropos* 23 (1928): 263–278.

Hastings, Adrian. *The Church in Africa 1450–1950*. Oxford: Clarendon, 1994.

———. *A History of African Christianity 1950–1975*. Cambridge: Cambridge University Press, 1979.

———. "Were Women a Special Case." In *Women and Missions: Past and Present*, edited by F. Bowie, D. Kirkwood, and S. Ardener, 109–125. Oxford: Berger, 1993.

Hauge, H. E. *Luo Religion and Folklore*. Oslo: Universitetsforlaget, 1974.

Hay, M. "Economic Change in Late Nineteenth Century Kowe, Western Kenya." *Haddith* 5. Stanford, CA: Stanford University Press, 1974.

———. "Luo Women and Economic Change during Colonial Period." In *Women in Africa: Studies in Social and Economic Change*, edited by N. Hafkin and G. B. Edna, 87–109. Stanford, CA: Stanford University Press, 1976.

Hay, Margaret, and Marcia Wright, eds. *African Women and the Law: Historical Perspectives*. Boston: Boston University, African Studies Centre, 1982.

Hay, Margaret, and Sharon Stichter. *African Women South of the Sahara*. New York: Longman, 1984.

Heilman, B., and N. Ndumbaro. "Corruption, Politics and Societal Values in Tanzania: An Evaluation of Mkapa Administration's Anti-Corruption Efforts." *African Journal of Political Science* 7, no. 1 (2002): 1–19.

Henige, D. *Oral Historiography*. New York: Longman, 1984.

Hewitt, Gordon. *The Problem of Success: A History of Church Missionary Society, Vol 1, 1910–1942*. London: SCM Press, 1971.

Hobley, C. W. "British East Africa: Anthropological Studies in Kavirondo and Nandi." *Journal of the Anthropological Institute of Great Britain and Ireland* 33 (1903): 325–259.

————. "Eastern Uganda Occasional Papers No. 1." *Journal of the Anthropological Institute of Great Britain and Ireland* 1 (1902): 33–35.

————. "Kavirondo." *The Geographical Journal* 12, no. 4 (1898): 361–372.

————. *Kenya from Chartered Company to Crown Colony*. London: Witherby, 1929.

Hodgson, D. L. "Once Intrepid Warriors: Modernity and Production of Masaai Masculinities." *Ethnology* 38, no. 2 (1999): 121–150.

Hodgson, D. L., and S. A. McCurdy. *"Wicked" Women and the Reconfiguration of Gender in Africa*. Oxford: James Currey, 2001.

Hoehler-Fatton, C. *Women of Fire and Spirit: History, Faith and Gender in Roho Religion in Western Kenya*. New York: Oxford University Press, 1996.

Holmes, E. R., and L. D. Holmes. *Other Cultures, Elder Years*. London: Sage Publishers, 1995.

Hoogvelt, A. *Globalisation and the Post-Colonial World: The New Political Economy of Development*. London: Macmillan, 1997.

Horton, Robin. *Patterns of Thought in Africa and the West*. Cambridge: Cambridge University Press, 1993.

Hotchkiss, Willis. *Sketches from the Dark Continent*. London: Headley Brothers, 1945.

Houtondji, P. *African Philosophy: Myth and Reality*. Indianapolis: Indiana University Press, 1983.

Huxley, E. *A New Earth*. New York: William Morow, 1960.

Ibeanu, O. "Ethnicity and Authoritarianism in Nigeria: Explaining the Passing of Authoritarianism in a Multi-Ethnic Society." *Journal of Political Science* 5, no. 2 (2000): 45–65.

Imam, A., A. Mama, and F. Sow, eds. *Engendering African Social Sciences*. Dakar: CODESRIA, 1997.

Ilife, J. *Africans: The History of the Continent*. Cambridge: Cambridge University Press, 1995.

Imbo, S. O. *An Introduction to African Philosophy*. Oxford: Rowman & Littlefield, 1998.

Isichei, Elizabeth. "Does Christianity Empower Women? The Case of Anaguta in Central Nigeria." In *Women and Missions: Past and Present*, edited by F. Bowie, D. Kirkwood, and S. Ardener, 209–228. Oxford: Berg, 1993.

Jacinta, A., Kapiyo et al. *The Gift of a School: Alliance Girls High School 1948–1998*. Nairobi: Christian Digest, 1998.

Jackson, C., and R. Pearson. *Feminist Vision of Development: Gender Analysis and Policy*. London: Routledge, 1998.

Jennings, M. "Recent History of Kenya." In *Africa South of the Sahara*, edited by Kathrine Murison, 564–572. London: Routledge, 2005.

Johnston, H. *The Uganda Protectorate*. London: Hutchinson, 1902.

Jones, J. *Education in East Africa*. London: Edinburgh House Press, 1938.

Kameri-Mbote, P., W. Kiai, and S. A. Khasiani. "The Women's Movement in Kenya." In *The Women's Movement in Kenya*, edited by S. A. Khasiani and E. L. Njino, 9–16. Nairobi: AAWord Publishers, 1993.

Kamau, Nyokabi. *Women and Political Leadership in Kenya: Ten Case Studies*. Nairobi: Heinrich Boll Foundation Publishers, 2010.

Kandiyoti, Deniz. "Gender, Power and Contestation: Rethinking Bargaining with Patriarchy." In *Feminist Visions of Development*, edited by C. Jackson and R. Pearson, 135–151. London: Routledge, 1998.

Kanogo, Tabitha. *African Womanhood in Colonial Kenya 1900–1950*. Oxford: James Currey, 2005.

———. "Kenya and Depression." In *A Modern History of Kenya, 1895–1980*, edited by W. R. Ochieng and B. A. Ogot, 112–143. Nairobi: Evans Brothers, 1989.

———. "Mission Impact on Women in Colonial Kenya." In *Women and Missions: Past and Present*, edited by F. Bowie, D. Kirkwood, and S. Ardener, 165–186. Oxford: Berg, 1993.

———. *Squatters and the Root of Mau-Mau, 1905–1963*. London: Ohio University Press, 1997.

Kanyoro, Musimbi R. A. "Interpreting Old Testament Polygyny through African Eyes." In *The Will to Arise: Women, Tradition and the Church in Africa*, edited by Mercy A. Oduyoye and Musimbi R. A. Kanyoro, 87–100. New York: Orbis, 1992.

———. *Introducing Feminist Cultural Hermenutics*. London: Sheffield Academic Press, 2002.

Kanyoro, Musimbi R. A., and N. J. Njoroge. *Groaning in Faith: African Women in the Household of God*. Nairobi: Acton Publishers, 1996.

Kanyoro, Musimbi R. A. et al. *Culture, Women and Theology*. Delhi: ISPCK, 1994.

Karanja, J. K. *Founding of an African Faith: Kikuyu Anglican Christainity, 1900–1945*. Nairobi: Uzima Press, 1999.

Kenyatta, Jomo. *Facing Mount Kenya: The Tribal Life of the Gikuyu*. London: Secker & Warburg, 1938.

Khasiani, S. A., and E. I. Njiro, eds. *The Women's Movement in Kenya*. Nairobi: Association of African Women for Research and Development, 1993.

Kihoro, Wanyiri. *The Price of Freedom: The Story of Political Resistance in Kenya*. Nairobi: MvuleAfrica Publishers, 2005.

King, K. J. *Pan-Africanism and Education: A Study of Race, Philanthropy and Education in the Southern States of America and East Africa*. Oxford: Clarendon Press, 1971

King, U., ed. *Feminist Theology from the Third World*. New York: Orbis, 1994.

————. *Religion and Gender.* Oxford: Blackwell, 1995.

Kinoti, A., and J. M. Waliggo, eds. *The Bible in African Christianity.* Nairobi: Acton Publishers, 1997.

Kipkorir, Benjamin. "Carey Francis at Alliance High School Kikuyu 1940–1962." In *Biographical Essays on Imperialism and Collaboration in Colonial Kenya,* edited by B. E. Kipkorir, 125–140. Nairobi: KLB, 1980.

Kiragu, Esther. "Prof. Julia Ojiambo: A Lifetime of Service to Kenya." *Parents* no. 354, January 2016, 29–33.

Kirkwood, D. "Protestant Missionary Women: Wives and Spinsters." In *Women and Missions: Past and Present,* edited by F. Bowie, D. Kirkwood, and S. Ardener, 25–28. Oxford: Berg, 1993.

Kiros, T. *Exploration of African Thought.* London: Routledge, 2001.

Ki-Zerbo, J., ed. *General History of Africa, Vol.1.* Berkley: University of California, 1990.

Kyeyune, D., ed. *New Trends for the Empowerment of the People.* Nairobi: Pauline Publications, 1997.

Kyle, K. *The Politics of Independence in Kenya.* London: Macmillan Press, 1999.

Labode, M. "From Heathen Kraal to Christian Home: Anglican Mission Education and African Girls 1850–1900." In *Women and Missions Past and Present,* edited by F. Bowie, D. Kirkwood, and S. Ardener, 126–144. Oxford: Berg, 1993.

Langford, S. N. "Mass-Education and Rural Africa." *International Review of Missions* 34, no. 134 (1945): 121–135.

Leaky, Louis. *The Stone Age Races of Kenya.* London: Oxford University Press, 1935.

Lestedi, G., and M. Mulinge. "Corruption in Sub-Saharan Africa: Towards a More Holistic Approach." *African Journal of Political Science* 7, no. 1 (June 2002): 51–77.

Lewis, J. *Empire-State Building: War and Welfare in Kenya, 1925–52.* Oxford: James Currey, 2000.

Lewis, L. J. *Educational Policy and Practice in British in Tropical Areas.* London: Nelson, 1954.

————. *Phelps-Stokes Reports on Education in Africa.* London: Oxford University Press, 1962.

Leys, C. *The Rise and Fall of Development Theory.* Oxford: James Currey, 1996.

Likimani, Muthoni G. *Passbook Number F.47927: Women and Mau-Mau in Kenya.* Nairobi: Noni's Publicity, 1984.

Lonsdale, John. "Agency in Tight Corners: Narrative and Initiative in African History." *Journal of African Cultural Studies* 13, no. 1 (2000): 6–8.

———. "Authority, Gender and Violence: The War within Mau Maus Fight for Land and Freedom." In *Mau Mau & Nationhood,* edited by J. Lonsdale and E. S. Atieno-Odhiambo, 46–75. Oxford: James Currey, 2003.

———. "The Conquest of State 1895–1905." In *A Modern History of Kenya, 1895–1980: In Honour of B. A. Ogot,* edited by W. R. Ochieng and B. A. Ogot, 13–44. Nairobi: Evans Brothers, 1989.

———. "The Dynamics of Ethnic Development in Africa, Moral and Political Argument in Kenya." In *Ethnicity and Democracy in Africa,* edited by Berman, D. Eyoh, and W. Kymlicka, 73–95. Oxford: James Currey, 2004.

———. "European Attitudes and African Pressures: Missions & government in Kenya between the Wars." In *Hadith,* edited by B. A. Ogot (1975): 229–242.

———. "Kikuyu Christianities: A History of Intimate Diversity." In *Christianity and the African Imagination,* edited by D. Maxwell, 157–197. Boston: Brill, 2002.

———. "Mission Christianity & Settler Colonialism in Eastern Africa." In *Christian Missionaries and the State in the Third World,* edited by H. B. Hansen and M. Twaddle, 194–210. Oxford: James Currey, 2002.

Lonsdale, J., and B. Berman. "Coping with Contradictions: The Development of the Colonial State in Kenya, 1895–1914." *Journal of African History* 20 (1979): 487–505.

———. *Unhappy Valley: Clan, Class and State in Kenya, Book 1.* Oxford: James Currey, 1991.

———. *Unhappy Valley: Conflict in Kenya and Africa, Book 2.* Oxford: James Currey, 1992.

Lumumba-Kasongo, T. "Corruption in Sub-Saharan Africa: Towards a Holistic Approach." *African Journal of Political Science* 7, no. 1 (2002): 56–68.

Magesa, L. *African Religion: The Moral Traditions of Abundant Life.* Nairobi: Pauline Publishers, 1997.

Maitra, P., and R. Ray. "The Joint Estimation of Child Participation in Schooling and Employment: Comparative Evidence from Three Continents." *Oxford Journal of Development* 30, no. 1 (2000): 41–62.

Makhoulf, H. H. "Globalisation: The Gap between Promise and Reality." *Journal of Development Alternatives* 23, no. 3/4 (2004): 57–65.

Makotsi, Pamela, ed. *A Journey of Courage: Kenya Women Experiences of 2002 General Elections.* Nairobi: AWC Features, 2004.

Malo, Shadrak. *Dhoudi Mag Central Nyanza* [Clans of Central Nyanza]. Kampala: Eagle Press, 1953.

———. *Dhoudi Moko Mag Luo.* Kisumu: Oluoch Publishing House, 1981.

Maloba, Wunyabari. "Nationalism and Decolonization, 1947–1963." In *A Modern History of Kenya,1895–1980*, edited by W. R. Ochieng and B. A. Ogot, 173–201. Nairobi: Evans Brothers, 1989.

Mandala, E. "Peasant, Cotton, Agriculture, Gender and Intergenerational Relationships: The Lower Tschiri (Shire) Valley of Malawi, 1940–1960." *African Studies Review* 25, no. 2/3 (1982): 27–44.

Martin, F. *The Feminist Question: Feminist Theology in the Light of Christian Tradition*. Grand Rapids, MI: Eerdmans, 1994.

Maundeni, Z. "Why Is African Renaissance Likely to Fail: The Case of Zimbabwe." *Journal of Contemporary African Studies* 22, no. 2 (2004): 189–204.

Maxon, R. M. *John Ainsworth and the Making of Kenya*. Washington, DC: University Press of America, 1980.

———. *A Political History: The Colonial Period*. Oxford: Oxford University Press, 2002.

———. "The Years of Revolutionary Advance, 1920–1929." In *A Modern History of Kenya, 1895–1980*, edited by W. R. Ochieng and B. A. Ogot, 71–111. Nairobi: Evan Brothers, 1989.

Maxwell, David, ed. *Christianity and the African Imagination*. Boston: Brill, 2002.

Mayor, A. W. *Thouondi Luo* [Luo Heroes]. Maseno: CMS, 1938.

Mazrui, Ali. *Cultural Forces in World Politics*. London: James Currey, 1990.

Mazrui, A., and K. L. Toby, eds. *The Africans: A Reader*. New York: Praeger, 1986.

Mazrui, Ali A., and Alamin Mazrui. *The Power of Babel: Language and Governance in the African Experience*. Oxford: James Currey, 1998.

Mbiti, John S. *African Religions and Philosophy*. London: Heinemann, 1970.

———. *Bible and Theology in African Christianity*. Nairobi: Oxford University Press, 1986.

———. *Concepts of God in Africa*. London: SPCK, 1977.

———. *Introduction to African Religion*. Oxford: Heinemann, 1991.

Mboya, Paul. *Luo Kitgi Gi Timbegi* [Luo Customs and Traditions]. Nairobi: East African Standard, 1938.

Mbuva, J. "Human Rights: In Light of African Women in Kenya." *Journal of Development Alternatives and Area Studies* 3, no.1 (2004): 33–43.

McIntosh, B. G. *Ngano: Nairobi Historical Studies*. Nairobi: East African Publishing House, 1969.

Mianda, G. "Colonialism, Education and Gender Relations in the Belgian Congo: The Évolué Case." In *Women in African Colonial Histories*, edited by J. Allman, S. Geiger, N. Musisi, 144–163. Bloomington: Indiana University Press, 2002.

Middleton, John, and Greet Kershaw. *The Kikuyu and Kamba of Kenya*. London: International African Institute, 1965.

Mikell, Gwendolyn. *African Feminism: The Politics of Survival in Sub-Saharan Africa*. Philadelphia: University of Pennsylvania Press, 1995.

Miles, B. M., and M. A. Huberman. *Qualitative Data Analysis*. London: Sage, 1994.

Miran, J. "Missionaries, Education and the State in the Italian Colony of Eretria." In *Christian Missionaries in the Third World*, edited by H. B. Hansen and M. Twaddle, 121–135. Oxford: James Currey, 2002.

Miruka, S. O. *Oral Literature of the Luo*. Nairobi: East African Education Publishers, 2001.

Mohanty, C. T. "Under Western Eyes: Feminist Scholarship and Colonial Discourses." *Feminist Review* 30 (1988): 61–88.

Molyneux, M. "Analysing Women's Movement." In *Feminist Vision of Development*, edited by C. Jackson and R. Pearson, 65–88. London: Routledge, 1998.

Moore, H. L. *Feminism and Anthropology*. Cambridge: Polity Press, 1998.

———. *A Passion for Difference*. Cambridge: Polity Press, 1994.

Mouw, R. J. *The God Who Commands: A Study of Divine Ethics*. Notre Dame, IN: University of Notre Dame Press, 1996.

Mudimbe, Valentine Y. *The Invention of Africa: Gnosis, Philosophy and the Order of Knowledge*. Bloomington: Indiana University Press, 1988.

Muhumuza, W. "Unfulfilled Promises? NGO's, Micro-Credit Programs and Poverty Reduction in Uganda." *Journal of Contemporary African Studies* 23, no. 3 (2005): 391–416.

Muruiki, Godfrey. *A History of the Gikuyu, 1500–1900*. Nairobi: Oxford University Press, 1974.

Musisi, N. B. "Colonial and Missionary Education: Women and Domesticity in Uganda." In *African Encounters with Domesticity*, edited by K. T. Hansen, 172–193. New Brunswick, NJ: Rutgers University Press, 1992.

———. "Taking Spaces/Making Spaces: Gender and the Cultural Construction of 'Bad Women' in the Development of Kampala-Kibuga 1900–62." In *Wicked Women and the Reconfiguration of Gender in Africa*, edited by D. Hodgson and Sheryl McCurdy, 78–99. Portsmouth, NH: Hienemann, 2002.

Mutua, William. *Development of Education in Kenya 1846–1963*. Nairobi: East African Literature Bureau, 1978.

Nabudere, W. D. "The African Renaissance in the Age of Globalisation." *African Journal of Political Science* 6, no. 2 (2001): 11–27.

Nasimiyu, Anne. "The History of Maendeleo ya Wanawake Movement in Kenya, 1952–1975." In *The Women's Movement in Kenya*, edited by S. A. Khasiani and E. I. Njino, 93–110. Nairobi: Association of African Women for Research and Development, 1993.

Nasimiyu, N. "Women in the Colonial Economy of Bungoma: Role of Women in Agriculture 1902–1960." *Journal of East African Development* 15 (1985): 57–73.

Nasimiyu, Anne J. "Polygamy: A Feminist Critique." In *The Will To Arise: Women, Tradition and the Church in Africa*, edited by Mercy A. Oduyoye and Musimbi R. A. Kanyoro, 101–118. New York: Orbis, 1992.

Nasimiyu, A. J., and D. W. Waruta, eds. *Mission in African Christianity.* Nairobi: Acton Publishers, 1998.

Nasongo, W., and Godwin Murunga. "Bent on Self-Destruction: Two Years into the Kibaki Regime in Kenya." *Journal of Contemporary African Studies* 24, no. 1 (2006): 1–28.

Ndisi, J. W. *A Study in the Economic and Social Life of the Luo in Kenya.* Lund: Uppsala University Press, 1974.

Neocosmos, M. "Towards Understanding New Forms of State Rule in (Southern) Africa in the Era of Globalization." *African Journal of Political Science* 6, no. 2 (2001): 29–57.

Njoroge, N. J. *An African Feminist Ethic of Resistance and Transformation.* Accra: Advent Press, 2000.

Njoroge, N. J., and M. W. Dube, eds. *Talitha Cum: Theologies of African Women.* Pietermaritzburg: Cluster Publications, 2001.

Nnaemeka, O. "Mapping African Feminism." In *Readings in Gender in Africa*, edited by A. Cornwall, 31–40. Oxford: James Currey, 2005.

Noble, T. *Social Theory and Social Change.* London: Palgrave, 2000.

Nolega, Salome. "Disarmament: UN Calls for Endevour." Address to the Special Session of UN 12 June, 1978.

Northcote, G. A. S. "The Nilotic Kavirondo." *Journal of Royal Anthropological Institute of Great Britain and Ireland* 37 (1907): 58–66.

Nuffield Foundation & Colonial Office. *African Education: A Study of Educational Policy and Practice in British Tropical Africa.* Oxford: Oxford University Press, n.d.

Nurse, D. "The Contribution of Linguistics to the Study of History in Africa." *Journal of African History* 38, no. 3 (1997): 359–391.

Nwachuku, D. N. "The Christian Widow in African Culture." In *The Will to Arise: Women, Tradition and the Church in Africa*, edited by Mercy A. Oduyoye and Musimbi R. A. Kanyoro, 54–73. New York: Orbis, 1992.

Nyamweri, Celia. "Reinventing Africa's National Heroes: The Case of Mekatilil, a Kenyan Popular Heroine." *African Affairs* 115, no. 461 (October 2016): 599–620.

Oakley, P., ed. *Evaluating Empowerment: Reviewing the Concept and Practice.* Oxford: INTRAC, 2001.

Obbo, C. *African Women: Their Struggle for Economic Independence.* London: Zed Press, 1981.

Ochieng, W. R. "Clan Settlement and Clan Conflict in Yimbo Location of Nyanza 1500–1915." In *Ngano: Studies in Traditional and Modern East African History*, edited by B. G. McIntosh, 49–71. Nairobi: EAPH, 1969.

———. "Colonial African Chiefs: Were They Primarily Self-Seeking Scoundrels?" In *Politics of Nationalism in Colonial Kenya*, edited by B. A. Ogot, 46–64. Nairobi: EAPH, 1972.

———. "Democracy and Government in Pre-Colonial Nyanza." In *New Trends for the Empowerment of the People*, edited by D. Kyeuye, 30–40. Nairobi: Pauline Publications, 1997.

———. *A History of Kenya.* London: Macmillan, 1985.

———. *An Outline History of Nyanza up to 1914.* Nairobi: EALB, 1974.

Ochieng, W. R., and B. A. Ogot. *A Modern History of Kenya, 1895–1980: In Honour of B. A. Ogot.* Nairobi: Evans Brothers, 1989.

Ochola-Ayayo, A. B. C. *Traditional Ideology and Ethics among the Luo.* Upsalla: Upsalla University Press, 1976.

Odaga, Asenath B. *Luo Sayings.* Kisumu: Lake Publishers, 1994.

———. *Poko Nyar Migumba.* Kisumu: Lake Publishers, 1978.

———. *Sigendni Mag Luo Mamit.* Kisumu: Lake Publishers, 2001.

———. *Simbi Nyaima Gi Sigendini Luo Moko.* Kisumu: Lake Publishers, 1984.

———. *Simba Nyaima Gi Sigendni Moko*, 5th edition. Kisumu: Lake Publishers, 2002.

———. *Thu Tinda Kisumu.* Kisumu: Lake Publishers, 1980.

Odera-Oruka, Henry. "Philosophy and Other Disciplines in African Thought and Practice." Journal of Philosophical Association of Kenya 1, no. 1 (1974): 27–36.

———. *Sage Philosophy: Indigenous Thinkers and Modern Debate on African Philosophy.* Leiden: E. J. Brill, 1990.

———. "Sagacity in African Philosophy." In *Africa Philosophy: The Essential Readings*, edited by T. Serqueberhan, 81–83. New York: Paragon House, 1991.

Odinga, A. Oginga. *Not Yet Uhuru: An Autobiography.* New York: Hill & Wang, 1967.

Odinga, A. Oginga, and H. O. Oruka. *Oginga Odinga: His Philosophy and Beliefs.* Nairobi: Initiatives Publishers, 1992.

Oduol, Jacqueline Adhiambo. "Research Priorities on Women in Development Issues in Kenya." In *From Strategies to Action: A Research Perspective*, 1–8.

By Association of African Women for Research and Development. AAWord Kenya, 1995.

Oduol, Wilhelmina. "Kenyan Women's Participation in the Women's Movement in Kenya." In *The Women's Movement in Kenya*, edited by S. A. Khasiani and E. L. Njino, 20–27. Nairobi: AAWord Publishers, 1993.

Oduyoye, Mercy A. *Daughters and Anowa: African Women and Patriarchy*. Maryknoll, NY: Orbis, 1999.

———. *Hearing and Knowing: Theological Reflections on Christianity in Africa*. Nairobi: Acton Publishers, 2000.

———. "Reflections from a Third World Women's Perspective: Women's Experience and Liberation Theologies." In *Feminist Theology from the Third World*, edited by Ursula King, 23–34. New York: Orbis, 1994.

———. "Women and Ritual in Africa." In *The Will to Arise: Women, Tradition and The Church in Africa*, edited by Mercy A. Oduyoye and Musimbi R. A. Kanyoro, 9–24. Maryknoll, NY: Orbis, 1992.

Oduyoye, Mercy A., and Musimbi R. A. Kanyoro. *Talitha Qumi! Proceedings of the Convocation of African Women Theologians 1989*. Ibadan: Daystar, 1990.

Oduyoye, Mercy A., and Musimbi R. A. Kanyoro, eds. *The Will to Arise: Women, Tradition and the Church in Africa*. Maryknoll, NY: Orbis, 1992.

Ogot, Bethwell A. "British Administration in Central Nyanza District of Kenya 1900–1960." *Journal of African History* 4, no. 2 (1963): 249–273.

———. "Britain's Gulag Review Article." *Journal of African History* 46, no. 3 (2005): 493–505.

———. *Building on the Indigenous: Selected Essays 1981–1998*. Kisumu: Anyange Press, 1998.

———. "The Construction of Luo Identity and History." In *African Words and African Voices*, edited by L. White, S. Miescher, and D. W. Cohen, 31–52. Indianapolis: Indiana University Press, 2001.

———. *East Africa*. Nairobi: EALB, 1978.

———. *Hadith 2: Proceedings of the 1968 Conference of the Historical Association of Kenya*. Nairobi: East African Publishing House, 1970.

———. *Hadith 3: Proceedings of the 1969/70 Conference of the Historical Association of Kenya*. Nairobi: East African Publishing House, 1971.

———. *Hadith 5: Economic and Social History of East Africa*. Nairobi: EALB, 1975.

———. *Hadith 6: History and Social Change in East Africa*. Nairobi: EALB, 1976.

———. *Hadith 7: Ecology and History in East Africa*. Nairobi: Kenya Literature Bureau, 1979.

———. *A History of the Southern Luo, Vol.1*. Nairobi: East African Publishing House, 1967.

———. "Mau Mau and Nationhood: The Untold Story." In *Mau Mau and Nationhood*, edited by E. S. Atieno-Odhiambo and J. Lonsdale, 8–36. Oxford: James Currey, 2003.

———. "Social and Economic History of the Luo of Kenya 1870–1910." Arts Research Prize Essay. Kampala: Makerere University Library, 1950.

———. *Politics of Nationalism in Colonial Kenya*. Nairobi: East African Publishing House, 1972b.

———. *War and Society in Africa*. Nairobi: East African Publishing House, 1972a.

———. *Zamani: A Survey of East African History*. Nairobi: East African Publishing House, 1973.

———. *Zamani: A Survey of East African History*. Revised edition. Nairobi: East African Publishing House, 1974.

Ogot, B. A., and M. Kieseran. *Zamani*. Nairobi: East African Publishing House, 1967.

Ogot, B. A., and W. R. Ochieng. *Decolonization and Independence in Kenya*. London: James Currey, 1995.

———. "Mumboism: An Anti-Colonial Movement." In *Politics and Nationalism in Colonial Kenya*, edited by B. A. Ogot, 55–68. Nairobi: East African Publishing House, 1972.

Ogot, B. A., and F. Welbourn. *A Place to Feel at Home: A Study of Two Independent Churches in Western Kenya*. London: Oxford University Press, 1966.

Ogot, Grace. *Aloo Kod Apul Apul*. Kisumu: Anyange Press, 1981.

———. *Ber Wat*. Kisumu: Anyange Press, 1981.

———. "Grace Ogot." *Weekly Review*, 21 October, 1983.

———. *Land without Thunder and Other Stories*. Nairobi: East African Publishing House, 1968.

———. *Land without Thunder*. 8th edition. Nairobi: East African Publishing House , 2003.

———. *Miaha*. Kisumu: Anyange Press, 1983.

———. *The Other Woman*. 4th edition. Nairobi: East African Publishing House, 2001.

———. *The Promised Land*. Nairobi: East African Publishing House, 1966.

———. *The Promised Land*. 8th edition. Nairobi: East African Publishing House , 2005.

———. *The Strange Bride*. 5th edition. Nairobi: East African Publishing House, 2003.

Ogundipe-Leslie, M. *Recreating Ourselves: African Women and Critical Transformation*. Trenton: African World Press, 1994.

Ojuka, A. "African Thought and Concept of Essence in African Thought and Practice." *Journal of Philosophical Association of Kenya* 1, no. 1 (1974): 19–36.

Okaro-Kojwang, K. M. "Origins and Establishment of Kavirondo Tax-Payers Association." In *Ngano: Nairobi Historical Studies*, edited by B. G. McIntosh, 111–128. Nairobi: East African Publishing House, 1969.

Okola, Zablon, and Michael Were. *Weche Moko Mag Luo* [Luo Traditions, Customs and Folklore]. Nairobi: CMS, 1936.

Okullu, Henry. *Church and Politics in East Africa.* Nairobi: Uzima Press, 1985.

———. *Church and State in Nation Building and Human Development.* Nairobi: Uzima Press, 1987.

Okumu, A. J. W. *The African Renaissance: History, Significance and Strategy.* Trenton, NJ: African World Press, 2002.

Oldham, J. H. "The African Continent: A Survey of Ten Years." *International Review of Missions* 13, no. 4 (October 1924): 418–419.

———. "The Christian Opportunity in Africa: Some Reflections on the Report of the Phelps-Stoke's Commission." *International Review of Missions* 14, no. 2 (April 1925): 173–187.

———. "Educational Policy of the British Government in Africa." *International Review of Missions* 14, no. 3 (1925): 421–427.

———. "Religious Education in the Mission Field." *International Review of Missions* 13, no. 4 (1924): 500–517.

Omachar, Barasa Samson. "Forgotten Educators in Colonial Kenya: An Australian Fanny Moller and Canon Pleydell Educational Mission 1923–1952." *International Journal of Education and Research* 3, no. 7 (July 2015): 396–384.

Ominde, Simeon. *The Luo Girl from Infancy to Marriage.* London: Macmillan, 1952.

———. *The Luo Girl from Infancy to Marriage.* 5th edition. Nairobi: KLB, 1987.

Omondi Patrick. "Woman Ordained." *Daily Nation*, 27 January, 1983.

Onyango Emily, ed. *For God and Humanuty: One Hundred Years of St. Paul's United Theological College.* Eldoret: Zapf Chancery, 2003.

Onyango-Ogutu, B., and A. Roscoe. *Keep My Words: Luo Oral Literature.* Nairobi: EAPH, 1982.

Ormsby-Gore, H. W. G. A. *Education Policy in British Tropical Africa: Memorandum Submitted to the Secretary of State for the Colonies by the Advisory Committee on Native Education in British Tropical Africa Dependencies.* London: HMSO, 1925.

Osogo, John. *A History of Abaluhiya.* Nairobi: Oxford University Press, 1966.

Østergaard, L., ed. *Gender and Development: A Practical Guide.* London: Routledge, 1982.

Otiende, J. *Education and Development in Kenya: A Historical Perspective.* Nairobi: Oxford University Press, 1986.

Oyewumi, Oyeronke. *The Invention of Women: Making an African Sense of Women Gender Discourses.* Minneapolis: University of Minnesota Press, 1997.

Oyugi, W. "Coalition Politics and Coalition Governments in Africa." *Journal of Contemporary African Studies* 24, no. 1 (2006): 53–59.

Pala, Achola Okeyo. "Daughters of Lakes and Rivers: Colonization and Land Rights of Women." In *Women and Colonization: Anthropological Perspectives*, edited by Mona Etienne and E. B. Leacock, 80–105. New York: Praeger, 1980.

———. "The Role of African Women in Rural Development: Research Priorities." *Journal of East Africa Research and Development* 5, no. 2 (1975): 137–161.

———. "Women's Access to Land and Their Role in Agriculture and Decision-Making on the Farm: Experiences of the Joluo of Kenya." *Journal of Eastern Africa Research and Development* 13 (1983): 69–85.

p'Bitek, Okot. *Song of Lawino: Song of Ocol.* Nairobi: Heinmann, 1972.

Peel, J. D. Y. "The Cultural Work of Yoruba Ethnogenesis." In *Women Wielding the Hoe: Lessons from Rural Africa for Feminist Theory and Development Practice*, edited by E. Tonkin, M. McDonald, and D. F. Bryceson, 114–122. Oxford: Berg, 2000.

———. "Gender in Yoruba Religious Change." *Journal of Religion in Africa* 32, no. 2 (May 2002): 136–166.

Peterson, Derek. *Creative Writing: Translation, Bookkeeping and the Work of Imagination in Colonial Kenya.* Portsmouth: Heinemann, 2004.

———. "Revivalism and Dissent in Colonial East Africa." In *The East African Revival: History and Legacies*, edited by K. Ward and E. Wild-Wood, 105–117. Kampala: Fountain Publishers, 2010.

Phiri, Isabel A. *Women, Presbyterianism and Patriarchy: Religious Experience of Chewa Women in Central Malawi.* Blantyre: Claim, 1997.

Phiri, I. A., B. G. Devarakshanam, and S. Nadar, eds. *Her-Stories: Hidden Histories of Women of Faith in Africa.* Pietermaritzburg: Cluster Publications, 2002.

Pietilä, Hilkka. *Engendering the Global Agenda: The Story of Women and the United Nations.* New York: NGLS, 2000.

Pirouet, M. L. *Black Evangelists: The Spread of Christianity in Uganda 1891–1914.* London: Rex Collings, 1978.

Pobee, John. *Towards an African Theology.* Nashville: Abingdon, 1974.

Pon, V., ed. *Introduction to Social Research.* Dares-Salaam: University Press, 1992.

Porter, A. *Religion versus Empire? British Protestant Missionaries and Overseas Expansion 1700–1914.* Manchester: Manchester University Press, 2004.

Potash, B. "Wives of the Grave: Widows in a Rural Luo Community." In *Widows in African Societies: Choices and Constraints*, edited by B. Potash, 44–65. Stanford: Stanford University Press, 1986.

Presley, Cora Ann. *Kikuyu Women, The Mau Mau Rebellion and Social Change in Kenya*. Stanford: Westview, 1992.

Price, T. "Missionary Agency in Colonial Development." *International Review of Missions* 29, no. 116 (1940): 463–469.

———. "Task of Mission Schools in Africa." *International Review of Missions* 27, no. 2 (1938): 233–238.

Provincial Unit of Research. *From Rabai to Mumias*. Nairobi: Uzima Press, 1994.

Quayson, A. *Postcolonialism: Theory, Practice or Process*. Oxford: Polity Press, 2000.

Quest, C., ed. *Liberating Women … from Modern Feminism*. IEA Health and Welfare Unit, 1994.

Radford-Ruether, R. *Women and Redemption*. London: SCM, 1998.

Ranger, T. "The Invention of Tradition in Colonial Africa." In *The Invention of Tradition*, edited by E. Hobsbawn and T. Ranger, 211–262. Cambridge: Cambridge University Press, 1983.

———. "The Invention of Tradition Revisited: The Case of Colonial Africa." In *Legitimacy and the State in Twentieth Century Africa*, edited by T. Ranger and O. Vaughan, 62–111. Basingstoke: Macmillan, 1993.

———. "The Nature of Ethnicity: Lessons from Africa." In *People, Nation and State: The Meaning of Ethnicity and Nationalism*, edited by E. Mortimer, 12–28. London: I. B. Tauris, 1999.

———. "Taking on the Missionary Task: African Spirituality and Mission Churches in Manicaland in 1930." In *Christianity in African Imagination*, edited by D. Maxwell, 93–126. Boston: Brill, 2002.

———. *Voices from the Rocks: Nature, Culture and History in the Matopos Hills of Zimbabwe*. Oxford: James Currey, 1999.

Ranger, T., and I. N. Kimambo, eds. *The Historical Study of African Religion*. London: Heinemann, 1972.

Ranger, T., and R. Werbner, eds. *Post-Colonial Identities in Africa*. London: Zed, 1996.

Reed, Collin. *Pastors, Partners and Paternalists: African Church Leaders and Western Missionaries in the Anglican Church in Kenya, 1850–1900*. New York: Brill, 1997.

Richards, Elizabeth. *Fifty Years in Nyanza, 1906–1956: The History of the CMS and the Anglican Church in Nyanza*. Maseno: CMS Jubilee Committee, 1956.

Robert, D. L. *American Women in Mission: A Social History of Their Thought and Practice*. Macon, GA: Mercer University Press, 1996.

Robertson, C., and K. Martin, eds. *Women and Slavery in Africa*. Madison: University of Wisconsin Press, 1983

Robson, C. *Real World Research: A Resource for Social Scientists and Practitioner Researchers*. Oxford: Blackwell, 1993.

Rodney, Walter. *How Europe Under-Developed Africa*. Washington, DC: Howard University Press, 1982.

Sabar, Galia. *Church State and Society in Kenya: From Mediation to Opposition 1963–93*. London: Frank Cass, 2002.

Sanneh, Lamin. *Translating the Message: The Missionary Impact on Culture*. New York: Orbis, 1989.

Savage, D. C., and F. J. Munro. "Carrier Corps Recruitment in British African Protectorate 1914–18." *Journal of African History* 7, no. 2 (1966): 313–342.

Schmidt, Elizabeth. *Peasants, Traders and Wives: Shona Women in the History of Zimbabwe 1870–1939*. London: James Currey, 1992.

Schwartz, Nancy. "Active Dead or Alive: Some Kenyan Views about the Agency of Luo and Luhyia Pre- and Post-Mortem." *Journal of Religion in Africa* 30, no. 4 (November 2000): 433–467.

Senior, M. "Women in African Village Church." *International Review of Missions* 37, no. 148 (1948): 403–409.

Serequeberhan, T., ed. *African Philosophy: The Essential Readings*. New York: Paragon House, 1991.

———. *The Hermeneutics of African Philosophy: Horizon and Discourse*. New York: Routledge, 1994.

———. *Philosophy and Post-Colonial African Philosophy: A Critical Reader*. Oxford: Blackwell, 1997.

Shadle, B. "Bridewealth and Female Consent: Marriage Disputes in African Courts, Gusiiland, Kenya." *Journal of African History* 44, no. 2 (2003): 241–262.

———. "Patronage, Millennialism and the Serpent God, Mumbo in South-West Kenya 1912–34." *Africa* 72, no. 1 (2002): 29–54.

Shaw, Carolyn M. *Colonial Inscriptions: Race, Sex and Class in Kenya*. Minneapolis: University of Minnesota Press, 1995.

Sheffield, J. R. *Education in Kenya: A Historical Study*. New York: Teachers College Press, 1973

Snell, G. S. *Nandi Customary Law*. London: Macmillan, 1954.

Southall, A. W. "Lineage Formation among the Luo." *International African Institute Memorandum* 26. London: Oxford University Press, 1952.

Sow, F. "The African Social Sciences and Gender Analysis." In *Engendering African Social Sciences*, edited by A. M. Imam, A. Mama, and F. Sow, 31–60. Dakar: CODESRIA, 1997.

Spear, T. "Neo-Traditionalism and the Limits of Invention in British Colonial Africa." *Journal of African History* 44, no. 1 (2003): 3–27.

Spear, T., and I. N. Kimambo, eds. *East African Expressions of Christianity.* Oxford: James Currey, 1999.

Spencer, L. "Christianity and Colonial Protest: Perceptions of WE Owen, Archdeacon of Kavirondo." *Journal of Religion in Africa* 33, no. 1 (1982): 47–60.

Spradley, J. P., and D. W. McCurdy. *Conformity and Conflict: Reading in Cultural Anthropology.* Boston: Allyn & Bacon, 2000.

Stam, P. N. "The Religious Conception of the Kavirondo." *Anthropos* 5, no. 2 (1910): 359–362.

Stassen, G. H. and D. P. Gushee. *Kingdom Ethics: Following Jesus in Contemporary Context.* Downer's Grove, IL: InterVarsity Academic, 2003.

Steady, F. C. "African Feminism: A Worldwide Perspective." In *Women in Africa and the African Diaspora*, edited by R. Terborg-Penn, S. Harley, and A. B. Rushing, 3–21. Washington, DC: Howard University Press, 1997.

Stock, E: *The History of Church Missionary Society, Vol. 1 1799–1848.* London: CMS, 1899.

———. *The History of Church Missionary Society, Vol. 2 1849–1861.* London: CMS, 1899.

———. *The History of Church Missionary Society, Vol. 3 1862–1888.* London: CMS, 1899.

———. *The History of Church Missionary Society, Vol. 4 1900–1914.* London: CMS, 1916.

Strayer, Robert. *The Making of Mission Communities in East Africa.* London: Heinemann, 1978.

Taras, C. R., and Rajat Ganguly. *Understanding Ethnic Conflict: The International Dimension.* London: Longman, 2006.

Tate, H. R. "The Native Law of Southern Gikuyu of British East Africa." *Journal of the Royal African Society* 9, no. 35 (April 1910): 233–254.

———. "Notes on the Kikuyu and Kamba Tribes of British East Africa." *Journal of the Anthropological Institute of Great Britain and Ireland* 34 (1904): 130–148.

Taylor & Francis Group, eds. *Africa South of the Sahara 2005*, 34th edition. London: Europa Publications, 2005.

———. *The Europa World Year Book 2003 Vol. II*, 44th edition. London: Europa Publication, 2003.

Temu, A. J. *British Protestant Missions.* London: Longman, 1972.

Thomas, L. M. *Politics of the Womb: Women, Reproduction and the State in Kenya.* Berkeley: University of California Press, 2003.

Thompson, W. *Postmodernism and History: Theory and History*. New York: Palgrave Macmillan, 2004.

Throup, D. *Economic and Social Origins of Mau-Mau 1945–53*. London: James Currey, 1987.

Tieku, T. K. "Explaining the Clash and Accommodation of Interests of Major Actors in the Creation of African Union." *African Affairs* 103, no. 411 (2004): 249–267.

Tiyambe, Zeleza. "The Establishment of Colonial Rule." In *A Modern History of Kenya, 1895–1980*, edited by W. R. Ochieng and B. A. Ogot, 35–70. Nairobi: Evans Brothers, 1989.

Toshiharu, A. "The Concepts of Chira and Dhoch among the Luo: Transition, Deviation and Misfortune." In *Themes in Socio-Cultural Ideas and Behaviour among Six Ethnic Groups of Kenya*, edited by N. Nobuhiro, 60–74. Tokyo: Hitotsubacshi University, 1981.

Tucker, Alfred. *Eighteen Years in Uganda and East Africa Vol. 2*. London: Edward Arnold, 1908.

Ukaegbu, C. C. "Entrepreneurial Succession and Post-Founder Durability: A Study of Private Manufacturing Firms in Igbo States of Nigeria." *Journal of Contemporary African Studies* 21, no. 2 (2003): 27–45.

United Nations. *The Beijing Declaration and Platform for Action: Fourth Conference of Women in Beijing China*. New York: UN, 1996.

Van Buren, Linda. "Economy of Kenya." In *Africa South of the Sahara 2005*, 34th edition, edited by Taylor and Francis, 150–164. London: Europa Publication, 2005.

Vansina, Jan. "Linguistic Evidence and Historical Reconstruction." *Journal of African History* 40, no. 3 (1999): 469–473.

———. "New Linguistic Evidence and the Bantu Expansion." *Journal of African History* 36, no. 2 (1995): 173–195.

———. *Oral Tradition as History*. Madison: University Press, 1985.

———. *Paths in the Rain Forest*. Madison: University Press, 1990.

Adenaike, C. K., and J. Vansina, eds. *In Pursuit of History: Fieldwork in Africa*. Portsmouth: Heinemann, 1996.

Vincent, L. "Bread and Honour: White Working Class Women and Afrikaner Nationalism in the 1930s" *Journal of Southern African Studies* 26, no. 1 (2000) 61–78.

Walker, A. *In Search of Our Mothers Garden*. San Diego: Harcourt, 1983.

Walls, A. *The Missionary Movement: A Christian History*. New York: Orbis, 1996.

Wamue, G. N. "Revisiting Our Indigenous Shrines through Mungiki." *African Affairs* 100 (2001): 453–467.

Wanjiku, Mukabi Kabira, and Elizabeth Akinyi Nzioki. *Celebrating Women's Resistance*. Nairobi: New Era Publications, 1993.

Wanyande, P. "Management Politics in Kenya's Sugar Industry: Towards an Effective Framework." *African Journal of Political Science* 6, no. 1 (2001): 123–140.

Warren, M. A. C. "Nationalism as an International Asset." *International Review of Missions* 44, no. 176 (1955): 385–393.

Welbourn, F. B. *East African Rebels.* London: SCM Press, 1961.

Were, Gideon. *A History of the Abaluyia of Western Kenya.* Nairobi: East African Publishing House, 1967.

Westermann, D. "The Place and Function of Vernacular in African Education." *International Review of Missions* 14, no. 1 (1925): 25–36.

Whisson, M. G. *Change and Challenge: A Study of Social and Economic Changes among the Luo.* Nairobi: KLB, 1964.

White, L. *Speaking with Vampires: Rumours as History in Colonial Africa.* Berkeley: University of California Press, 2000.

White, L., S. Miescher, and D. W. Cohen. *African Words and African Voices.* Indianapolis: Indiana University Press, 2001.

White, R. E. O. *Biblical Ethics: The Changing Continuity of Christian Ethics,* vol. 1. Exeter: Paternoster Press, 1979.

Wilde, J. C. "The Experience in Central Nyanza District." In *Experiences with Agricultural Development in Tropical Africa,* edited by J. C. Wilde, 123–141. Baltimore: John Hopkins Press, 1967.

Willis, J. J. "The Presentation of Christianity to Primitive People: A Statement by Christian Converts of Kavirondo Addressed to their Heathen Friends." *International Review of Missions* 14, no. 15 (1915): 382–395.

Wilson, G. M. *Luo Customary Laws and Customs.* Nairobi: Government Printers, 1961.

———. *Luo Customary Law Marriage.* Nairobi: KLB, 1961.

———. *Marriage Laws and Customs 1955. Report to the Kenyan Government.* Nairobi: Government Printers, 1955.

Wipper, A. "Equal Rights for Women." *Journal of Modern African Studies* 9, no. 3 (October 1971): 429–442.

———. "The Politics of Sex." *African Studies Review* 14, no. 3 (December 1971): 463–482.

———. *Rural Rebels.* Nairobi: Oxford University Press, 1977.

Wogaman, J. P. *Christian Ethics: A Historical Introduction.* Louisville, KY: Westminster John Knox Press, 1993.

Wolterstorff, N. *Educating for Responsible Action.* Grand Rapids, MI: Eerdmans, 1980.

World Bank. "Data & Statistics Yr. 2004." Available at http://www.worldbank.org/CountryReport/Kenya. Accessed February 2006.

———. *World Development Report 2005: A Better Investment Climate for Everyone.* New York: Oxford University Press, 2005.

Wright, M. *Strategies of Slaves and Women: Life Stories from East Central Africa.* London: James Currey, 1993.

———. "Women and the Charismatic Community: Defining the Attraction." *Sociological Analysis* 53, no. S (Special Presidential Issue Conversion, 1992): S35–S49.

Wrong, Margaret. "Literacy and Literature for African Peoples." *International Review of Mission* 33, no.130 (1944): 193–199.

———. "The Church's Task in Africa South of the Sahara." *International Review of Missions* 36, no.142 (1946): 206–231.

Yin, K. R. *Case-Study Research: Designs and Methods.* London: Sage Publications, 2003.

Yngstrom, I. "Women, Wives and Land Rights in Africa: Situating Gender beyond the Household in the Debate over Land Policy and Changing Tenure Systems." *Oxford Development Studies* 30, no. 1 (2000): 21–40.

Zeleza, T. "Gender Biases in African Historiography." In *Engendering African Social Sciences*, edited by A. Imam, A. Mama, and F. Sow, 81–116. Dakar: CODESRIA, 1997.

Unpublished Theses and Manuscripts

Butterman, J. M. "Luo Social Formations in Change: Karachuonyo and Kanyamkago 1800–1945." PhD dissertation, Syracuse University, 1979.

Cohen, D. "Pim's Work: Some Thoughts on the Construction of Relations and Groups: The Luo of Western Kenya." Paper presented to a conference on "The History of Family in Africa," at the School of Oriental and African Studies, London, September 1981.

Emerson, C. "Early Kenyan Christianities: Geography, Ethnicity and Denomination." Undergraduate dissertation. University of Cambridge, 2002.

Francis, Carey. "Polygamy." Unpublished manuscript, 1942.

Hay, M. J. "Economic Change in Luo Land: Kowe, 1890–1945." PhD dissertation, University of Wisconsin, Madison, 1972.

Indalo, P. "A Critical Study of the Contribution of the Rev. Canon Ezekiel Apindi to the Growth of the Church in Nyanza." Unpublished manuscript, SPUTC Library, 1978.

Ndeda, M. A. Jalango. "The Impact of Male Labour Migration of Rural Women: A Case-Study of Siaya District 1891–1963." PhD dissertation, Kenyatta University, 1991.

Labode, G. M. "African Christian Women and the Anglican Missionaries in South Africa 1850–1963." PhD dissertation, Oxford University, 1992.

Lonsdale, John. "A Political History of Nyanza: 1883–1945." PhD dissertation, Cambridge University, 1964.

Mombo, Esther. "A Historical and Cultural Analysis of The Position of Abaluhyia Women in Kenyan Quaker Christianity 1902–1979." PhD dissertation, University of Edinburgh, 1999.

Musandu, Phoebe. "Daughter of Odoro: Grace Onyango and African Women's History." Master's thesis, Miami University, 2006.

Odira, A. "A History of Kanyada People up to 1914." Unpublished manuscript, Kenyatta University, n.d.

Odiyo, E. O. "State Formation among the Luo: The Case of Alego, 1500–1920." MPhil thesis, Moi University, Eldoret, 1991.

Ogacho, S. "The Participation of the Africans in the Establishment of the Anglican Church in Nyanza 1906–1955." BD research paper, SPUTC Limuru, 1989.

Olang, D. "A History of the Karachuonyo c.1500–1900." BA graduating essay, University of Nairobi, 1972.

Oloo, P. C. "History of Settlement: An Example of Luo Clans in Alego 1500–1918." BA graduating essay, University of Nairobi, 1972.

Omachar, B. S. "The Contribution of the Church Missionary Society to the Development of Education: A Case Study of Ng'iya Girls' School 1923–1927." Master's thesis, Moi University, 2014.

Opinya, O. "History of Kano: A Study of the Stranger Elements of Wang'aya, Sidho and Kasagam." BA graduating essay, University of Nairobi, 1969.

Rabongo, J. A. "The Establishment and Growth of the Anglican Church in Ramba Parish of the Diocese of Maseno-South 1906–1940." BD research paper SPUTC, Limuru 1983.

Ranger, T. "Christian Missions, Capitalism and Empire, The State of The Debate." Lecture at Oxford Centre of Mission Studies, 21 June 2005.

———. "African Initiated Churches." Lecture at Oxford Centre of Mission Studies, 2005.

Schiller, L. D. "Gem and Kano: A Comparative Study of Stress in Two Traditional African Political Systems in Nyanza Province, Western Kenya c.1850–1914." Seminar Paper, Department of History, University of Nairobi, 1977.

Stoner-Eby, A. M. "African Leaders Engage Mission Christianity: Anglicans in Tanzania 1876–1926." A dissertation in history, University of Pennsylvanian, 2003.

Tiplady Higgs, Eleanor. "Mothers Union in Kenya 1955–2015." Unpublished paper presented to Mothers Union in the Diocese of Carslie, London: SOAS, 2015.

Urban-Mead, W. E. "Religion, Women and Gender in Brethren in Christ Church, Matabeleland, Zimbabwe 1898–1978." PhD dissertation, Columbia University, 2004.

Wamagatta, Evanson. "The Presbyterian Church of East Africa: An Account of Its Gospel Missionary Society Origins." PhD dissertation, West Virginia University, 2001.

Langham
PARTNERSHIP

Langham Literature, with its publishing work, is a ministry of Langham Partnership.

Langham Partnership is a global fellowship working in pursuit of the vision God entrusted to its founder John Stott –

> *to facilitate the growth of the church in maturity and Christ-likeness through raising the standards of biblical preaching and teaching.*

Our vision is to see churches in the majority world equipped for mission and growing to maturity in Christ through the ministry of pastors and leaders who believe, teach and live by the Word of God.

Our mission is to strengthen the ministry of the Word of God through:
- nurturing national movements for biblical preaching
- fostering the creation and distribution of evangelical literature
- enhancing evangelical theological education

especially in countries where churches are under-resourced.

Our ministry

Langham Preaching partners with national leaders to nurture indigenous biblical preaching movements for pastors and lay preachers all around the world. With the support of a team of trainers from many countries, a multi-level programme of seminars provides practical training, and is followed by a programme for training local facilitators. Local preachers' groups and national and regional networks ensure continuity and ongoing development, seeking to build vigorous movements committed to Bible exposition.

Langham Literature provides majority world preachers, scholars and seminary libraries with evangelical books and electronic resources through publishing and distribution, grants and discounts. The programme also fosters the creation of indigenous evangelical books in many languages, through writer's grants, strengthening local evangelical publishing houses, and investment in major regional literature projects, such as one volume Bible commentaries like the *Africa Bible Commentary* and the *South Asia Bible Commentary*.

Langham Scholars provides financial support for evangelical doctoral students from the majority world so that, when they return home, they may train pastors and other Christian leaders with sound, biblical and theological teaching. This programme equips those who equip others. Langham Scholars also works in partnership with majority world seminaries in strengthening evangelical theological education. A growing number of Langham Scholars study in high quality doctoral programmes in the majority world itself. As well as teaching the next generation of pastors, graduated Langham Scholars exercise significant influence through their writing and leadership.

To learn more about Langham Partnership and the work we do visit **langham.org**

In this book, Rev Canon Dr Onyango has brought to light women's agency in navigating layers of systems that first affirmed them in the community life and then excluded them from being heard in the area of education. The triple culture within which women operated in seeking formal education is well narrated. Most importantly the objective analysis of culture, especially the Luo culture, shows the learning processes between African women students and the missionaries who taught them. The African women's agency runs through the book and adds to the perspectives of women and the growth and development of a new community. The intersections between the African and Western learning systems run through the chapters of the book and are an indication of the author's effort using them in as much as they impacted education for girls. This is an important book in teaching about women and education in Kenya during the period discussed, but it also has parallels to some of the education patterns in society today. Education has been and continues to be an important factor in empowering women to be key leaders in society.

Esther Mombo, PhD
Director, International Partnerships and Alumni Relations,
Faculty of Theology, St Paul's University, Nairobi, Kenya

Emily Onyango is a pioneer in the history of girls' education in Kenya. With good evidence based on state and missionary archives and the recollections of some memorable women, she tells an extraordinary story of initial cultural courage by young Kenyan women, of persevering female missionary dedication, of difficult gendered negotiations in home and employment and, in the end, of the confident, if still embattled, sense of achievement by a growing number of Kenyan women.

John Lonsdale, PhD
Emeritus Professor, Modern African History,
Fellow of Trinity College,
University of Cambridge, UK